Damian Williams

speakout

Intermediate
Teacher's Resource Book

TEACHER'S RESOURCE BOOK CONTENTS

STUDENTS' BOOK CONTENTS

LISTENING/DVD	SPEAKING	WRITING
listen to someone describing their family history	talk about family events; talk about people in your life	write an email of introduction; learn to use formal and informal styles
listen to a set of instructions and do a test	discuss the differences between men and women	
listen to a set of interviews; learn to understand and use two-word responses	talk about type of interviews and interview experiences; role-play an interview	
BBC The Money Programme: Second Life: watch and understand a documentary about life online	discuss and create a new identity	write answers to a questionnaire
listen to a radio programme about important roles in films	talk about life experiences; talk about your life story	
listen to news reports	talk about an important news story/event	write a news report; learn to use time linkers: as soon as, while, during, until and by the time
listen to people telling anecdotes; learn to keep a story going	tell a true story or a lie	
BBC Hustle: watch and listen to a drama about a burglar and a famous painting	discuss fictional crime dramas; tell a narrative	write a short newspaper article
	discuss attitudes now in comparison to ones you had earlier in life	write messages; learn to use note form
listen to predictions about the future of communication	talk about how things will change in the future	
listen to telephone conversations involving misunderstandings	learn to reformulate and retell a story about a misunderstanding; role-play resolving a misunderstanding	
BBC The Virtual Revolution: watch and understand a documentary about the impact of the internet	talk about communication preferences	write a memo
	discuss the qualities needed for different jobs; complete a survey and discuss the results	
listen to two people describing dream jobs gone wrong	talk about past habits	write a covering letter; learn to organise your ideas
listen to people making decisions in a meeting	learn to manage a discussion; participate in a meeting and create a business plan	
BBC Gavin and Stacey: watch and understand a comedy programme about a man's first day in a new job	describe a day in your life	write about daily routines
	discuss how technology has changed the world; talk about different types of transport and their uses	write an advantages versus disadvantages essay; learn to use discourse markers
listen to people answering difficult general knowledge questions	do a short general knowledge questionnaire; answer questions on your area of expertise	
listen to conversations about technical problems; learn to respond to requests	role-play asking and responding to requests	
BBC Top Gear: watch and understand a programme about a race between a car and two people	present and describe a new machine	write an advertisement for a new machine

COMMUNICATION BANK page 158   AUDIO SCRIPTS page 164

STUDENTS' BOOK CONTENTS

LISTENING/DVD	SPEAKING	WRITING
listen to a radio programme about therapies	talk about your emotions; discuss what advice to give people in a variety of situations	
	discuss what you would do in different hypothetical situations	write a letter of advice; learn to qualify what you say
listen to conversations where people receive news	learn to introduce and respond to news; role-play giving someone news	
The Worst Week: watch and understand a comedy programme about a man's terrible day	talk about memorable moments	write about one of your happiest memories
listen to and understand a radio programme about success	discuss how people can be successful; talk about something you've been doing	
listen to a three-way conversation about memory	talk about your abilities	write a summary; learn to make notes for a summary
listen to a discussion about intelligence; learn to refer to what you said earlier	choose the right candidate for the job; give opinions and examples	
The One Show: Water Ski Challenge: watch and understand a programme about an incredible experience	describe an achievement	write about an achievement for an internet post
	describe your neighbourhood and discuss how it could be improved	
listen to descriptions of online communities	compare real-world and online activities	write a website review; learn to use complex sentences
listen to people describing guest/host experiences; learn to accept apologies	discuss problematic social situations	
Tribe: Anuta: watch and understand a documentary programme about a man's visit to a remote community	create an ideal community	write a web advert for members of your ideal community
	describe a big moment in history	write a short essay; learn to structure paragraphs
listen to people describing past decades	talk about your personal history	
listen to people doing a quiz about history; learn to react to information	compile and do a quiz	
The Divine Michelangelo: watch and understand a documentary programme about a great artist	talk about people who influenced you	write a wiki entry about an influential person
	discuss environmental issues and solutions	
listen to descriptions of the world's best food cities	recommend a city for food; talk about your attitude to food	write a restaurant review; learn to link ideas
listen to people giving advice/warnings; learn to make generalisations	ask for and give travel advice	
Nature's Great Event: The Great Melt: watch and understand a programme about the Arctic's melting ice caps	talk about a special or an endangered place	write an email campaigning for action

COMMUNICATION BANK page 158   AUDIO SCRIPTS page 164

Before we started writing *Speakout*, we did a lot of research to find out more about the issues that teachers and students face and how these can be addressed in a textbook for the 21st century. The issues that came up again and again were motivation, authentic content and the need for structured speaking and listening strategies.

As English teachers, we know how motivating it can be to bring the real world into the classroom by using authentic materials. We also know how time consuming and difficult it can be to find authentic content that is truly engaging, at the right level and appropriate for our students. With access to the entire archive of the BBC, we have selected some stunning video content to motivate and engage students. We have also created tasks that will encourage interaction with the materials while providing the right amount of scaffolding.

We realise that the real world is not just made up of actors, presenters and comedians, and 'real' English does not just consist of people reading from scripts. This is why *Speakout* brings real people into the classroom. The Video podcasts show people giving their opinions about the topics in the book and illustrate some of the strategies that will help our students become more effective communicators.

Speakout maximises opportunities for students to speak and systematically asks them to notice and employ strategies that will give them the confidence to communicate fluently and the competence to listen actively. While the main focus is on speaking and listening, we have also developed a systematic approach to reading and writing. For us, these skills are absolutely essential for language learners in the digital age.

To sum up, we have tried to write a course that teachers will really enjoy using; a course that is authentic but manageable, systematic but not repetitive – a course that not only brings the real world into the classroom, but also sends our students into the real world with the confidence to truly 'speak out'!

From left to right: Frances Eales, JJ Wilson, Antonia Clare and Steve Oakes

OVERVIEW OF THE COMPONENTS

STUDENTS' BOOK

- Between 90 and 120 hours of teaching material
- Language Bank with reference material and extra practice
- Vocabulary bank to expand vocabulary
- Audioscripts of the class audio

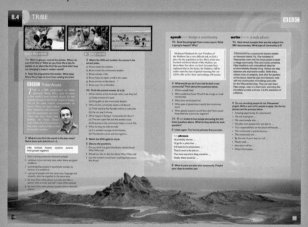

CLASS AUDIO CDs

- Audio material for use in class
- Test audio for the Mid-course and End of Course Tests

DVD & ACTIVE BOOK

- DVD content
- Digital Students' Book
- Audio, video and Video podcasts

WORKBOOK

- Grammar and vocabulary
- Functional language
- Speaking and listening strategies
- Reading, writing and listening
- Regular review and self-study tests

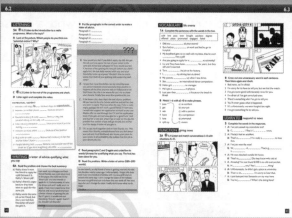

AUDIO CD

- Audio material including listening, pronunciation and functional practice

MYSPEAKOUTLAB

- Interactive Workbook with hints and tips
- Unit tests and Progress Tests
- Mid-course and End of Course Tests
- Video podcasts with interactive worksheets

TEACHER'S RESOURCE BOOK

- Teaching notes
- Integrated key and audioscript
- Five photocopiable activities for every unit
- Mid-course and End of Course Test

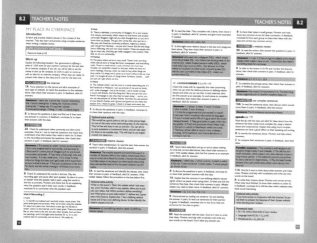

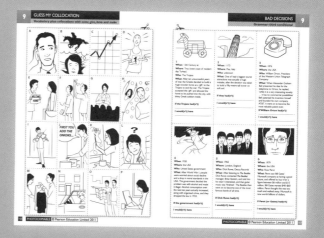

SPEAKOUT ACTIVE TEACH

- Integrated audio and video content
- Video podcasts
- Test master containing all course tests
- Answer reveal feature
- Grammar and vocabulary review games
- A host of useful tools
- Large extra resources section

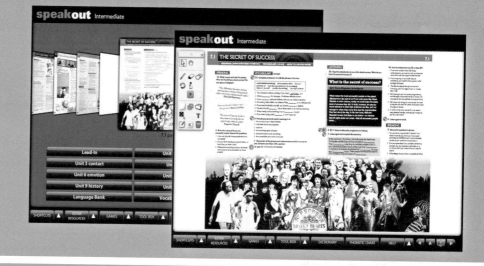

SPEAKOUT WEBSITE

- Information about the course
- Sample materials from the course
- Teaching tips
- Placement test
- A range of useful resources
- Video podcasts

A UNIT OF THE STUDENTS' BOOK

UNIT OVERVIEW

Every unit of Speakout starts with an Overview, which lists the topics covered. This is followed by two main input lessons which cover grammar, vocabulary and the four skills. Lesson three covers functional language and focuses on important speaking and listening strategies. Lesson four is built around a clip from a BBC programme and consolidates language and skills work. Each unit culminates with a Lookback page, which provides communicative practice of the key language.

INPUT LESSON 1

Lesson one introduces the topic of the unit and presents the key language needed to understand and talk about it. The lesson combines grammar and vocabulary with a focus on skills work.

> Lexical sets are introduced in context. Practice of new words often includes pronunciation work.

> The target language and the CEF objectives are listed to clearly show the objectives of the lesson.

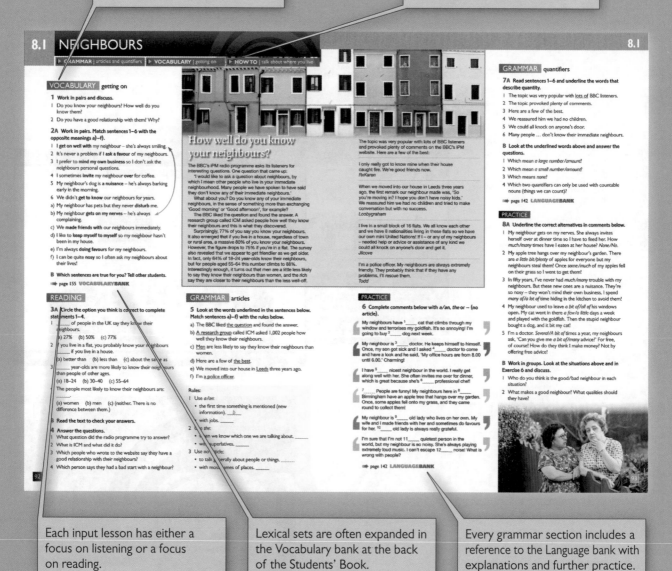

> Each input lesson has either a focus on listening or a focus on reading.

> Lexical sets are often expanded in the Vocabulary bank at the back of the Students' Book.

> Every grammar section includes a reference to the Language bank with explanations and further practice.

INPUT LESSON 2

Lesson two continues to focus on grammar and vocabulary while extending and expanding the topic area. By the end of the second lesson students will have worked on all four skill areas.

Clear grammar presentations are followed by written and oral practice as well as pronunciation work.

All lessons include a focus on speaking where the emphasis is on communication and fluency building.

8.2
8.2

GRAMMAR relative clauses

4 Read about the origins of a website. Why did the website become successful?

The rise and rise of YouTube

Early in 2005, three friends, Chad Hurley, Steve Chen and Jawed Karim, who were also colleagues, were having problems trying to email a video clip. Within two hours they came up with an idea which would solve the problem and change internet history. They decided to create a video sharing platform and YouTube was born. It's a familiar story for anyone who follows the development of the internet: technology-minded entrepreneurs under thirty; a garage or bedroom, where dreams become reality; little money and a big communicative need. The site was an instant success. The key was a number of features: links to the videos, which made them easy to email; tell-a-friend functions; a feature that allowed YouTube videos to be played on other social networking sites; and another feature that let users comment on the videos. This helped to develop the site's sense of community: YouTube was a place where you posted videos but also chatted about them, complained, smiled (☺) or laughed out loud (LOL). Two years after the launch, Google Inc., bought YouTube for $1.65 billion.

5A Look at the underlined clauses in the sentences below. Which is a defining relative clause and which is a non-defining relative clause?

a) Chad Hurley, Steve Chen and Jawed Karim, who were colleagues, were having problems trying to email a video clip.
b) YouTube was a place where you posted videos.

B Read rules 1 and 2 to check your answers. Then complete rule 3 with *which, who, where* and *that*.

Rules:
1 Defining relative clauses tell us exactly which thing, person or place we are talking about.
2 Non-defining relative clauses add extra information to a sentence. They tell us what a thing, person or place is or does. The sentence is still grammatically possible without the extra information.
3 _____ is used to talk about places.
_____ is used to talk about people.
_____ is used to talk about places.
_____ can be used to talk about places, people or things (in defining relative clauses only).

C Read the text in Exercise 4A again. Find and underline eight relative clauses. What type of relative clauses are they: defining (D) or non-defining (ND)?
➡ page 142 LANGUAGEBANK

PRACTICE

6A Circle the correct alternatives to complete the text.

For people who liked to send and receive very short messages, Twitter.com was a dream come true. This social networking site, [1]*that/which was/who was* the fastest growing site in 2009, became amazingly popular in a short space of time. So how does it work? You write your message, [2]*of which must be/what must be/which must be* no longer than 140 characters, onto your profile via a web, SMS or phone application. Then the message, [3]*what is called/this is called/which is called* a 'Tweet', is sent automatically to your subscribers or 'followers'. The people [4]*use/that use/are who use* Twitter say it's fantastic. Jerry Jones, [5]*who works for/who works where/which works for* an internet company, describes it as 'a mini-revolution'. He says that when Twitter arrived, it was the moment [6]*which online/for online/when online* communication changed. No more boring blogs, [7]*what go/where people go/who people go* on and on about nothing. 'Me and my friends, [8]*who all use/all use/we use* Twitter, have a saying: Keep your Tweet short and sweet!'

B Discuss the questions.
1 Do you or does anyone you know use Twitter?
2 What social networking websites do you know?
3 Which are the most popular now?

7A ▶ 8.3 Listen for the pauses where there are commas. Tick the sentence you hear.
1 a) The travel site which we developed is really popular.
b) The travel site, which we developed, is really popular.
2 a) Those children who spend too much time on the net don't communicate well.
b) Those children, who spend too much time on the net, don't communicate well.
3 a) Video sharing sites which are free are a great resource for students.
b) Video sharing sites, which are free, are a great resource for students.
4 a) On that dating site where I met my wife there are hundreds of single people.
b) On that dating site, where I met my wife, there are hundreds of single people.
5 a) Bloggers who write regularly often get their stories from news websites.
b) Bloggers, who write regularly, often get their stories from news websites.

B Work in pairs. Take turns to choose a sentence from Exercise 7A and read it aloud. Your partner says which sentence you read, a) or b).

SPEAKING

8A Look at the activities in the box below. Do you prefer doing them online or in the real world? What are their advantages/disadvantages?

shopping	meet new people	find out the news	learn a language
book flights/hotels	watch films/programmes	speak to friends
look up information	explore new places

B Work with other students. Discuss your opinions.
I prefer shopping online because I don't have to leave my house, park the car and deal with crowds of people. It's really convenient and easy.

WRITING a website review

9A Read the website review and answer the questions.
1 What type of website is it?
2 Why does the writer recommend it?
3 Who uses the website? Why?

Website of the Month for January is **magportal.com**. It's a website which you can use to find magazine articles on lots of different topics. One reason I'd recommend it is the range of subjects, which include health, finance, entertainment, science and technology, sports and even pets and animals.

The best thing about magportal.com is that the design is very simple, which makes it really easy to use. There's a menu of categories and a search engine if you want something specific. Another excellent feature is that you can get articles by typing the date – the most recent ones are shown first – or the name of a specific magazine.

I know several journalists who use magportal.com for research. I suggest that readers try it out; there's something for everyone.

B Number the features of a review in a logical order.
a) Say the purpose of the website. ___
b) Say who you'd recommend the website to. ___
c) Introduce the name of the website. ___
d) Say what special features the website has. ___

C Find and underline three phrases we use to recommend something.

LEARN TO use complex sentences

10A Compare the pairs of sentences. Which sounds more fluent: a) or b)?
1 a) It's a website. You can use it to find magazine articles. The articles are on lots of different topics.
b) It's a website which you can use to find magazine articles on lots of different topics.
2 a) I know several journalists. They use magportal.com. They use it for research.
b) I know several journalists who use magportal.com for research.

speakout TIP

Think about using complex sentences. Simple sentences can be effective, but when we use many simple sentences together, it sounds childish: *I swim every day. I love the water. It's good exercise.* We can make sentences more complex by using conjunctions (*and, because, but,* etc.) and relative clauses: *I swim every day because I love the feel of the water and it's also good exercise.* How have the b) sentences in Exercise 10A been made more complex?

B Rewrite sentences 1–4 to make them sound more fluent.
1 The website is well-designed. The good design makes it user-friendly.
2 The site has too much animation. This makes it very slow. It takes a long time to upload.
3 The website's content comes from its users. Users send in their photos.
4 The site feels friendly. It has user profile areas. Here, users can say who they are.

C Work in pairs and compare your answers.

11A What is your 'Website of the Month'? Choose a website and think about the questions below.
1 What type of website is it (photo sharing, social networking, etc.)?
2 Why do you like it?
3 How often do you visit it?
4 Is there a community of users?
5 Who would you recommend it to?

B Write your review (120–150 words). Show it to other students. Which websites sound interesting to you?

96
97

Grammar and vocabulary sections often include a listening element to reinforce the new language.

Every pair of input lessons includes at least one writing section with focus on a variety of different genres.

Regular Speakout tips help students to develop their study skills both inside and outside the classroom.

FUNCTIONAL LESSON

The third lesson in each unit focuses on a particular function, situation or transaction as well as introducing important speaking and listening strategies.

The target language and the CEF objectives are listed to clearly show the objectives of the lesson.

Students learn a lexical set which is relevant to the function or situation.

The lesson ends with a speaking activity which gives students the chance to practise the new language.

The functional language is learnt in context, often by listening to the language in use.

Students learn important speaking and listening strategies which can be transferred to many situations.

Conversation flow charts provide scaffolding that allows students to explore the new language.

DVD LESSON

The fourth lesson in each unit is based around an extract from a real BBC programme. This acts as a springboard into freer communicative speaking and writing activities.

A preview section gets students thinking about the topic of the extract and introduces key language.

A series of different tasks helps students to understand and enjoy the programme.

The Speakout task builds on the topic of the extract and provides extended speaking practice.

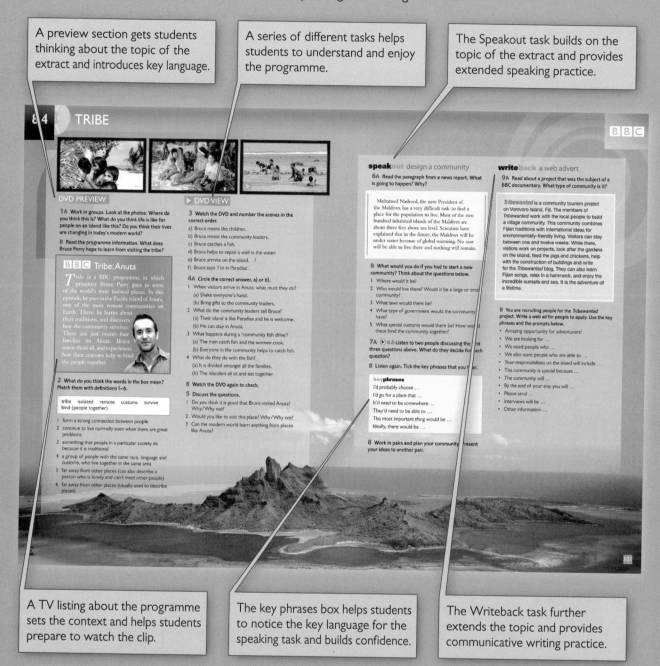

A TV listing about the programme sets the context and helps students prepare to watch the clip.

The key phrases box helps students to notice the key language for the speaking task and builds confidence.

The Writeback task further extends the topic and provides communicative writing practice.

LOOKBACK PAGE

Each unit ends with a Lookback page, which provides further practice and review of the key language covered in the unit. The review exercises are a mixture of communicative activities and games. Further practice and review exercises can be found in the Workbook. The Lookback page also introduces the Video podcast, which features a range of real people talking about one of the topics in the unit.

WORKBOOK

The Workbook contains a wide variety of practice and review exercises and covers all of the language areas studied in the unit. It also contains regular review sections as well as self-study tests to help students consolidate what they have learnt.

The Workbook contains regular listening practice using the accompanying audio CD.

The Workbook features extensive practice of vocabulary, grammar, reading, writing and listening.

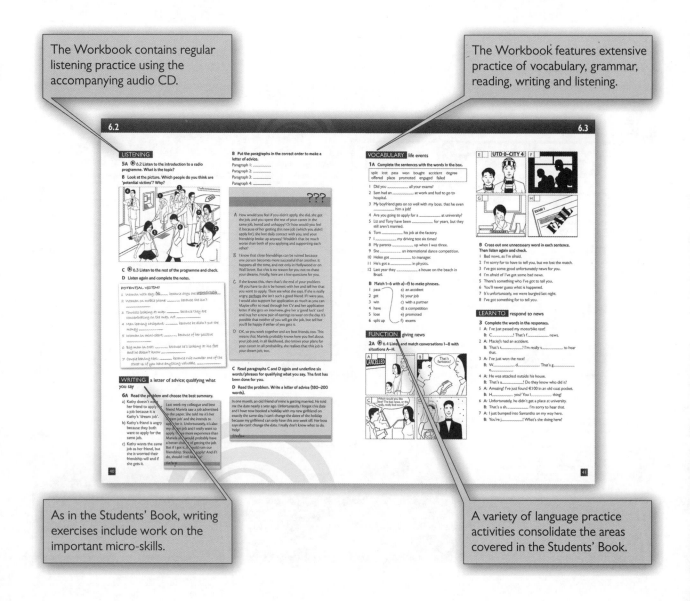

As in the Students' Book, writing exercises include work on the important micro-skills.

A variety of language practice activities consolidate the areas covered in the Students' Book.

MYSPEAKOUTLAB

MySpeakoutLab provides a fully blended and personalised learning environment that benefits both teachers and students. It offers:

- an interactive Workbook with hints, tips and automatic grade book.
- professionally written Unit Tests, Progress Tests, Mid-course and End of Course tests that can be assigned at the touch of a button.
- interactive Video podcast worksheets with an integrated video player so students can watch while they do the exercises.

ACTIVETEACH

Speakout ActiveTeach contains everything you need to make the course come alive in your classroom.
It includes integrated whiteboard software which enables you to add notes and embed files.
It is also possible to save all of your work with the relevant page from the Students' Book.

An answer reveal function lets you show the answers to an exercise at the touch of a button.

Shortcuts to the relevant pages of the Language bank and the Vocabulary bank make navigation easy.

All audio and video content is fully integrated and includes subtitles as well as printable scripts.

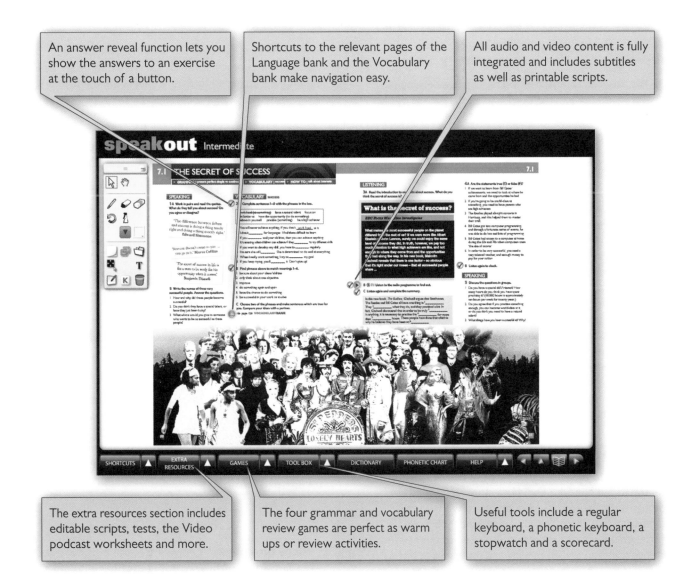

The extra resources section includes editable scripts, tests, the Video podcast worksheets and more.

The four grammar and vocabulary review games are perfect as warm ups or review activities.

Useful tools include a regular keyboard, a phonetic keyboard, a stopwatch and a scorecard.

WEBSITE

The Speakout website will offer information about the course as well as a bank of useful resources including:

- introductory videos by the authors of the course.
- sample materials.
- teaching tips.
- placement test.
- CEF mapping documents.
- Video podcasts for all published levels.

speakout is designed to satisfy both students and teachers on a number of different levels. It offers engaging topics with authentic BBC material to really bring them to life. At the same time it offers a robust and comprehensive focus on grammar, vocabulary, functions and pronunciation. As the name of the course might suggest, speaking activities are prominent, but that is not at the expense of the other core skills, which are developed systematically throughout.

With this balanced approach to topics, language development and skills work, our aim has been to create a course book full of 'lessons that really work' in practice. Below we will briefly explain our approach in each of these areas.

TOPICS AND CONTENT

In *Speakout* we have tried to choose topics that are relevant to students' lives. Where a topic area is covered in other ELT courses we have endeavoured to find a fresh angle on it. It is clear to us that authenticity is important to learners, and many texts come from the BBC's rich resources (audio, visual and print) as well as other real-world sources. At lower levels, we have sometimes adapted materials by adjusting the language to make it more manageable for students while trying to keep the tone as authentic as possible. We have also attempted to match the authentic feel of a text with an authentic interaction. Every unit contains a variety of rich and authentic input material including BBC Video podcasts (filmed on location in London, England) and DVD material, featuring some of the best the BBC has to offer.

GRAMMAR

Knowing how to recognise and use grammatical structures is central to our ability to communicate with each other. Although at first students can often get by with words and phrases, they increasingly need grammar to make themselves understood. Students also need to understand sentence formation when reading and listening and to be able to produce accurate grammar in professional and exam situations. We share students' belief that learning grammar is a core feature of learning a language and believe that a guided discovery approach, where students are challenged to notice new forms works best. At the same time learning is scaffolded so that students are supported at all times in a systematic way. Clear grammar presentations are followed by written and oral practice. There is also the chance to notice and practise pronunciation where appropriate.

In *Speakout* you will find:

- **Grammar in context** – We want to be sure that the grammar focus is clear and memorable for students. Grammar is almost always taken from the listening or reading texts, so that learners can see the language in action, and understand how and when it is used.

- **Noticing** – We involve students in the discovery of language patterns by asking them to identify aspects of meaning and form, and complete rules or tables.

- **Clear language reference** – As well as a summary of rules within the unit, there is also a Language bank which serves as a clear learning reference for the future

- **Focus on use** – We ensure that there is plenty of practice, both form and meaning-based, in the Language bank to give students confidence in manipulating the new language. On the main input page we include personalised practice, which is designed to be genuinely communicative and to offer students the opportunity to say something about themselves or the topic. There is also regular recycling of new language in the Lookback review pages, and again the focus here is on moving learners towards communicative use of the language.

VOCABULARY

Developing a wide range of vocabulary is key to increasing communicative effectiveness; developing a knowledge of high-frequency collocations and fixed and semi-fixed phrases is key to increasing spoken fluency. An extensive understanding of words and phrases helps learners become more confident when reading and listening, and developing a range of vocabulary is important for effective writing. Equally vital is learner-training, equipping students with the skills to record, memorise and recall vocabulary for use.

In *Speakout* this is reflected in:

- **A prominent focus on vocabulary** – We include vocabulary in almost all lessons whether in a lexical set linked to a particular topic, as preparation for a speaking activity or to aid comprehension of a DVD clip or a listening or reading text. Where we want students to use the language actively, we encourage them to use the vocabulary to talk about their own lives or opinions. At lower levels, the Photo bank also extends the vocabulary taught in the lessons, using memorable photographs and graphics to support students' understanding.

- **Focus on 'chunks'** – As well as lexical sets, we also regularly focus on how words fit together with other words, often getting students to notice how words are used in a text and to focus on high-frequency 'chunks' such as verb-noun collocations or whole phrases.

- **Focus on vocabulary systems** – We give regular attention to word-building skills, a valuable tool in expanding vocabulary. At higher levels, the Vocabulary plus sections deal with systems such as affixation, multi-word verbs and compound words in greater depth.

- **Recycling and learner training** – Practice exercises ensure that vocabulary is encountered on a number of occasions: within the lessons, on the Lookback page, in subsequent lessons and in the Photo bank/Vocabulary bank at the back of the book. One of the main focuses of the Speakout tips – which look at all areas of language learning – is to highlight vocabulary learning strategies, aiming to build good study skills that will enable students to gain and retain new language.

FUNCTIONAL LANGUAGE

One thing that both teachers and learners appreciate is the need to manage communication in a wide variety of encounters, and to know what's appropriate to say in given situations. These can be transactional exchanges, where the main focus is on getting something done (buying something in a shop or phoning to make an enquiry), or interactional exchanges, where the main focus is on socialising with others (talking about the weekend, or responding appropriately to good news). As one learner commented to us, 'Grammar rules aren't enough – I need to know what to say.' Although it is possible to categorise 'functions' under 'lexical phrases', we believe it is useful for learners to focus on functional phrases separately from vocabulary or grammar.

The third lesson in every unit of *Speakout* looks at one such situation, and focuses on the functional language needed. Learners hear or see the language used in context and then practise it in mini-situations, in both a written and a spoken context. Each of these lessons also includes a Learn to section, which highlights and practises a useful strategy for dealing with both transactional and interactional exchanges, for example asking for clarification, showing interest, etc. Learners will find themselves not just more confident users of the language, but also more active listeners.

SPEAKING

The dynamism of most lessons depends on the success of the speaking tasks, whether the task is a short oral practice of new language, a discussion comparing information or opinions, a personal response to a reading text or a presentation where a student might speak uninterrupted for a minute or more. Students develop fluency when they are motivated to speak. For this to happen, engaging topics and tasks are essential, as is the sequencing of stages and task design. For longer tasks, students often need to prepare their ideas and language in a structured way. This all-important rehearsal time leads to more motivation and confidence as well as greater accuracy, fluency and complexity. Also, where appropriate, students need to hear a model before they speak, in order to have a realistic goal.

There are several strands to speaking in *Speakout*:

- **Communicative practice** – After introducing any new language (vocabulary, grammar or function) there are many opportunities in *Speakout* for students to use it in a variety of activities which focus on communication as well as accuracy. These include personalised exchanges, dialogues, flow-charts and role-plays.

- **Focus on fluency** – In every unit of *Speakout* we include opportunities for students to respond spontaneously. They might be asked to respond to a series of questions, to a DVD, a Video podcast or a text, or to take part in conversations, discussions and role-plays. These activities involve a variety of interactional formations such as pairs and groups.

- **Speaking strategies and sub-skills** – In the third lesson of each unit, students are encouraged to notice in a systematic way features which will help them improve their speaking. These include, for example, ways to manage a phone conversation, the use of mirror questions to ask for clarification, sentence starters to introduce an opinion and intonation to correct mistakes.

- **Extended speaking tasks** – In the *Speakout* DVD lesson, as well as in other speaking tasks throughout the course, students are encouraged to attempt more adventurous and extended use of language in tasks such as problem solving, developing a project or telling a story. These tasks go beyond discussion; they include rehearsal time, useful language and a concrete outcome.

LISTENING

For most users of English (or any language, for that matter), listening is the most frequently used skill. A learner who can speak well but not understand at least as well is unlikely to be a competent communicator or user of the language. We feel that listening can be developed effectively through well-structured materials. As with speaking, the choice of interesting topics and texts works hand in hand with carefully considered sequencing and task design. At the same time, listening texts can act as a springboard to stimulate discussion in class.

There are several strands to listening in *Speakout*:

- **Focus on authentic recordings** – In *Speakout*, we believe that it is motivating for all levels of learner to try to access and cope with authentic material. Each unit includes a DVD extract from a BBC documentary, drama or light entertainment programme as well as a podcast filmed on location with real people giving their opinions. At the higher levels you will also find unscripted audio texts and BBC radio extracts. All are invaluable in the way they expose learners to real language in use as well as different varieties of English. Where recordings, particularly at lower levels, are scripted, they aim to reflect the patterns of natural speech.

- **Focus on sub-skills and strategies** – Tasks across the recordings in each unit are designed with a number of sub-skills and strategies in mind. These include: listening for global meaning and more detail; scanning for specific information; becoming sensitised to possible misunderstandings; and noticing nuances of intonation and expression. We also help learners to listen actively by using strategies such as asking for repetition and paraphrasing.

- **As a context for new language** – We see listening as a key mode of input and *Speakout* includes many listening texts which contain target grammar, vocabulary or functions in their natural contexts. Learners are encouraged to notice this new language and how and where it occurs, often by using the audio scripts as a resource.

- **As a model for speaking** – In the third and fourth lessons of each unit the recordings serve as models for speaking tasks. These models reveal the ways in which speakers use specific language to structure their discourse, for example with regard to turn-taking, hesitating and checking for understanding. These recordings also serve as a goal for the learners' speaking.

READING

Reading is a priority for many students, whether it's for study, work or pleasure, and can be practised alone, anywhere and at any time. Learners who read regularly tend to have a richer, more varied vocabulary, and are often better writers, which in turn supports their oral communication skills. Nowadays, the Internet has given students access to an extraordinary range of English language reading material, and the availability of English language newspapers, books and magazines is greater than ever before. The language learner who develops skill and confidence in reading in the classroom will be more motivated to read outside the classroom. Within the classroom reading texts can also introduce stimulating topics and act as springboards for class discussion.

There are several strands to reading in *Speakout*:

* **Focus on authentic texts** – As with *Speakout* listening materials, there is an emphasis on authenticity, and this is reflected in a number of ways. Many of the reading texts in *Speakout* are sourced from the BBC. Where texts have been adapted or graded, there is an attempt to maintain authenticity by remaining faithful to the text type in terms of content and style. We have chosen up-to-date, relevant texts to stimulate interest and motivate learners to read. The texts represent a variety of genres that correspond to the text types that learners will probably encounter in their everyday lives.

* **Focus on sub-skills and strategies** – In *Speakout* we strive to maintain authenticity in the way the readers interact with a text. We always give students a reason to read, and provide tasks which bring about or simulate authentic reading, including real-life tasks such as summarising, extracting specific information, reacting to an opinion or following an anecdote. We also focus on strategies for decoding texts, such as guessing the meaning of unknown vocabulary, understanding pronoun referencing and following discourse markers.

* **Noticing new language** – Noticing language in use is a key step towards the development of a rich vocabulary and greater all-round proficiency in a language, and this is most easily achieved through reading. In *Speakout*, reading texts often serve as valuable contexts for introducing grammar and vocabulary as well as discourse features.

* **As a model for writing** – In the writing sections, as well as the Writeback sections of the DVD spreads, the readings serve as models for students to refer to when they are writing, in terms of overall organisation as well as style and language content.

WRITING

In recent years the growth of email and the internet has led to a shift in the nature of the writing our students need to do. Email has also led to an increased informality in written English. However, many students need to develop their formal writing for professional and exam-taking purposes. It is therefore important to focus on a range of genres, from formal text types such as essays, letters and reports to informal genres such as blog entries and personal messages.

There are four strands to writing in *Speakout*:

* **Focus on genres** – In every unit at the four higher levels there is a section that focuses on a genre of writing, emails for example. We provide a model to show the conventions of the genre and, where appropriate, we highlight fixed phrases associated with it. We usually then ask the students to produce their own piece of writing. While there is always a written product, we also focus on the process of writing, including the relevant stages such as brainstorming, planning, and checking. At Starter and Elementary, we focus on more basic writing skills, including basic written sentence patterns, linking, punctuation and text organisation, in some cases linking this focus to a specific genre.

* **Focus on sub-skills and strategies** – While dealing with the genres, we include a section which focuses on a sub-skill or strategy that is generally applicable to all writing. Sub-skills include paragraphing, organising content and using linking words and pronouns, while strategies include activities like writing a first draft quickly, keeping your reader in mind and self-editing. We present the sub-skill by asking the students to notice the feature. We then provide an opportunity for the students to practise it.

* **Writeback** – At the end of every unit, following the DVD and final speaking task, we include a Writeback task. The idea is for students to develop fluency in their writing. While we always provide a model, the task is not tied to any particular grammatical structure. Instead the emphasis is on using writing to generate ideas and personal responses.

* **Writing as a classroom activity** – We believe that writing can be very usefully employed as an aid to speaking and as a reflective technique for responding to texts – akin to the practice of writing notes in the margins of books. It also provides a change of pace and focus in lessons. Activities such as short dictations, note-taking, brainstorming on paper and group story writing are all included in *Speakout*.

PRONUNCIATION

In recent years, attitudes towards pronunciation in many English language classrooms have moved towards a focus on intelligibility: if students' spoken language is understandable, then the pronunciation is good enough. We are aware, however, that many learners and teachers place great importance on developing pronunciation that is more than 'good enough', and that systematic attention to pronunciation in a lesson, however brief, can have a significant impact on developing learners' speech.

In *Speakout*, we have taken a practical, integrated approach to developing students' pronunciation, highlighting features that often cause problems in conjunction with a given area of grammar, particular vocabulary items and functional language. Where relevant to the level, a grammatical or functional language focus is followed by a focus on a feature of pronunciation, for example, the weak forms of auxiliary verbs or connected speech in certain functional exponents. Students are given the opportunity to listen to models of the pronunciation, notice the key feature and then practise it.

TEACHING INTERMEDIATE LEARNERS

Intermediate can be a tremendously rewarding level to teach. In contrast to lower levels, the students now have enough English to really express themselves. They can begin to use and understand humour; they can engage in discussions about serious issues; and they can use language creatively. At intermediate, the class begins to relax a little, as students start to communicate more freely without needing so much input and guidance from the teacher. There is a shift of focus from what they don't know (everything, at the lower levels) to what they do know, and what they are able to do with it. At the same time, for many students the intermediate level marks a 'plateau'. They are able to deal with most of the basic functions they need and, consequently, many learners never get beyond this level.

While intermediate students have already covered the most important grammatical areas and probably learned a good deal of basic vocabulary, there will almost certainly be major gaps in their knowledge and in their ability to produce effective spoken and written discourse.

At this level, other elements become important beyond simply getting a message across. For example, there is the issue of register: can the student modulate his or her speech to fit both formal and informal occasions? There is range: is the student-as-speaker confident attempting a variety of speech acts such as describing a place, giving instructions, or narrating a story? There is also range of input: is the student-as-listener/watcher able to cope with different genres of authentic material such as radio programmes, DVD clips, and live interaction? These questions underpin the approach to the teaching of skills in an intermediate class.

Besides skills, one of the most important areas for intermediate students to work on is vocabulary. While they may 'know' the meaning of many words where one word equates with one idea, they often do not know collocations and idioms that use those same words. For example, they know the words take and part, but not the expression take part in something. The English language has thousands of these expressions, and it is at the Intermediate level that students really begin to grapple with the depth and breadth of the language.

In terms of grammar, the approach needs to encompass both consolidation and gradual broadening of the repertoire. Structures that have been 'half-learnt' at lower levels should be revisited with the goal of developing automaticity so that the student does not have to search for the right forms. At the same time, there is plenty of new grammar (and new uses for old grammar!) to keep intermediate students challenged.

It has often been noted that intermediate can be a wide-ranging level. There may be large discrepancies between students in terms of what they are capable of doing with the language. While some may still struggle with, say, reading a course book text, others are able to read whole books in English. Besides being aware of differences in level, teachers also need to focus on individual needs. At the beginner levels all students have similar needs (basic language skills), but many students at intermediate will start

to have specific requirements depending on their reasons for learning English, whether for work, exams, travel, or fun. Try to use this variety to benefit the class. There is much scope for peer teaching (both language and content), project work, and extended group work based on mixed abilities and interests in intermediate classes.

Here are our top tips for teaching at this level:

- Help the students to become independent learners through the use of strategies. Try to get students interacting with the language on their own by using authentic materials such as video, songs, and Internet downloads.

- Challenge the students in different ways. Intermediate students probably know a lot about how they learn best and the types of activities that motivate them. Although teachers cannot please everyone all the time, we can provide a wide range of activity types, including both analytical exercises and hands-on experiential learning.

- Do a lot of work on collocation. At this level, the students should be able to work with phrases and chunks of language.

- Use teaching strategies to counteract a feeling articulated by many Intermediate students that 'I'm not learning anything new'. Keep records of all new vocabulary learned (use a Word Wall or vocabulary cards) and regularly recycle the words/expressions; video learners doing speaking activities at different stages of the course; and keep portfolios of their written work.

- Invite students to extend shorter responses. Set pre-speaking goals such as 'each student should speak for two minutes' or assign group monitors to keep conversations flowing. For written assignments, set word counts that go beyond students' normal output. Particularly in classes where students don't get much of a chance to interact in English outside the class, it's vital that the students use their opportunities to speak the language.

- Identify and deal with fossilised errors. These start to become an issue at intermediate. Use various techniques: keep a common mistake file and revisit it regularly. Use extended post-speaking activities in which the students self-correct and analyse their language use. Besides using it for correction, use this slot to highlight examples of interesting and successful language use.

- Keep encouraging and motivating students. You can do this through comments on student journals or letters, one-to-one tutorials, or while giving feedback to the whole class. While progress may sometimes seem slow at this level, one of the keys to teaching intermediate students is to see the level as a transition point rather than an end point.

Antonia Clare, Frances Eales, Steve Oakes and JJ Wilson

TEACHER'S NOTES INDEX

OVERVIEW

1.1 WHO DO YOU THINK YOU ARE?
GRAMMAR | question forms
VOCABULARY | family
HOW TO | talk about your family

COMMON EUROPEAN FRAMEWORK
Ss can enter unprepared into conversation on topics that are familiar, of personal interest or pertinent to everyday life; can write personal letters describing experiences and impressions.

1.2 MEN AND WOMEN
GRAMMAR | review of verb tenses
VOCABULARY | relationships
HOW TO | talk about people in your life

COMMON EUROPEAN FRAMEWORK
Ss can understand the majority of radio broadcast material about familiar topics delivered slowly and clearly; can summarise and give their opinion about and answer questions of detail; can take an active part in informal discussion in familiar contexts.

1.3 TELL ME ABOUT YOURSELF
FUNCTION | talking about yourself
VOCABULARY | interview advice
LEARN TO | use two-word responses

COMMON EUROPEAN FRAMEWORK
Ss can provide concrete information required in an interview; can carry out a prepared interview, checking and confirming information.

1.4 SECOND LIFE ● BBC DVD
speakout | create a new identity
writeback | answer a questionnaire

COMMON EUROPEAN FRAMEWORK
Ss can catch the main points in TV programmes when the delivery is relatively slow and clear; can exchange, check and confirm accumulated factual information on familiar routine and non-routine matters; can convey information and ideas on abstract as well as concrete topics, check information and ask about or explain problems.

1.5 LOOKBACK
Communicative revision activities

BBC VIDEO PODCAST
What does 'family' mean to you?

This video podcast extends discussion of the unit topic to family. Ss can view people describing their family and what 'family' means to them. Use this video podcast at the start or end of Unit 1.

WHO DO YOU THINK YOU ARE?

Introduction
Ss revise/practise question forms (*yes/no* questions, subject and object questions and questions with a preposition) in the context of talking about their family in the present and past. They also practise writing formal and informal emails.

SUPPLEMENTARY MATERIALS
Resource bank p127

Warm up
With new classes, it's important to build rapport so that the Ss feel comfortable with each other and with you. Write three facts about yourself on the board, two true and one false. Invite Ss to ask questions to find out further information about the facts and then guess which one is false.

SPEAKING

1A The aim of this activity is to help you assess Ss' language and speaking skills, as well as their use of question forms, which will be reviewed later in the lesson. Elicit some ideas for questions they might ask, e.g. *What's your job? What do you like doing at the weekend?* Ss then work in pairs to ask as many questions as they can in two minutes.

B Ss use the facts they noted down to introduce their partner to the class. Check they are using the third person -s correctly.

> **Teaching tip**
> When nominating Ss to speak, do it randomly (rather than round the class) to prevent Ss from switching off before their turn.

VOCABULARY family

2A Go through the first example with the class. Ss match the questions and answers alone, then check their answers in pairs. Elicit the correct answers and check the meaning of new words. Drill the pronunciation chorally and individually.

> **Answers:** 1 a) 2 h) 3 f) 4 j) 5 g) 6 e) 7 b) 8 i) 9 c) 10 d)

B Arrange Ss into small groups and ask them to discuss the questions together. When they have finished, elicit an answer for each question.

> **Teaching tip**
> In group discussions, monitor carefully and note down any common errors and/or examples of good language. After feedback, go through the errors as a class, without naming who made them. Ask Ss to try and correct the errors themselves. Drill any examples of good language.

> ➡ **VOCABULARYBANK** p148 Family
> **1** Focus attention on the family tree. Read the example with the class, then Ss complete the family tree with the words in the box. In feedback, elicit Ss' answers. *Stronger classes* can do the exercise at home.
>
> **Answers:** (from left to right, top to bottom): grandparents on my mother's side, stepfather, in-laws, ex-husband, sister-in-law, stepdaughter, nephew, niece

READING

3A Ask Ss if they know much about their family history, or if they would like to. Focus attention on the logo and title and elicit their suggestions as to what the programme is about. Write some of their ideas on the board.

B Give Ss three minutes to read the text quickly and check their predictions. Explain that they will have a chance to read again for more detail afterwards.

Answer: They discover that their family histories include every type of person imaginable: heroes, liars, geniuses, soldiers, inventors and even kings.

C Focus attention on the photos and ask Ss if they have seen any of these celebrities before. Ss read the text again more carefully and work alone to find the answers to the questions. They can then check their answers with a partner. In feedback, elicit the answers, asking Ss to tell you which part of the text gives the information.

Answers: 1 Matthew Pinsent 2 Davina McCall 3 Colin Jackson 4 Kim Cattrall 5 Jodie Kidd 6 Nigella Lawson

D Point out the paragraph numbers at the side of the text and give Ss 3–4 mins to find the words and phrases in the text, working alone then checking with a partner. Elicit the answers and check comprehension by using focused questions, such as *What kind of jobs can earn you a fortune? Which position wins a gold medal – 1st, 2nd or 3rd? What things might organising security involve?* etc. Drill the new vocabulary.

Answers: 1 a fortune 2 gold medallist 3 organising security 4 tragic 5 abandoned 6 sentenced

4 Put Ss into small groups to discuss the questions. Monitor and provide any vocabulary Ss need. In feedback, nominate Ss from each group to tell the class their opinions.

LISTENING

5A Introduce the topic of the listening and check Ss understand what they have to do. Explain that they don't have to understand every word and that they will have a chance to listen again later. Ss listen and write the family members he talks about.

Teaching tip

In listening activities, don't play the recording too many times, as this isn't like real-life listening. Before playing the recording again, let Ss check their answers in pairs, as they may be able to get the answers they didn't hear.

Answers: He talks about his grandmothers, paternal grandfather, wife and two sons.

B Before playing the recording again, ask if Ss can remember any of the questions the man was asked. Ss listen again and answer the questions. They can then check their answers with a partner. Play the recording again and check Ss' answers.

Answers: 1 one – his grandmother 2 Holland 3 soldiers, churchmen or sailors 4 three – his wife and two sons 5 himself

---

Unit 1 Recording 1

W=Woman M=Man

W: So, do you know a lot about your family history?

M: I do actually. Yes, erm, cos, one thing we have got is a family tree, so, erm, I've put it all on the computer. So, er, I know quite a lot about them.

W: Did you ever meet your great-grandparents, for example?

M: No, I never met them. Erm, in fact, I've only ever met one grandparent.

W: Oh?

M: Yeah, they all died rather young so I only had … I met my granny. Erm, that was from my mother's side. Mellows, they were from Yorkshire.

W: Oh, I was going to say, where did your ancestors come from?

M: Well, yeah, no, erm, my mother's side they all came from Yorkshire, but my father's family, er, originally came from Holland. They came over with, er, with William of Orange in 1689.

W: Ah! That's fascinating!

M: And my ancestor was William of Orange's, erm, closest advisor. And, er, so that was for the glorious revolution.

W: Wow! And what happened to the other ancestors? Do you know anything about your other side?

M: What?

W: What might have happened to …

M: What, my mother's side?

W: … more recently perhaps?

M: Well, all of, most of my ancestors were either soldiers, erm, or in the church, or sailors and, erm, very dull apparently. My father's side, incredibly dull lot until, er, my father's ah father married ah a woman whose ah surname was Knowle and they're all eccentrics – barking mad – lovely and great fun, so I like to think that I'm descended from that lot, rather more than the boring lot.

W: So on that note, which members of your family do you feel close to, would you say?

M: Well, I've only got, I don't have. Both my parents are dead now so, my immediate family is the answer to that question, my wife and my two sons who are twenty-five and twenty-one years old.

W: And who tells the best family stories?

M: Me!

W: I thought so!

GRAMMAR question forms

6A Ask Ss to look at the example questions 1–6. Check the meaning of *auxiliaries, prepositions* and *subject* by eliciting examples. Ss then read the grammar questions a)–e) and answer them using the example questions.

Teaching tip

Stronger classes can work alone, then compare their answers in pairs. You could also ask them to think of more examples for each type of question. *Weaker classes* may need more support. Read the notes with the Ss and check they understand how the word order changes in question forms. In each exercise, elicit the first answer as an example and check Ss can form the questions correctly before they do the rest of the exercises. In *mixed-ability classes, stronger Ss* could work with *weaker Ss*. This challenges the *stronger Ss* and reinforces their knowledge by having to explain it.

Check the answers with the class. Be prepared to clarify any points Ss aren't sure about, using examples.

Answers: a) 1 know 2 meet 3 come 4 happened 5 feel 6 tells b) 1 Do (present) 2 Did (past) 3 did (past) 5 do (present) c) 1 and 2 d) 3 and 5 e) 4 and 6

➡➡ **LANGUAGEBANK** 1.1 p128–129

Stronger classes could read the notes at home. Otherwise, check the notes with Ss, especially the word order in questions and the position of prepositions. In each exercise, elicit the first answer as an example. Ss work alone to complete the exercises, then check their answers in pairs. In feedback, elicit Ss' answers and drill the questions. Ss can refer to the notes to help them.

> **Answers:** 1 1 Where do you live? 2 Who won the game? 3 Does he eat meat? 4 What are they doing? 5 What are you writing about? 6 When did you arrive? 7 Who ate the chocolate? 8 Did you like the film?
> 2 1 Who killed the President? 2 What were you thinking about? 3 What happened to the old theatre? 4 Where did your great-grandparents come from? 5 Did your ancestors come from here? 6 Has she worked here for a long time? 7 Who is making all that noise? 8 Which house are you looking for?

B Ss listen to the questions from Ex 6A and decide if the *wh*-question words are said in a higher or lower voice.

> **Answer:** a higher voice

C Play the recording again and ask Ss to imitate the questions as they hear them. Repeat this until Ss feel comfortable pronouncing the questions.

> **Watch out!**
> Intonation can be frustrating for Ss due to the lack of hard and fast rules. But intonation is important for expressing meaning, sometimes more so than the words we use. Reassure Ss that the best way to learn it is by shadowing natural spoken language.

PRACTICE

7A Do the first question together as an example and write it on the board. Ss work alone to make questions, then check their answers in pairs. Elicit the answers.

> **Answers:** 1 Do you see your family every day? 2 Did your grandparents teach you anything? 3 Who always remembers your birthday? 4 Who taught you to read? 5 What do you do to relax? 6 Where do you want to go on your next holiday? 7 What three words describe you? 8 What makes you happy? 9 Who knows you best? 10 When did you first speak English?

B Drill the questions with the class. Ss choose three of the questions and walk around asking them to other Ss in a mingling activity. Invite Ss to share with the class any interesting answers they found out.

SPEAKING

8A Demonstrate the activity by writing two dates, two names and two places which are important to you on the board and explaining why they are important. Give Ss 5 mins to write their own dates, names and places and make notes about them. Monitor carefully to help with vocabulary, especially with *weaker classes*.

B Arrange Ss into groups of four and ask them to explain their information to their group. Monitor and encourage Ss to ask follow-up questions. Note down any common errors for later feedback. Nominate Ss from each group to tell the class any interesting facts they found out.

WRITING emails of introduction

9A Ss discuss the questions in pairs. In feedback, nominate some Ss to share their answers with the class.

B Focus attention on the subject lines of each email and ask Ss why they think the people are writing. Ss read and check. When eliciting the answers, ask them which lines tell us this.

> **Answers:** Nicholas Collett is writing to introduce himself to his new colleagues. The second sentence tells us. Julia is writing because she wants Max to show her around a new town. Sentence 6 tells us.

10 Ss read the five stages of email writing and the emails again, then answer the question in pairs. In feedback, elicit Ss' answers.

> **Answers:** 1 Both emails aim for their audience. They choose a formal or informal style, depending on the situation. 2 Both emails are short and to the point. 3 It is easy to understand the reason for writing. 4 & 5 We cannot see from the emails whether they have been drafted and edited, but the fact that points A to C have been covered suggests that they have.

LEARN TO write formal and informal emails

11A Ss look back at the two emails in Ex 9B and decide which is formal and which is informal. Elicit the answers and ask Ss how they can tell.

> **Answers:** The first email is formal. The second is informal. We know because of the answers to Ex 11B below.

> **Teaching tip**
> Due to historical influences on British English, longer, Latin-based words tend to be more formal, while shorter, Germanic-based words tend to be more informal. Because of this, Spanish, Italian, French and Portuguese speakers tend to find formal words easier to understand.

B Ss look back at the two emails and answer the questions in pairs. In feedback, elicit Ss' answers.

> **Answers:** 1 F 2 I 3 I 4 F

C Do the first note together as an example. Ss refer back to the emails to find the missing words, then check their answers in pairs. Elicit Ss' answers.

> **Answers:** 1 Dear (colleagues) 2 How are you? 3 opportunity 4 Hope to hear from you soon. 5 Yours sincerely,

12 Give Ss 3–4 mins to read the information and take notes. Check that Ss are clear about what they need to write and give them 10–15 mins to write a draft of their emails. Monitor carefully and help Ss with any vocabulary they need. Note down any common errors and go over them with the class at the end. Ss exchange drafts with a partner and give each other suggestions for improving their emails.

> **Homework ideas**
> • Ex 8A/B: write about your partner's (or your) important dates, names and places.
> • Ex 12: write a final draft of your email.
> • Language bank 1.1 Ex 1–2, p129
> • Vocabulary bank p148
> • Workbook Ex 1–6, p4–5

MEN AND WOMEN

Introduction

Ss revise and practise the present simple, present continuous, past simple and past continuous in the context of talking about the differences between men and women. They also learn and practise common collocations with *take*, *get*, *do* and *go*.

> **SUPPLEMENTARY MATERIALS**
>
> Resource bank p125, p126 and/or p128
>
> Ex 6A: bring dictionaries for Ss to use.

Warm up

Lead into the lesson via the blog illustrations. Ss work in pairs and discuss stereotypes of men and women.

SPEAKING

1A Ss discuss the questions in groups. In feedback, nominate Ss to share their ideas with the class and give feedback.

B Check Ss understand *to impress*, *(be) in charge*, *doorbell* and *outfit*. Give Ss 2–3 mins to read the blog, then discuss the comments in groups. Elicit their opinions in feedback.

GRAMMAR review of verb tenses

2A Focus attention on the underlined verbs in the examples. Ss work alone to match them to the names of the tenses, then check their answers in pairs. In feedback, elicit Ss' answers and check they know how to form the continuous tenses correctly.

> **Answers:** 1 c) 2 d) 3 a) 4 b)

B Do the first rule together as an example, then Ss complete the rest in pairs. Check answers and clarify if necessary.

> **Answers:** 1 c) 2 b) 3 a) 4 d)

C Go through the rules with the class, then give Ss 2–3 mins to underline three examples in the blog. Elicit the answers and other examples of 'state verbs' (verbs that are not usually used in continuous tenses) and write them on the board.

> **Answers:** Men <u>like</u> to have all their stuff; Women <u>know</u> what to do; Women <u>remember</u> every outfit

> ⟹ **LANGUAGEBANK** 1.2 p128–129
>
> **1A** Teach/elicit *translator* and *conference* before Ss do the exercise.
>
> **B** Elicit the first answer with the class as an example and check Ss are forming the tense correctly. Ss complete the sentences, then check their answers in pairs.
>
> **Answers:** 1 1 speak 2 'm attending 3 was doing 4 heard 5 arrived 6 don't speak 7 met 8 was looking 9 do you know 10 found
> 2 1 're winning 2 was travelling 3 died 4 wasn't listening 5 don't work 6 's burning 7 Did you see 8 causes

PRACTICE

3A Go through the first sentence together as a class. *Stronger classes* can do the exercise alone, then check their answers in pairs, but *weaker classes* could work in pairs. Elicit Ss' answers.

> **Answers:** 1 am 2 grew up 3 am learning 4 got 5 seemed 6 am enjoying 7 met 8 was looking 9 are 10 sing

B Arrange Ss into pairs and elicit the questions they need to ask to find out the information, e.g. *What do you do? What are you doing at the moment?* etc. With *weaker classes*, you could write these on the board. Ss then ask the questions and write their partner's profile.

LISTENING

4A Ss cover the text and focus on the title and questions. Elicit their predictions as to what the documentary is about. Give them 1 min to read the text alone and answer the questions in pairs. In feedback, elicit Ss' answers.

> **Answers:** 1 To discover what makes us who we are.
> 2 Twenty-five children and their families. For twenty years.
> 3 To discover whether a male brain is different from a female brain.

B Explain that Ss have to listen and follow the instructions and draw a picture.

C Ss listen and compare their picture with the one on p158. Check comprehension.

D In pairs, Ss read the sentences and decide if a man or woman says each one. Ss then listen and check their answers.

> **Answers:** 1 W 2 M 3 M 4 M 5 W 6 W

Unit 1 Recording 3

P=Presenter

Part 1

P: Is your brain male or female? A strange question? Maybe, maybe not. In a moment, you will be asked to draw a picture of a bike. Make sure you have a pen or pencil. Pause now and play when you're ready.

Part 2

P: OK, you have exactly one minute to draw a picture of a bicycle. Go! Make it as beautiful or normal as you like. Include as much detail as you can. You've got forty-five seconds left.

You've got another fifteen seconds.

You've got five seconds left … four, three, two, one, zero, stop. Right, stop drawing please. Now, you have to write down on your piece of paper, whether you, the artist, are male or female. That's all we need to know for the experiment. Now turn to page a hundred and fifty-eight to see what a real bike looks like. Please pause the recording now.

Unit 1 Recording 4

P=Presenter

Part 3

P: Now, count up the parts on your drawing. Did you include wheels? A handlebar? A saddle? A chain? A crossbar? Pedals? Did your bike have at least five parts? And could it work? Now for the difference between the men's drawings of a bicycle and the women's – female drawings often include a person riding the bike; men's drawings don't usually include a person. This is a clear indication that women think people are important. Men, on the other hand, are more interested in getting the machine right.

Unit 1 Recording 5

P=Presenter W1=1st woman M1=1st Man W2=2nd woman

Part 4

P: Here are some comments from men and women who did the test.

W1: Hmmm. Well, I only got four parts right. How many did you get right?

M1: I only got four. How many did you get?

W2: I've got, I've got five, but none of us got the chain, did we, so …

M1: Mine hasn't even got pedals …

W2: No, mine hasn't got pedals …

M1: Pedals nor chains so mine will never work!

W2: But if you've got pedals and no chain it's not going to work anyway …

M1: It'll have to be going downhill …

W2: And also that, um, that means the explanation for men making the bike work doesn't work because you, you …

M1: That's right … of the two women and one man none of us drew …

W2: Have made the bike work.

M1: … yeah and none of us drew a person … so the explanation about women wanting to put a person on there is hasn't proven correct for you two …

W1: No, not with us … no.

M1: And mine is meant to be all about functionality and it hasn't … ah, I've got a little bird on my handle bars though …

W2: It's a very clear drawing though, yours …

W1: I think mine is more male than yours, maybe?
Yes …

M1: I think you're right …

W2: Yours is much more accurate … yours is the most accurate one.

M1: The way you've used the biro to just kind of make the lines more solid … that's quite a masculine …

W1: And you've got lights on yours and you've got, you've got five, five parts.

W2: Yeah.

5 Arrange Ss into small groups to discuss the questions. In feedback, nominate Ss to share their ideas with the class.

VOCABULARY relationships

6A Check Ss understand *boss and employee* in the first example. Ss work in pairs to match the rest of the words to the questions. If you've brought dictionaries, give them out for Ss to use. Elicit Ss' answers and check comprehension.

> **Answers:** 1 boss and employee 2 godfather and godmother 3 fiancée and fiancé 4 mentor and pupil 5 team-mates 6 classmates 7 member 8 partner

B Ss discuss the questions in small groups. Monitor and help Ss with any vocabulary they need. Nominate Ss from each group to share their opinions with the class.

C Ss listen to the words and number them in the order they hear them. Elicit the correct order.

> **Answers:** 1 employee 2 mentor 3 godmother 4 boss 5 fiancé 6 member

D Check Ss understand *syllable* in the rubric. Ss work alone to find the words with two syllables and underline the stressed syllable, then check their answers in pairs. Elicit Ss' answers.

> **Answers:** Two syllable words: <u>men</u>tor, <u>pu</u>pil, <u>part</u>ner, <u>class</u>mates, <u>team</u>-mates, <u>mem</u>ber

speakout TIP

Read the tip with the class and practise saying the two-syllable words using the technique described.

Unit 1 Recording 6

1 I think I'm a good employee as I always do my best at work.
2 At my school we have a system of mentors who help the younger pupils and I'm one of the mentors. 3 My nice news is that I recently became godmother to my best friend's little girl. 4 I'm the boss of a small company that sells phone cards. 5 I'll introduce you to my fiancé later. We got engaged two weeks ago. 6 I took up judo six months ago and I'm a member of a local club.

SPEAKING

7A Read the examples with the class. Give Ss 5 mins to take notes. Monitor and help with vocabulary and write new words/phrases on the board.

B Arrange Ss into small groups and ask them to share their information. Monitor carefully and take notes on their language for later feedback.

VOCABULARY *PLUS* collocations

8A Introduce the topic and focus attention on the quiz. In pairs, Ss complete the quiz.

B Ss turn to p158 and check their answers. Nominate Ss to tell the class how many they got correct.

> **Answers:** 1 c) 2 c) 3 a) 4 c) 5 b) 6 a) 7 b) 8 b)

9A Ss work alone to find five expressions in the quiz, then check their answers in pairs. In feedback, elicit Ss' answers.

> **Answers:** gone on a diet, doing exercise, get married, take responsibility for, doing the housework

B Check Ss understand the expressions in italics. They then work alone to put the expressions in the word webs, then check their answers in pairs. Elicit Ss' answers in feedback.

> **Answers:** (in correct order) 1 Do: exercise, housework, research, someone a favour 2 Take: a taxi, part in something, after someone, responsibility for 3 Get: married, a job/degree, here, on with someone 4 Go: on a diet, grey, home, for a drink/a walk/a meal, off something

> ⫸ **VOCABULARYBANK** p148 Collocations
>
> With *weaker classes*, elicit one or two examples with the class first, then Ss complete the word webs in pairs. *Stronger classes* can do the exercise at home.
>
> **Answers:** 1 Do: exercise, your best, the cleaning, nothing for you 2 Get: a prize, fired, food poisoning, excited 3 Take: sugar, ages, a look, the blame 4 Go: crazy, badly, on holiday, together

SPEAKING

10A Elicit Ss' ideas for the first phrase as an example. Ss work alone and write their classmates' names next to the phrases.

Teaching tip

With **large classes** and/or **multilingual classes,** it can be difficult for Ss to remember the names of their classmates. For this activity, write all the Ss' names in a list on the board.

B Ss discuss their ideas in small groups. When they have finished, nominate Ss to tell the class their ideas and check if other students agree.

Homework ideas
- Ex 1C: write some more opinions for men and women.
- Ex 7A: write about your own relationships.
- Language bank 1.2 Ex 1–2, p129
- Vocabulary bank p148
- Workbook Ex 1–6, p6–7

TELL ME ABOUT YOURSELF

Introduction

Ss learn and practise ways of talking about themselves in interviews. They also learn to use formal and informal two-word responses.

SUPPLEMENTARY MATERIALS

Resource bank p129

Warm up

Lead in to the topic by telling Ss about an interview experience you've had, whether it was for a job or another reason. Encourage Ss to ask you follow-up questions to find out more information.

SPEAKING

1A Check Ss understand the types of interview listed and elicit which of the interviews Ss can see in the picture. Encourage Ss to give reasons for their choices.

Answer: job interview

B Arrange Ss into small groups and ask them to discuss the questions. Monitor and help with vocabulary. In feedback, nominate Ss from each group to share their ideas with the class.

Teaching tip

When conducting feedback after discussion activities, going through every question with every student wastes valuable class time. Instead, ask Ss to decide on the most interesting piece of information they found out and share this with the class. This will also give Ss an opportunity to process/think about what they heard during the discussion.

VOCABULARY interview advice

2A In pairs, Ss categorise the expressions. *Stronger Ss* can work alone, but *weaker Ss* may need more help. Elicit Ss' answers and check comprehension using examples, e.g. *If you dress smartly, what clothes will you wear? What kind of research can you do?* etc.

Suggested answers: dress smartly 3; speak clearly 1; answer briefly 2; shake hands firmly 1; send references 3; arrive on time 3; avoid eye contact 2; do some research 3; show enthusiasm 1; be prepared 3

B In the same pairs, give Ss 2 mins to think of as many more things as they can. When they have finished, elicit their ideas and write them on the board. Ask other Ss if they agree.

Teaching tip

Ss could do brainstorming activities as a race. Set a strict time limit and ask Ss to write down as many ideas as they can. The pair with the most relevant ideas wins.

FUNCTION talking about yourself

3 Go through the questions and elicit Ss' predictions. Give Ss 5 mins to read the text and answer the questions in pairs. In feedback, elicit Ss' answers.

Answers: 1 They send flowers, chocolates and other things to get noticed. 2 Before: be prepared (do some research), dress appropriately, arrive on time. During: shake hands firmly and make eye contact, speak clearly and give full answers, show enthusiasm.

Culture notes

Harvard is a prestigious university in the USA, particularly in the fields of Business and Law. Competition for entry is very high.

4A Go through the questions and check Ss know what they need to listen for. Ss listen to the extracts, then check their answers in pairs. In feedback, elicit Ss' answers.

Answers: 1 Interview 1 = English course; Interview 2 = job interview; Interview 3 = university course
2 In Interview 2, Jade gives very short answers and doesn't show enthusiasm.

B In pairs, Ss answer the questions with what they can remember from the first listening. Play the recordings again for Ss to check their answers. *Weaker classes* may need to listen again twice. Elicit Ss' answers.

Answers: 1 speaking and listening 2 special classes with a special focus like English idioms, conversation and pronunciation 3 games 4 different ages together 5 if it's possible to take online classes 6 There's a lot of reading and writing.

Watch out!

In Conversation 3, the student says … *actually, I do have a query*. Point out to Ss that when we emphasise things, we often add an auxiliary and stress it in the sentence.

Unit 1 Recording 7

Conversation 1

T=Teacher S=Student

T: And what about your expectations of the course?

S: Well, as I said, I've studied English for many years and spent time in Britain, but that was a few years ago. So for me the most important thing is to just refresh … and try to remember my English and practise speaking and listening.

T: OK. You've got a very good level of English so we'd put you in the advanced class. Is there anything else?

S: Could I ask a question?

T: Of course.

S: I can take the morning class from 9.00 to 12.00. Is that right?

T: Yes, that's right.

S: And in the afternoon there are options? Optional classes?

T: Yes, these are special classes with a special focus like English idioms, conversation, pronunciation. We have the full list here.

S: I see. Thank you.

T: No problem. OK, well, thank you very much.

Conversation 2

I=Interviewer A=Applicant

I: There are a couple of things I'd like to ask about, Jade. Your CV says you have some experience of looking after children?

A: Yes, I was a tutor on a summer camp last year.

I: Can I ask you about that? What type of things did you do?

A: Um, well, I organised games.

I: Games for?

A: The children.

I: OK. And what age were the children?

A: Um … seven to ten.

I: OK. And you enjoyed it?

A: Yes.

I: What aspect, what part did you enjoy, would you say?

A: I suppose I'd have to say I liked the games best.

I: And any problems?

A: Um, no.

I: What about the different ages? We often find that different ages together can be difficult.

A: It depends. In my opinion, you can usually get the older children to help the younger ones.

Conversation 3

I=Interviewer S=Student

I: I think that's about it. Do you have any questions? Any queries?

S: Um, yes, actually I do have a query.

I: Yes, go ahead.

S: It's about online classes at the university.

I: Right.

S: If I'm accepted, I saw that there are … urm, that it's possible to take some courses online.

I: That's right.

S: So I wouldn't need to attend classes?

I: Not for the online courses. But, erm … well, one thing I'd like to say is that the online courses are, in many ways, more difficult than face-to-face courses. Certainly in terms of reading and writing, they're really quite demanding.

5A Focus attention on the example and elicit the function of the expression (to introduce a question). Ss underline three more expressions and check their answers in pairs. In feedback, elicit Ss' answers.

Answers: Could I ask a question? There are a couple of things I'd like to ask about. Can I ask you about that? I do have a query.

B Focus attention on the example and elicit the function of the expression (to introduce an opinion). Ss circle three more expressions and check their answers in pairs. In feedback, elicit Ss' answers.

Answers: So for me the most important thing is to … I suppose I'd have to say … In my opinion, … one thing I'd like to say is that …

▶ **LANGUAGEBANK** 1.3 p128–129

Ss can refer to the notes on p128 when they do the exercises. *Weaker classes* should do the exercises in class before continuing with the lesson. Drill the expressions in the chart with the class.

Answers: 1 A: There are a couple of things I'd like *to* ask about. B: I'd *have* to say *Millennium Dreamer*.
A: Can I ask you *about* that? A: Could I ask *a* question about your image? B: No. *One thing* I'd like to say is that these images are invented by the media. *In* my opinion, good actors …

6 Do the first sentence together as an example and write it on the board. Ss work alone to put the words in order to make sentences or questions, then check their answers in pairs. Elicit Ss' answers. Early finishers could write the answers up on the board.

Answers: 1 I do have a query. 2 Could I ask a question?
3 There are a couple of things I'd like to ask about.
4 Can I ask you about that? 5 In my opinion this isn't true.
6 I'd have to say I agree. 7 One thing I'd like to say is that the course is difficult. 8 For me the most important thing is to study.

LEARN TO use two-word responses

7A Focus attention on the example, then give Ss 2 mins to match the other expressions alone, then check their answers in pairs. Elicit Ss' answers and drill the expressions chorally and individually. Check comprehension of *I see = I understand*.

Answers: 1 d) 2 b) 3 e) 4 c) 5 a)

B Elicit which expressions are more formal and which ones Ss use regularly. Refer Ss to audio script 1.7 on p164 and ask them to find the expressions. Elicit what is said before each response.

Answer: Expressions a)–e) are more formal.

Teaching tip

Two-word responses are relatively easy for Ss to learn and help them sound more natural when they speak. Encourage Ss to use them whenever they can.

SPEAKING

8A Divide the class in half. One half are Student As and the other half are Student Bs. Student As read the information on p15 and prepare their questions. Student Bs read the information on p158 and prepare for the interview. Monitor and help with language and ideas. When they are ready, put Ss into A/B pairs and ask them to role-play the interview. Encourage Ss to use the functional language from the unit. Monitor and note down any common errors and good language for later feedback. When they have finished, ask if the candidates were successful.

B Ss change roles and role-play the interview again. When they have finished, ask if the candidates were successful and go over any common errors and drill examples of good language.

Teaching tip

When practising functional language, encourage Ss to use the phrases by asking one student in each pair to note down every time their partner uses one of the phrases. In feedback, elicit how many times they used them.

Homework ideas

- Ex 7B: write a conversation using the expressions.
- Language bank 1.3 Ex 1, p129
- Workbook Ex 1–3, p8

SECOND LIFE

Introduction

Ss watch an extract from the BBC current affairs programme *The Money Programme,* in which they investigate *Second Life,* an internet-based virtual world where people can reinvent themselves and interact with other people. Ss learn and practise how to create a new identity and introduce themselves and write their answers to a questionnaire.

SUPPLEMENTARY MATERIALS

Warm up: if you have access to the internet in class, load up www.secondlife.com (correct at the time of going to press).

Warm up

If you have access to the internet in class, load up www.secondlife.com (correct at the time of going to press) and explore some of the pages, e.g. *World Map, What is Second Life?* etc.

If you don't have access to the internet, write the following questions on the board for Ss to discuss: *Have you heard of Second Life? Have you ever played it? What things can you do in Second Life? Do you think it's an interesting idea or a waste of time?* Elicit Ss' answers when they have finished.

▶ DVD PREVIEW

1A Ss discuss the statements in pairs. Elicit their answers but don't give any feedback at this stage.

B Do the first word together as an example. Ss match the words in bold to the words/phrases in the box. Elicit the answers and check comprehension, giving further examples if necessary.

Answers: 1 change 2 beautiful 3 choose 4 clothes 5 meet and talk to 6 people who live in one place 7 type of money from one country

C Refer Ss back to their answers to Ex 1A and give them 1 min to read the programme information to check their answers. Elicit Ss' answers and check any unknown vocabulary in the text.

Answer: You can do all seven of the activities.

▶ DVD VIEW

2 Focus attention on the pictures and elicit ideas as to what is happening in each one. Play the DVD. Ss watch and put the pictures in the correct order, then check their answers in pairs. In feedback, elicit Ss' answers.

Answers: D, C, E, A, B

3A Match the first picture to the correct sentence together as an example. Ss then work in pairs to match the rest of the pictures to the correct sentences.

B Play the DVD again. Ss watch and check their answers. In feedback, elicit Ss' answers.

Answers: 1 D 2 C 3 E 4 A 5 B

4 Arrange Ss into small groups to discuss the questions. Monitor and help with vocabulary if needed. When they have finished, nominate Ss from each group to tell the class their ideas.

DVD 1 Virtual World/Real Millions

V=Voice-over GY=Ginsu Yoon MM=Matt Martin

V: Have you ever dreamt of reinventing yourself as a completely different person? Well, I've done it. This is me inside a virtual world called Second Life. It's a place full of strange islands and towns and buildings created by people who live here. And the rules are: there are no rules. Once you've created an account, which you do for free, you create an avatar, which is basically a digital version of yourself. The fun starts choosing your new body, or avatar. There's something for all tastes. You can be female, male, or even something called a 'Furry' – half animal, half human.

GY: You can edit your appearance to look however you want. You can look tall or short or fat or skinny. It turns out that there are not a lot of unattractive people in Second Life.

V: You can easily alter your face and get a hair-do. I could look like Brad Pitt or even Les Dawson if I wanted. You could be whatever colour you want and can tweak your features – big ears, big nose, or anything else you feel like making bigger. Finally you pick an outfit. Not really me. In the end I just went for a spiky-haired, suit-wearing disco dancer. No change there. My avatar can explore Second Life by walking around. But it's more fun flying and with maps I can find almost anything I want.

MM: Second Life is all about creating your own on-line personality and socialising: whether that's with big groups, small groups. It's going to online concerts, going into online stores and trying on shoes, it's dressing up.

V: Second Life claims to have over three million individual residents from all over the world living there. You can go up to anyone and chat. This avatar's owner is in Germany and these two are from India.

speakout create a new identity

5A Focus attention on the questions and make sure Ss know what to listen for. Ss listen and answer the questions, then check their answers in pairs. In feedback, elicit Ss' answers.

Answers: 1 on BBC breakfast TV 2 She made herself with dark hair rather than blonde. 3 a businesswoman 4 her personality 5 a shop

B Go through the key phrases and ask Ss if they can remember which ones she used. Ss listen again and check. Elicit the answers and drill the phrases chorally and individually.

Answers: create a sort of a different version of yourself. I created a new image of myself. I didn't change my appearance that much. One thing I decided to alter was my … ; One thing that hasn't changed is …

Teaching tip

Use rhythm when drilling whole phrases. Start by drilling only the stressed syllables with a clear rhythm, e.g. *DIFF – VERS – ME.* Keeping the same rhythm, add in the other syllables, e.g. *It's a DIFFerent VERSion of ME.* This helps Ss pronounce the weak forms more naturally.

C Check Ss understand the vocabulary, especially *height, weight, hang out* and *motto*. Give Ss 5 mins to complete the profile of their avatar. Monitor and help with vocabulary and check Ss complete the profile in note form.

D When they are ready, ask Ss to stand up and mingle, introducing their new selves to other Ss. Encourage them to ask further questions and note down any errors or examples of good language for later feedback. When they have finished, elicit any interesting information and ask if they had anything in common with other Ss. In feedback, go through any errors with the class and drill any examples of good language.

Unit 1 Recording 8

A=Annabel Winter

A: I heard about Second Life, um, BBC breakfast TV and um I decided to sort of get on it because I wanted to see what it'd be like to interact in a, a virtual world so, um and also to see how it was presented onscreen on our computers. So, um, I went on and you can create your own avatar which means to create a, a sort of a different version of yourself, so um, I … it … I, I … created a new image of myself, um I didn't change my appearance that much. You can choose different parts of, ah the body so you can change your face, I made myself, I made myself with dark hair rather than with blonde. I'm not sure why. Um, one thing I decided to alter was my job. I, um, decided to be a businesswoman rather than, um, an actress … um, but one thing that hasn't changed is my personality. You get to talk to people online um as your avatar, so obviously my responses are um still as me. Um, but you can also set up, ah … your own buildings, you can, you can, um, pay for and build your own buildings, so you can be your own businesswoman in your own shop and people can come in and actually buy things from your shop. So it's really interesting to sort of interact as this alternative being, different version, different version of me.

write**back** answer a questionnaire

6A Check Ss understand the questions and explain that they can either answer as themselves or as their avatars. While Ss write their answers, monitor and encourage them to write full answers, i.e. one or two sentences for each. Help with vocabulary where necessary.

B When they have finished, arrange Ss into small groups and ask them to show their answers to other Ss. They then read the questionnaires and decide if the answers are for themselves or their avatars. Nominate Ss from each group to tell the class any interesting information they found out.

> **Homework ideas**
> - Ex 5C: write your avatar's profile.
> - Ex 6A: write a final draft of your answers, as a short text.

LOOKBACK

Introduction

Ss revise and practise the language of Unit 1. The notes below provide ideas for exploiting the exercises and activities but your approach will depend on your aim, e.g. whether you use the activities as a diagnostic or progress test or as revision/ fluency practice. If done as a test then it would not be appropriate to monitor or help Ss.

FAMILY

1A Ss complete the sentences using the words in the box, then check their answers in pairs. In feedback, elicit Ss' answers.

> **Answers:** 1 history 2 ancestors 3 great 4 after 5 inherited 6 roots 7 relative 8 related 9 side 10 extended

B Ss tick which sentences are true for them, then compare their answers in pairs. Monitor and encourage them to ask follow-up questions. Elicit any interesting answers.

> **Alternative approach**
> Instead of ticking which sentences are true for them and comparing in pairs, Ss could lie and say that all the sentences are true for them. Their partner then asks questions to try and catch them out and guesses if the sentence is true or false.

QUESTION FORMS

2A Ss correct the mistakes alone, then check their answers in pairs. Elicit the correct answers.

> **Answers:** 1 When *did you start* studying English? 2 *Who helped* you to learn English? 3 *Do you enjoy* learning languages? 4 *Did you learn* anything important from your teachers? 5 correct 6 In your job or studies, is there anything you are not happy *with*? 7 correct 8 correct

B In pairs, Ss choose four of the questions and ask their partner. While they are speaking, monitor and note down any errors and examples of good language. In feedback, elicit any interesting answers and give feedback on their language use.

REVIEW OF VERB TENSES

3 Ss find and correct the five mistakes, then check their answers in pairs. Elicit the answers and ask Ss if they or anyone they know is in a band.

> **Answers:** 1 correct 2 saw 3 correct 4 asked 5 'm going 6 correct 7 correct 8 started 9 correct 10 like 11 correct 12 correct

> **Alternative approach**
> You could do this as a team game. Arrange Ss in small group and ask them to do the exercise orally, making sure they don't write any answers down. When they have finished, ask each group to think of a team name and write them on the board. Each turn, call out one of the numbers randomly. Each team must call out the correct answer, or *Correct!* The first team to answer correctly gets a point, which you mark on the board next to their team name. Make sure Ss still don't write the answers at this stage. The team with the most points wins. After the game ask Ss to work alone to do the exercise in their books.

RELATIONSHIPS

4A Do the first word together as an example, then Ss reorder the letters. Elicit Ss' answers. Early finishers could write the words up on the board.

> **Answers:** 1 godmother 2 fiancé 3 pupil 4 partner 5 fiancée 6 member 7 classmate 8 godfather 9 boss 10 employee 11 mentor 12 team-mate

B Give Ss 2–3 mins to prepare and make notes on any additional information they can give. Monitor and help with vocabulary if necessary. In pairs, Ss share their information and ask questions. In feedback, elicit any interesting answers.

TALKING ABOUT YOURSELF

5A Focus attention on the first example. Ss work alone to complete the conversations with the pairs of words, then check their answers in pairs. Elicit Ss' answers and ask them what situations they think the conversations take place in.

> **Answers:** 1 A: I have a *query about* the class. Do I have to bring a pen? 2 A: Could *I ask* a question? Where does the tennis class meet? 3 A: I'd have *to say* I'm not sure you're qualified. Why should we employ you for the library position? 4 A: There are a couple of things I'd *like to ask*. Firstly, can you work on Saturdays? 5 A: One *thing I'd* like to say is that you look good for your age. You're thirty-one. How old were you last year? 6 A: Can I ask *you about* your latest film, *Philadelphia*? Where is it set?

B In pairs, Ss use the expressions on p15 to write a conversation. Monitor and help with vocabulary. When they are ready, they show it to another pair, who guesses the situation.

C In groups, Ss perform their conversations. Monitor and note down any errors and examples of good language. In feedback, nominate some pairs to perform their conversations for the class. In feedback, correct any common errors and drill examples of any good language.

OVERVIEW

FACT OR FICTION?

Introduction

Ss revise and practise the present perfect simple and past simple and vocabulary to describe types of story in the context of life stories. They also learn and practise common uses of prepositions.

SUPPLEMENTARY MATERIALS

Resource bank p131 and p132

Warm up: bring a trailer for a film about a famous person's life (a biopic).

Warm up

To start the lesson and contextualise the topic in a motivating way, show Ss a trailer for a film about a famous person's life. It could be one of the films in Ex 2A, or a similar one. Show the trailer and ask Ss if they can identify the film and if they have seen it.

SPEAKING

1 Introduce the activity by giving Ss an example of a film that has taught you about history. Ss then work in small groups to share their own experiences.

2A Focus on the quiz and read the introduction with the class. Ss do the quiz in pairs. Elicit some answers, then direct Ss to p158 to check their answers.

Answers: 1 Fiction 2 Fiction 3 Partly true 4 Partly true 5 Partly true

B Discuss the question as a class.

VOCABULARY types of story

Teaching tip

When introducing topic vocabulary, first gauge how much the Ss already know. Write *types of story* on the board and give an example, e.g. *action/adventure*. Elicit further examples and write them on the board.

3A Do the first example with the class. Ss match the words in the box to the correct definitions, then compare their answers in pairs. In feedback, check Ss' answers, drilling each word with the class.

Answers: biopic d), docudrama i), disaster h), romantic comedy g), period drama f), fantasy/science fiction c), psychological thriller b), action/adventure a), mystery/crime e)

B Ss discuss the questions in pairs. In feedback, nominate Ss to share their partner's answers with the class.

LISTENING

4A Introduce the topic of the listening and check Ss understand what they have to do. Explain that they don't have to understand every word and that they will have a chance to listen again later. Ss listen and answer the questions, then compare answers in pairs before class feedback.

> **Answers:** 1 Hollywood biopics 2 People like watching films which give them more information about a person or event which they already know something about. People can learn about history in an entertaining way.

B Put Ss into pairs and focus attention on the photos. Ask which people Ss are familiar with and if they have seen the films. Ss discuss the questions in pairs. In feedback, elicit Ss' ideas.

Unit 2 Recording 1

R=Rosie (A film historian) P1=1st presenter P2=2nd presenter

P1: Hi and welcome to *The Film Show*, where today we're looking at the Hollywood biopic and why it's become so popular. Now, Hollywood has always used true stories in its films. In fact, they began making successful films in the 1920s and since then there have been thousands of films based on true stories.

P2: That's right, but in recent years, there've been more and more biopics. Directors have turned to the lives of famous people as a source of material. So, why is it that some of the best films in recent years have been based on true events, or inspired by real people?

P1: Today, we're talking to Rosie Truman, an actor and a film historian. Rosie, why do you think Hollywood is doing so many biopics?

R: Well, one reason is that it seems that audiences really enjoy films about people that they already know something about, but they want to know more. So, from these films we've learned something. We've learned about the difficult lives of some of the biggest music legends, like Ray Charles and Johnny Cash. We've learned about their history and how they grew up. And we've learned about the lives of politicians, like George Bush, or sporting heroes, like Muhammad Ali. It's a way in which Hollywood can actually teach us about history in an entertaining way. And it's interesting.

P2: Yes, I think that's right.

5 Ss listen to the second part of the programme and answer the questions, then check their answers in pairs. In feedback, elicit Ss' answers.

> **Answers:** 1 Helen Mirren, Will Smith 2 Audrey Tatou
> 3 Will Smith 4 Josh Brolin

Unit 2 Recording 2

R=Rosie (A film historian) P1=1st presenter P2=2nd presenter

P2: But what about the actors, Rosie? I mean, many of the actors have won Oscars for their roles in these films. What's it like for them?

R: Well, I think actors just love these roles. I mean, that's another reason why the films work so well. For an actor, this is a great challenge – you know, taking on a role like this. And it's very exciting to be asked to play a character who everyone already knows. Look at Helen Mirren. She won an Oscar for her role-playing the Queen and it's probably one of her greatest successes.

P1: Oh, absolutely! And I mean there have been some fantastic performances.

P2: Yes, that's right …

P1: So, how do they do it? How does an actor prepare for a role like this? Do they get the chance to meet the person that they're going to play? I mean … What happens?

R: Well, yes, obviously, if that person is still alive, then that's a great way for the actor to study the character: how this person moves, how they respond to people. In fact, I know that Helen Mirren met the Queen for tea, you know, very English. And she has talked about how this really helped her to understand her character. And Will Smith, who played Muhammad Ali … well, when they met, they got on really well and … and they became friends.

P2: But what about playing a difficult character, like George Bush, for example?

R: Yes, it's funny actually, when you're playing a character everyone knows, you have to work really hard at it. And especially on the voice, to get it exactly right. Josh Brolin played George Bush. And when he was preparing for the character, he talked to himself all day in a Texan accent. He even phoned up hotels in Texas, just so he could learn the accent.

P1: Really? That's funny. What about actors who can't meet the character in person? What do they do?

R: Well, there are lots of other ways to prepare. Audrey Tatou, for example. She played Coco Chanel. So she couldn't meet her in person, but she watched hours and hours of film footage. She watched her in interviews and she looked at the photographs. In a way, you have a little bit more freedom to do what you want with the character, when people are not so familiar, you know, with how the person behaves and with their voice. Tatou wanted to look like Coco Chanel when she was on screen, so that we would recognise the image.

P2: That's right. And it was a beautiful film.

R: It was and you know one of the things …

6A Ss work alone to complete the sentences from memory, then compare answers in pairs.

B Ss listen again, this time to the whole programme and check their answers. In feedback, elicit Ss' answers and write them on the board.

> **Answers:** 1 true stories 2 1920s 3 true events 4 difficult
> 5 Oscars 6 tea 7 accent 8 image

Unit 2 Recording 3

Recording 3 is Recording 1 and Recording 2 combined. See above for audio scripts.

GRAMMAR present perfect/past simple

7A Elicit the examples from the first two sentences. Give Ss 2–3 mins to underline the other examples alone, then check their answers in pairs. In feedback, elicit Ss' answers.

> **Answers:** Present perfect: 1 has always used 3 have been based 4 we've learnt 5 have won Past simple: 2 began 6 met 7 phoned up 8 wanted

B Ss complete the rules with the present perfect or past simple. Check Ss' answers.

> **Answers:** Rule 1: present perfect Rule 2: present perfect Rule 3: past simple Rule 4: past simple

C Do the first sentence as an example. In pairs, Ss match the other sentences to one of the rules. Elicit Ss' answers and be prepared to give more examples if necessary.

> **Answers:** Rule 1: sentences 4, 5 Rule 2: sentences 1, 3 Rule 3: sentences 2, 6 Rule 4: sentences 7, 8

▮▶ **LANGUAGEBANK** 2.1 p130–131

Point out that we often use the **present perfect** to introduce a story, then switch to the **past simple** to give details.

1A Elicit the first answer as an example. Ss then tick the correct sentences in pairs.

B Elicit the first conversation as an example and write it on the board. Ss write the conversations, then check their answers in pairs and practise them.

Answers: 1 1 b) 2 a) 3 b) 4 b) 5 a) 6 a)
2 1 A: Have you ever been here before? B: No, I haven't. 2 A: Have you seen the film *The Reader?* B: No, I haven't seen it yet. 3 A: Has he been to Budapest? B: Yes, he went last summer. 4 A: Have you finished that book yet? B: Yes, I've already started the next one. 5 A: Have you seen Maria? B: Yes, she left a message for you. 6 A: Has he decided what job he wants to do yet? B: No, he hasn't.

8A Ss listen to the pairs of phrases and repeat them. Draw attention to the differences.

B Ss listen and write the sentences they hear. Pause the recording after each sentence to give Ss enough time to write the sentences. When they have finished, Ss compare their sentences in pairs.

Answers: 1 I lived there for ten years. **2** We've never met before. **3** He won an Oscar. **4** They've spent all the money. **5** You decided to stay. **6** I've learnt a lot.

Teaching tip

Make feedback more student-centred by asking Ss to come to the board to write their answers, especially if some Ss finish early. If possible, have several Ss come to the board at the same time to avoid putting one student on the spot.

C If they need to, Ss listen once more to check their sentences. Drill the sentences with the class.

Unit 2 Recording 5

1 I lived there for ten years.
2 We've never met before.
3 He won an Oscar.
4 They've spent all the money.
5 You decided to stay.
6 I've learnt a lot.

PRACTICE

9 Do the first sentence together as an example. Ss complete the text with the correct forms of the verbs in brackets alone, then check their answers in pairs. In feedback, elicit Ss' answers.

Answers: 1 haven't (always) been **2** didn't meet **3** has (always) wanted **4** experienced **5** left **6** lost **7** slept **8** has come **9** met **10** asked **11** became **12** has spent **13** has (also) written

SPEAKING

10A Elicit Student A's first question and write it on the board. Divide the class in half. One half write Student A's questions and the other half turn to p160 and write Student B's questions. Monitor and help where necessary. *Stronger classes* can do the exercise orally.

Answers: Student A: 1 Have you ever been on TV/in a newspaper? 2 Have you ever done something embarrassing in public? 3 Have you ever written a poem/story? 4 Have you ever been to a country on a different continent? 5 Have you ever collected something as a hobby? 6 Have you ever seen someone commit a crime?
Student B: 1 Have you ever won an award/competition/some money? 2 Have you ever eaten something very unusual? 3 Have you ever broken a bone in your body? 4 Have you ever locked yourself out of the house? 5 Have you ever ridden a horse/donkey/camel/motorbike? 6 Have you ever climbed a mountain/run more than 2km?

B Arrange Ss into pairs and explain the activity. Ss take it in turns to ask their questions and try to find five things they have in common. In feedback, elicit any common answers.

SPEAKING

11A Demonstrate the activity by giving some of your own details. Give Ss 10 mins to make notes and think of ideas. Monitor and help with ideas if necessary.

B Put Ss into pairs. They take it in turns to explain the films of their lives. Monitor and help with vocabulary where necessary.

C Ss take it in turns to ask questions about their partner's film. In feedback, nominate Ss to share any interesting facts.

VOCABULARY *PLUS* prepositions

12 Do the first example together. Ss work alone to put the words in the correct word webs, then check their answers in pairs. In feedback, elicit Ss' answers.

Answers: 1–2 the weekend/lunchtime **3–5** July/the winter/the summer/the twenty-first century **6–8** Saturday/Monday morning/New Year's Day

speakout TIP

Read the tip with the class and drill the phrases.

13 Explain that in each sentence one preposition will fit all the gaps. Ss work alone to complete the sentences, then check their answers in pairs. In feedback, elicit Ss' answers.

Answers: 1 by **2** on **3** for **4** by

14 In pairs, Ss match the expressions with their meanings. In feedback, elicit Ss' answers and give further examples.

Answers: 1 h) **2** e) **3** i) **4** j) **5** c) **6** a) **7** d) **8** f) **9** g) **10** b)

15A Give Ss 10 mins to write questions using the expressions. Monitor and help where necessary.

B When they have finished, put Ss into pairs to ask and answer their questions. In feedback, nominate Ss to share their partner's answers with the class.

▮▶ **VOCABULARYBANK** p149 Prepositions

Use the pictures to teach/elicit *motorway, bridge, city centre* and *cathedral*. Match the first description to the correct picture as an example, then Ss match the rest in pairs.
Answers: 1 C **2** A **3** E **4** B **5** D

Homework ideas
- Language bank 2.1 Ex 1–2, p131
- Vocabulary bank p149
- Workbook Ex 1–6, p9–10

WHAT REALLY HAPPENED?

Introduction

Ss revise and practise narrative tenses in the context of conspiracy theories and talking about important events. They also practise using time linkers in writing a news report.

SUPPLEMENTARY MATERIALS

Resource bank p130 and p133

Warm up: and Ex 7A: bring a range of tabloid/broadsheet newspapers or articles from news websites.

Warm up

Discuss recent major news stories with the Ss. Ask *Which stories have been in the news recently in your country? How have they affected you?* If possible, bring in newspapers or articles from news websites for Ss to discuss.

SPEAKING

1 Read and check the questions with the class. Put Ss into groups of three to discuss their answers. In feedback, nominate Ss to give the answers for their group to the class.

2A Elicit what Ss can see in each photo and which stories they refer to. Ss listen and check.

Answers: Moon landing, Princess Diana's crash, the shooting of President John F Kennedy (JFK)

B In pairs, Ss discuss what they know about these stories. In feedback, elicit Ss' answers.

Unit 2 Recording 6

P=Presenter N1=1st news clip N2=2nd news clip N3=3rd news clip N4=4th news clip

P: Hello. I know what I was doing. Do you?

N1: Buckingham Palace has announced the death of Diana, Princess of Wales. The Princess, who was thirty-six, died late last night in a car crash in central Paris.

N2: It's one small step for man, one giant leap for mankind.

N3: Breaking news in here at five live. There are reports that a plane has crashed into the World Trade Center in New York. That's a plane is reportedly crashed into the World Trade Center in New York, setting it on fire …

N4: President Kennedy and Governor John Connally of Texas were shot today from an ambush as President Kennedy's motorcade left the centre of Dallas …

READING

3A Read the definition with the class and check Ss understand it. Focus attention on the photos and make sure Ss cover the texts. Ss discuss the questions in pairs. In feedback, elicit Ss' answers.

B In this exercise, Ss practise their prediction skills. Ss read the articles and check their answers.

Answers: 1 Man on the Moon: the astronauts didn't land on the Moon, photographs were taken in a studio.
A Royal Affair: Princess Diana was killed by MI6 because of her relationship with Dodi Al-Fayed.
Death of Kennedy: Lee Harvey Oswald was not acting alone when he killed JFK. Suspects include Fidel Castro and the FBI.
2 Official reports have concluded that President Kennedy was killed 'as the result of a conspiracy'.

4A Elicit what Ss can remember, but don't give any answers yet. Give Ss 3–4 mins to read the texts again and check their answers. In feedback, elicit Ss' answers.

Answers: 1 Princess Diana 2 President Kennedy 3 Lee Harvey Oswald 4 Lee Harvey Oswald, President Kennedy 5 the FBI, Fidel Castro 6 the astronauts, Princess Diana

B Demonstrate the activity using the first word as an example, eliciting what Ss can remember about *shadows*. In pairs, Ss discuss what they can remember about the words and phrases. In feedback, nominate Ss from each pair to give their answers.

Answers: shadows: in the photos of the Moon landing these were falling in different directions.
stars: there are no stars visible in the photos of the Moon landing.
a love story: Princess Diana was having a love affair with Mr Dodi Al-Fayed.
alcohol: the driver of the car, Henri Paul, was drunk when he crashed the car.
photographs/photographers: people have doubts about the photographs of the Moon landing. Photographers were following Princess Diana's car when it crashed.
a man with a gun: President Kennedy was shot by a man with a gun.
a flag: the flag in the photos looks as if it is waving, but there is no wind on the Moon.
the FBI: the FBI are suspects in the conspiracy theory. Their original report and investigation was criticised.

C Ss discuss the questions in pairs. Monitor and provide any vocabulary Ss need. In feedback, elicit Ss' opinions.

GRAMMAR narrative tenses

5A Give Ss 2–3 mins to find the examples and answer the questions. In pairs, Ss compare their answers. In feedback, check Ss' answers and provide further examples if necessary.

Answers: past simple; crashed, claimed, planned; past continuous: was driving, was having
1 past simple 2 past continuous

B Give Ss 2–3 mins to read the conclusion and answer the questions in pairs. In feedback, elicit Ss' answers and provide further examples if necessary.

Answers: 1 concluded 2 had not planned; had happened 3 past perfect

C Read the rule with the class and elicit the correct alternative for Ss to underline.

Answer: before the past time event we are talking about

⇒ **LANGUAGEBANK** 2.2 p130–131

Stronger classes could read the notes and do the exercises at home. *Weaker classes* can do the exercises in class. Focus attention on the timelines to help Ss understand the tenses and read the notes with the class, paying particular attention to when we don't need to use the past perfect.

1A Ss choose the correct alternatives, then check their answers in pairs.

B Focus attention on the first sentence and elicit the mistake. Ss correct the remaining sentences, then check their answers in pairs. In feedback, elicit reasons why the sentences are wrong.

Answers: 1 1 died 2 had been 3 hadn't played 4 was living 5 was studying 6 came 7 replied 8 turned **2** 1 … when I ~~had~~ heard … 2 … I *had* left my keys at home 3 We *were driving* through the tunnel … 4 … I realised *I'd* seen it before. 5 I *had* never been to Egypt before … 6 … everybody else *was* leaving. 7 We ~~had~~ waited for nearly an hour … 8 I *was looking* through …

PRACTICE

6 Do the first sentence with the class as an example. Ss work alone to complete the text with the rest of the phrases, then compare answers in pairs. In feedback, elicit Ss' answers and encourage them to say why they chose each answer.

Answers: 1 d) 2 a) 3 c) 4 g) 5 h) 6 b) 7 f) 8 e)

VOCABULARY the news

7A Introduce the topic of newspaper headlines and discuss some typical features used in headlines, e.g. present tenses used, prepositions often dropped, dramatic language, etc. If you have brought newspapers/articles from news websites, pass them round the class for Ss to look at and elicit some common features. Match the first headline with the correct explanation as an example. Ss work alone to match the rest of the headlines with the correct explanations, then compare their answers in pairs. In feedback, elicit Ss' answers and check they understand the words in bold.

Answers: 1 g) 2 a) 3 j) 4 i) 5 e) 6 d) 7 h) 8 b) 9 c) 10 f)

B Demonstrate the activity by describing some news stories you have read/heard recently using the vocabulary in bold from Ex 7A. Put Ss into pairs to discuss other stories. In feedback, nominate Ss to tell you any interesting stories they heard.

⇒ **VOCABULARYBANK** p149 News

Teach/Elicit *held hostage*, *security depot*, *hand over* and *lorry*. Give Ss 3–4mins to read the text. Elicit the first definition with the class as an example, then Ss match the phrases and definitions in pairs. Stronger classes can do the exercise at home.

Answers: 1 proceeded to 2 gang 3 arrested 4 armed robbers 5 raid 6 at gunpoint 7 security guards 8 escape 9 eye witnesses 10 attempted 11 raise the alarm 12 forced 13 getaway vehicle

SPEAKING

8A Give Ss 5–10 mins to think about their stories and write notes.

B Put Ss into groups of three to share their stories. Monitor and check their use of narrative tenses, noting down any common errors for later feedback. In feedback, nominate a student from each group to summarise their stories for the class.

9A Focus attention on the title and the photo and ask Ss to predict what the news report is about. Then give Ss 5–10 mins to find the answers and underline the parts of the text which helped them.

Answers: 1 Maxi Sopo 2 He was wanted for fraud in the United States. He escaped to Mexico, but was found when he talked about his life on Facebook. 3 He made a friend through Facebook, who was a former policeman (justice official). When the man discovered where Sopo was living, he told the police. 4 Mexico 5 Last month (according to the report) 6 The man is in custody in Mexico City.

B Go through the sentences with the class and check Ss know what they are looking for. Ss work in pairs to find the examples in the text. In feedback, elicit Ss' answers.

Answers: 1 line 10, lines 11–14 2 line 20 3 lines 1–5 4 lines 6–10

LEARN TO use time linkers

10A Ss find examples of the time linkers in the news report and underline them. Check Ss' answers.

Answers: as soon as (line 18) while (line 6) during (line 15) until (line 9) by the time (line 7)

B Ss match the time linkers to the questions. Demonstrate by using the sentences in the text to illustrate the meaning.

Answers: 1 by the time 2 until 3 while 4 during 5 as soon as

C Do the first sentence together as an example. Ss then complete the rest of the sentences alone and compare their answers in pairs. In feedback, elicit Ss' answers.

Answers: 1 as soon as 2 while 3 during 4 until 5 By the time

11A Elicit questions for the first headline e.g. *Where was she travelling to? How much money did she find? Did she give it to the police?* In pairs, Ss write their questions on a piece of paper.

B Ss pass their paper to another pair.

C Ss look at the questions they have been given and write notes. Focus attention on the ideas in Ex 9B. Give Ss 10–15 mins to write their news reports.

speakout TIP

When Ss have written their reports, read the tip with the class and ask them to check they have included everything.

D Display the finished reports and ask Ss to read the stories and choose which story they like best.

Homework ideas
• Ex 8A: write your news story as a news report, following the example in Ex 9A.
• Ex 11C: write a final draft of your news report.
• Language bank 2.2 Ex 1–2, p131
• Vocabulary bank p149
• Workbook Ex 1–5, p11–12

I DON'T BELIEVE IT!

Introduction

Ss learn and practise ways of telling a story in the context of telling lies. They also learn how to keep a story going by responding with interest.

SUPPLEMENTARY MATERIALS

Resource bank p134

Ex 5A: write the sequencers on sets of cards for Ss to use.

Warm up

Think of something interesting that happened to you recently and prepare to tell the story to the class, but with one false detail. Explain what you are going to do to Ss. Ss listen to your story and then ask questions to discover the false detail.

VOCABULARY say/tell

1A Ss discuss the questions in pairs. In feedback, build up a list on the board of ways in which you can tell if someone is lying, e.g. *they touch their nose, they look uncomfortable*.

Teaching tip

When we read texts in our own language, we use different subskills depending on why we are reading, e.g. for pleasure, to extract specific information, etc. Set a clear task to ensure Ss practise reading in the same way.

B Ss read the text and identify if any of their ideas in the list in Ex 1A are in the text. In feedback, ask Ss to tell you which ideas are mentioned in the text and tick them off from the list on the board. Check comprehension of any new vocabulary from the text.

Answers: When someone is lying they:
keep their hands still
don't look at you straight in the eyes
don't use 'me' words

Teaching tip

Reading texts is an excellent way for Ss to build their vocabulary. However, after Ss have read a text, avoid asking *Are there any words you don't understand?* as the word *understand* has powerful connotations. A better question is *Are there any new words you'd like to check?*

2A Match the first sentence halves together as an example. Ss match the rest of the sentence halves alone, then compare their answers in pairs. In feedback, elicit Ss' answers and check *a white lie* and *the punch line*.

Answers: 1 f) 2 d) 3 e) 4 b) 5 c) 6 a)

B Go over the examples with the class. Ss then write the phrases in the chart. In feedback, elicit Ss' answers and drill the phrases chorally and individually, paying attention to the linking in the phrases.

Teaching tip

When drilling new language, vary your drilling techniques. You can mix choral and individual drilling, substitute words in the phrase being drilled, or backchain. Backchaining is when you isolate the end of a phrase then gradually build it up again, working backwards. This ensures you use natural stress patterns.

Answers: say: hello, sorry, what you mean
tell: jokes, a (white) lie, a (funny) story

C Read the statements with the class and check they understand them. Put Ss into groups of three to discuss if they agree or disagree with the statements and why. In feedback, nominate a student from each group to share their opinions with the class.

FUNCTION telling a story

3A Focus attention on the pictures and elicit what Ss can see in each one. Put Ss in pairs and give them 2–3 mins to discuss what they think happened in the story. In feedback, elicit Ss' ideas.

B With *weaker classes*, teach/check *pills, the tube, swollen up, blotches, an allergic reaction* and *spots* using the pictures to help. Ss listen to the story and check their ideas from Ex 3A and put the pictures in the correct order. In feedback, elicit Ss' answers.

Answers: A 4 B 3 C 2 D 1

4A Focus on the example. Ss then add the sequencers to the table. In feedback, elicit Ss' answers and drill the phrases.

Answers: beginning: This happened when I; describing what happened: The next thing I knew, Anyway, Before long and then, all of a sudden; ending: In the end,

4B Play the story again, but explain that this time Ss have to listen for the sequencers and tick them as they hear them.

Answers: ✓ Well; In the beginning; So; Anyway; And then, all of a sudden; The next thing I knew

Unit 2 Recording 7

W=Woman M=Man

M: OK, so, tell me all about it …

W: Well, in the beginning, I was at home and … um … this was just one morning before a very important interview …

M: Uh-huh.

W: And … um … I didn't feel well, so my mother had given me some pills and um … then I didn't think anything more about it. So, anyway, erm … I then got on to the tube, um … to go for my interview.

M: Right and what happened then?

W: Well, um … clearly I must have fallen asleep, because I wasn't feeling great by this time. And um, I'm starting to feel sleepy, so I'm thinking I must have fallen asleep. Anyway, erm … I was getting some funny looks, even before I fell asleep, but anyway. I fell asleep and then I realised, before long, um … I must have been having a dream, I suppose, about my mother. And all of a sudden, I've woken up, but I haven't just woken up, I've woken up shouting the word, 'Mum!'.

M: No! You're joking!

W: At the top of my voice, in a packed, quiet tube.

M: Oh no!

W: Yes and everybody's staring at me and that did not help, er, matters. Anyway, I've got off the tube and I've then arrived at my interview, put all that behind me, I'm not, I'm still not feeling a hundred per cent perfect, but nevertheless arrived at my interview on time and go in and think, actually 'This is going rather well. They're not saying an awful lot and come to think of it, they're looking at me in a rather strange way.'

M: Right … Then what?

W: Well, the next thing I knew, I have left the interview and said 'thank you very much for seeing me, blah-di-blah … and gone to the ladies' room. And there in the mirror, I could see what everyone was looking at and why they couldn't say anything,

M: What was it?

W: My face had swollen up!

M: Ah! No way!

W: It was bright red and …

M: No!

W: and covered in blotches, spots …

M: Oh! You're kidding!

W: Yes and the pills that my mother had given me were so out-of-date that they had caused an allergic reaction …

M: Oh! How embarrassing!

W: I know.

⫸ **LANGUAGEBANK** 2.3 p130–131

Stronger classes could read the notes and do the exercises at home. *Weaker classes* can do the exercises in class. Go through the phrases in the chart and elicit possible continuations before doing the exercise.

Answers: 1 1 this happened when 2 So, what happened? 3 Well 4 Anyway 5 The next thing I knew 6 So 7 You must be joking 8 don't believe it 9 In the end 10 really funny

5A Focus attention on the opening sentence. In pairs, Ss practise retelling the story. Monitor and check they are using the sequencers correctly.

Teaching tip

To ensure Ss practise the target language, write the sequencers on cards, one set for each pair. Each time Ss use one of the sequencers, they lay the card down on the desk. Ask Ss to try to use all of the sequencers when telling their stories.

B Ask Ss if they think it was a true story or a lie and why they think so. Play the recording and elicit the answer.

Answer: It was false.

UNIT 2 Recording 8

M=Man W1=1st woman W2=2nd woman

M: OK. What do we reckon? True or false?

W2: Erm … I don't know. I think it might be false because … I don't know …

M: Yeah, she was a little bit slow in telling the story …

W2: I don't know if your mum would give you out-of-date pills …

M: Yeah, would a mother giver her daughter out-of-date pills?

W2: I think false.

M: It sounded like she was trying to think of what to say next, so … you think false, I think false.

W1: Yes, it was false!

LEARN TO keep a story going

6A Introduce the topic by asking Ss how they feel when they are talking to an unresponsive person (they should answer negatively). Go through the first example with the class. Ss then complete the extracts with the correct phrases, then compare their answers in pairs. In feedback, elicit Ss' answers.

Answers: 1 a) 2 i) 3 d) 4 c) 5 j) 6 f)

B Play the recording once for Ss to listen and notice how the intonation is used.

C Play the recording again, but pause after each phrase for Ss to repeat, mimicking the intonation used. Play the recording a third time and pause after each phrase again but, this time, ask Ss to try and sound bored. Ask them if they notice the difference.

speakout TIP

Read the tip with the class, then say the phrase *How amazing!* for them to repeat, sounding interested.

Optional extra activity

Write on the board *1 So, I got on the bus to work and saw an old school friend who I hadn't seen for years.*

2 I sat down next to her and said; 'Hi, How are things with you?'

3 She looked and me a bit strangely, but replied, 'Fine, thanks!'

4 I asked her, 'How's your brother these days?'

5 She said; 'Fine thanks, but do I know you?'

6 I realised I'd made a mistake and didn't know her!

Ss take it in turns to say each sentence to their partner, who chooses a phrase from Ex 6A and reacts in a bored or interested way. When they have finished, Ss swap roles and repeat the activity. In feedback, nominate one or two pairs to perform their conversations for the class.

SPEAKING

7A Check Ss understand the situations, especially *got stuck* and *chased*. Give Ss 2–3 mins to choose a situation.

B Ss work alone to prepare their stories, using the questions and any other ideas they have. Monitor and help with vocabulary and write any new words/phrases on the board. Remind Ss to use the sequencers from Ex 4A.

C Ss tell each other their stories in groups of four and the other Ss in the group should respond using the language from Ex 6A, using intonation to sound interested. When they have finished, the other Ss in the group guess if the story is true or a lie. Monitor and note down any common errors for later feedback.

D Ss reveal to their group if they told a true story or a lie. In feedback, nominate Ss from each group to share any interesting facts they discovered and correct any common errors with the class.

Homework ideas

• Write the story you told in Ex 7C, or choose a different situation from Ex 7A and write a story.

• Language bank 2.3 Ex 1–2, p131

• Workbook Ex 1–3, p13

HUSTLE

Introduction

Ss watch an extract from the BBC drama *Hustle*, in which a burglar steals a painting and tries to take it through customs. Ss learn and practise how to tell a story and write it up as a newspaper article.

SUPPLEMENTARY MATERIALS

Ex 7: find a real story from a newspaper or news website about a theft for Ss to look at first.

Warm up: bring/download some pictures of the following paintings: *Mona Lisa* by Leonardo da Vinci, *Sunflowers* by Van Gogh, *The Scream* by Edvard Munch, *Le pigeon aux petits pois* by Picasso, *La Pastorale* by Matisse and *Portrait of Suzanne Bloch* by Picasso.

Culture notes

The Mona Lisa was stolen from The Louvre in Paris by Vincenzo Peruggia, an Italian workman who was angered by the number of Italian pieces in the French museum. The painting was missing for two years.

Sunflowers was one of twenty paintings taken from the Van Gogh Museum in 1991 in an armed raid. The painting was found hours later, abandoned in a car.

The Scream was stolen in 2004 from the Munch Museum in Oslo by two masked gunmen. They were arrested several months later, but the painting wasn't recovered until 2006.

Le pigeon aux petits pois was stolen in 2007 from the Musee d'Art Merne in Paris, along with *La Pastorale* by Matisse and three other artworks. They have yet to be recovered.

Portrait of Suzanne Bloch was stolen from the São Paulo Museum of Art in 2007. The whole theft took three minutes. The paintings were recovered from a town outside São Paulo in 2008.

Warm up

Show the pictures you have brought (see supplementary materials) and ask *What do these paintings have in common?* (They have all been stolen at some point.) Write the following questions on the board: *Do you know who painted the pictures? Do you know how/why they were stolen? Why do people steal works of art? If you were going to steal a painting, how would you do it?* Ss discuss the questions in pairs. In feedback, elicit Ss' answers and share some of the information from the **Culture notes**.

DVD PREVIEW

1 Check Ss understand the questions. In pairs, Ss discuss them. Monitor and help with any vocabulary they need. In feedback, nominate Ss to share their ideas with the class.

Culture notes

The BBC drama *Hustle* was first screened in 2004. It's about a group of con artists who specialise in 'long cons' – extended deceptions which require greater commitment, but which return a higher reward than simple confidence tricks. It stars several well-known British actors: Adrian Lester (Mickey Stone), Robert Glenister (Ash Morgan), Matt Di Angelo (Sean Kennedy) and Kelly Adams (Emma Kennedy).

2 Ss cover the programme information and look at the photos. Elicit their predictions about who the man is and what they think he has done/is going to do. Give Ss 1 min to read the information and check their predictions. Elicit what problems the Ss think Finch had when he stole the painting.

Teaching tip

When we read a text in our own language, it is usually because the title and/or photos have aroused our interest and we subconsciously activate our background knowledge of the subject so that new information in the text connects with our existing knowledge. Ss need to practise and use this skill with texts in English too.

▶ DVD VIEW

3A Focus attention on the example. Give Ss 2–3 mins to match the other words alone, then compare their answers in pairs. In feedback, elicit Ss' answers and write them on the board.

Answers: 1 e) 2 a) 3 g) 4 f) 5 d) 6 c) 7 b)

Teaching tip

Collocations are difficult for Ss to learn because of the lack of common rules regarding which words go together, e.g. *a heavy smoker, make the bed*. Encourage Ss to learn the collocation as a single item, as they would a single word. This makes it easier to remember and use it.

B Play the DVD for Ss to check which of the collocations from Ex 3A they don't see. Tell Ss to focus on the collocations and not to worry about language they didn't understand. They'll watch the DVD again in Ex 4A. Give Ss a chance to compare their answers, then go through the collocations you wrote on the board in Ex 3A, ticking the ones that appeared and crossing the ones that didn't.

Answer: 4 f) (burglar alarm) does not appear in the clip.

4A Go through the questions and check *breaks into* and *sets off*. In pairs, Ss discuss their answers to the questions from what they can remember. Play the DVD again for Ss to check their answers.

Answers: 1 He climbs over the wall. 2 Walking round the outside of the house. 3 He tries to steal the painting. 4 A monkey 5 He climbs back over the wall. 6 The customs officers stop Finch and search his bags. 7 They are looking for the painting but they don't find it. 8 They plan to follow Finch.

B Ss compare their answers in pairs. If necessary, play the DVD again. Elicit the answers and ask *What do you think he did with the painting? What do you think happens next?*

DVD 2 Hustle

D=Detective T=Thief C=Customs man

C: Excuse me, sir, could you follow me, please?
D: Where is it?
T: Where's what?
D: You know what.
T: Sorry. Can I put my trousers back on now? Can I just … ?
D: I want him followed. If he makes contact with anyone, I want to know about it. You understand me? Well, what are you waiting for?

speakout a narrative

5 Ss now invent details for the rest of the story. Elicit some ideas for the first two questions. Ss then discuss their answers to the questions in groups of three and one of them writes them down.

Alternative approach
Rather than sharing their stories with the class in feedback, arrange Ss in A/B pairs. Student B tells Student A their story. After 3–4 mins, clap your hands and ask Student Bs to move to the next Student A. Continue until Ss are back with their original partner. Student A then tells Student B everything they can remember about the stories they heard and together they choose their favourite one. This will take longer, but Ss will be much more active throughout.

6A Ss listen to the story, then answer the questions in pairs. In feedback, elicit Ss' answers and compare them to Ss' stories in Ex 5B.

Answers: 1 Finch has stolen a Van Gogh painting.
2 He has stolen it for a Russian art dealer, who offered to pay him huge amounts of money for the painting.
3 No, Finch isn't a very good thief. In fact, he's been in prison before. 4 When he's in the airport in Rio, he realises that security men are watching him, so he hides the painting inside a locker. 5 In the locker in the airport. 6 When he leaves the airport in the UK, he realises that he is being followed by customs officers. 7 He arranges for a friend to collect the painting from the Brazilian airport and to meet him in Argentina, where they can sell the painting and then share the money. 8 Yes. His friend saw there was a reward being offered for the painting. So he told the police about the plan and therefore Finch was arrested when he got to the airport.

B Give Ss 1 min to read the key phrases, then play the recording again for them to check which phrases they hear. In feedback, elicit Ss' answers and drill the key phrases.

Answers: ✓ In this story, …; The problem is that …; In fact, …; However …; What he doesn't know is that …; Because of this, …

C In pairs, Ss tell the story again, using the key phrases in Ex 6B and the questions in Ex 5. Monitor and encourage Ss to use the key phrases. In feedback, nominate one or two Ss to tell their stories to the class.

Unit 2 Recording 10

C=Chris Harris
C: OK. Well, in this story, the painting which Finch has stolen is a Van Gogh. Er, he has stolen it for a Russian art dealer, who offered to pay him huge amounts of money for the painting. The problem is that Finch isn't a very good thief. In fact, he's been in prison before. So, when he's in the airport in Rio, he realises that security men are watching him. They're talking on their radios. Also, he sees a newspaper which has headlines about the stolen painting. He decides to put the painting inside a locker in the airport. Er … He keeps the key and flies back to the UK hoping that in a few weeks' time, he can go back to Brazil and collect the painting. However, when he leaves the airport in the UK, he realises that he is being followed by customs officers. Oh, also, he meets the art dealer who wants the painting and the dealer threatens to break his legs if he doesn't get the painting. So, Finch is worried, but he has an idea. He tells a friend of his about the painting and gives him the key to the locker. He arranges for the friend to fly to Brazil and collect the painting and to meet him in Argentina, where they can share the money. What he doesn't know is that the friend has seen that there is a reward being offered for the painting. So he decides to call the police and tell them about the plan. Because of this, when Finch arrives at the airport, he is arrested.

writeback a newspaper article

7A Teach/Elicit *poet* and *evidence*. Focus attention on the headline and elicit Ss' predictions/what they know about this story. Ss work alone to read the text and answer the questions, then check their answers in pairs. In feedback, elicit Ss' answers.

Answers: The painting was stolen by Vincenzo Peruggia, because he was angry at how many Italian paintings were being displayed in France. In the end the painting was shown throughout Italy before finally being returned to France in 1913.

7B Remind Ss of the vocabulary for news stories in Ex 7A on p24 and the key phrases in Ex 6B on p29. Ss write their newspaper stories alone. Monitor and help with vocabulary, writing any new words/phrases on the board. When they have finished, Ss show their stories to other Ss and suggest changes.

Homework ideas
• Ex 5: write the story you invented.
• Ex 7B: write a final draft of your newspaper article.

2.5 LOOKBACK

Introduction

Ss revise and practise the language of Unit 2. The notes below provide ideas for exploiting the exercises and activities but your approach will depend on your aim, e.g. whether you use the activities as a diagnostic or progress test or as revision/ fluency practice. If done as a test then it would not be appropriate to monitor or help Ss.

TYPES OF STORY

1A Do the first sentence together to demonstrate. Ss work alone to add the missing vowels, then compare their answers in pairs. Elicit Ss' answers and write the words on the board.

> **Answers:** 1 action 2 biopic 3 romantic comedy 4 period dramas 5 psychological thriller 6 detective 7 science fiction 8 docudramas

B As an example, choose one of the genres and tell Ss some of your favourite films in that genre. Ss work alone and choose five of the genres, then write 'best ever' lists for each one. If Ss don't know the names of the films in English, tell them to write the names in their language but be prepared to describe the film. Monitor and help where necessary.

PRESENT PERFECT/PAST SIMPLE

2A Give Ss 1 min to read the phrases and check they understand them. Ss choose eight of the phrases and write a sentence for each. Make sure they choose things they have and haven't done to ensure they practise both the positive and negative forms. Monitor and make sure Ss are forming the sentences correctly.

B Go through the example and point out the use of the past simple to give details. Ss work in pairs to give more information about their experiences. Monitor and note down any common errors for later feedback. In feedback, nominate Ss to share any interesting facts they found out.

THE NEWS

3A Ss choose the correct options alone, then compare their answers in pairs. In feedback, elicit Ss' answers and check they understand the vocabulary.

> **Answers:** 1 strike 2 demonstration 3 Hostages 4 earthquake 5 Fugitive 6 crash 7 attacked 8 shot

B Put Ss into pairs. First demonstrate the activity with two of the words from Ex 3A. Ss then continue in their pairs. One student says a word and their partner responds by inventing a headline. In feedback, elicit a few of their headlines.

> **Alternative approach**
> Ss choose four of the words and write headlines using them. When they are ready, they read out the headline to their partner, but instead of the word chosen, they say *blank*. Their partner guesses the word.

NARRATIVE TENSES

4A Elicit the first answer as an example. Ss complete the story alone, then compare their answers in pairs. In feedback, elicit Ss' answers and check the pronunciation.

> **Answers:** 1 woke 2 had forgotten 3 was having 4 rang 5 hadn't finished 6 had asked 7 left 8 was standing 9 were looking 10 realised 11 had forgotten 12 was wearing

B Go through the questions with the class. Give Ss 2–3 mins to prepare what they are going to say and make notes. In pairs, Ss tell their stories. In feedback, elicit any interesting answers.

TELLING A STORY

5A Go through the example with the class and elicit the next missing word in conversation 1. Ss work alone to add the rest of the missing words, then compare their answers in pairs. Check answers so that the conversations they use in Ex B are correct.

> **Answers:** 1 A: This *happened* when I was living in Hong Kong. B: Oh really? *What* happened? 2 A: I was having a shower when all *of* a sudden I saw a huge spider. B: Oh no. What *did* you do? 3 A: Anyway, before *long* someone called the police. B: Really? What *happened* next? 4 A: The next *thing* I knew, the man was running towards me and shouting. B: *I* don't believe it! 5 A: *So/Well*, anyway I was going up the ski-lift and I fell off. B: *How* embarrassing! 6 A: So, in *the* end, I had to pay all the money back. B: *Oh* dear.

B Focus attention on the first conversation and ask *What could have happened?* Elicit Ss' ideas and demonstrate how they can expand the conversation, using the language from Lesson 2.3. In pairs, Ss choose three of the conversations to expand. Monitor and help where necessary.

C Put the pairs together into groups of four and Ss perform their conversations to each other. In feedback, nominate one or two pairs to perform their conversations to the class.

> **Alternative approach**
> Ex 5C: Ss perform only their extensions to the conversations and the other pair listens and guesses which conversation they have expanded.

> **Homework ideas**
> • Workbook Review and check 1, p14–16
> • Workbook Test 1, p17

OVERVIEW

This video podcast extends discussion of the unit topic to communication. Ss can view people describing the best communicators they know. Use this video podcast at the start or end of Unit 3.

YOU'RE GOING WHERE?

Introduction
Ss learn and practise future forms to describe plans and learn vocabulary related to communication in the context of teenagers. They also learn and practise how to write messages.

SUPPLEMENTARY MATERIALS
Resource bank p135 and p137
Ex 8A: bring dictionaries for Ss to use.
Ex 12: bring small pieces of paper for Ss to write their messages on.
Speakout TIP: write some recent text messages you've sent/received on the board.

Warm up
Write on the board *How to survive being a teenager*. In pairs, Ss write five pieces of advice for being a teenager. Monitor and help with vocabulary, writing any new words/phrases on the board. Rearrange Ss to work with a new partner and share their ideas. In feedback, ask Ss to share their favourite idea with the class.

SPEAKING

1 Read and check the questions with the class. Give Ss 3–4 mins to discuss the questions. In feedback, elicit Ss' ideas and have a brief class discussion. Write their ideas on the board so that they can refer back to them in Ex 2A.

READING

2A Focus attention on the title and the photos and elicit Ss' ideas as to what the text is about. In pairs, Ss read the text, then compare it with their ideas in Ex 1. In feedback, tick off any of the problems mentioned on the board and elicit the main problem mentioned in the text.

Answer: The main problem is the fact that the writer's teenage children never tell their mother their plans and this causes her to worry.

B Ss complete the summary, referring back to the text if they need to. Elicit Ss' answers.

Answers: 1 (teenage) children 2 plans 3 don't answer/know 4 changing/flexible 5 change 6 late

Optional extra activity
Vary the pace by doing the gap-fill exercise as a team game. Ss first do the exercise orally in small groups, but don't write any of the answers down. When they are ready, give each group a board pen. Each round, you call out one of the numbers randomly and one student from each group comes to the board to write the answer. The first team with the correct answer on the board gets a point and the team with the most points at the end wins. After the game, Ss can do the exercise alone to reinforce the answers.

C Read through the sentences and elicit Ss' answers, but don't confirm any answers yet. Give Ss 3–4 mins to read the text and check their answers. In feedback, elicit Ss' answers. With *weaker Ss*, you may need to help them identify the parts of the text that give them the correct information.

Answers: 1 T 2 F 3 T 4 F 5 T

D Find the first word together with the class to demonstrate. Ss find the rest of the words in the text, then compare answers in pairs. Elicit the words/phrases in feedback, drill them and write them on the board.

Answers: 1 changing his mind about 2 cope with 3 nosy 4 panic 5 last-minute arrangements 6 if you can't beat them, join them

3 Ss discuss the questions in small groups. Monitor and provide vocabulary where necessary, writing new words/ phrases on the board. In feedback, nominate Ss from each group to tell the class their opinions.

GRAMMAR the future (plans)

4A Do the first example with the class. Read the first conversation using *might* together, then elicit which rule it goes with. Ss complete the other rules alone, then compare their answers in pairs. Elicit the correct answers, giving further examples where necessary.

Answers: Rule 1: present continuous Rule 2: *going to* + verb Rule 3: *might* + verb Rule 4: *will* + verb

Teaching tip

When introducing grammar, it's useful for Ss to discover the rules rather than simply hear them. Focus attention on examples used in context so that they have the opportunity to discover the rules for themselves.

B Ss find further examples of the forms in the text and underline them, then compare their answers in pairs. In feedback, elicit Ss' answers and ask Ss to show you where they are in the text.

Answers: 1 When are you coming back? How are you getting home? 'I'm going out on Saturday,' says my sixteen-year-old. I don't know what I'm doing.
2 He's never quite sure where he's going to be; Simon, I'm going to follow your lead.
3 The next time I arrange to meet someone, I'll be late.
4 Or I might not turn up at all.

⟹ LANGUAGEBANK 3.1 p132–133

Stronger classes could read the notes and do the exercises at home. Otherwise, read the notes carefully with Ss, giving further explanations/examples where necessary. Remind Ss that it's much more common to use *might* when we're not sure than *maybe+will*, e.g. *I might go out tonight*, not *Maybe I will go out tonight*.

In each exercise, do the first sentence as an example. Ss complete the exercises alone, then check their answers in pairs. Ss can refer to the notes to help them.

Answers: 1 1 are 2 going 3 re 4 is playing 5 coming 6 are you 7 'll ask 8 might
2 1 *Are you going* out this weekend? 2 I'm sorry I can't come. *I'm playing* tennis after work. 3 I don't feel very well. I think *I'll stay* at home. 4 What *are* you going to do? 5 We're going for a picnic, so I hope it doesn't rain. 6 Is that the phone? Don't worry – I'll get it.
7 They might *go* to a concert. 8 I'm sorry we can't come, but *we're visiting* my mother this weekend.

Watch out!

Talking about the future can be complicated for Ss, as many different future forms can be used, depending on how we see the event and how we want others to see it. At this stage, keep it simple and focus on a few forms with common uses, e.g. for making plans.

5A Ss listen and complete the sentences. Pause the recording after each one to give Ss time to write their answers. After listening, Ss compare their answers in pairs. If necessary, play the recording again for Ss to check their answers.

Answers: 1 are you going to do 2 're going to visit 3 are you going to look 4 're going to have 5 Are you going to come 6 's going to leave

B Play the recording again for Ss to listen to the pronunciation. Explain that in fast speech *going to* is usually pronounced /ˈɡʊnə/, but this is not always appropriate in more formal situations.

C Play the recording again, pausing after each sentence for Ss to practise saying them. Make sure they pronounce *going to* as in the recording.

Teaching tip

To practise rapid speech, start by focusing on the stressed syllables only, then building up the phrases with the unstressed words at the same speed. This will help Ss keep a natural rhythm when saying the phrases rapidly.

Unit 3 Recording 1

1 What are you going to do at the weekend?
2 We're going to visit my brother and his family.
3 Where are you going to look for them?
4 They're going to have a party on Friday.
5 Are you going to come with us tomorrow?
6 I'll ask Marion when she's going to leave.

PRACTICE

6 Do the first example with the class and elicit why this is the correct answer. Ss choose the correct alternatives, then compare their answers in pairs. In feedback, elicit the answers and why they are correct.

Answers: 1 are you two doing 2 might 3 I'm going to have 4 are going 5 is bringing 6 we'll have 7 is going to bring 8 is coming 9 I'll text 10 I'll call 11 I'll speak

7A Go through the examples with the class. Ss read the situations and write one or two sentences for each. Monitor and check they are using the correct future forms.

B When they have finished, Ss read out their sentences in pairs. Encourage Ss to ask follow-up questions to find out as much information as possible. In feedback, ask each student to share one interesting fact they found out about their partner.

VOCABULARY communication

8A Focus attention on the example and elicit the answer to the second sentence. Ss match the words to the sentences, then compare their answers in pairs. If you've brought dictionaries, give them out for Ss to use. In feedback, elicit Ss' answers and drill the words.

Answers: 1 gossip 2 apologise 3 chat 4 boast 5 argue 6 warn 7 compliment 8 moan

B Read sentence I with the class and elicit who is talking. Ss decide who is talking in the other sentences in pairs. In feedback, elicit Ss' answers.

Answers: 1 T 2 P 3 P 4 P 5 P/T 6 P 7 P/T 8 P

C Play the recording for Ss to listen to the intonation. Play the recording again and pause after each sentence for Ss to repeat, imitating the intonation.

▬▶ **VOCABULARYBANK** p150 Communication

1A Read the first example and elicit the key phrase in the second sentence. Ss underline the rest of the phrases alone, then check their answers in pairs.

B In pairs, Ss match the definitions to the phrases. In feedback, elicit Ss' answers and give further examples if necessary.

Stronger classes can do the exercises at home.

Answers: 1A 1 get hold of you 2 have a chat with 3 got in touch with 4 get what you mean 5 goes on and on 6 stayed in touch 7 said sorry for 8 have arguments about
B 1 c) 2 a) 3 g) 4 e) 5 h) 6 f) 7 d) 8 b)

SPEAKING

9A To demonstrate the activity, tell Ss some of the typical things you did when you were a teenager. Give Ss 5 mins to think about when they were teenagers and make notes. Monitor closely to help with vocabulary, especially with *weaker Ss*.

B Give Ss 5 mins to make notes. With *weaker Ss*, first give them some examples from your own life to demonstrate. Monitor and help with vocabulary where necessary.

C In pairs, Ss compare their experiences. Monitor and note down any common errors for later feedback and encourage Ss to make generalisations about differences between their lives now and when they were teenagers. In feedback, nominate Ss to share any interesting experiences and ask if the pairs had any answers in common. Correct any common errors with the class.

Alternative approach
If your Ss are mostly teenagers, they could discuss the points in Ex 9A and Ex 9B about their life now.

WRITING messages

10 Introduce the topic by drawing a word web on the board with *messages* in the middle. Elicit different ways of writing messages, e.g. *email, on the fridge, sms,* etc. and write them on the board. In pairs, Ss discuss the questions. Monitor and help with vocabulary where necessary. In feedback, elicit Ss' answers and have a brief discussion.

Possible answers: 1 to pass on phone messages, give information, make requests, make arrangements
2 note 1 – friends/flatmates; note 2 – work colleagues; note 3 – husband and wife/family members; note 4 – mother or father and sons
3 Notes tend to be informal in style.

speakout TIP
Read the tip with the class, then write *Be home 10p.m.* on the board and elicit the missing words (*I'll* and *at*). You could also write on the board some recent text messages you've sent/ received and elicit the missing words.

LEARN TO use note form

11A Focus attention on the first message in Ex 10 and elicit the missing words (*I've, I'll*). Ss work alone to add the other words from the box to the messages, then compare their answers in pairs. In feedback, elicit Ss' answers.

Answers: 1 I've, I'll 2 Can you 3 I, Your 4 We'll

B Do the first message together as an example. Ss rewrite the other messages alone, then compare their answers in pairs. In feedback, nominate Ss to read out their shortened messages.

Possible answers: 1 Hungry? Lunch at Pavarotti's 1pm? Rx 2 Going to Elton John concert. Want a ticket? Tonya 3 Pete can't come for dinner. Call him on 01954627823 Jayne 4 Sorry, can't come to the film tonight. Too much work. Enjoy it. Bess

12 Read and check the situations with the class. Ss write the messages alone, then compare their answers in pairs. In feedback, nominate Ss to read out their messages.

Optional extra activity
To make the writing more communicative, Ss write messages to each other to arrange to do things at the weekend/in the evening. If you brought small pieces of paper to class, Ss can write their messages on them with the name of the Ss they are writing/responding to. Go round and deliver them for Ss, noting any common errors for later feedback. In feedback, elicit what Ss have arranged and correct any common errors with the class.

Homework ideas
• Ex 9C: write about differences between when you were a teenager and now.
• Write a list of advice for parents on how to deal with teenage children.
• Language bank 3.1 Ex 1–2, p133
• Vocabulary bank p150
• Workbook Ex 1–6, p18–19

GETTING CONNECTED

Introduction

Ss learn and practise future forms to describe predictions and future time markers in the context of science and technology. They also learn and practise idioms.

> ### SUPPLEMENTARY MATERIALS
>
> **Resource bank** p136 and p138
>
> **Ex 9** and **Ex 10**: bring dictionaries for Ss to use.
>
> **Warm up**: bring any gadgets you have (e.g. mobile phone, mp3 player, laptop) to class.

Warm up

Bring any gadgets you have to class and show them to Ss, telling them what you like/dislike about them. Ss talk about any gadgets they have in small groups.

LISTENING

1 Focus attention on the pictures and elicit the names of the objects (*telephone, record player, pen and ink, television or TV, cassette player, video cassette*). Write the words on the board. In pairs, Ss discuss the questions. In feedback, elicit what has replaced the objects and Ss' opinions on them.

2A Read/Check the questions with the class. Ss then discuss the questions in pairs. In feedback, nominate Ss to share their ideas with the class.

B Explain that Ss will listen to people discussing the same questions as in Ex 2A. Tell Ss to listen for any of their own ideas.

C Ss read the notes and find three factual mistakes, then compare their answers in pairs. Play the recording again for Ss to check their answers.

> **Answers:** 1 English to Japanese (and back) 2 in 10 years 3 The woman thinks it'll be in the short term.

3 Ask Ss to find the first word in the audio script and read the words around it. Elicit their ideas as to its meaning. Ask *If you use an intermediary, do you speak directly to the person? (No)*. Ss discuss the meanings of the other words in pairs. In feedback, elicit their ideas and check comprehension.

> ### Teaching tip
>
> With *weaker Ss*, give them more help when guessing meanings from context. Ask *Is it a noun, verb or adjective? Which other words does it collocate with? What was said before/after it?*

Unit 3 Recording 3

Conversation 1

W1=1st woman M1=1st man W2=2nd woman M2=2nd man

W1: Erm, so there are many, many ways we communicate with people at the moment and, um, in the near future – I wanted to talk about something that, um, is going to be with us which is, um, a system for translating foreign languages. Um, so potentially you could be on the phone talking to someone from another country who's speaking in a different language and it's being, um, translated into your ear so you can communicate that way. What do we th …

M1: Like an intermediary or something?

W1: Um, yes …

M1: Or by technology?

W1: By technology so you can do this on Skype you know where you've got the erm, the camera filming you and you are talking to someone um in another country … How, how do we feel about that?

M1: Well, it might work in the future but it certainly doesn't work at the moment. I mean if you go to a website that's in a foreign language and you can get these, you know, these online translation services …

M2: It, erm …

W2: It's not quite right.

M1: It's very funny.

M2: He gets it wrong.

M1: He gets it completely wrong, especially English to Japanese and back from it.

W1: See, you see will this type of communication affect the way we work and … and?

W2: Well, businesses, I mean it works very well for businesses because you will be able to communicate with someone from a different company in a different country and maybe … erm, that will stop barriers in that way.

Conversation 2

W=Woman M=Man

W: I heard a TV programme the other day and they said that they don't think that handwriting will exist in the next ten years. What d'you think about that?

M: Oh really? What, what did they suggest would take its place?

W: Er, well, for things like, erm, signatures, you know, for bank cards, or whatever, or signing things, erm, they suggested that we would use thumbprints or er, digital …

M: Kind of retina scans, things like that?

W: Yeah, that's it, yeah.

M: Well, I personally think that handwriting will be with us y'know for a long time. Erm, I think in years to come, people will still carry a pen around in their top pocket rather than anything else and erm, that will be the quickest, easiest and most straightforward way to communicate.

W: Well, maybe in the short term but if you think about – I don't know – sort of kids ten, twelve years old, they're using more and more y'know computers at school and things and they might actually just stop writing, stop the practice of writing.

Conversation 3

W1=1st woman M1=1st man W2=2nd woman M2=2nd man

W1: Well, before I give my opinion I'd like to know what you all think about the future of television.

M1: Well, it won't be on a television set, that's for sure.

W2: No, it'll be on a computer.

M2: Absolutely.

M1: Through broadband on a, on a computer and it'll be on demand. Y'know, the difference between push and pull technology.

W1: Yes, I absolutely agree that it will be on demand, but I don't think that it will still be … I don't think … I think there'll be a place for computers, for YouTube, all those things, but ultimately it will not replace a very large screen in your living room.

M1: But the large screen in your living room will still be there. It's just the method of delivery and whether or not it's broadcast to you when you don't want it or whether you …

W2: Oh, I absolutely agree.

M1: … pick it up when you do want it.

M2: How soon do you think it'll change then? I mean are we talking long term? Short term?

M1: It won't be in a month … It won't be in a month or two and it won't be in the short term, but certainly in the long term this will be the future.

W1: I think, I think it will be in the short term, actually. I would say in the next …

W2: Everything is so quickly changing, isn't it?

W1: Yes, absolutely.

M1: You've already got y'know on-demand, with the iPlayer and …

W1: Yes …

M1: and YouTube where y'know if you want to see it you can go and see it when you want to see it.

W1: And that is phenomenally successful.

VOCABULARY future time markers

4A Read the first two examples with the class and elicit what the phrases are used for, i.e. to mark a period of time in the future. Ss work alone to underline the future time markers in the other sentences, then compare their answers in pairs.

Answers: 1 in the near future 2 in the next ten years 3 in a month or two 4 in the long term 5 in the short term 6 in ten years' time 7 a long time from now 8 next year 9 shortly

> **Watch out!**
> Check/teach the use of the apostrophe in *ten years' time*, compared to *one year's time*.

B Read/Check the headings with the class and go over the examples. In pairs, Ss categorise the other phrases in Ex 4A.

Answers: 1 in ten years' time, next year 2 in the near future, in the next ten years, shortly, in a month or two, in the short term 3 a long time from now, in the long term

C Ss discuss the questions in pairs. Encourage Ss to ask follow-up questions and give reasons.

GRAMMAR the future (predictions)

5A Check *a turning point* with the class. Give Ss 1 min to read the preview, then tell you what the programme is about.

Answer: the science of the future.

B Read the example with the class. Ask *Is it certain or possible? (certain) How do we know? (the use of will)*. Repeat with sentence 2. Ss look at the other sentences in pairs.

Answers: 1 C 2 P 3 P 4 C 5 P

C Ss complete the rules alone, using the sentences in Ex 5B, then compare their answers in pairs. In feedback, elicit Ss' answers.

Answers: 1 will 2 be 3 could 4 to

> ⟱ **LANGUAGEBANK** 3.2 p132–133
>
> Read the notes carefully and check the use of *be* in *is/are likely to*. Give further examples where necessary. Ss work alone to complete the exercises, then check their answers in pairs.
>
> **Answers:** 1 1 We might not win the cup this year. 2 I'm likely to be late. 3 That company is going to close in July. 4 He is unlikely to call after 10.00. 5 I won't give up exercise. 6 There may be a problem with the flight. 7 She's going to get angry when she sees this. 8 Will you visit us? 9 I hope he comes to the party. 10 Prices could rise if they complete the development.
> 2 1 Jenny *might not* be able to … 2 … are *likely to* lose their jobs … 3 … cars *will be* able to fly. 4 … *may arrive* at any moment. 5 The children *aren't going* to stay with me … 6 I *won't know* my exam results until August. 7 It's *not likely* that we'll arrive before 6.00 … 8 That painting *is going* to fall …

PRACTICE

6A Read the example with the class and elicit the second answer. Ss choose the answers alone, then check in pairs.

Answers: 1 a) 2 c) 3 c) 4 b) 5 c) 6 c) 7 a) 8 a) 9 c) 10 b)

B Discuss the first prediction with the class as an example and elicit Ss' ideas. In small groups, Ss discuss the other predictions.

SPEAKING

7A Focus attention on the picture and elicit what Ss can see in it. Elicit Ss' ideas as to how realistic it is.

B Read the topics in the box with the class. Give Ss 3–4 mins to think about their ideas and make notes.

C Read the example with the class and ask if Ss agree or disagree and why. In pairs, Ss discuss their ideas from Ex 7B.

VOCABULARY PLUS idioms

8A Read the definition and the first sentence with the class. Ss underline the other idioms alone, then compare their answers in pairs. Check and drill the idioms with the class.

Answers: 1 small talk 2 work against the clock 3 on our mind 4 be everyone's cup of tea 5 close to my heart

B Ss work alone to decide if the statements are true or false.

C In pairs, Ss discuss the statements. When they have finished, they turn to p160 to check.

Answers: 1 F 2 T 3 T 4 F

speakout TIP

Read the tip and explain that if Ss overuse idioms, it can sound unnatural/forced.

9 Ss discuss the meanings in pairs. If you've brought dictionaries, give them out for Ss to use.

Answers: 1 in hot water = in trouble 2 put my foot in it = say something embarrassing that gets you into trouble 3 working against the clock = needing to finish something in a short time 4 running out of time = not having enough time to finish something

10 Ss work alone to match the idioms to their definitions, then compare their answers in pairs. In feedback, elicit Ss' answers and drill the idioms with the class.

Answers: 1 b) 2 c) 3 a) 4 f) 5 e) 6 d)

11A Correct the first question together as an example. Ss work alone, then check their answers in pairs.

Answers: 1 the *a* hand 2 *a dark horse* 3 put your *foot* in it 4 close *to* your heart 5 work against the clocks 6 in *hot* water?

B Give Ss 2–3 mins to write their answers. Monitor and help where necessary. In pairs, Ss compare their answers.

> ⟱ **VOCABULARYBANK** p150 Idioms
>
> **1A** In pairs, Ss match the idioms to the pictures.
>
> **B** Ss complete the sentences, then check answers in pairs.
>
> **C** In pairs, Ss discuss the meanings. In feedback, elicit Ss' answers. *Stronger classes* can do the exercises at home.
>
> **Answers: 1A** A break the ice B learn (something) by heart C go window shopping D travel light E let your hair down F be in two minds
> **B** 1 learn (it) by heart 2 in two minds 3 break the ice 4 travels light 5 window shopping 6 let your hair down

---

Homework ideas
- Language bank 3.2 Ex 1–2, p133
- Vocabulary bank p150
- Workbook Ex 1–8, p20–21

IN OTHER WORDS …

Introduction

Ss learn and practise ways of dealing with misunderstandings when finding out information. They also learn how to reformulate to make their message clearer.

SUPPLEMENTARY MATERIALS

Resource bank p139

Warm up: prepare a story about a time when you had a misunderstanding.

Warm up

Tell Ss about a time when you had a misunderstanding with someone and encourage them to ask you follow-up questions to find out more information. Ss then share their own experiences in pairs. In feedback, nominate Ss to share their partner's experience with the class.

SPEAKING

1A Ask Ss to cover the text and focus attention on the picture. Elicit what Ss can see and where they think it is. Give Ss 2 mins to read the text, then discuss in pairs what they think happened next. Check comprehension of the text by asking *How many people were celebrating in the restaurant? Why were they celebrating? Why did Johnny Carson go over? Who went to pay the bill?* In feedback, nominate Ss to share their predictions with the class.

B Ss turn to p160 and read the ending. Ask *Who actually paid the bill? Why did he pay it? How much was it? Was Johnny Carson angry about the misunderstanding?*

C Ss cover the text and use the words in the box to practise retelling the story in pairs. In feedback, ask one or two **stronger Ss** to retell the story to the class.

VOCABULARY misunderstandings

2A Read the example with the class. Ss match the sentences alone, then check their answers in pairs. In feedback, elicit Ss' answers.

Answers: 1 f) 2 d) 3 e) 4 h) 5 c) 6 b) 7 g) 8 a)

B In pairs, Ss discuss the meanings of the words in bold. Monitor and encourage them to share their own experiences. In feedback, elicit the definitions and ask Ss to share their experiences.

FUNCTION dealing with misunderstandings

3A Ss listen to four conversations and say what type of misunderstandings they hear. Explain that they shouldn't worry about understanding every word and that they'll have a chance to listen again in Ex 3B. Play the recording. Then ask Ss to compare their answers in pairs. In feedback, elicit Ss' answers.

Answers: 1 a wrong number 2 the wrong hotel 3 the wrong time 4 the wrong date

B Ss listen again and answer the questions. Give them time to compare their answers in pairs, then play the recording again if needed. In feedback, elicit Ss' answers.

Answers: 1 Tom 2 Willy's Burger Bar 3 over the phone 4 the Sheldon Hotel 5 7.00 6 5.00 7 a car 8 the fourth of July

C Elicit the first answer together as an example. Ss complete

the expressions alone, then compare their answers in pairs. Don't confirm any answers yet.

D Play the recording for Ss to check their answers. In feedback, elicit Ss' answers. Play the recording again for Ss to repeat, pausing after each sentence. Ask them to focus on repeating the phrases with the same intonation.

Answers: 1 that 2 me 3 name 4 again 5 mean 6 saying 7 tell me

Unit 3 Recording 4

Conversation 1

W=Woman M=Man

W: Hi. Me again. I've sent an attachment with all the figures for the last six months. That should be all you need.

M: Sorry – I didn't catch any of that.

W: I've sent the figures in an attachment. Is that Tom?

M: You've lost me. Who is this?

W: This is Ana Lucia. Is that Tom?

M: No, this is Willy's Burger Bar. What number are you trying to get?

W: 845 6795.

M: I think you've got the wrong number.

W: Oh I'm sorry.

Conversation 2

M=Man W=Woman

M: I've got a reservation in the name of David Cullinan.

W: Just one moment. Umm, could you repeat the last name?

M: Cullinan. C-u-l-l-i-n-a-n.

W: Cullinan. I can't find the name. Did you make the reservation over the phone?

M: Yes, just yesterday.

W: Sorry, let me just see if there are any messages here. I won't be a moment. I'm sorry. We've got no reservations in the name of Cullinan and we're fully booked tonight.

M: So you're saying I can't stay here. This is the Sheldon Hotel, yes?

W: No, this is The *Felton*. With an 'f'.

M: Really? So I'm in the wrong hotel.

W: The Sheldon is on Queen's Road, just around the corner.

M: Oh no. Sorry, can you say that again – where is it?

W: On Queen's Road, just around the corner.

Conversation 3

G=Girl F=Father

G: You've missed the best bits. You're late.

F: What exactly do you mean? The show starts at 7.00, doesn't it?

G: No, it finishes at 7.00!

F: Didn't you say it starts at 7.00?

G: No, it starts at 5.00 and finishes at 7.00!

F: So what you mean is I've missed the whole show.

G: Yes.

Conversation 4

M=Man W=Woman

M: We've got nothing for you, I'm afraid.

W: I don't get what you're saying. You're a car rental company, right?

M: Yes, but today's a holiday and all the cars have been booked already.

W: Do you mean to tell me that there's nothing at all? No cars available?

M: There's nothing till tomorrow, I'm afraid.

W: But I definitely booked a car for today, the third of July.

M: It's the fourth of July today. In other words, your booking was for yesterday.

W: It can't be. Is it?

M: It's the fourth today, madam.

W: Oh no, I've got the date wrong.

⇒ **LANGUAGEBANK** 3.3 p132–133

Stronger classes could read the notes and do the exercises at home. *Weaker classes* can do the exercises in class. Drill the phrases in the chart. Elicit the first answer, then Ss match the sentences and questions in pairs. In feedback, elicit Ss' answers.

Answers: 1 1 e) 2 g) 3 a) 4 b) 5 f) 6 d) 7 c)

4A Read the example with the class. Ss add the missing words, then check their answers in pairs. With *weaker Ss*, write the missing words on the board in random order for them to add. In feedback, elicit Ss' answers and drill the phrases.

Answers: 1 Do you *mean* to say we're going to be locked out all night? 2 You've *lost* me. Who are all these people? 3 What exactly *do* you mean? 4 I don't *get* what you're saying. 5 I didn't *catch* any of that. What's the number? 6 Can you *say* that again? I didn't hear. 7 Could you *repeat* the last part? I didn't hear you.

B Put Ss into pairs and give them 5 mins to think about what A says next in each conversation. Monitor and help with vocabulary where needed. When they are ready, Ss practise the conversations in pairs. In feedback, nominate Ss to perform their conversations for the class.

Alternative approach
In feedback, Ss just read out their extensions to the conversations. Other Ss listen and guess which conversation it is.

LEARN TO reformulate

5A Here Ss learn how to reformulate their ideas. Read the example with the class. Ask *Why does the speaker use this phrase?* (to repeat what they heard in a different way, to check that they understand correctly). Ss underline the phrases alone, then check their answers in pairs. In feedback, elicit Ss' answers and write them on the board.

Answers: 1 So you're saying 2 So what you mean is 3 Do you mean to tell me; In other words

B Focus attention on the phrases on the board from Ex 5A and draw curves linking the words. Play the recording once for Ss to listen and focus on the linking.

C Play the recording again and pause after each sentence for Ss to repeat. Listen to how they are linking the words and, if necessary, drill the phrases further.

Teaching tip
Linking is useful, not only for pronunciation but also for listening skills and helps Ss distinguish words in rapid speech. Explain this to Ss.

Unit 3 Recording 6

1 So you're saying I can't stay here.

2 Didn't you say it starts at 7.00?

3 So what you mean is I've missed the whole show.

4 Do you mean to tell me that there's nothing at all?

5 In other words, your booking was for yesterday.

SPEAKING

6A Put Ss into A/B pairs. Review the language in Ex 3C and 5A and give Ss 2–3 mins to read through the situation and think about what they will say. When they are ready, Ss role-play the situation in pairs. Monitor and check Ss are using the language correctly, with natural intonation and linking.

B When they have finished, Ss swap roles and practise a new conversation using the details on p162. In feedback, nominate one or two pairs to perform their conversations for the class.

C Rearrange Ss so that they are working with a different partner. Read the situation with the class. Student A thinks of a problem and begins the role-play. When they have finished, they swap roles and role-play a new problem. Monitor and note down any errors for later correction.

Teaching tip
Stronger Ss can go straight into the role-play. *Weaker Ss* may need time to prepare their ideas and what they want to say.

In feedback, nominate one or two pairs to perform their dialogues for the class.

Optional extra activity
Ss could do Ex 6C as a mingling activity, walking round and practising the conversation with different Ss.

Homework ideas
• Write a story about when you (or someone you know) had a misunderstanding.
• Language bank 3.3 Ex 1, p133
• Workbook Ex 1–3, p22

THE VIRTUAL REVOLUTION

Introduction

Ss watch an extract from a BBC documentary about the impact of the internet. Ss learn and practise speaking about how they prefer to communicate and write a memo.

SUPPLEMENTARY MATERIALS

Warm up: write the questions described below on the board.

Warm up

Write on the board the names of the first three websites you visit every time you go on the internet and encourage Ss to ask you questions about each one. Ss then write their own three and share them with a partner. In feedback, nominate Ss to share their partner's information with the class.

▶ DVD PREVIEW

1 Ss discuss the question in pairs. Monitor and help with vocabulary, writing any new words/phrases on the board. In feedback, nominate one or two Ss to share their ideas with the class and have a brief discussion.

2A Go through the sentences and ask if any of them were mentioned in Ss' discussions in Ex 1.

B In pairs, Ss discuss the meanings of the words/expressions in bold. In feedback, check Ss understand each of the expressions and drill the phrases.

Answers: 1 creates wealth: makes money 2 challenge authority: question people in power 3 spy: monitor people/ organisations secretly; censor: cover up information 4 web addicts: people who can't stop using the internet 5 opens up new realms of knowledge: makes new facts available 6 pioneers: the first people to do something; key players: the most important people 7 e-shopping: shopping online

3 Give Ss 2 mins to read the introduction. Ss discuss the questions in pairs. In feedback, elicit Ss' answers.

Answers: The programme is about the impact of the internet. She speaks to some of the best-known internet pioneers.

▶ DVD VIEW

4 Teach/Elicit *pioneers* and *censorship*. Give Ss 2–3 mins to read the sentences. Check comprehension. Play the DVD for Ss to put the sentences in order. After viewing, Ss compare their answers in pairs. In feedback, elicit Ss' answers.

Teaching tip

Tell Ss to focus on putting the extracts in order and not to worry about language they don't understand. They'll watch the DVD again in Ex 5B.

Answers: a) 5 b) 4 c) 1 d) 3 e) 2

5A In pairs, Ss match the people to the extracts.

B Play the DVD again for Ss to check their answers. Ss then compare their answers in pairs and, if necessary, play the DVD again.

Answers: 1 a) g) 2 d) 3 e) 4 f) 5 b) 6 c)

C Ss discuss the questions in small groups. Monitor and note down any common language errors for later feedback. In feedback, nominate Ss from each group to share their opinions with the class. Correct any common errors.

DVD 3 The Virtual Revolution

B=Bill Gates SW=Steve Wozniak AG=Al Gore MZ=Mark Zuckerberg SF=Stephen Fry AK=Aleks Krotoski

AK: The web is the defining technological revolution of our lifetimes. Almost two billion of us are now online and in the ten years that I've been studying the web and writing about it as a journalist, I've seen it take our world and shake it apart.

The web has created unimaginable wealth, yet encouraged millions to work for nothing.

It's challenged authority, yet allowed regimes to spy and censor as never before.

And it's been blamed for creating a generation of web addicts. It opened up new realms of knowledge.

In this series I'll be meeting all the pioneers and key players: everybody from Google to Facebook; Twitter to Amazon, the people who've helped bring about this seemingly unstoppable levelling of power, culture and values that's having such an impact on all of our daily lives.

BG: Well the web is how mankind communicates nowadays.

SW: It's like the internet has become a brain. It's the smartest brain in the world.

AG: It is an empowering tool that has more potential than any other that human civilisation has ever developed.

MZ: The world is just gonna keep on getting more and more open and there's gonna be more information available about everything.

SF: This is astounding technology and we should just take a moment to celebrate the power and the reach that it gives us.

AK: And so this is the story of the web. But it's more than that. This is also the story of how the web is remaking our world.

A quarter of the planet now uses the web. On any given day in the British Isles, over 35 million of us will log on. The web is where we spend our money; around a billion pounds a week. Britain's most active e-shoppers are in Swansea, with Kirkwall in the Orkneys in second place.

It's where we fall in love, with five million of us using a dating website every month. Manchester and Central London have proportionally the most online lonely hearts. And the web is where we express opinion: eighteen million of us read blogs, Dumfries the least, West London the most.

The web is a revolution.

speakout communication preferences

6A Focus attention on the list, especially the first four topics. Play the recording for Ss to note which form of communication the woman prefers for each topic. Ss then check their answers in pairs. If necessary, play the recording again. In feedback, elicit Ss' answers.

Answers: Giving good news: face-to-face, but if you can't meet them then a phone call or email is fine. Giving bad news: face-to-face, but if it's difficult then an email. Never by text. Arranging social activities: text or phone, as it's more convenient. Sending a 'Thank you' message: Letter (or card). People appreciate the effort and might keep it.

B Go through the phrases and drill them with the class, paying attention to stress and linking. Ss listen again and tick the phrases they hear, then check their answers in pairs. In feedback, elicit Ss' answers.

> **Answers:** ✓ It depends on … ; It's much better to … ; On the other hand; In those circumstances I'd rather … ; It's more convenient; People really appreciate …

C Give Ss 5 mins to prepare their notes. Monitor and help with vocabulary, writing any new phrases on the board.

D Review the language from Ex 6B and drill again if necessary. Ss discuss their opinions in small groups. Monitor and note down any common errors for later correction. In feedback, nominate Ss from each group to share their opinions with the class and ask which ways of communicating are most popular. Correct any common errors.

Unit 3 Recording 7

L=Lisa Brown

L: I use the internet all the time to communicate, but I think for giving good news it's much, much nicer to be there and to do it face-to-face, though obviously it depends on what type of good news it is. Maybe the news is for someone you don't know personally or someone in a different country or city so you can't deliver it face-to-face. If that's the case, an email or a phone call are fine.

I'd say the same thing about giving bad news. If you know the person, it's much better to give it face-to-face. On the other hand, some bad news can be really difficult to give face-to-face. It can be embarrassing if someone's going to start crying in front of you or if they're going to get upset. So in those circumstances I'd rather send an email because it's less personal. I don't think I'd ever give bad news by text.

For arranging social activities I usually text my friends or do it over the phone. It's more convenient. People have such bad memories we kind of need to see arrangements written down. Also, we're always changing our plans at the last minute so we really need our phones switched on all the time.

For sending a 'thank you' message I think it's really nice to send a letter or, in my case, usually a card. I still send handwritten cards sometimes and I think people really appreciate them because it shows you made an effort, whereas just sending a text or something isn't much of an effort. And it's not like they're going to keep the message for more than two minutes. But they might keep a card.

writeback a memo

7A Introduce the topic by asking *How do you think you would cope if you couldn't use email once a week, both in your work/ studies and at home?* and elicit Ss' ideas. Explain the situation and give Ss 1 min to read the notes and discuss the reasons in pairs. In feedback, elicit Ss' answers.

> **Answers:** To encourage face-to-face communication and phone conversations, reduce time spent on emails and change the routine.

B Ss write their memos alone. Monitor and help with vocabulary where needed. When Ss have finished, they show their memo to a partner and discuss any language errors/ suggestions for changes. Monitor and help where needed.

Teaching tip

A good way to motivate Ss when writing is to use a speed-writing technique. In pairs, one student writes and the other provides ideas. They have exactly 5 mins to write their text. Count down each minute, putting gentle pressure on Ss and stop them after 5 mins. Ss then have 1 min to change/correct their writing, but cannot add any more text. Ss then join another pair and read their writing, circling any errors and underlining any suggestions for changes and consult the other pairs, explaining their comments. Ss write a final draft alone or for homework.

Homework ideas
- **Ex 7B**: write a final draft of your memo.
- Design a class website.

LOOKBACK

Introduction

Ss revise and practise the language of Unit 3. The notes below provide ideas for exploiting the exercises and activities but your approach will depend on your aim, e.g. whether you use the activities as a diagnostic or progress test or as revision/ fluency practice. If done as a test then it would not be appropriate to monitor or help Ss.

COMMUNICATION

1 Read the examples with the class. In pairs, Ss take turns to think of three situations for each verb. Monitor and help with vocabulary, writing any new words/phrases on the board. In feedback, nominate Ss to share some of their situations with the class.

> **Alternative approach**
> Ss choose five of the verbs and write a situation for each. In small groups, they read out their situations (but not the verbs) and other Ss guess the verb.

THE FUTURE (PLANS)

2A Elicit the first answer as an example. Ss complete the paragraphs alone, then check their answers in pairs. In feedback, elicit Ss' answers.

> **Answers:** 1 'm finishing 2 I'll be 3 'm going to have
> 4 are going 5 might 6 going to 7 having 8 are coming
> 9 'm organising 10 will

B Give Ss 5 mins to write their paragraphs. With *weaker Ss*, give them a list of topics to choose from e.g. *work, home, travel, studies, a party*. Monitor and help with vocabulary. When they have finished, Ss read their paragraphs to a partner. In feedback, nominate one or two Ss to share their paragraphs with the class.

FUTURE TIME MARKERS

3A Match the first pair together as an example. Ss match the parts of the sentences alone, then check their answers in pairs. In feedback, elicit Ss' answers and drill the phrases.

> **Answers:** 1 d) 2 a) 3 f) 4 e) 5 c) 6 b)

B Ss write their sentences alone, then check their answers in pairs. *Stronger Ss* can change all six sentences. In feedback, nominate Ss to share one interesting fact they found out about their partner.

THE FUTURE (PREDICTIONS)

4A Read the first two sentences with the class and elicit the mistakes. Ss find and correct the other mistakes, then check in pairs. In feedback, elicit Ss' answers.

> **Answers:** 1 Man *will not/won't* fly for fifty years. (1901)
> 2 There isn't going *to be* any German reunification this century. (1984) 3 Democracy *will be* dead by 1950. (1936)
> 4 By 1980 all power (electric, atomic, solar) is likely *to be* almost free. (1956) 5 correct 6 Man *will never* reach the moon. (1957) 7 Television *won't matter* in your lifetime or mine. (1936) 8 The internet *may become* useful for business, but never for the general public. (1989)

B Read the examples with the class and check Ss understand what to do. Ss change the sentences alone, then check their answers in pairs. In feedback, elicit Ss' answers.

> **Answers:** 1 Man will fly within fifty years. 2 There is going to be German reunification this century. 3 Democracy won't be dead by 1950. 4 By 1980 all power (electric, atomic, solar) isn't likely to be almost free. 5 The Japanese car industry is likely to be successful in the US market. 6 Man will reach the Moon. 7 Television will matter in your lifetime and mine. 8 The internet will become useful for business and also for the general public.

DEALING WITH MISUNDERSTANDINGS

5A Do the first sentence together as an example. Ss put the words in the responses in order, then check their answers in pairs. *Weaker Ss* may need extra help when monitoring. In feedback, elicit Ss' answers.

> **Answers:** 1 I don't get what you're saying, What exactly do you mean? 2 I didn't catch any of that. Can you say that again? 3 You've lost me. Do you mean to say they're meeting without me?

B Ss practise the conversation in pairs. Monitor and check their pronunciation. When they have finished, Ss swap roles and practise again. In feedback, nominate one or two pairs to perform the conversation for the class.

OVERVIEW

4.1 MILLIONAIRES

GRAMMAR | *must/have to/should*

VOCABULARY | personal qualities

HOW TO | talk about work

COMMON EUROPEAN FRAMEWORK
Ss can read straightforward factual texts on subjects related to his/her field of interest; can give brief comments on the views of others; can compare and contrast alternatives, discussing what to do, where to go, who or which to choose, etc.

4.2 DREAM JOB

GRAMMAR | *used to, would*

VOCABULARY | strong adjectives

HOW TO | talk about past habits

COMMON EUROPEAN FRAMEWORK
Ss can understand straightforward factual information about common everyday or job-related topics, identifying both general messages and specific details; can convey information and ideas on abstract as well as concrete topics, check information and ask about or explain problems.

4.3 THAT'S A GOOD IDEA

FUNCTION | reaching agreement

VOCABULARY | business

LEARN TO | manage a conversation

COMMON EUROPEAN FRAMEWORK
Ss can make his/her opinions and reactions understood as regards possible solutions or the question of what to do next, giving brief reasons and explanations.

4.4 GAVIN AND STACEY ⊙ BBC DVD

speakout | a day in the life …

writeback | your daily routine

COMMON EUROPEAN FRAMEWORK
Ss can understand the large part of a TV comedy show on topics of personal interest such as starting work when the delivery is in standard dialect; can exchange, check and confirm accumulated factual information on familiar routine and non-routine matters within his/her field; can write clear, detailed texts on a variety of subjects related to his/her field of interest.

4.5 LOOKBACK

Communicative revision activities

BBC VIDEO PODCAST
Is your job a 'dream job'?

This video podcast extends discussion of the unit topic to dream jobs. Ss can view people describing their dream jobs. Use this video podcast at the start or end of Unit 4.

4.1 MILLIONAIRES

Introduction
Ss learn and practise modals of obligation and vocabulary related to personal qualities in the context of millionaires. They also learn and practise confusing words.

SUPPLEMENTARY MATERIALS

Resource bank p140, p141 and p142

Warm up: bring/download photos of Richard Branson, Mark Zuckerberg and Bill Gates.

Warm up
Bring/Download pictures of Richard Branson, Mark Zuckerberg and Bill Gates and elicit who they are. In pairs, Ss discuss what they know about them. In feedback, nominate Ss to share their ideas and feed in information from the **Culture notes** below. Alternatively, if you can't get hold of pictures of the millionaires above, then write on the board *How to become a millionaire*. Ss brainstorm ways to get rich in pairs. In feedback, Ss share their ideas with the class and other Ss choose their favourite ones.

Culture notes
Sir Richard Branson is an English entrepreneur who was born in London in 1950. At 16 he set up a school magazine and in 1970 he founded Virgin as a mail-order record retailer. In 1972 he opened a recording studio. Virgin Records went on to sign many famous groups including *The Sex Pistols* and *The Rolling Stones*. His company now owns over 200 companies in over 30 countries, in diverse areas ranging from leisure and travel to finance. He has recently launched Virgin Galactic, which will offer short trips into space.

Mark Zuckerberg is an American entrepreneur who was born in New York in 1984. He co-founded the social networking site Facebook. Harvard University, where he was studying, published a yearbook known as the 'Facebook', containing headshots and profiles of all students. Zuckerberg had the idea of turning this into a website. Originally only accessible to Harvard students, it eventually became accessible to the general public and a worldwide phenomenon. He is now worth more than $1.5 billion.

Bill Gates is chairman of Microsoft Corporation and was born in Seattle in 1955. He began programming computers at the age of 13. At Harvard University, he developed a version of the BASIC programming language for the first microcomputer and in 1975 left university to set up Microsoft. The Microsoft Corporation is now a worldwide brand with revenues of over $50 billion. Bill Gates is consistently ranked among the world's richest people.

VOCABULARY personal qualities

1A Introduce the topic by eliciting what personal qualities people need to be successful and writing them on the board. Give Ss 3–4 mins to read the texts and guess the jobs. In feedback, elicit Ss' answers and ask if any of the qualities they predicted are in the texts.

Answers: football coach, teacher, entrepreneur

B Elicit the first answer to demonstrate. Ss work alone to match the words to the definitions, then check their answers in pairs. Elicit Ss' answers and drill the new words. Give further examples/explanations where necessary.

> **Answers:** 1 hard-working 2 indecisive 3 think outside the box 4 competitive 5 ambitious 6 motivated 7 a risk taker 8 a good leader 9 a good communicator

C In pairs, Ss discuss which qualities they have and add any other qualities they have which aren't mentioned. Monitor and help with vocabulary, writing any new words/phrases on the board. In feedback, nominate Ss to share their partners' opinions with the class.

> ⟹ **VOCABULARYBANK** p151 Personal qualities
>
> **1A** Elicit the first answer from the class as an example. Ss work alone to complete the rest of the sentences, then check their answers in pairs. In feedback, elicit Ss' answers and drill the words.
>
> **B** Ss discuss the questions in pairs.
>
> *Stronger classes* can do the exercises at home.
>
> > **Answers: 1A** 1 independent 2 moody 3 sensible 4 punctual 5 easy-going 6 honest 7 lazy 8 clever/bright 9 reliable 10 aggressive
> > **B** positive: reliable, sensible, easy-going, clever/bright, honest, punctual, independent; negative: aggressive, lazy, moody

READING

2A Introduce the topic and ask *Do you think millionaires have any common personal qualities? What are they?* Ss read the statements and decide in pairs if they are true or false. In feedback, elicit Ss' answers, but don't correct them yet.

B Give Ss 5 mins to read the article and check the answers. Tell them not to worry about new words yet, as they'll read the article again in Ex 3. In feedback, elicit Ss' answers and ask Ss to justify them.

> **Teaching tip**
> Using strict time limits helps ensure that Ss practise reading the text in the way you want them to and don't get stuck on new vocabulary. Tell Ss not to worry about new words at the moment. They'll work on vocabulary in Ex 3.

> **Answers:** 1 F 2 T 3 T 4 F 5 F 6 F

3 Do the first phrase with the class as an example. Point out the paragraph numbers in brackets that will help them locate the words/phrases. Ss work alone to find the words/phrases in the text, then check their answers in pairs. In feedback, elicit the words, write them on the board and drill the correct pronunciation.

> **Answers:** 1 come from relatively poor backgrounds 2 refuse to switch off 3 having a good work-life balance 4 put in the hours 5 find a bargain 6 do your own thing

> **Watch out!**
> Check Ss understand *do your own thing,* as in some languages this phrase means *mind your own business* and has a negative meaning.

4A Read the example with the class and elicit one more idea. In pairs, Ss take turns to come up with more ideas. Monitor and help with vocabulary, writing new words/phrases on the board if necessary. In feedback, nominate Ss to share their ideas with the class.

> **Possible answers:** Millionaires do: think a lot about money, come from poor backgrounds, have a clear idea of what they want to do, leave school early to start businesses, enjoy their work, work more than sixty hours a week, stay in contact with the office when they're on holiday, take risks, do anything they can to get what they want, spend their money carefully, like to find a bargain on the high street, eat at home, drive Mercedes, go on three holidays a year. Millionaires don't: work hard at school, have to be born rich, get good results at school, take too many holidays, switch off when on holiday, have a good work-life balance, break the law, spend money on expensive designer clothes, spend money on expensive meals in restaurants, care what other people think of them.

B Elicit the names of some famous millionaires that Ss know and write them on the board. Ss discuss the question in pairs. In feedback, elicit their ideas.

> **Optional extra activity**
> If you brought in pictures of famous millionaires for the warm up, show them to Ss again here. Draw three word webs on the board and write *Richard Branson, Mark Zuckerberg* and *Bill Gates* in each one. Elicit what Ss can remember about each one and add notes to the word webs. Ss discuss the question in Ex 4B and compare with the people on the board. In feedback, elicit Ss' ideas and have a brief discussion.

GRAMMAR   *must/have to/should* (obligation)

5 Focus attention on the example, then Ss match the other words to their meanings. In feedback, elicit Ss' answers and drill the modals.

> **Teaching tip**
> When drilling modals, focus on silent letters, i.e. *should* sounds like *good* and not like *shoulder*.

> **Answers:** 1 b) 2 and 3 c) 4 a) 5 e) 6 d)

> ⟹ **LANGUAGEBANK** 4.1 p134–135
>
> *Stronger classes* could read the notes and do the exercises at home. *Weaker classes* can do the exercises in class. Check the notes carefully with Ss, especially the difference between *mustn't* and *don't have to*, giving further examples where necessary. Teach/elicit *malaria, mosquito net, container, bite* and *raccoon*. Ss work alone to complete the exercises, then check their answers in pairs. Ss can refer to the notes to help them.
>
> > **Answers: 1** 1 should 2 has to 3 must 4 mustn't 5 shouldn't 6 has to 7 don't have to 8 must
> > **2** 1 a) 2 f) 3 h) 4 b) 5 c) 6 g) 7 d) 8 e)

PRACTICE

6A Read the example with the class. Ss write the sentences alone, then check their answers in pairs. In feedback, nominate Ss to read out their sentences. With *weaker classes,* write the sentences on the board as they read them out.

> **Answers:** 1 Postmen have to get up early in the morning. 2 Window cleaners mustn't be afraid of heights. 3 Nurses should be patient and care about other people. 4 Businessmen often have to travel a lot. 5 Politicians shouldn't do their job because they want fame. 6 Teachers must enjoy working with children. 7 Doctors have to train for several years before they can work. 8 Teachers don't have to work in the school during the holidays. 9 Policemen have to be good communicators.

> **Optional extra activity**
> Arrange Ss into two teams and give each team a board pen. Each turn, read out the prompts for Ss to come to the board and write the sentence. The first student to write the sentence correctly on the board wins a point for their team. The team with the most points at the end wins.

> ➡ **VOCABULARYBANK** p151 Working life
>
> Focus attention on the pictures and ask *What job do you think each photo shows?* Ss match the pictures to the descriptions, then discuss the meaning of the words in bold in pairs. In feedback, elicit Ss' answers and check Ss understand the words. *Stronger classes* can do the exercise at home.
>
> > **Answers:** 1 B Personal assistant 2 C Accountant 3 A Window cleaner
> > **B** work nine-to-five: work regular hours; checking and responding to emails: reading emails and sending answers back; answering phone enquiries: answering people's questions on the phone; organising: arranging; work long hours: work a lot of hours every day; attending meetings: going to meetings; dealing with problems: solving problems; advise clients: help customers with their questions; write updates and reports: write new information; an outdoor job: a job that involves working outside; a physical job: a job that requires manual work; work for myself: not work for a company; work flexible hours: choose the times that you work

B Demonstrate by telling Ss about some of your friends' jobs. Ss write information about three of their friends' jobs, then compare in pairs. Monitor and check Ss are using the modals correctly. In feedback, nominate Ss to share their descriptions with the class.

> **Optional extra activity**
> Ss write the descriptions without mentioning the job. When they are ready they read their descriptions to their partner, who guesses the job.

SPEAKING

7A Give Ss 2 mins to read the survey and check any new vocabulary. In pairs, Ss discuss the questions. Monitor and note down any common errors for later feedback.

B Ss turn to p159 and check their scores and the explanations, then discuss the questions in pairs. In feedback, elicit any interesting answers and correct any common errors with the class.

VOCABULARY *PLUS* confusing words

8 Read the vocabulary notes with the class, then Ss complete the sentences. Check Ss understand that *work* is uncountable and *job* is countable. In feedback, elicit Ss' answers.

> **Answers:** 1 job 2 work

> **Watch out!**
> *Work* can be plural when referring to *works of art,* for example. Don't mention this unless Ss ask about it.

9A Do the first one together as an example and ask *Which verb involves one person? (remember); Which verb involves two people? (remind).* Ss do the rest of the exercise alone, then check their answers in pairs. In feedback, elicit Ss' answers and check they understand the verbs.

> **Answers:** 1 remembered 2 remind 3 left 4 hear 5 listening 6 fun

B Ss turn to p159 and read the notes. Monitor and help with any questions Ss have.

speakout TIP

Read the tip with the class. Ss choose four pairs of words from Ex 9 and write sentences in their notebooks. Monitor and help with vocabulary. In feedback, nominate a few Ss to share their sentences with the class.

10A Elicit the first answer with the class as an example. Ss complete the rest of the questions on their own. In feedback, elicit Ss' answers.

> **Answers:** 1 jobs 2 forget 3 listen 4 remind 5 earn 6 fun

B Ss ask and answer the questions in pairs. Encourage them to ask follow-up questions to find out more information. In feedback, nominate Ss from each pair to share one interesting fact they found out about their partner.

> ➡ **VOCABULARYBANK** p151 Confusing words
>
> Ss complete the sentences, then check their answers using a dictionary, if available. In feedback, elicit Ss' answers and drill the words.
>
> *Stronger classes* can do the exercise at home.
>
> > **Answers:** 1A 1 a) actually b) currently 2 a) course b) career 3 a) lend b) borrow 4 a) discussion b) argument 5 a) miss b) lose

> **Homework ideas**
> • Ss write descriptions of jobs, as in Ex 6B.
> • Language bank 4.1 Ex 1–2, p135
> • Vocabulary bank p151
> • Workbook Ex 1–5, p23–24

DREAM JOB

Introduction

Ss learn and practise *used to* and *would* to describe past habits in the context of childhood dreams. They also learn strong adjectives to describe things more effectively.

SUPPLEMENTARY MATERIALS

Resource bank p143

Ex 11: bring some real job advertisements from a local newspaper or the internet.

Warm up

Write on the board *famous musician, sports star, chocolate tester, video game tester, model* and *film critic*. Ss discuss what personal qualities people need to succeed in each job. In feedback, nominate Ss to share their ideas with the class and ask if Ss would like to do any of these jobs.

LISTENING

1 Focus attention on the pictures and elicit what Ss can see in each one. Elicit/Teach *fashion show, three-course meal, vineyard* and *grapes* and write them on the board. Ss discuss the questions in pairs. In feedback, elicit Ss' answers.

Answers: A restaurant critic B winemaker C model

2A Teach/Elicit *photo shoots* and *frost*. Ss listen and match the people to the jobs. Tell Ss not to worry if they don't understand the whole recording, as they'll listen again in Ex 2C. In feedback, elicit Ss' answers.

Answers: 1 C 2 A 3 B

B Ss discuss the question in pairs. In feedback, elicit what they can remember.

Answers: Angie – modelling is actually very hard work
Pauline – restaurant food gets boring/she was putting on weight
Monty – the work is tiring and there are no holidays/bad weather can ruin the grapes

C Give Ss 2–3 mins to read the questions and write the answers they can remember. Ss listen again and check their answers, then compare them in pairs. Play the recording again if necessary. In feedback, elicit Ss' answers.

Answers: 1 A 2 P 3 P 4 A 5 M 6 A 7 M 8 M 9 A 10 P

Unit 4 Recording 1

A=Angie P=Pauline M=Monty

A: As a child, I always wanted to be a model. I used to look at all of the **beautiful** women in the magazines and on television. And I used to think it looked so exciting. To spend all day wearing beautiful clothes and going to exciting locations for photo shoots. And I've always loved fashion, so the idea that I could go to fashion shows in Paris, New York, etc, was just **amazing** for me. What I didn't realise is that actually being a model is really, really hard work. The hours are very long, especially when you have to travel. Sometimes, we travel for fifteen hours or more and when we arrive we need to start work straightaway. And the problem is that you need to look good all the time. But often, you're feeling **terrible**.

P: I have a passion for food, so being a restaurant critic seemed like the perfect job for me. I could spend my days sitting in some of the best restaurants, eating **delicious** food and get paid for it. The only problem, which I didn't realise at the time, is that actually you can get bored of eating restaurant food. I used to eat three-course meals every day, or sometimes twice a day. And I would often cook

at home. So I put on loads of weight. I was **furious**! I used to spend hours in the gym, doing exercise to try and work off the food I was eating. But it was **impossible**. So, in the end, I gave it up.

M: I used to work in a bank, so when I lost my job I decided it was time to do something that I would really enjoy. To follow a dream, if you like. I had this wonderfully romantic idea of owning my own vineyard, making wine and spending my life in the beautiful Tuscan countryside. But the reality is very different. I had no idea how tiring the job would be. For a start, there're no holidays. For five months of the year, you don't even have weekends. You work seven days a week and you're **exhausted** all the time. And the other problem is the weather. Bad weather can ruin everything. So, in the winter, you have to get up at two o'clock in the morning when it's **freezing** outside, to turn on the frost control. And in September, a bad storm can ruin the grapes in just a few minutes. At least when I worked in an office, I didn't use to worry about the weather. Having said that, I love my life. And the science of making wine is absolutely **fascinating**. I wouldn't change my job for anything.

VOCABULARY strong adjectives

3 Ss turn to p168 and find the strong adjectives in bold in the audio script. Ss work alone to match them to the gradable adjectives in Ex 3 on p47, then check their answers in pairs. In feedback, elicit Ss' answers and drill the adjectives.

Answers: 1 amazing 2 terrible 5 exhausted 7 freezing
8 delicious 9 furious 10 fascinating 11 beautiful
12 impossible

Watch out!

With gradable adjectives we can use *very, a bit, quite,* etc. to grade the meaning. We can't do this with strong adjectives, but we can emphasise their meaning with *absolutely*.

4A Elicit the first answer as an example. Ss then complete the conversations on their own and check in pairs. In feedback, elicit Ss' answers.

Optional extra activity

Do an adjective bingo activity. Ss draw a simple 3 x 3 chart in their notebooks and write a strong adjective in each square. Each turn, call out a gradable adjective and Ss cross out the corresponding strong adjective if they have it in their chart. When a student completes their chart they shout 'Bingo!'

Answers: 1 delicious 2 boiling 3 furious 4 beautiful
5 fascinating 6 impossible

B Do the first word with the class as an example. Ss listen and mark the stressed syllables. In feedback, elicit Ss' answers and drill each adjective.

Answers: 1 de<u>li</u>cious 2 <u>boil</u>ing 3 <u>fur</u>ious 4 <u>beau</u>tiful
5 <u>fas</u>cinating 6 im<u>pos</u>sible

C Play the recording again and pause after each response for Ss to shadow the intonation.

GRAMMAR *used to, would*

5A Introduce the topic by telling Ss what job(s) you dreamt about doing when you were a child. Teach/elicit *cardboard box, blast off* and *butterfly*. Give Ss 3–4 mins to read the texts and answer the questions in pairs. In feedback, elicit Ss' answers.

Answers: Chang imagined having his own rocket; he is now a rocket scientist. Lowri wanted to look after animals; she is now a veterinary surgeon.

B Read/Check the rules with the class. Ss work alone to match the examples to the rules, then check their answers in pairs. In feedback, elicit Ss' answers and give further explanations/examples if necessary.

Answers: 1 d) 2 a) and c) 3 b)

▶ **LANGUAGEBANK** 4.2 p134–135
Stronger classes could read the notes and do the exercises at home. Otherwise, check the notes with Ss, especially the use of stative and active verbs with *used to*, but only active verbs with *would*. In each exercise, do the first sentence as an example. Ss complete the exercises alone, then check their answers in pairs. Ss can refer to the notes to help them.

Answers: 1 1 play 2 take 3 never used to play 4 wouldn't enjoy 5 would have 6 used to study/didn't use to study
2 1 used to think 2 didn't use to have 3 Did people really use to enjoy 4 would put/used to put
5 didn't use to use/wouldn't use 6 used to fight/would fight 7 used to make/would make 8 did people use to eat

PRACTICE

6A Elicit the first two answers with the class as examples. Make sure Ss use *would* if both answers are possible. Ss complete the texts alone, then check their answers in pairs. In feedback, elicit Ss' answers.

Answers: 1 used to love 2 would practise 3 would use 4 would thank 5 used to live 6 would go 7 took 8 watched 9 would ask

B Ss listen to the sentences, paying attention to the pronunciation of /juːstə/. Drill /juːstə/ on its own, making sure Ss pronounce it smoothly. Play the recording again and pause after each sentence for Ss to repeat.

C Ss discuss the sentences in pairs. Monitor and check pronunciation of *used to*. In feedback, nominate Ss to share one interesting fact about their partner with the class.

SPEAKING

7 Read the questions and the example with the class. Ss discuss the questions in pairs. In feedback, nominate Ss to share their partner's answers with the class.

Teaching tip
With *weaker Ss* and *quiet Ss*, give them time to prepare their answers alone before sharing them with their partner. This will ensure they have more to say during the discussions.

WRITING a covering letter

8 Ask Ss to cover the text and focus on the title. Ask *What do you think this job involves? Would you like to do this job?* Give Ss 2–3 mins to read the text and discuss the questions in pairs. In feedback, elicit Ss' ideas.

Suggested answer: 1 Someone who enjoys travelling, is independent, loves nature, is a good communicator and has IT skills.

9A Ss read the covering letter, then answer the questions in pairs. In feedback, elicit Ss' ideas.

Suggested answer: This person would be good for the job because she is a good communicator, she has IT skills, as well as experience of working with nature and organising projects.

Culture notes
When applying for a job in the UK, it's normal to send a concise CV (*Curriculum Vitae*), listing your qualifications and experience and also to attach a covering letter to draw the employer's attention to relevant parts of your CV. Another type of application is a *résumé*, which is like a CV but targeted towards the requirements of a specific job.

B Ss read the letter again and find examples of formal or informal expressions. In feedback, elicit the examples, check comprehension and write them on the board.

Answers: The wording is formal.
Examples of formal expressions:
I'm writing to you regarding …
I would like to submit an application for the post.
Please find my CV attached.
I believe that I meet all the requirements you outline in your advertisement.
If you require any further information, or would like to arrange an interview, …
I look forward to hearing from you at your earliest convenience.
Yours sincerely,

C Do the first phrase together as an example. Ss work alone to find the expressions, then check their answers in pairs. In feedback, elicit Ss' answers and write them on the board.

Answers: 1 regarding 2 I would like to submit an application for the post 3 I believe that I meet all the requirements you outline in your advertisement.
4 hands-on experience 5 Proven ability in 6 at your earliest convenience

D Give Ss 3–4 mins to find and underline any other useful expressions, then compare their answers in pairs. In feedback, elicit/check the expressions they chose and write them on the board for reference for Ex 11.

LEARN TO organise your ideas

10 Give Ss 2–3 mins to read the notes. They then match them to the parts of the letter. In feedback, elicit Ss' answers.

Answers: a) 3 b) 1 c) 4 d) 2 e) 5

11 Ss turn to p163 and read the job advertisements. If you have brought in authentic job advertisements, Ss can also read these. Check/Teach any new vocabulary. Ss write their letters, using the sample and the vocabulary on the board to help. Monitor and help with any other vocabulary Ss need. When they have finished, put Ss into pairs and ask Ss if they would give their partner the job.

Homework ideas
• Ex 7: write about your childhood dreams.
• Ex 11: write a letter for one of the other jobs on p163.
• Language bank 4.2 Ex 1–2, p135
• Workbook Ex 1–8, p25–26

THAT'S A GOOD IDEA

Introduction

Ss learn and practise ways of reaching agreement in meetings. They also learn how to manage a discussion.

SUPPLEMENTARY MATERIALS

Resource bank p144

Ex 4A: write the words on pieces of paper and put each sentence in an envelope.

Warm up: bring/download pictures of the inventions described below.

Warm up

Bring/Download pictures of some or all of the following: *pet massager, fish training kit, the loo read, thumbthing, laser-guided scissors, doggles and motorised ice cream cone.* All of these pictures are available on a google image search. If you can't bring pictures, write the names on the board. In pairs, Ss discuss how useful each one is. In feedback, nominate Ss to share their opinions with the class and ask them to pick their favourite.

Culture notes

pet massager – a device for massaging pets

fish training kit – a kit including a 'field' and goalposts to train your fish to play sports

the loo read – a portable table for reading newspapers in the bathroom

thumbthing – a device you clip on your thumb which helps you to keep a book open with one hand

laser-guided scissors – a pair of scissors with a laser to guide you to cut a perfect edge

doggles – wrap-around sunglasses for dogs

motorised ice-cream cone – a plastic ice cream cone which spins round

---

VOCABULARY business

1A Ss cover the text and look at the photos. Ask Ss to use the photos to predict what the text is about and elicit their ideas. Write the ideas on the board. Then give Ss 3–4 mins to read the text and check the ideas on the board. In feedback, elicit Ss' answers and teach/check any new vocabulary.

Answers: The programme is about contestants competing to become an apprentice to successful businessman, Lord Alan Sugar.

Culture notes

The BBC reality show *The Apprentice* was first screened in 2005. Each week a group of people compete for a job working for Lord Alan Sugar, founder of the electronics company, Amstrad. The contestants have to work as a team to complete tasks and each week one of the contestants gets fired.

B Elicit the first word as an example. Ss complete the questions alone, then check their answers in pairs. In feedback, elicit Ss' answers and drill the questions.

Answers: 1 businessmen   2 team   3 boss   4 interview
5 compete   6 salary   7 fired

C Ss discuss the questions in pairs. Monitor and help with vocabulary, writing any new words/phrases on the board. In feedback, nominate Ss to share their answers with the class.

FUNCTION reaching agreement

2A Give Ss 1 min to read the options and check/teach any new vocabulary. Ss listen and choose the options then compare in pairs. Play the recording again if necessary. In feedback, elicit Ss' answers.

Answers:
Name: Buon Appetito
Company based: outside central London
Type of catering: events catering
Speciality Food: Mediterranean (Italian)

B Give Ss 2 mins to read the phrases and try to remember which ones were used. Ss listen again and tick the correct options. In feedback, elicit Ss' answers.

Answers: 1 a)   2 b)   3 a)   4 a)   5 b)   6 b)

Unit 4 Recording 4

W1=1st woman   M1=1st man   M2=2nd man   W2=2nd woman

W1: First of all we need to decide what food we want to sell.

M1: OK, well, the way I see things, the most important thing is to make sure, in the catering industry, what we want to do, is we want to make sure that we make a seventy percent profit on everything we sell, right? So, we need to think about food that doesn't cost very much to produce …

M2: OK, so no smoked salmon, or …

W2: Exactly. But I think we should decide on a name for the company first, like 'Lotus foods' or 'Saffron', something which sounds exotic.

W1: Hmm. I'm not sure that I agree. Let's focus on the issue of a theme for our food, you know like Indian, or Mediterranean first, because that will influence the name.

M2: That's a good point. Also, I suggest we think about how we're going to sell. Because if we're going to events, then the type of food we cook might change, but we could have a name like *Food4events*.

W1: Good idea.

M1: Sorry, I missed that.

M2: We could call the company *Food4events* and cater for events, weddings and parties. That kind of thing.

W1: I think that's a great idea. Does everyone agree with that?

All: Yes. That's fine. Yup. That's fine by me.

W1: OK. So, moving on to the next point, where do we work from?

M1: We need to be somewhere central, like in central London and then we can travel to events from there.

W2: Sorry, but I'm not sure that central London is a good idea. It's very expensive. I suggest we look outside the city, where it's cheaper to rent office-space.

M2: Yes, I see what you mean. You're right – we don't need to be based in the centre of the city.

W2: Exactly.

W1: OK, so let's recap: the company is called Food4events and we sell at parties, events, weddings, etc. We're based outside London. Erm … What else do we need to think about?

M2: How is our company going to be different from others?

W1: Ah … I think we need to come back to the kind of food we want to sell. I really feel that we need to specialise, so perhaps we could be Italian.

W2: How about Mediterranean?

M1: Yes, Mediterranean's really popular.

W1: OK – good point. I like the idea of Mediterranean, actually.

M2: OK. <u>Why don't we call it</u> *Italy On The Move*?

M1: Or *Buon Appetito*?

W1: I like that. It sounds good. Oh, let's go with Italian, so it's an Italian catering company and it's called *Buon Appetito*. That will make us different from the others and we can have Luca as our head chef! So, let's sum up what we've decided. The company …

3 Read the examples in the table with the class and do the first one as an example. In pairs, Ss add the phrases. In feedback, elicit Ss' answers and drill them.

Answers:
Giving opinions:
I (really) feel that …
The way I see things …
The way I see it …
Commenting on other opinions:
I (don't) see what you mean.
That's a good idea.
That's a good point.
Exactly!
That's fine by me.
That's OK by me.
I'm not sure that I agree, actually.
I'm not sure that … is a good idea.
Suggestions:
What about …?
I suggest we focus on …
I suggest we think about …
I think we should think about …
How about if we (call it) …?
Why don't we (call it) …?

→ LANGUAGEBANK 4.3 p134–135

Stronger classes could read the notes and do the exercises at home. With *weaker classes,* drill the phrases from the chart and elicit possible ways to continue the questions. Read the example. Ss then work alone to complete the sentences and check their answers in pairs. In feedback, elicit Ss' answers and drill the sentences.

Answers: 1 I think we should begin. 2 Why don't we look at the emails first? 3 I don't see what you mean. 4 It's fine/OK by me. 5 The way I see things, … 6 That's a good point.

4A Elicit the first sentence as an example. Ss work alone to put the words in the correct order, then check their answers in pairs. In feedback, elicit Ss' answers and write them on the board.

Alternative approach
If you have prepared the words on pieces of paper and put them in envelopes, Ss can do this as a team race. Arrange Ss into small groups and give each group an envelope. When you say 'Start', Ss empty the envelopes and put the words in the correct order. The first team to finish gets a point. Redistribute the envelopes and repeat this process until all groups have done all of the sentences.

Answers: 1 I <u>think</u> we should <u>decide</u> on a <u>name</u>. 2 That's a <u>good</u> <u>point</u>. 3 I <u>see</u> what you <u>mean</u>. 4 I <u>suggest</u> we <u>focus</u> on the <u>products</u>. 5 That's <u>fine</u> by <u>me</u>. 6 I'm <u>not</u> <u>sure</u> that I <u>agree</u>. 7 <u>Why</u> don't we <u>think</u> <u>about</u> it? 8 <u>What</u> about a <u>name</u> for the <u>business</u>?

B Play the first sentence and elicit the stressed words. Underline the stressed words on the board. Ss listen to the rest and underline the stressed words, then check their answers in pairs. Elicit Ss' answers and underline the stressed words on the board. Play the recording again and pause after each phrase for Ss to repeat.

Answers: See underlined words in answers to Ex 4A.

LEARN TO manage a discussion

5A Elicit the first answer as an example. Ss complete the phrases and check in pairs.

B Ss listen and check their answers, then compare their answers in pairs. If necessary, play the recording again. In feedback, elicit Ss' answers and drill the phrases.

Answers: 1 first of all 2 let's focus on 3 moving on to the next point 4 let's recap 5 I think we need to come back to 6 let's sum up

6 Elicit the first answer with the class as an example. Ss work alone to correct the mistakes, then check their answers in pairs. In feedback, elicit Ss' answers.

Answers: 1 A: First of *all* we need to decide what we want to cook. B: That's a good *point/idea*. How many people are coming to the party? 2 A: OK. So, let's focus *on* cooking something really simple. B: Yes, *that's OK by* me. 3 A: So, moving *on* to the next point. Who's going to bring what? B: I think we need to come back *to* what kind of food we want. 4 A: So let's *recap*. We're cooking pasta and people are bringing salads. B: OK, let's sum *up* what we've decided so far.

SPEAKING

7A Give Ss 5 mins to read the task and note down their ideas. Monitor and help with vocabulary, writing any new words/phrases on the board.

B Arrange Ss into groups of three. If this doesn't work with your class size, have some groups of four and repeat role C. Give Ss 1 min to read their role and check they understand what to do.

C Review the language for reaching agreement and managing a discussion from the unit and read how to start the discussion with the class. Ss discuss and agree on their plans in their groups. Monitor closely and note down any common errors for later feedback.

D When the groups are ready, ask student Bs to share their ideas with the class. Elicit other Ss' favourite plans and correct any common errors with the class in feedback.

Alternative approach
Do Ex 7D as a role-play. Each group presents their business plan to the rest of the class (the bank managers) with a view to getting a start-up loan for their business. Encourage the bank managers to ask more questions and to say at the end whether or not they will give the loan.

Homework ideas
• Ex 7A: write your ideas as a business plan.
• Language bank 4.3 Ex 1, p135
• Workbook Ex 1–3, p27

GAVIN AND STACEY

Introduction

Ss watch an extract from the BBC sitcom *Gavin and Stacey*, in which Gavin starts a new job. Ss learn and practise how to describe a typical day in their life, write a web entry about their daily routine.

SUPPLEMENTARY MATERIALS

Warm up: bring/download some photos of Barry, Wales.
Ex 3: write the sentences on separate cards, one set for each pair of students.
Ex 5D: write the topics on separate cards, one set for each group of students.

Culture notes

Barry is a small town in the south of Wales, near the capital, Cardiff. It has a population of nearly 50,000 and was traditionally the home of heavy industry. Having lost a lot of the industry, it is now a seaside resort with several beaches. It is also the birthplace of the Australian Prime Minister, Julia Gillard.

Warm up

Divide the class in half. Half the class write a list of *Dos* and the other half write a list of *Don'ts* for the first day in a new job. Monitor and help with vocabulary, writing any new words/phrases on the board. When they have finished, arrange Ss in pairs to share their advice. In feedback, nominate Ss to share their ideas with the class.

▶ DVD PREVIEW

1A Teach/check *welcome pack*, *motto* and *parcel*. Go through the example with the class. Ss then work alone to match the phrases and check their answers in pairs. In feedback, elicit Ss' answers.

Answers: 1 b) 2 d) 3 e) 4 f) 5 c) 6 a)

B Ss cover the text and look at the photos. Elicit what they can see and what they think happens in the programme. Give Ss 1 min to read the programme information and check.

Culture notes

The BBC sitcom *Gavin and Stacey* was first screened in 2007. It follows the story of a man and woman who met over the phone at work, fell in love and eventually got married. It was written by James Corden and Ruth Jones, who also co-star as Gavin and Stacey's friends Smithy and Nessa. It stars a number of well-known British comedians: Mathew Horne (Gavin), Joanna Page (Stacey) and Rob Brydon (Bryn). It is set in Barry, Wales and Essex and includes many of the stereotypes of people from those areas. It has won several British comedy awards.

2 Ss discuss the questions in pairs. In feedback, nominate Ss to share their ideas with the class.

▶ DVD VIEW

3 Give Ss 1 min to read through the events. Ss watch and tick which of the things happen, then compare in pairs. In feedback, elicit Ss' answers.

Answers: 1, 2, 3, 5, 7, 9 and 10 happen.

Teaching tip

Kinaesthetic learners learn best through physical activity. When doing ordering activities, it can be useful to write the sentences out on cards for Ss to arrange in order while they watch the DVD. This will also change the pace of the activities and add variety here.

4A Ss discuss the questions in pairs from memory. In feedback, elicit Ss' answers, but don't give any answers yet, as they'll watch the DVD again in Ex 4B.

B Play the DVD again for Ss to check their answers, then compare in pairs. If necessary, play the DVD again. In feedback, elicit Ss' answers.

Answers: 1 She is worried he'll meet lots of girls. 2 A name plate for his door. 3 He gets a lot of personal calls shortly after starting work. 4 He invites him to play rugby. 5 A lunch box full of sandwiches. 6 His wife sends him a good luck balloon.

DVD 4 Gavin and Stacey

G=Gavin St=Stacey MD=Mr Davies P=Pamela GD=Gavin's dad Sm=Smithy OH= Owain Hughes B=Bryn

G: Hiya.
St: Hiya. It's me. It's Stacey.
G: I know.
St: How's it going? What's it like?
G: I've literally just sat down. I said goodbye to you 35 minutes ago.
St: Have you met anyone yet? What are they like? Are there girls everywhere? They'll be all over you.
G: Don't be silly.
St: It's just new territory for me, babes.
G: I've been at work for 11 minutes. I promise I'll call you at lunch. OK?
St: OK. I love you.
G: I love you too.
MD: Gavin. Huw Davies. Welcome to Cardiff.
G: Mr. Davies. Good to see you again.
MD: Oh, please, call me Huw. Now, is this your first office of your own?
G: Yeah, it is.
MD: Excellent news! I tell you what, call maintenance and get them to stick this on your door. It's a big moment.
G: Aw, cheers. Thanks!
MD: Now, I'll take you round in a bit, show you what's what and who's who. Did you get your welcome pack?
G: Er … yeah. I think so.
MD: Excellent news. Get that. Could be important. Phone system: real easy. Boom, boom. And then Line 1. Go.
G: Er … Gavin Shipman.
P: Hello, my little prince.
G: Hiya. Look, um …
P: How's it going, darling? Are people being nice to you?
G: It's my mother. I'm just with my new boss.
P: What's he like?
G: Look, I'll call you at lunch or after work when it's not on the company's time.
P: All right. Well call me on the …
G: Sorry about that.
MD: Hey listen … everyone has to take a personal call once in a while. And when it's family, it's family. Now, your fire regs and what have you. Very simple. In the event of a fire, my motto is …
G: Run for your life?
MD: No. Go to your nearest assembly point. Right. You're on your own with this one. Go for it.

G: Hello, Gavin Shipman.
GD: Are you all right, mate?
G: It's my dad. Er, Dad, I'm actually with my boss.
GD: Oop. Apologies. Say no more. Call me later.
G: Cheers. See ya.
       I'm so sorry about that. It's just, you know with the move down here and that.
MD: Listen, I completely understand.
G: Gavin Shipman.
Sm: Gavilah!
G: Right. Ready when you are.
MD: Excellent news. OK. Let's show you around.
G: I'm just gonna leave that there.
MD: And the surprising thing about Terry is, although he doesn't look it, he is in fact, our nominated First Aider.
OH: Huw!
MD: Ah! Now here's somebody you've not met yet. Owain Hughes. Owain heads up the website.
G: Hi. Nice to meet you. Gavin Shipman.
OH: Owain Hughes. Hey, er, we have a little seven-a-side on a Thursday if you fancy joining us.
G: Oh right, yeah. I'd like that.
OH: I mean it's nothing too serious, you know, at the end of the day it's touch rugby but some of the guys …
G: Oh sorry. I thought you meant football.
OH: No, we play rugby.
MD: It's rugby, it is.
Man's voice: Gavin! Gavin! They won't let me in! I wanted to surprise you! Got you a packed lunch.
G: Bryn, I don't need a … I'm sorry. This is my uncle … in-law.
Bryn: I'll see you, Gav.
OH: Bye, Bryn.
MD: See you.
Office worker: Mr Shipman? A parcel for you, just arrived.
G: Oh, thanks.
MD: Open it, then!
G: It's from my wife.

speakout a day in the life …

5A Teach/Check *kindergarten*, *muffins* and *have a nap*. Ss listen and decide if she likes her job. In feedback, ask *What's her job? Does she like it?* and elicit Ss' answers.

Answers: Candace is a kindergarten teacher. She likes her job.

B Elicit the first answer with the class as an example. Ss complete the sentences alone, then check their answers in pairs. Don't elicit the answers yet.

C Ss listen to the recording again and check their answers in pairs. In feedback, elicit Ss' answers and drill the sentences.

Answers: at, latest, thing, ready, once, plans, by
✓ all phrases

Optional extra activity
Arrange Ss in small groups. Before Ss prepare to talk about a normal day in their lives, copy each of the topics in Ex 5D onto separate cards. Distribute one set of cards to each group, face down in the middle. Ss take it in turns to pick up a card and tell the rest of the group about this aspect of their daily lives. Encourage the other group members to ask follow-up questions. Monitor and note any common errors for later correction with the class. Rearrange Ss into different groups for Ex 5D and 5E.

D Go through the topics with the class then give Ss 5 mins to plan their ideas and write notes. Monitor and help with vocabulary where needed, writing any new words/phrases on the board.

E Ss share their ideas in small groups. Encourage other Ss to ask follow-up questions. Monitor and note down any common errors for later feedback. In feedback, nominate Ss from each group to share their information with the class and correct any common errors.

Unit 4 Recording 7
C=Candace Parker
C: I'm a kindergarten teacher with a class of two-year-olds. So, um, my daily routine: well, I wake up about six thirty, take a shower and have breakfast with my husband. I have to be at the Child Development Centre by seven thirty so I leave home by twenty past at the latest. Luckily, I don't have far to drive. The first thing I do is check my mail at work to see if there are any messages. Then I go to the classroom and switch on the lights and I check everything is ready for the children. They usually start coming in about eight. The first hour is play-time, so we're on the floor with the toys. At nine o'clock we get the children seated at the table for their breakfast, which is usually muffins and apple sauce, or bread and cheese and fruit juice. Then we clean up. If the weather's good we take the children out to the playground. This is probably the best part of the day because everyone's happy to be outside. We try to do this at least once a day. We have lunch at midday and then most of the children have a little nap for about an hour. After that, we do some art work or play music to the children or read to them. Then it's snack time around three thirty: just biscuits and more fruit juice. Then the parents usually arrive at four to take the children home. When all the children have gone, I write down what we did during the day and clean up a little and then I make plans for the next day. And that's it! I'm usually home by five. Then I relax by reading or watching TV. It's a lovely job.

writeback your daily routine

6A In pairs, Ss read the text and answer the questions. In feedback, elicit Ss' answers and check any new vocabulary.

B Ss write about their own daily routine, using the sentence starters from Ex 6A to help them. Monitor and help with vocabulary where needed. When they have finished, Ss show their texts to a partner, who reads and suggests changes.

Teaching tip
Before they start writing, get Ss into the habit of planning the layout first to ensure they have organised their ideas well.

Homework ideas
• Ex 6B: write a final draft of the text about your daily routine.
• Write a list of advice for the first day of a new job.

LOOKBACK

Introduction

Ss revise and practise the language of Unit 4. The notes below provide ideas for exploiting the exercises and activities but your approach will depend on your aim, e.g. whether you use the activities as a diagnostic or progress test or as revision/fluency practice. If done as a test then it would not be appropriate to monitor or help Ss.

PERSONAL QUALITIES

1 Read the example with the class and demonstrate with a stronger student. In pairs, Ss take turns to test each other. In feedback, elicit some of their definitions.

Teaching tip

With *weaker classes*, give them 5 mins to choose five of the words and write their definitions first. Monitor closely and help with vocabulary where needed. Ss then use their written definitions to test each other.

Optional extra activity

If you think Ss need further practice of the vocabulary, ask them to work alone to think of a job, then write down three of the qualities from the box in Ex 1 which they think you might need for this job. Arrange Ss in pairs. Ss take it in turns to say their jobs, then their partner has five guesses to guess the three expressions they chose. In feedback, elicit Ss' answers.

MUST/HAVE TO/SHOULD (OBLIGATION)

2A Do the first sentence together as an example. Ss work alone to choose the correct alternatives, then check their answers in pairs. In feedback, elicit Ss' answers.

Answers: 1 have to 2 must 3 don't have to 4 should 5 mustn't 6 shouldn't

B Give Ss 3–4 mins to complete the sentences. Monitor and help with vocabulary, writing new words/phrases on the board.

Alternative approach

Ss complete the sentences as in Ex 2B, but make three of them true and three of them false. Ss take it in turns to read out their sentences to their partner, who guesses which are true and which are false.

C Ss compare their ideas in pairs. In feedback, nominate Ss to share their partner's ideas with the class.

STRONG ADJECTIVES

3A Do the first sentence together as an example. Ss work alone to replace the words, then check their answers in pairs. In feedback, elicit Ss' answers.

Answers: 1 exhausted 2 boiling 3 furious 4 impossible 5 brilliant, awful 6 tiny 7 fascinating 8 delicious

B In pairs, Ss take turns to test each other.

Optional extra activity

Do a board race with the class. Split the class in half and have Ss stand in two lines, facing the board. Give Ss at the front of the lines a board pen each. Each turn, call out a gradable adjective. Ss from each team come to the board to write the corresponding strong adjective. The first student to write each one correctly wins a point for their team. The team with the most points at the end wins.

USED TO, WOULD

4A Do the first sentence together as an example. Make sure Ss use *would* if both are possible. Ss do the exercise on their own, then check their answers in pairs. In feedback, elicit Ss' answers.

Answers: 1 My family *used to live* in Paris, but we moved when I was a teenager. 2 I *would spend* a lot of time with my grandparents when I was younger. 3 For my first job, I washed dishes in a restaurant. 4 I didn't *use to think* money was important. Now, I have lots of bills to pay. 5 We *used to have* a lot more free time before we had children. 6 My best friend at school *used to live* just across the road from me.

B Give Ss 3–4 mins to look back at the sentences and change four of them so they are true for them. Monitor and make sure they are using *used to* and *would* correctly.

C In pairs, Ss compare sentences and find three things in common. In feedback, nominate Ss to share their ideas with the class and explain anything they have in common with their partner.

REACHING AGREEMENT

5A Do the first conversation with the class as an example. Ss complete the conversations alone, then check their answers in pairs. In feedback, elicit Ss' answers and drill the phrases.

Answers: 1 A: The way I *see* things all cars should be banned from city centres. B: *Exactly.* 2 A: I really *feel* that we need to look at immigration. B: That's a good *point*. 3 A: The *way* I see it the company is making too much money. B: I don't see what you *mean*. 4 A: I *think* we should ask for more money. B: I'm not *sure* I agree, actually. 5 A: I *suggest* we try to meet again next week. B: *That's* fine by me.

B Ss practise the conversations in pairs. Monitor and check their intonation, drilling remedially where necessary.

6 Give Ss 2–3 mins to read the questions and think about their answers. Ss discuss the questions in small groups and try to reach agreement. In feedback, nominate Ss from each group to share their opinions with the class and have a brief discussion.

Homework ideas
- **Workbook** Review and check 2, p28–30
- **Workbook** Test 2, p31

OVERVIEW

5.1 MACHINES
GRAMMAR | comparatives/superlatives
VOCABULARY | technology
HOW TO | talk about technology

COMMON EUROPEAN FRAMEWORK
Ss can compare and contrast alternatives, discussing what to do, where to go, who/which to choose etc.; can write an essay which develops an argument, giving reasons in support of/against a particular viewpoint and explaining the advantages and disadvantages of various options.

5.2 ASK THE EXPERTS
GRAMMAR | question tags
VOCABULARY | questions
HOW TO | confirm information

COMMON EUROPEAN FRAMEWORK
Ss can generally follow the main points of extended discussion; can give or seek personal views and opinions in discussing topics of interest; can give brief comments on the views of others.

5.3 IT'S OUT OF ORDER
FUNCTION | polite requests
VOCABULARY | problems and solutions
LEARN TO | respond to requests

COMMON EUROPEAN FRAMEWORK
Ss can understand what is said to him/her in the standard spoken language; can explain why something is a problem, discuss what to do next, compare and contrast alternatives.

5.4 TOP GEAR ◉ BBC DVD
speakout | present a new machine
writeback | an advertisement

COMMON EUROPEAN FRAMEWORK
Ss can understand most of a documentary in a standard dialect; can give a clear, systematically developed presentation, highlighting significant points and adding supporting detail; can write straightforward, detailed descriptions familiar subjects.

5.5 LOOKBACK
Communicative revision activities

BBC VIDEO PODCAST
Are you good at solving problems?

COMMON EUROPEAN FRAMEWORK
This video podcast extends discussion of the unit topic to modern technology. Ss can view people talking about technology and how it has changed their lives. Use this video podcast at the start or end of Unit 5.

MACHINES

Introduction
Ss learn and practise comparatives and superlatives in the context of technology. They also learn and practise how to write an advantages/disadvantages essay and use discourse markers.

SUPPLEMENTARY MATERIALS
Resource bank p147
Ex 8A: write the phrases on cards for Ss to stick on the board/wall.
Warm up: bring/download photos of the forms of transport below.

Warm up
Bring/Download photos of the following forms of transport: *becak, gondola, hovercraft, tram, electric car* and *canal barge.* Write on the board *Which is the fastest/the best for the environment/the cheapest/the slowest/the most comfortable?* Ss discuss the questions in pairs. In feedback, nominate Ss to share their ideas with the class.

VOCABULARY technology

1A Ss discuss the questions in pairs. In feedback, nominate Ss to share their ideas with the class and have a brief discussion.

B Read the example with the class and elicit one more answer. In pairs, Ss categorise the words/phrases. In feedback, elicit Ss' answers, giving explanations/examples where necessary.

Answers: energy: electricity, nuclear power, solar power
machines: washing machine, vacuum cleaner, motorbikes, commercial aeroplanes
medicine/science: antibiotics, genetic engineering, vaccinations, space travel
IT: computer networks, communications satellites

C Drill the examples with the class, focusing on the stressed syllables. Ss underline the stressed syllables in pairs.

Teaching tip
When Ss are identifying the stress in words it can be useful for them to say the word out loud first.

D Ss listen and check their answers, then compare their answers in pairs. Elicit Ss' answers. Play the recording again, pausing after each word for Ss to repeat.

Answers: electricity, nuclear power, antibiotics, vaccinations, computer networks, motorbikes, genetic engineering, washing machine, vacuum cleaner, space travel, commercial aeroplanes, solar power, communications satellites

E Focus attention on the first word web and elicit more examples, e.g. *gas* and *wind power.* Give Ss 5 mins to add more words to the word webs. Monitor and help with vocabulary, writing new words/phrases on the board. When they are ready, Ss compare ideas in small groups and discuss which they have used in the last twenty-four hours. In feedback, nominate Ss from each group to share their ideas with the class.

▶ **VOCABULARYBANK** p152 Technology

Ss cover the words/phrases. Focus attention on the pictures and elicit what Ss can see. Ss match the words/phrases to the pictures in pairs.

Stronger classes can do the exercise at home.

Answers: 1 F 2 C 3 E 4 I 5 B 6 J 7 G 8 H 9 D 10 A

READING

2 Ss work alone to read the text and identify the inventions mentioned, then check their answers in pairs. Tell Ss not to worry about new words at this stage, as they'll read the text again in Ex 3A. In feedback, elicit Ss' answers.

Answers: The article mentions: electricity, the computer (computer networks), motorbikes, space travel
The article also talks about: cars, cinema, television, high-rise buildings, new fabrics, electric guitar, amplifier

3A Ss read the article again and answer the questions alone, then check their answers in pairs. In feedback, elicit Ss' answers and teach/check any new words/phrases.

Answers: 1 The military or the rich. 2 Long-distance travel became easier (more affordable) and inventions such as the cinema, television and computer brought the world to us. 3 They have become bigger and taller. More people are moving into cities and technology has improved, so the buildings are getting taller. 4 It was cheaper and more colourful than other materials. 5 Motorbikes give teenagers a sense of freedom, because they can travel away from home. 6 The electric guitar.

B Write *medicine*, *education*, *home* and *travel* on the board. Give Ss 3–4 mins to think of inventions under each category and write them down. In small groups, Ss share their ideas and try to agree on the most important one(s). In feedback, nominate Ss from each group to share their ideas with the class.

GRAMMAR   comparatives/ superlatives

4A Focus attention on the two underlined examples in the text. Ss work alone to find and underline more examples, then check their answers in pairs. In feedback, elicit Ss' answers and write them on the board.

Answers: the most surprising, easier, more affordable, (a little bit) smaller, the tallest, (a lot) taller, (much) cheaper, more colourful, further, the most important, faster, louder, better

Watch out!

Paragraph 2 includes another comparative form: *not as easy as*. With **stronger classes**, explain the meaning: *not to the same amount as*. With **weaker classes**, read the examples together in the **Language bank** on p136.

B Give Ss 2–3 mins to look at their examples and complete the rules. In feedback, elicit Ss' answers.

Answers: 1 Adjectives with one syllable: comparatives: add -er, superlative: add *the* _____-est
2 Adjectives with two or more syllables: comparatives: add *more* + adjective, superlatives: add *the most* + adjective

C Read the sentences with the class. Ss then complete the rules in pairs. In feedback, elicit Ss' answers.

Answers: 1 big 2 small

▶ **LANGUAGEBANK** 5.1 p136–137

Stronger classes could read the notes and do the exercises at home. Otherwise, check the notes with Ss, especially the alternative ways of forming comparatives and superlatives. In each exercise, elicit the first answer as an example. Ss work alone to complete the exercises, then check their answers in pairs. In feedback, elicit Ss' answers. Ss can refer to the notes to help.

Answers: 1 1 quicker 2 further/farther 3 less confident 4 the naughtiest 5 easier 6 bigger 7 tallest 8 more difficult 9 more dangerous 10 the best
2 1 My brother is a bit taller than I am. 2 The journey took us far longer than we expected. 3 It's by far the most expensive restaurant I've ever been to. 4 Your shoes are similar to my shoes. 5 People here are a lot healthier now that they have clean water.

PRACTICE

5A Do the first statement with the class as an example. Ss work alone to complete the rest of the statements, then check their answers in pairs. In feedback, elicit Ss' answers and drill the phrases.

Answers: 1 a lot easier 2 much safer, far healthier 3 a lot quicker, the best 4 cheapest, (the) most flexible 5 most important 6 much busier

B Demonstrate by giving an example with the class, e.g. *computers – They have made it easier to communicate, but our working lives have become busier as we can do more work every day.* In pairs, Ss choose an invention and write sentences. Monitor and encourage them to use comparatives and superlatives, as in the sentences in Ex 5A and help with vocabulary.

C When they are ready, nominate Ss from each pair to share their sentences with the class. At the end, Ss vote for the best/worst inventions.

SPEAKING

6A Before looking at the photos, Ss turn to p161 and read the introduction to the challenge, then ask a student to summarise the challenge to the class. Ss turn back to p57 and look at the photos. Teach/Check *mph (miles per hour)* and *mpg (miles per gallon)*. Ask Ss which vehicles exist at the moment and elicit the answer.

Answers: The space plane and rocket pack do not exist yet. All the other vehicles exist.

Culture notes
mph stands for *miles per hour*. 50 miles = 80 kilometres.
mpg stands for *miles per gallon*. 1 gallon = 4.54609188 litres.

B Ss read the challenges on p161 and discuss them in pairs. Monitor and encourage Ss to use comparatives and superlatives when discussing their answers. In feedback, elicit Ss' answers.

C Ss discuss the questions in small groups. Monitor and note down any common errors for later feedback. In feedback, nominate Ss from each group to share their opinions with the class. Correct any common errors.

WRITING   advantages/disadvantages essay

7A Divide the class in half. One half lists advantages and the other half lists disadvantages. Give Ss 5 mins to note down their ideas. Monitor and help with vocabulary. When they have finished, put Ss into pairs of advantage/disadvantage Ss to share their ideas and add any more they can think of to their partner's list. In feedback, elicit Ss' ideas and write them on the board.

B Give Ss 3–4 mins to read the essay and compare it with their ideas. In feedback, go through the ideas on the board from Ex 7A and tick any that are mentioned.

C Ss read the essay again and match the paragraphs with the descriptions. In feedback, elicit Ss' answers.

Answers: a) 3 b) 4 c) 1 d) 2

D Do the first guideline with the class as an example. Ss complete the rest of the guidelines alone, then check their answers in pairs. In feedback, elicit Ss' answers and give further explanations where necessary.

Answers: 1 notes 2 logical order 3 beginning 4 examples
5 personal opinions

LEARN TO   use discourse markers

8A Read the examples in the table with the class and check comprehension. Ss put the examples from the essay in the table, then check in pairs. In feedback, elicit Ss' answers.

Answers:
introduce advantages:
The most important advantage is …
One of the main advantages …
introduce disadvantages:
The main disadvantage is …
The problem is that …
contrasting ideas:
Although, …
However, …
additional reasons:
As well as that, …
And another thing, …
Another disadvantage
In addition to …
personal opinion/conclusion:
In general, …
As far as I'm concerned, …
In my opinion, …

Alternative approach
To cater for kinaesthetic learners, you could write the phrases on cards. Divide the board up into the same sections as the table, then give out the cards. Ss come to the board and stick the cards in the correct section on the board.

B Ss work alone to choose the correct alternatives, then check in pairs. In feedback, elicit Ss' answers.

Answers: 1 The main advantage 2 in addition to this
3 However 4 On the other hand 5 This means that
6 In my opinion 7 However

9 Ss choose one of the topics and make lists of the advantages and disadvantages. Monitor and help with vocabulary, writing new words/phrases on the board. When they have enough ideas, give Ss 10 mins to write a draft of their essays. When they have finished, Ss swap essays with a partner, who reads and makes suggestions on language/content. Monitor and help where necessary. Ss can either write a final draft in class or for homework.

Homework ideas
- **Ex 3B:** write about the most important inventions of the last 100 years.
- **Ex 9:** write a final draft of your essay, or write an essay about one of the other topics.
- **Language bank 5.1** Ex 1–2, p137
- **Vocabulary bank** p152
- **Workbook** Ex 1–6, p32–33

ASK THE EXPERTS

Introduction

Ss learn and practise question tags in the context of asking questions. They also learn and practise how to form adjectives with suffixes.

SUPPLEMENTARY MATERIALS

Resource bank p145, p146 and p148

Ex 2A and Ex 2C: bring dictionaries for Ss to use.

Warm up

Tell the following joke to Ss: *One night there was a loud storm, as a mother was putting her young child to bed. The boy was frightened and said in a weak voice, 'Mummy, I'm scared. Can you sleep with me tonight?' His mother replied, 'Sorry dear, I can't. I have to sleep with Daddy.' After a long silence, the boy said, 'What a coward Daddy is.'* Ask Ss if they know any jokes involving children and to share them with the class.

SPEAKING

1A Ss cover the questions and look at the photos. Elicit what they can see. Ss match the questions to the photos. In feedback, elicit Ss' answers.

Answers: 1 A 2 F 3 E 4 B 5 D 6 C

B Give Ss 2 mins to try and answer the questions in pairs. In feedback, elicit Ss' ideas, but don't give them the correct answers yet.

C Ss turn to p160 to check their answers. In feedback, elicit any surprising facts.

VOCABULARY questions

2A Read the first example with the class. Ss work alone to match the verbs to the situations, then check in pairs. If you've brought dictionaries, give them out for Ss to use. In feedback, elicit Ss answers and drill the verbs.

Answers: 1 question/wonder 2 respond/reply 3 discuss/debate 4 research/investigate 5 inquire/look into

B Read the example with the class to demonstrate. Ss answer the question in pairs. In feedback, elicit Ss' answers.

Answers: *debate, reply, research, question* and *wonder* are also nouns

C Read the example with the class. If you can, bring enough dictionaries for Ss to use in pairs. Ss find the noun forms and decide which verb doesn't have a noun form. In feedback, elicit Ss' answers and write them on the board.

Answers: *discussion, response, investigation, inquiry. Look into* does not have a noun form.

D Do the first sentence with the class as an example. Ss work alone to choose the correct alternatives, then check their answers in pairs. In feedback, elicit Ss' answers and drill the words, paying attention to any changes in word stress.

Teaching tip

When the part of speech changes, the stress may also change, e.g. *investigate* and *investigation*. Make sure Ss record the different stress patterns in their notebooks.

Answers: 1 investigation 2 reply 3 debate 4 research 5 question 6 look into

LISTENING

3A Introduce the topic by asking if any Ss have small children and eliciting some of the questions they ask. Ss discuss the questions in small groups. In feedback, nominate Ss from each group to share their ideas with the class.

B Teach/Check *rainbow*, *jellyfish* and *doughnuts*. Give Ss 3–4 mins to read the text and answer the question. In feedback, elicit Ss' answers.

Answer: He got the idea from questions his son asked him.

4A Read the questions with the Ss. Ss listen to the recording and number the questions in the order they hear them, then check in pairs. In feedback, elicit Ss' answers.

Answers: 2, 1, 5, 4, 3

B Give Ss 3–4 mins to think about their answers to the questions. Ss then discuss them in pairs. In feedback, elicit Ss' ideas, but don't give any answers yet.

5A Ss listen to the recording and compare it with their answers. Tell Ss not to worry if they don't understand all the language and that they'll listen again in Ex 5B. In feedback, ask if anyone had the same answers as in the recording.

B Before listening again, ask Ss what they can remember for each question. Ss listen again and take notes, then compare answers in pairs. If necessary, play the recording again. In feedback, elicit Ss' answers.

Answers: 1 are stronger 2 10,000 3 the engines shut down, stop working completely 4 they all grew up and wanted to do things their own way 5 economic reasons, fear

---

Unit 5 Recording 3

W1=1st woman M1=1st man W2=2nd woman

W1: Why are the windows round on ships?

M1: Round windows are stronger, aren't they?

W2: Are they? I've no idea.

W1: That's right. According to the book, they're less likely to break.

W2: Ah.

M1: There you go.

W1: What about this second one? How many hairs are there on the human head?

W2: Erm … A million?

M1: No, it's not that many, is it?

W2: It depends whose head, doesn't it?! On my dad's there are about three.

W1: The answer is about 10,000.

M1: Oh, really?

W2: I think that's a bit of a stupid question because it depends, doesn't it?

M1: Well, it was a four-year-old who asked the question.

W2: Oh yeah, that's true.

W1: Next question: What happens when your plane flies over a volcano?

W2: Ummm.

M1: Nothing happens, does it? Well, it depends on whether the volcano is erupting? Or whether it's active.

W2: Yeah.

W1: Well, according to the book, Jamieson asked a pilot. And the pilot said as he was flying over the volcano, his engines shut down, stopped working completely.

W2: Scary. Did he get hot?

W1: Hmm, it doesn't say. But he obviously survived. So there you go. Anyway, what about this one? Why did The Beatles break up?

W2: Dunno. They got old, didn't they?

M1: No, John Lennon went off with Yoko Ono, didn't he?

W1: Well, Jamieson wrote to Yoko Ono and she replied, 'Because they all grew up, wanted to do things their own way and they did.'

W2: Oh that's interesting.

M1: I'm amazed she replied.

W1: Me, too. OK, last one. After watching a violent video game, the little boy asked why is there war?

W2: Great question.

M1: That's a really good question.

W2: Hmm, because men like fighting?

M1: Political reasons. One country wants the land or the oil or the gold.

W1: Well, Jamieson asked lots of experts. Most of them didn't or couldn't answer. Then he asked an American army colonel, who said there are four big reasons: different ideologies, a sense of honour, economic reasons and fear.

M1: Uh-huh.

W2: Good question for a four-year-old.

M1: And a good answer.

GRAMMAR question tags

6A Ss complete the questions in pairs, then check their answers with the audio script on p168.

> **Answers:** 1 aren't 2 is 3 doesn't 4 does 5 didn't 6 didn't

B Ss read the rules and underline the correct alternatives, then check their answers in pairs. In feedback, elicit Ss' answers, giving further examples/explanations.

> **Answers:** 2 the present 3 pronoun 4 negative 5 positive

> ⇒ **LANGUAGEBANK** 5.2 p136–137
>
> *Stronger classes* could read the notes and do the exercises at home. *Weaker classes* can do the exercises in class. Also remind Ss that in a sentence with *Let's …* the question tag is *shall we?* e.g. *Let's go out, shall we?*
>
> > **Answers: 1** 1 g) 2 d) 3 e) 4 a) 5 b) 6 h) 7 c) 8 f)
> > **2** 1 *were you?* 2 *won't it?* 3 *didn't she?* 4 *don't they?* 5 *don't I?* 6 *haven't you?* 7 *didn't I?* 8 *won't he?* 9 *didn't you?* 10 *aren't they?*

PRACTICE

7 Read the examples with the class to demonstrate. Ss work alone to complete the question tags, then check their answers in pairs. In feedback, elicit Ss' answers.

> **Answers:** 1 aren't 2 are 3 do 4 don't 5 did 6 has 7 won't 8 isn't 9 didn't 10 haven't 11 weren't 12 was

8A Play the recording and ask *In which question is the speaker sure?* (the first); *In which question isn't the speaker sure?* (the second). Play the recording again for Ss to notice the intonation and repeat the question tags.

B Ss listen and write *S* if the person is sure and *NS* if the person isn't sure, then check in pairs. In feedback, elicit Ss' answers. Play the recording for Ss to repeat.

> **Answers:** The speaker is sure about 1, 4, 6, 7, 8, 9, 10 and 11.

C Ss choose six questions and decide if they are sure or unsure about the answers, then ask their partner. Monitor and check Ss intonation.

SPEAKING

9 Arrange Ss into small groups and read the first instruction with the class. Ss follow the instructions in their groups. Monitor and help with questions. In feedback, nominate Ss from each group to share information they found out.

VOCABULARY *PLUS* word building: adjectives

10A Give Ss 2 mins to read the text and find out the answer. In feedback, elicit Ss' answers.

> **Answer:** an ice cream seller ran out of spoons and dishes so he bought some wafers to put the ice cream in.

B Elicit the first example with the class, then Ss find three more adjectives in the text and add them to the word web. Elicit Ss' answers and write them on the board.

> **Answers:** -ive: creative -less: hopeless -able/-ible: profitable -ful: thankful

Check Ss understand the adjectives in the word web. Ss work alone to think of more examples, then compare in pairs. Elicit Ss' answers, drill them and write them on the board.

> **Possible answers:** -y: easy, rainy -able/-ible: affordable, visible -ful: beautiful, helpful -ive: attractive, productive -less: careless, helpless -ic/-ical: heroic, historical

speakout TIP

Read the tip with the class and elicit more examples from the Ss' own L1(s). In *multilingual classes*, Ss can do this in pairs, then share their ideas with the class in feedback.

11 Elicit the first answer with the class as an example. Ss work alone to complete the text, then check in pairs. In feedback, elicit Ss' answers and write them on the board.

> **Answers:** 1 valuable 2 responsible 3 hopeless 4 effective 5 easy 6 rainy 7 successful 8 useful

12A Ss work alone to complete the words, then check in pairs. In feedback, elicit Ss' answers.

> **Answers:** 1 peaceful 2 hopeless 3 careful 4 messy 5 creative 6 knowledgeable

B Ss ask and answer in groups of four to find people for each of the sentences. In feedback, elicit Ss' answers.

> ⇒ **VOCABULARYBANK** p152 Word-building
>
> **1A** Check Ss understand the words in the chart.
>
> **B** Ss complete the sentences, then check their answers in pairs. Elicit Ss' answers and drill the words.
>
> > **Answers: 1B** 1 competition 2 improvement 3 responsibility 4 loneliness 5 depression 6 imagination 7 stupidity 8 entertainment 9 kindness 10 instruction

Homework ideas

- Ex 1A: research some interesting facts to share.
- Language bank 5.2 Ex 1–2, p137
- Vocabulary bank p152
- Workbook Ex 1–7, p34–35

IT'S OUT OF ORDER

Introduction

Ss learn and practise ways of making polite requests when solving problems. They also learn how to respond to requests.

SUPPLEMENTARY MATERIALS

Resource bank p149

Warm up: write the phrases below on the board

Warm up

Write some or all of the following phrases on the board, depending on how many Ss you have: *open a bank account, drive a car, send a text message on your phone, book a cheap flight, make your favourite recipe, avoid getting a computer virus, use a credit card, lose weight, make coffee, watch a DVD.* Put Ss in pairs and assign a topic to each pair. Give Ss 5 mins to write simple instructions on how to do their topic. Monitor and help with vocabulary where necessary. In feedback, Ss share their instructions with the class.

VOCABULARY problems and solutions

1A Demonstrate by telling Ss two pieces of technology you have used and possible problems with them. Ss discuss the questions in pairs. In feedback, nominate Ss to share their ideas with the class and have a brief discussion.

B Look at the first picture and elicit the problem. Write the phrase on the board. Ss identify the other problems in the photos in pairs. In feedback, elicit answers with the class and write them on the board.

Possible answers: A The printer is jammed/needs fixing. B The vacuum cleaner doesn't work/is broken. C The phone needs recharging. D The computer's crashed/frozen. E The ATM machine is out of order.

C Do the first two with the class as examples. Ss work alone to decide if the sentences are problems or solutions, then check in pairs. Elicit Ss' answers and which photos each sentence can be used with.

Answers: 1 P 2 P 3 P 4 P 5 P 6 S 7 P 8 P 9 P 10 S 11 S 12 S
A 4, 7, 9 and 10 B 1, 4, 7 and 9 C 2 D 6 and 8 E 3, 4 and 9

D Ss discuss the questions in pairs. Monitor and help with vocabulary, writing any new words/phrases on the board. In feedback, nominate Ss to share their experiences with the class.

2A Draw a word web on the board and write *computer problems* in the middle. Elicit possible problems and write them on the board, e.g. *breaks down, crashes or freezes, wireless problems, slow computer, takes too long to load, printing problems, problems with specific programs, overheats.* In pairs, Ss discuss which of the problems they have had and describe what they did. In feedback, elicit Ss' answers.

B Give Ss 5 mins to read the text, then answer the question in pairs. In feedback, elicit Ss' answers and ask *Have you ever done any of these things?*

Answers: People shout at colleagues, hit the computer, throw parts of the computer and/or swear at the computer.

FUNCTION polite requests

3A Ss listen to the conversations and identify the problems, then check their answers in pairs. Tell them not to worry if they don't understand all the language, as they'll listen again in Ex 3B. In feedback, elicit Ss' answers.

Answers: 1 A cash machine doesn't work. 2 Her laptop had crashed/keeps losing documents. 3 His vacuum cleaner makes a funny noise. 4 The ticket machine is not working (has taken money).

B Give Ss 2 mins to look at the table and complete what they can from memory. Ss listen again and complete the phrases, then check in pairs. Play the recording again if necessary. In feedback, elicit Ss' answers and write the phrases on the board. Point out the use of the gerund after *mind* in 6 and 7.

Watch out!

Point out that when we ask *Would you mind … ?* it means *Is it a problem for you if …?* Answering *No* means it's OK.

Answers: 1 hold 2 give 3 speak 4 problem 5 machine 6 looking 7 calling

---

Unit 5 Recording 6

Conversation 1

M=Man W=Woman

M: Arggh. Oh no.

W: What's the matter?

M: Oh. This cash machine's not working. <u>Do you know if</u> there's another machine somewhere? I really need to get some money.

W: Hmm … I'm not sure. There might be one in the shopping centre.

M: Thanks.

Conversation 2

W=Woman M=Man

W: Argh!

M: What's the matter?

W: My laptop's just crashed, again. That's the third time it's happened. <u>Would you mind looking at it for me?</u>

M: Sure.

W: Thanks. It's so annoying. I keep losing my documents. <u>Do you know what the problem is?</u>

M: Let me have a look. There's a lot of stuff on here. Why don't you save the documents onto a memory stick?

W: That's a good idea.

M: And then do you want me to try …

Conversation 3

W=Woman M=Man

W: Customer Services. Good Morning.

M: Um, yes. I've got a problem with my vacuum cleaner.

W: <u>Could you tell me what the problem is,</u> sir?

M: Yes, I can. It keeps making a funny noise. And it's just not working properly.

W: You say it keeps making a funny noise …

M: Yes, that's right.

W: OK. Let's see if I can find someone who can help you. <u>Could you hold the line, please?</u>

M: Yes, of course.

Conversation 4

M=Man W=Woman

M: Oh. I don't believe it! Excuse me, this machine's not working.

It's just taken my money. <u>Could you give me a refund?</u>

W: I'm afraid I can't do that.

M: Why not?

W: Well, I'm not allowed to give refunds.

M: But I've just lost my money. And I still need a ticket.

W: I can sell you a ticket, but I can't give you a refund.

M: Well, <u>could you tell me who I should speak to?</u>

W: Yes, of course. You need to speak to the manager.

M: OK. <u>Would you mind calling him for me?</u>

W: Of course not. I'll just call him.

C Play the recording and pause after each request for Ss to repeat.

➡ LANGUAGEBANK 5.3 p136–137

Stronger classes could read the notes and do the exercises at home. *Weaker classes* can do the exercises in class.

Drill the requests and responses on p136. Check the notes with Ss, especially the meaning of *Would you mind…?* questions and typical responses. Focus attention on the exercise on p137 and elicit the first mistake as an example. Ss complete the exercises alone, then check their answers in pairs. Ss can refer to the notes to help them.

> **Answers: 1** 1 A: Excuse me, could you ~~is~~ hold the door for me? B: Yes, ~~I do~~ of course. 2 A: Do you know when the next train ~~does to~~ leaves? B: I'm not ~~OK~~ sure. 3 A: Would you ~~to~~ mind staying behind after the meeting? B: ~~It's~~ Sure. That's fine. 4 A: Could ~~is possible~~ you tell me what Tim's phone number is? B: Let me have a ~~to~~ look. 5 A: Would you mind ~~to~~ looking after my bag while I go to the bathroom? B: No, of course not ~~mind~~. 6 A: Could you tell ~~for~~ me the way to the station? B: Yes, ~~so~~ I can.

LEARN TO respond to requests

4A Do the first conversation together as an example. Ss work alone to complete the responses, then check their answers in pairs.

B Ss turn to p169 to check their answers with the audio script. In feedback, elicit Ss' answers and drill the responses.

> **Answers: 1** I'm not sure **2** Sure **3** Let me have a look **4** Yes, I can. **5** Yes, of course. **6** I'm afraid I can't … Yes, of course. Of course not.

5A Elicit the first answer as an example and write it on the board. Ss work alone to write the requests, then check their answers in pairs.

B Ss listen and check their answers. Pause the recording after each conversation to give Ss time to correct any mistakes. In feedback, elicit Ss' answers.

> **Answers: 1** Would you mind turning the music down? **2** Do you know if there's anyone in the office? **3** B: Do you know when he's coming back? A: I'm not sure. **4** A: Could you tell me how this machine works? B: Yes, of course. **5** A: Would you mind helping me? B: Of course not. **6** A: Could you tell me who I should speak to? B: Let me have a look.

C Ss listen again and decide if the voice starts high or low. In feedback, elicit Ss' answers, then play the recording again, pausing after each one for Ss to repeat.

Unit 5 Recording 8

Conversation 1

A: I can't concentrate. Would you mind turning the music down?

B: Sure. Sorry about that.

Conversation 2

A: I need to speak to the manager. Do you know if there's anyone in the office?

B: Let me have a look.

Conversation 3

A: I'm afraid Mr Soul isn't here at the moment.

B: Do you know when he's coming back?

A: I'm not sure. Do you want me to check?

B: Thank you.

Conversation 4

A: Could you tell me how this machine works? I don't know how to turn it on.

B: Yes, of course.

Conversation 5

A: I need to take this machine to the repair service. Would you mind helping me?

B: Of course not. Leave it here.

Conversation 6

A: My computer has frozen. Could you tell me who I should speak to?

B: OK. Let me have a look.

SPEAKING

6A Arrange Ss into A/B pairs. Review the language for polite requests in Ex 3B and responding to requests in Ex 4A. Give Ss 3–4 mins to read the situations and think about what they are going to say. Monitor and help where necessary. When they are ready, Ss practise the conversations in pairs. Monitor and note down any common errors for later feedback.

B Ss change roles and role-play the second situation in the same way as in Ex 6A. In feedback, nominate one or two pairs to perform their role-plays for the class.

C Ss work in pairs to plan their own role-play. Monitor and help with ideas where needed. When Ss have finished, nominate pairs to perform their role-plays for the class and ask Ss to vote for the best one. Correct any common errors.

> **Teaching tip**
> With *weaker classes*, give them prompts to help them plan, e.g. *Where are you? What problem do you have? What's the solution?* etc.

> **Homework ideas**
> - Ex 1D: write about a problem you had and how you solved it.
> - Language bank 5.3 Ex 1, p137
> - Workbook Ex 1–3, p36

TOP GEAR

Introduction

Ss watch an extract from the BBC television series *Top Gear*, in which the presenter races two freerunners in a Peugeot 207 in Liverpool. Ss also learn and practise how to give a short presentation and write an advertisement for a new product.

SUPPLEMENTARY MATERIALS

Ex 6: bring some authentic advertisements for Ss to look at before they write.

Warm up: bring/download photos of people doing parkour/freerunning. If you have internet access in class, show people doing parkour on www.youtube.com (correct at the time of going to press).

Culture notes

Parkour, or freerunning, is a non-competitive sport which involves continuous movement in a straight line, passing smoothly over obstacles in your way. It involves running, jumping, climbing and other complicated techniques. It originated in France. A person who participates is called a *traceur* (if a man) and *traceuse* (if a woman).

Culture notes

Liverpool is a well-known city in the north-west of England. It is famous as the birthplace of The Beatles and for its docks on the River Mersey. People who live there are known as *Liverpudlians*, or informally as *Scousers*, which comes from a local stew dish called *Scouse*. Several parts of the city have been granted world heritage site status by UNESCO and it is a popular centre of tourism.

Warm up

Show Ss the photos or video clip and write the following questions on the board: *Do you know what this sport is? Have you ever seen people doing it? Would you like to try it? Have you ever done any other 'extreme' sports?* Ss discuss the questions in pairs. In feedback, nominate Ss to share their ideas with the class. Tell Ss they'll watch a DVD programme with people doing parkour in it.

DVD PREVIEW

1 In pairs, Ss look at the pictures and discuss the questions. In feedback, elicit their ideas and have a brief class discussion, feeding in information from the **Culture notes** on parkour/freerunning. Elicit/Check *as the crow flies*.

2 Give Ss 2–3 mins to read the text and discuss in pairs who they think will win. In feedback, write *Peugeot 207* and *freerunners* on the board and go round the class eliciting Ss' predictions and tallying them on the board.

Culture notes

The BBC programme *Top Gear* was first screened in 1977 and was relaunched in 2002. It started as a conventional car review programme, but over time it has developed a reputation for its humorous style and innovative ideas for ways of testing new cars. The show is presented by Jeremy Clarkson, Richard Hammond and James May. It has won several awards.

Optional extra activity

Before playing the DVD, draw two columns on the board and at the top of them write *James May* and *The Freerunners*. Elicit via a show of hands who thinks James May will win the race and who thinks the freerunners will win and write a tally of the votes in the columns. Play the DVD, but pause just as James May arrives at the Liver Building and elicit the Ss' votes again. Play the end of the DVD for Ss to find out who won.

▶ DVD VIEW

3 Play the DVD. Ss watch and put the events in the correct order, then check in pairs. In feedback, elicit Ss' answers and who won the race.

Answers: a) 1 b) 5 c) 2 d) 3 e) 4

4 Ss work in pairs to complete the phrases from memory. Play the DVD again for Ss to check. In feedback, elicit Ss' answers.

Answers: 1 good 2 trousers 3 city 4 shopping 5 win 6 won

DVD 5 Top Gear

V=Voice-over JM=James May YM=Young men

V: Tonight: Is a Peugeot faster than two men?

JM: Here it is. It's called the 207 and it's Peugeot's biggest small car yet.

As we can see, it's a very pretty car but is it any good?

I'm going to test this ginormous city car on the streets of Liverpool. And to spur me on a bit, I'm going to have a race and it's against the latest French development in urban transport solutions. A couple of young men in silly trousers. Are you ready?

YM: Ready. Yeah.

JM: Three ... two ... one ... go!

I should probably explain that these are not just any young men. They are masters of something called 'parkour'.

It's a French invention and involves that sort of thing.

Running around in the city leaping across buildings and benches. You know. Keeps them off the street.

Our race will run from the edge of Liverpool to the finish line at the Liver Building. For me it'll be about six miles.

Their journey of course is pretty much as the crow flies.

What am I doing? Mm ... 25 miles an hour. They'll have difficulty matching that!

So, anyway, the car. Well it's got a nice driving position, the steering's nice and weighty, the seat is excellent and there's quite a bit more room in here than in the old one.

But there is a problem, something you really feel on the city streets.

It's almost 300lbs heavier than the old car.

It's really sluggish low down. That's annoying.

There they are!

But I didn't catch them for long.

Oh please!

Come on! We're not all shopping!

I had just two miles to go in the sluggish Peugeot.

I must have averaged ten or 12 miles an hour. I should win.

I was close. But so were they.

Come on!

That must be the Liver Building.

And they're not here! They are not here. No sign of combat trousers man.

I've won!

Oh, for Pete's sake!

speakout present a new machine

5A Give Ss 5 mins to write their lists and think about their answers, then compare ideas in pairs. In feedback, elicit Ss' ideas for questions 1 and 2 and have a brief discussion. Don't ask them to show their pictures at this stage, as they'll present them in Ex 5E.

B Ss listen and note down what the invention is and what it does. In feedback, elicit Ss' answers and ask Ss if they would buy one.

Answers: The invention is called *Robo-chef* and it prepares meals automatically.

Unit 5 Recording 9

J=James Carn

J: I'm going to tell you about Robo-Chef. Basically, Robo-Chef can prepare and cook all your favourite recipes. It works like this. First of all, it washes and prepares all the vegetables, then it prepares your dish and cooks it for you on your cooker. Robo-Chef comes complete with hundreds of menus already programmed. But you can also programme Robo-Chef with your own recipes, or, if you want to try something new, you can download new recipes whenever you like. All you have to do is choose the dish you want, decide how many people you want Robo-Chef to cook for and what time you want the meal to be ready. So, let's say you would like a vegetable lasagne for six people, ready by eight o'clock. Then, just make sure you have all the ingredients in the kitchen, press the button and that's it. You can go out to work and when you come home in the evening, your delicious supper will be ready. What could be easier? Robo-Chef is the chef of the future.

C Give Ss 1 min to read the phrases, then play the recording for them to check which ones he uses. Ss then compare their answers in pairs. In feedback, elicit Ss' answers and drill the phrases.

Answers: ✓ I'm going to tell you about …, Basically, …, It works like this …, First of all, …, All you have to do is …, Make sure you …

D Ss prepare their presentations in pairs. First they discuss and make notes together, then decide who will work on each task. When they are ready, Ss check through the whole presentation together to make sure each part fits and decide who will present each section. Monitor and help with vocabulary, writing new words/phrases on the board. Make sure Ss think of a name for their machine and write these on the board while Ss are preparing.

E When they are ready, Ss come to the front of the class in pairs and present their machines to the class. When they have finished, ask Ss to vote for their favourite machines and build up a tally on the board next to the names of the machines.

writeback an advertisement

6A Teach/elicit *shower-head*. Give Ss 2–3 mins to read the text and answer the questions in pairs. If you have brought some authentic advertisements, distribute them for Ss to read and elicit some common features.

Answers: It's a shower-head with an mp3 player attached to it. You download your favourite tunes or radio programmes at night and in the morning the shower will play them automatically.

B Ss write a draft of an advertisement for their invention. Monitor and help with vocabulary, writing any new words/ phrases on the board. Ss can refer to the example in Ex 6A and the key phrases to help. When Ss have finished, they show their advertisements to other Ss, who choose their favourite one.

Teaching tip

When Ss have written a first draft, it's a good idea to encourage peer-correction. However, in order for it to be effective, Ss need clear guidance on what to look for e.g. vocabulary from the unit, grammar, sentence length, punctuation, etc. Make sure Ss are clear about what to look for before they peer-correct.

Homework ideas
• Ex 6B: write a final draft of your advertisement.

LOOKBACK

Introduction

Ss revise and practise the language of Unit 5. The notes below provide ideas for exploiting the exercises and activities but your approach will depend on your aim, e.g. whether you use the activities as a diagnostic or progress test or as revision/fluency practice. If done as a test then it would not be appropriate to monitor or help Ss.

TECHNOLOGY

1A Do the first sentence with the class as an example. Ss work alone to complete the rest of the sentences, then check their answers in pairs. In feedback, elicit Ss' answers and write the words on the board.

Answers: 1 nuclear power, electricity 2 Space travel
3 washing machine 4 vaccinations 5 genetic engineering
6 antibiotics

B Ss choose three sentences they disagree with and tell their partner why. In feedback, elicit Ss' opinions and discuss.

Alternative approach
Ss could do this as a mingling activity, sharing their opinions with different Ss around the class.

Teaching tip
Stronger classes can discuss if they agree/disagree with all of the statements.

COMPARATIVES/SUPERLATIVES

2A Give Ss 1 min to read the text, then do the first sentence together as an example. Ss complete the rest of the sentences alone, then check their answers in pairs. In feedback, elicit Ss' answers and write the structures on the board.

Answers: 1 as long 2 far more difficult 3 far more expensive 4 much more educated

B Write the following topics on the board to help Ss: *medicine, entertainment, communication, speed of transport, average wage, education.* Ss write their sentences alone, then compare them in pairs. Monitor and check Ss are forming comparatives and superlatives correctly. In feedback, nominate Ss to share their partner's sentences with the class.

Teaching tip
In *monolingual classes,* Ss write about their country then compare with other Ss to see if they agree. In *multilingual classes,* each student writes about their own country then shares their information with other Ss.

Optional extra activity
Before class, prepare a list of things which can be compared using language from the unit and adjectives e.g. *nuclear power/space travel (safe), cars/the internet (important),* etc. Arrange Ss in small groups and ask each group to appoint a 'secretary' who is responsible for writing the answers. When they are ready, write one of your pairs of things to be compared (and adjective) on the board. When Ss have written a comparative sentence they call out 'compared!' and other groups stop writing. If the group has written a correct sentence, award them a point and move on to the next items on the list. If their sentence isn't correct, don't give any feedback and continue until another group has written a sentence.

QUESTIONS

3A Read the example with the class. Ss work alone to put the letters in the correct order, then check their answers in pairs. In feedback, elicit Ss' answers and write the words on the board.

Answers: 1 discussed 2 questions 3 respond 4 look into
5 inquired 6 wonder 7 debate 8 investigate

B Demonstrate by completing one or two of the sentences with your own details and sharing them with the class. Give Ss 3–4 mins to finish the sentences. Monitor and help with vocabulary, writing new words/phrases on the board. When they are ready, Ss share their sentences in small groups and see if they have any common answers. In feedback, nominate Ss from each group to share their sentences with the class.

QUESTION TAGS

4A Read the example with the class. Remind Ss of the rules for forming questions tags on p60. Ss complete the question tags alone, then check their answers in pairs. In feedback, elicit Ss' answers and write them on the board.

Answers: 1 didn't she? 2 doesn't he? 3 hasn't he?
4 wasn't he? 5 was she? 6 did he? 7 isn't it? 8 will she?

B Read the example with the class to demonstrate. In pairs, Ss guess who the rest of the sentences are about. In feedback, elicit Ss' answers and write them on the board.

Answers: 1 JK Rowling 2 Bono 3 Tom Hanks 4 Michael Jordan 5 Mother Teresa 6 Fidel Castro 7 Madonna
8 Hillary Clinton

C Demonstrate the activity with a stronger student, then Ss play twenty questions in small groups. Monitor and check Ss are using question tags correctly.

Teaching tip
With *weaker classes,* ask Ss to write common questions with question tags first.

POLITE REQUESTS

5A Ss match the requests and responses alone, then check their answers in pairs. In feedback, elicit Ss' answers.

Answers: 1 b) 2 c) 3 e) 4 a) 5 d)

B Review the language for polite requests and responding to requests from Lesson 5.3 with the class. Ss practise the conversations in pairs. Monitor and check they are using the language correctly. In feedback, nominate one or two pairs to perform their conversations for the class.

Teaching tip
With *weaker classes,* Ss can write out their conversations before practising them.

OVERVIEW

FEELING STRESSED?

Introduction

Ss learn and practise zero and first conditionals in the context of emotions. They also learn and practise using -ing/-ed adjectives and multi-word verbs.

SUPPLEMENTARY MATERIALS

Resource bank p150, p151 and/or p152

Ex 10B: bring dictionaries for Ss to use.

Warm up

Divide the class into small groups. Ask each group to choose a name and write it on the board. Give Ss 5 mins to brainstorm and write down as many emotions as they can, e.g. *happiness, fear, excitement, anxiousness, tiredness,* etc. They could express these as feelings, if it's easier, e.g. *happy, afraid, excited, anxious, tired,* etc. In feedback, award points for each correctly spelled emotion/feeling and write the words on the board. The group with the most points wins. Check Ss understand whether the words on the board are positive or negative emotions/feelings. Drill the words.

SPEAKING

1A Tell Ss to cover the text and look at the photos. Elicit what emotions are shown in each one, but don't give any answers yet.

B Ss read the text and match the emotions to the photos, then check their answers in pairs. With *weaker classes*, do the first one together as an example. Elicit Ss' answers.

Answers: A surprise (5) B fear (1) C anger (2)
D disgust (6) E joy (4) F distress (3)

C Give an example of when you felt one of these emotions. Ss then discuss the question in pairs. In feedback, nominate Ss to share their experiences with the class.

VOCABULARY -ing/-ed adjectives

2A Give Ss 1 min to read the questions and check they understand all the vocabulary. Ss discuss the questions in pairs. In feedback, nominate Ss to share their partner's answers with the class.

B Ss look at the quiz again and answer the questions in pairs. Elicit Ss' answers.

Answers: 1 -ed 2 -ing

C Read the example with the class. Ss complete the sentences alone, then check their answers in pairs. Elicit Ss' answers.

Answers: 1 worrying 2 exhausted 3 embarrassing
4 boring 5 confusing 6 relaxed

D Change two of the sentences so they are true for you and read them out to the class as examples. Ss change two of the sentences for themselves. Monitor and help with vocabulary as necessary. Ss then compare their sentences with a partner. In feedback, nominate Ss to share their partner's sentences.

▶ **VOCABULARYBANK** p153 Emotions

1 Check the first definition and elicit the second. Ss complete the rest of the definitions in pairs.

Stronger classes can do the exercise at home.

> **Answers:** 1 1 interested 2 excited 3 astonishing
> 4 tiring 5 fascinating 6 disappointed 7 depressing
> 8 satisfied 9 frustrated 10 terrified

LISTENING

3 Read the definition with the class and give/elicit some examples of therapies, e.g. *psychoanalysis, group therapy, music therapy*, etc. Play the recording. Ss answer the questions, then check their answers in pairs. Elicit Ss' answers.

> **Answers:** 1 destruction therapy and laughter therapy
> 2 Destruction therapy is used to help people when they are
> stressed or angry, or to help build a team. Laughter therapy
> is used in hospitals to help people with pain.

Unit 6 Recording 1

R=Radio presenter C=Clip P=Professor M=Man

R: Welcome to *Start the Day*!

C: Hello – can I help you?

Your call is important to us.

Hello – can I help you?

Your call is important to us. Sorry, all our operators are busy at the moment. Please hold.

M: They put you in a queue for ages, listening to this terrible music. When you finally speak to someone, you're so angry, you just want to shout …

R: Anger. We all know the feeling. A report out last year shows that people are getting angrier. One in ten people say that they have trouble controlling their temper. Traffic jams, airports, call centres, computer crashes – they can all leave us feeling angry and anger is difficult to control. Or is it? Professor Miller from The Metropolitan University is here to tell us about two very different therapies to help deal with stress. First of all, destruction therapy. What's that about?

P: Well, basically, the idea is that a lot of people, when they get angry, they don't know what to do with their anger – they don't deal with it very well. They just keep it inside. But, if you don't deal with your anger, sooner or later it will explode. So with destruction therapy, you use your anger to destroy something, but in a controlled way and the idea is that if you do that, it helps you to feel better.

R: OK, I get angry a lot. Can destruction therapy help me?

P: Perhaps. We can try it. What we do is we take you to a place full of old cars. When we get there, I'll give you a hammer and you can use it to smash a car to pieces.

R: Really? Is it that simple? If I smash the car to pieces, will I feel better?

P: Yes, a little. But that's only the beginning. Then, I'll ask you to think about a situation in the past when you felt really angry. And when you think about that anger situation, you'll hit the car much harder. And the therapy will be much more satisfying. When we finish the session, you'll feel much better.

R: That's amazing and businesses are using this kind of therapy in Spain, is that right?

P: Yes, there are some old hotels in Spain. You can pay to go and destroy the hotel. So, some companies who feel that their workers are stressed, or they need to build a team, send their workers to destroy the hotel. And it's a good way for them to get rid of that stress. It works.

R: That's incredible. But there's another idea I wanted to ask you about. People say that laughter is the best medicine. And nowadays, laughter therapy is used in hospitals to help people with pain.

P: That's right.

R: So, how does that work?

P: Well, if people laugh about something, they feel better. On average, children laugh up to 400 times a day, but when we grow up, we only laugh about seventeen times a day. And it's not enough, because when you laugh, your body produces chemicals – and these chemicals make you feel happier. And they also make you feel less pain. So, in Mexico, for example, they use laughter therapy in hospitals. A group of people go around the hospital, visiting the patients and basically, they make them laugh, by telling them jokes, or doing something funny.

R: And does it really work? Do people feel better afterwards?

P: Absolutely! They feel better and they don't need medicine.

R: That's brilliant. So, in Mexico, laughter really is the best medicine?

P: Yes, it looks like it. That's right …

4A Ss decide if the statements are true or false, then check their answers in pairs.

B Play the recording again. Ss check their answers to Ex 4A, then check their answers in pairs. In feedback, elicit Ss' answers.

> **Answers:** 1 F *One* out of ten people have trouble. 2 T
> 3 F The therapy will be more *satisfying*. 4 F They pay
> workers to *destroy* hotels. 5 F They use *laughter* therapy in
> hospitals. 6 T 7 F Children laugh about *400* times a day.

C Ss discuss the questions in pairs. Monitor and note down any common errors for later feedback. In feedback, nominate Ss to share their opinions and correct any common errors.

GRAMMAR zero and first conditionals

5A Elicit the first answer as an example. Ss mark the sentences alone, then compare their answers in pairs. In feedback, elicit Ss' answers.

> **Answers:** a) GS b) FS c) FS d) GS

B Ss underline the correct alternatives alone, then check their answers in pairs. In feedback, elicit Ss' answers and give further examples if necessary.

> **Answers:** 1 general 2 specific

▶ **LANGUAGEBANK** 6.1 p138–139

Stronger classes can read the notes and do the exercises at home. Otherwise, check the notes with Ss, especially the difference between *if* and *when* and the meaning of *unless*. In each exercise, do the first sentence as an example. Ss complete the exercises alone, then check their answers in pairs. Ss can refer to the notes to help them.

> **Answers:** 1 1 pass, 'll/will be 2 visit, looks after
> 3 leaves, 'll/will worry 4 don't find, won't go 5 don't
> water, 'll/will die 6 'll/will be, comes 7 get, ask
> 8 won't come, invite 9 's/is, like 10 listen, want
> 2 1 unless 2 unless 3 is 4 if 5 'll feel 6 know
> 7 scream 8 opens

6A With *weaker classes*, play the first sentence and elicit the correct alternative as an example. Ss listen to the sentences and choose the correct alternatives, then check their answers in pairs. If necessary, play the recording again.

> **Answers:** 1 I get 2 I'll tell 3 we'll eat 4 I'll phone 5 I go

B Play the recording again but pause after each sentence for Ss to repeat. If necessary, drill the sentences yourself so that Ss can see how the sounds are produced.

PRACTICE

7A With *weaker classes*, do 1 a) and b) first as examples. Ss complete the sentences alone, then check their answers in pairs. Monitor and check Ss are forming the conditionals correctly. In feedback, elicit Ss' answers.

> **Answers:** 1 a) makes (0) b) 'll feel (1st) 2 a) 'll give (1st) b) finish (0) 3 a) 'll get (1st) b) get (0) 4 a) like (0) b) 'll stop (1st)

B Make two of the sentences true for you and read them out as examples. Give Ss 5 mins to complete the sentences so that they are true for them. Monitor and help with vocabulary and write any new words/phrases on the board. Ss then tell each other their sentences in pairs. In feedback, nominate Ss to share two of their partner's sentences with the class.

> **Alternative approach**
> Ss make some of the sentences true and some false. Their partner has to guess which are true and which are false.

SPEAKING

8A Read the sentences with the class and check they understand them. Put Ss in pairs and give them 5 mins to discuss and write down three pieces of advice for each situation. Monitor and help with ideas and vocabulary.

B Ss then work in small groups to share their ideas and choose the best piece of advice for each situation. Monitor and note down any common errors, especially with zero and first conditionals. In feedback, nominate Ss from each group to share their group's best ideas. Correct any common errors.

VOCABULARY *PLUS* multi-word verbs

9A Introduce multi-word verbs and elicit any that Ss already know. Then write *clothes*, *computers* and *love* on the board and ask if Ss can think of any multi-word verbs related to each topic. Ss match the topics to the paragraphs alone, then check their answers in pairs. Elicit Ss' answers.

> **Answers:** 1 Love and friendship 2 Computers 3 Clothes

> **Teaching tip**
> There are thousands of multi-word verbs and Ss may find them confusing because so many have non-literal meanings. De-mystify them by pointing out that Ss know a lot of them already, e.g. *stand up, write down, pick up, turn over, switch on*, etc.

speakout TIP

Read the tip with the class and ask Ss if they use any of these methods already. Explain that there is no 'correct' way to learn multi-word verbs. It's a case of experimenting and finding out which way works best for them.

B Read the example in the word web with the class. Ss complete the word webs alone, then check their answers in pairs. In feedback, elicit Ss' answers and give further explanations. Drill the verbs, paying attention to linking.

> **Answers:** on: click on, try on, get on; off: take off, go off, log off; up: chat up, scroll up, dress up; down: settle down, shut down, dress down

10A Check Ss understand the dictionary abbreviations *sth*, *phr v* and *Br E*. Ss read the definitions and answer the questions alone, then check their answers in pairs. In feedback, elicit Ss' answers. Point out that *shut down* can be either transitive (*Have you shut the computer down?*) or intransitive (*the company shut down*).

> **Answers:** 1 try on 2 get on 3 get on (with)

> **Watch out!**
> Multi-word verbs can be either transitive (they take an object), e.g. *look up* (*a word in a dictionary*), or intransitive (they don't take an object), e.g. *settle down*. It is important for Ss to know whether or not the verb takes an object. Remind them to check this when they look up multi-word verbs in a dictionary. Different dictionaries might show this in different ways, e.g. by including *sth* in between the two parts of the verb, e.g. *try sth on*, or by giving [I] for *intransitive* or [T] for *transitive* after the verb, e.g. *try on [T]*.

B If you've brought dictionaries, give them out for Ss to use. Ss tick the correct sentences alone, then check their answers in pairs. In feedback, elicit Ss' answers.

> **Answers:** 1 a) ✔ b) ✔ 2 a) ✔ b) ✗ 3 a) ✔ b) ✔

> **Teaching tip**
> Multi-word verbs are very common, so encourage Ss to look out for them when they are reading or listening and record them in the way that's best for them.

C Choose two of the verbs and use them in example sentences. Give Ss 5 mins to write their sentences. Monitor and check they are using the multi-word verbs correctly. When they have finished, Ss compare sentences in pairs. In feedback, nominate Ss to read out one of their partner's sentences.

> **➡ VOCABULARYBANK** p153 Multi-word verbs
>
> **1A** Write on the board *off, out, after* and *in*. Elicit multi-word verbs that have these particles and write them on the board. Ss look at sentences 1–10 to see if any of these multi-word verbs are included. Ss work alone to match the multi-word verbs to the definitions, then check their answers in pairs. In feedback, elicit the answers.
>
> **B** Ss cover the sentences and look at the pictures. Elicit what Ss can see. In pairs, Ss match the pictures to the sentences.
>
> *Stronger classes* can do the exercises at home.
>
> > **Answers:** 1A 1 b) 2 f) 3 a) 4 d) 5 g) 6 j) 7 h) 8 c) 9 i) 10 e)
> > B A 10 B 9 C 3 D 5 E 6 F 1

> **Homework ideas**
> • Ex 8A: write a list of advice for one of the situations.
> • Language bank 6.1 Ex 1–2, p139
> • Vocabulary bank p153
> • Workbook Ex 1–6, p37–38

THE PEOPLE WATCHERS

Introduction

Ss learn and practise the second conditional in the context of hypothetical situations. They also learn and practise verb–noun collocations.

SUPPLEMENTARY MATERIALS

Resource bank p153

Warm up: bring some photos of busy street scenes.

Warm up

Write on the board *Name, Age, Job* and *Likes doing at the weekend*. Put Ss into pairs. If your class looks onto the street, Ss look at people in the street and make guesses about them under the headings on the board. Alternatively, download some photos of busy street scenes and ask Ss to speculate about the people in the photos in pairs. In feedback, elicit Ss' ideas and ask if they ever do this when they are alone in public.

READING

1A Ss discuss the questions in pairs. In feedback, elicit Ss' ideas but don't give any answers yet.

B Teach/Elicit *dress up as sth*, *jump a queue*, *a complete stranger*, *bargain*, *fake* and *a badge*. Give Ss 5–6 mins to read the article and check their ideas. Tell Ss not to worry if they don't understand all the vocabulary as they'll read the article again in Ex 2.

Answers: 1 'People-watching' means looking at strangers in public to see how they behave. 2 Spies, teachers, psychologists

2A From memory, Ss answer the questions in pairs. If they need to, they can refer back to parts of the text, but should avoid reading the whole article again. In feedback, elicit Ss' answers.

Answers: 1 Two psychologists and a neuroscientist. 2 Why do we do what we do? 3 Because they thought they were getting one free. 4 None. 5 Start small and increase the size of your requests.

B Read the headings with the class and elicit what Ss can remember about each one. Don't confirm any answers yet. Give Ss 10 mins to read the article carefully and take notes alone. Monitor and help with any new vocabulary.

Answers: 1 Dr Wiseman, two psychologists, a neuroscientist and members of the public 2 People selling cakes to the public, a fake hairdresser who didn't cut any hair, a person persuading people to dress up as a tree 3 Everyone loves getting a bargain; don't always listen to experts, but trust your own eyes; if you want a favour, first ask for a small favour

Teaching tip

Review language and/or skills before Ss practise them again. Recycling language and skills helps Ss move from 'understanding' something to 'knowing' and being able to use it.

C In pairs, Ss cover the text and take it in turns to explain the article from their notes. Monitor and help as necessary. In feedback, nominate Ss to explain their notes to the class.

Alternative approach

Arrange the class into three large groups and assign one of the headings in Ex 2B to each group. Ss in each group work alone to read the article and take notes under their heading. When they have finished, arrange Ss into groups of three with one member from each of the three groups. Ss take it in turns to explain their notes, while other Ss in the group listen and take notes.

VOCABULARY verb–noun collocations

3A Elicit the first answer as an example. Ss match the verbs and nouns alone, then check their answers in pairs. In feedback, elicit Ss' answers and drill the collocations.

Answers: 1 g) 2 a) 3 b) 4 f) 5 e) 6 d) 7 c)

B Ss answer the questions in pairs. In feedback, elicit Ss' answers and give further examples if necessary.

Answers: 1 hold a sale 2 get a seat 3 raise money 4 watch a programme 5 cut hair 6 do experiments 7 jump a queue

GRAMMAR second conditional

4A Give Ss 3–4 mins to read the text and answer the question. They then check their answers in pairs. In feedback, elicit Ss' answers and write new words on the board.

Answers: The reviewer likes it because it asks some interesting questions and it's light, easy on the eye and fun.

B Ss complete the rules alone, then check their answers in pairs. In feedback, elicit Ss' answers and give further examples/explanations if necessary.

Answers: 1 hypothetical, imaginary 2 past 3 *would* 4 *could*

C Ss turn back to p71 and find further examples of the second conditional. They underline them, then check their answers in pairs. Elicit Ss' answers and drill the sentences.

Answers: If you wanted to persuade someone to dress up as a tree in public, what would you do? If you wanted to raise money for charity on the streets, who would you ask to help you? What would you do if you wanted to sell cakes and nobody was buying them? What would you do if you needed to think creatively …? If you wanted to know how to get a seat … you could find out by watching. If you bought a cake, you would get another one free. People would do better if they didn't always listen to 'experts'.

⏩ LANGUAGEBANK 6.2 p138–139

Check the notes with Ss. In both exercises, elicit the first answer as an example. Ss complete the exercises alone, then check their answers in pairs. In feedback, elicit Ss' answers.

Answers: 1 1 sold, wouldn't 2 Would your parents come, organised 3 wouldn't be, didn't pass 4 lost, you'd need to 5 'd be, they didn't eat 6 wrote, would you call 7 didn't have, they'd find 8 wouldn't work, didn't give 9 would she live, she had 10 could, he wouldn't need 2 1 If we walked to the game, we'd be late. 2 If the team entered the competition, it'd lose. 3 If you borrowed his car, he'd get angry. 4 If we called her now, we'd wake her up. 5 If we started the project again, we'd waste money. 6 If we extended our holiday, we'd miss school.

5A Give Ss 2 mins to read the conversations and predict the missing words. Elicit Ss' predictions but don't give any answers yet. Ss listen and check their answers, then compare them in pairs. In feedback, elicit Ss' answers.

Answers: 1 would you do 2 I'd 3 wouldn't be

B Read the questions with the class, then play the recording again for Ss to answer the questions. Elicit Ss' answers and drill the different forms of *would*.

Answers: 1 The full form is used: *would* /wʊd/ 2 The contracted form is used: *'d* /əd/ 3 The contracted form is usually used: *wouldn't* /ˈwʊdənt/

PRACTICE

6 Teach/Elicit *flute* and *UFO*. Read the example with the class and check Ss understand that they may need to change the form of the verbs. Ss complete the sentences alone, then check their answers in pairs. In feedback, elicit Ss' answers and drill the sentences.

Answers: 1 write, didn't have 2 had, 'd learn 3 could, 'd go 4 didn't rain, 'd like 5 wouldn't be, failed 6 would you work, didn't work 7 would you do, saw 8 saw, tell

7A Complete the first one with the class as an example and check Ss understand they need to write a different student's name for each sentence. Monitor and check Ss are forming the second conditional correctly.

B Do an example first to demonstrate and check Ss understand how to form questions from their sentences. Ss stand up and find the Ss they wrote about and ask them their question. Monitor and note down any common errors. In feedback, nominate Ss to share their true sentences with the class and correct any common errors.

SPEAKING

8A Give Ss 2–3 mins to read the questions and check any new vocabulary. Ss discuss the questions in pairs. Monitor and help with vocabulary and write any new words on the board.

B Reorganise Ss into pairs with different partners. Ss share their answers from Ex 8A and decide which dilemmas were the most difficult. In feedback, nominate Ss to share their ideas with the class.

Teaching tip

When doing speaking activities, it can be beneficial to play background music. It makes the activity more authentic (there is often background music or noise in cafés, etc.); it fills the silence between you giving instructions and Ss starting the activity and provides the momentum for Ss to start speaking; and when you want Ss to stop speaking, stopping the music creates a silence which makes Ss stop and take notice. Instrumental music is best. Avoid anything too heavy or anything in the Ss' language(s).

WRITING a letter of advice

9 Give Ss 3–4 mins to think about the questions. Monitor and help with vocabulary as needed. Ss share their experiences in small groups. In feedback, nominate Ss from each group to answer the questions about their group members.

10A Ss read the dilemma alone, then discuss possible solutions in pairs. In feedback, elicit Ss' ideas.

B Ss read the responses alone, then discuss the questions in pairs. In feedback, elicit Ss' answers.

C Ss tick the sentences alone, then compare their answers in pairs. In feedback, elicit Ss' answers.

Answers: 1 ✓ 2 ✗ 3 ✓ 4 ✓ 5 ✓

D Ss find the things they ticked in Ex 10C in the letters in Ex 10B and underline them. They then check their answers in pairs. In feedback, elicit Ss' answers.

Answers: 1 *Yes* text: 'You have the money. She has the ideas, the energy and the expertise.' *No* text: 'So your cousin wants money.' 3 *Yes* text: 'If I were you, I wouldn't worry about her age.' 'And if you're really worried, maybe tell her you want 50% of the money back within two years.' *No* text: 'If I were you, I'd ask a lot of questions first. I'd find out how much research she has done, how well she knows the market and who else is involved.' 4 *Yes* text: 'As a young person, in all likelihood she knows more about the internet than you do.' *No* text: ' … over 90% of new companies disappear within the first year.' 5 *Yes* text: 'What do you have to lose apart from a bit of money?' *No* text: 'Can you wait that long to get your money back? And think about this: if it wasn't your cousin asking, would you lend the money?'

LEARN TO qualify what you say

11A Ss find the words and phrases in the letters in Ex 10B and answer the questions in pairs. In feedback, elicit Ss' answers and drill the phrases.

Answers: 1 *probably* means there is a strong possibility. 2 *in all likelihood* and *in all probability* have the same meaning

Teaching tip

Remind Ss that qualifying what they say is important because if they don't do it, they can sound over-confident and aggressive.

B In pairs, Ss read the sentences, then discuss their feelings about them. In feedback, nominate Ss to share their ideas with the class and have a brief discussion. Read the example with the class, then Ss add the words/phrases from Ex 11A and compare their sentences in pairs. In feedback, nominate Ss to read out their sentences to the class.

12A Give Ss 3–4 mins to read the problem and check they understand it. Ss discuss and make a list of possible solutions in pairs. In feedback, nominate Ss to share their ideas with the class and ask which are the best ones.

B Give Ss 10 mins to write a letter of advice, using the letters in Ex 10B as examples and the qualifying phrases in Ex 11A.

C In small groups, Ss read out their letters and choose the best one. In feedback, nominate Ss from each group to describe the best advice letter to the class and correct any common errors.

Homework ideas
- Ex 12B: write a final draft of your letter of advice.
- Language bank 6.2 Ex 1–2, p139
- Workbook Ex 1–6, p39–40

THAT'S GREAT NEWS!

Introduction

Ss learn and practise how to give and respond to personal news.

SUPPLEMENTARY MATERIALS

Resource bank p154

Warm up

Write on the board *When was the last time you received good news? What was it? What happened? What's the best news you've ever received?* Ask Ss to discuss their answers in small groups. In feedback, nominate Ss from each group to share their experiences with the class.

VOCABULARY life events

1A Ss read the phrases and decide if they are good or bad news, then check their answers in pairs. In feedback, elicit Ss' answers and drill the phrases.

Answers: 1 G 2 B 3 G 4 G 5 G 6 B 7 B 8 B 9 G 10 G 11 G 12 G

B Ss discuss the question in pairs. Monitor and help with vocabulary where needed. In feedback, nominate Ss to share their partner's answers with the class.

2A Give Ss 3–4 mins to work alone to make a list of ways of giving bad news, e.g. *sit down*, *prepare the person*, etc. then compare their lists in pairs. In feedback, elicit Ss' ideas and write them on board.

B Check Ss understand the phrases in the box. Ss complete the article alone, then check their answers in pairs. In feedback, elicit Ss' answers and tick any of the ideas on the board that Ss mentioned.

Answers: 1 bad news 2 making people too upset 3 good news 4 Prepare your listener 5 give a reason 6 tone of voice

C In pairs, Ss discuss which pieces of advice they agree with. Encourage them to refer to their own experiences. In feedback, nominate Ss to share their opinions with the class.

FUNCTION giving news

3A Elicit Ss' ideas about what is happening in the pictures. Ss listen and match the conversations to the pictures then check their answers in pairs. In feedback, elicit Ss' answers.

Answers: 1 B 2 E 3 C 4 F 5 G 6 D 7 A

B Ss answer the question in pairs. In feedback, elicit Ss' answers and ask them to summarise each situation.

Answers: 1 good news – they are getting married; bad news – they are not inviting this person 2 good news – they were impressed with the interview; bad news – they've offered the job to someone else 3 good news – she won 1,000 euros on the lottery; bad news – she's going to spend it all on bills 4 good news – he is OK; bad news – he crashed the other person's car 5 good news – she has been offered a place at university; bad news – she is leaving home 6 good news – she got the promotion; bad news – she has to cancel the holiday 7 bad news – Steve's lost his job; good news – he is going to get £30,000 from the company

---

Unit 6 Recording 4

Conversation 1

W=Woman M=Man

W: We've got something to tell you.

M: What's that?

W: We're getting married.

M: Wow! That's fantastic. Congratulations!

W: There's one thing I've got to tell you though.

M: Really? What's that?

W: I'm afraid you're not invited.

M: Oh. That's a shame.

W: It's going to be a very small wedding.

M: I see.

Conversation 2

W=Woman M=Man

W: Hello. You came in for a job interview last week.

M: Yes, that's right.

W: Firstly, I'd like to say that we were very impressed with your interview.

M: Oh. Thank you.

W: However, I'm sorry to have to tell you, but we've offered the job to someone else.

M: Oh. That's a shame. Thanks, anyway.

W: I'm afraid the other candidate had more experience.

M: I understand.

W: But, we'd like to keep your details, in case another job comes up in the future.

M: OK.

Conversation 3

W1=1st woman W2=2nd woman

W1: You'll never guess what.

W2: What?

W1: I've just won some money on the Spanish lottery.

W2: Oh, you're joking?!

W1: No, really.

W2: That's amazing! How much did you win?

W1: One thousand euros.

W2: Oh, you lucky thing! How fantastic! How are you going to spend it?

W1: Actually, I've got so many bills to pay, I'll spend it on that.

W2: Well, it's good news anyway.

Conversation 4

M1=1st man M2=2nd man

M1: I'm afraid I've got some bad news.

M1: What is it?

M2: I've crashed the car.

M1: Oh no. That's terrible. Are you OK?

M2: Yes, I'm fine.

M1: That's lucky.

M2: But, I'm afraid the car isn't.

M1: Oh, that doesn't matter. You can get the car fixed.

M2: Unfortunately, it was your car.

M1: My car? You mean you crashed my car? How did that happen?

M2: Well, you see I …

Conversation 5

W=Woman M=Man

W: I've got some good news for you.

M: What is it?

W: You know I was waiting to hear from the university?

M: Yes.

W: Well, I'm really pleased to tell you they've offered me a place.

M: That's wonderful news. Well done! I'm so pleased for you.

W: There's only one problem.

M: What's that?

W: It means I'm leaving home.

M: Yes, of course. But it's fantastic news.

Conversation 6

W=Woman M=Man

W: Guess what!

M: What?

W: I got the promotion.

M: That's fantastic!

W: Yes, but there's something I've got to tell you.

M: What's the matter?

W: I'm sorry, but we'll have to cancel the holiday.

M: What do you mean?

W: Unfortunately, I can't go on holiday. I've got too much work to do.

M: Oh no. That's really annoying. I was looking forward to it.

W: I know. I'm really sorry.

Conversation 7

W1=1st woman W2=2nd woman

W1: Bad news, I'm afraid.

W2: What is it?

W1: Steve's lost his job.

W2: Oh no. That's awful. I'm really sorry to hear that.

W1: Do you want to hear the good news though?

W2: Yes.

W1: The company is paying him £30,000.

W2: Really?

W1: He's going to travel around the world.

W2: That's amazing.

4A Give Ss 2–3 mins to read the phrases and try to remember which ones were used. Ss listen again and write the conversation numbers. With *weaker classes*, pause the recording after each 'giving news' phrase.

Answers: I've got some good news (for you). 5; I'm really pleased to tell you … 5; You'll never guess what. 3; Bad news, I'm afraid. 7; I'm sorry to have to tell you, but … 2; I'm afraid … 4; Unfortunately, … 6; I'm afraid I've got some bad news … 4; There's something I've got to tell you. 6; You know …? Well, … 5; I've/We've got something to tell you. 1

B Write the first phrase on the board, play the recording and mark where the stressed syllables are. Ss listen to the rest of the recording and underline the stressed syllables. They then check their answers in pairs. In feedback, elicit Ss' answers.

Answers: I've <u>got</u> some <u>good</u> <u>news</u> for you. I'm <u>really</u> <u>pleased</u> to <u>tell</u> you … You'll <u>never</u> <u>guess</u> <u>what</u> … <u>Bad</u> <u>news</u> I'm <u>afraid</u>. I'm <u>sorry</u> to have to <u>tell</u> you. I'm <u>afraid</u> I've got some <u>bad</u> <u>news</u> … <u>Unfortunately</u>, there's <u>something</u> I've got to <u>tell</u> you …

C Ss listen again and answer the questions. In feedback, elicit Ss' answers. Ss then practise saying the phrases in pairs. Monitor and check they are saying them naturally.

Answer: high voice for good news, low voice for bad news

➡ LANGUAGEBANK 6.3 p138–139

Stronger classes could read the notes and do the exercise at home. Otherwise, drill the phrases from the chart, checking Ss are using natural intonation. Ss work alone to complete the conversations, then check their answers in pairs. In feedback, elicit Ss' answers. Ss can then practise the conversations in pairs.

Answers: 1 guess, joking, lucky 2 Have 3 something, sorry 4 afraid, shame, annoying

5 Elicit the first answer as an example. Ss work alone to put the words in order, then check their answers in pairs. In feedback, elicit Ss' answers and drill the sentences.

Answers: 1 Bad news, I'm afraid – we lost the match. 2 I'm really pleased to tell you that you got the job. 3 I'm afraid we're going to be late. 4 There's something I've got to tell you. 5 You'll never guess what. 6 I've got some good news for you. 7 Unfortunately, the concert was cancelled. 8 You know we lost the cat? Well, we found him again.

LEARN TO respond to news

6 Check Ss understand the words in the box. Ss complete the conversations alone, then check their answers in pairs. In feedback, elicit Ss' answers.

Answers: 1 Congratulations 2 shame 3 joking, lucky 4 terrible 5 done, pleased 6 sorry 7 annoying

speakout TIP

Read the tip with the class and explain that varied intonation can make Ss sound more polite or enthusiastic. Drill the responses with the class.

7A Ss listen and follow the intonation patterns.

B Ss practise saying the phrases in pairs.

C Ss listen and mark the stressed syllables, then check their answers in pairs. In feedback, elicit Ss' answers. Ss listen again and tick which phrases use a higher voice. Elicit Ss' answers, then Ss practise saying the phrases in pairs.

Answers: 1 You <u>lucky</u> <u>thing</u>! (high) 2 That's <u>terrible</u>. (low) 3 <u>Well</u> <u>done</u>. (high) 4 I'm <u>so</u> <u>pleased</u> for you. (high) 5 That's <u>really</u> <u>annoying</u>. (low) 6 That's <u>awful</u>. I'm <u>really</u> <u>sorry</u> to <u>hear</u> that. (low)

SPEAKING

8A Put Ss into A/B pairs. Give Ss 2 mins to read their role and think about what they're going to say. Review the language for giving and responding to news. Ss practise the dialogue in pairs. Nominate one or two pairs to perform their role-play.

B Ss prepare and practise their own role-plays. Monitor and note down any common errors. In feedback, nominate more confident pairs to perform their role-plays for the class and correct any common errors.

Alternative approach

Ss could do this as a mingling activity, walking round and giving good/bad news for other Ss to respond to.

Homework ideas

- Ex 1B: write about one of your experiences.
- Language bank 6.3 Ex 1, p139
- Workbook Ex 1–3, p41

MY WORST WEEK

Introduction

Ss watch an extract from the BBC television comedy *The Worst Week*, in which a man who is getting married loses a wedding ring. Ss learn and practise how to talk about a memorable moment in their lives and write a website entry on the same topic.

SUPPLEMENTARY MATERIALS

Warm up: write the list of things below on the board.

Warm up

Write on the board *buy rings, book the church, book a venue for the reception, order flowers, buy a dress, choose the music, arrange the food, choose a best man* and *write a speech.* Ask *Which of these things do people do when organising a wedding your country/ies? Can you add anything else to the list? Who usually organises each thing?* Ss discuss the questions in small groups. In feedback, nominate Ss from each group to share their ideas.

DVD PREVIEW

1 Teach/Elicit *a complete nightmare.* Ss read the text alone, then answer the questions in pairs.

Answers: It should be special because it's the week before his wedding. During the week, lots of things go wrong for Howard (he kills his in-law's dog, puts his fiancée's granny in hospital and loses the wedding ring twice).

Culture notes

The BBC sitcom *The Worst Week of my Life* was first screened in 2004. It follows the story of the seven days leading up to the marriage between Howard Steel, a publishing executive and his fiancée Mel, the daughter of a high court judge. The couple are plagued with bad luck and it seems that if anything can go wrong, it will. The comedy was written by Mark Bussell and Justin Sbresni and stars a number of well-known British comedians: Ben Miller (Howard), Sarah Alexander (Mel) and Janine Duvitski (Eve, Howard's assistant).

▶ DVD VIEW

2 Give Ss 1–2 mins to read the sentences. Check any new vocabulary. Play the DVD. Ss watch and put the events in the correct order. They then check their answers in pairs. In feedback, elicit Ss' answers.

Answers: a) 5 b) 6 c) 2 d) 1 e) 4 f) 3

3A Ss read the sentences and, from memory, write who says each one.

B Play the DVD again for Ss to check their answers to Ex 3A. In feedback, elicit Ss' answers.

Answers: 1 M 2 H 3 E 4 H 5 H 6 E 7 E

4A Ss complete the sentences alone. Monitor and help with vocabulary and write any new words/phrases on the board.

B Ss compare their sentences in pairs. In feedback, nominate Ss to share their ideas with the class.

Answers: 1 the wedding plans. 2 the ring. 3 not getting married herself. 4 the ring gets stuck. 5 the ring being stuck on her finger. 6 the ring goes down the plug hole.

DVD 6 The Worst Week of My Life

M=Mel H=Howard E=Eve

M: Mum said we mustn't forget to get something for the bridesmaids.

H: It's on my list.

M: And she asked, 'Have you called the video man?'

H: Yeah, yeah. I spoke to him last night. Raring to go.

M: And, er, don't forget the ring.

H: I'm picking it up on my way to work.

M: So this is it.
   Big week.

H: Yeah.

M: Nervous?

H: I'm terrified. What about you?

M: Oh God! Why didn't we just get married on a beach somewhere, just the two of us!

H: Hey, 'cause your family want you to have the most wonderful day of your life.

E: Oh, morning Howard!

H: Morning! Good weekend?

E: Yes. I made 22 jars of greengage jam. I left one on your desk.

H: Oh! Thank you.

E: Oh and Mel called, asked if you've got the ring.

H: Just picked it up from the jewellers.

E: Could you call her?

H: Absolutely.
   Was there something else?

E: I just wondered if I could have a little look at it.

H: Oh! Here. Help yourself.

E: Oh. It's lovely!

H: It's been in Mel's family for 150 years. They have this rather charming tradition where they pass it down from generation to generation. Eve? What is it?

E: Oh, I'm sorry. I always get like this about weddings.

H: Oh, don't cry.

E: I always wanted a fairytale wedding of my own.

H: Well, there's still time.

E: Do you really think so?

H: Yes!

E: I don't think so.

H: Just you believe it. One day you'll have a ring just like this on your finger.

E: Oh, in my dreams.

H: Try it on. See what it feels like.

E: Oh I can't do that! It's bad luck.

H: Come on.

E: Oh, it's lovely.

H: Hi, Mel! I was just about to call you. Yeah. I picked it up on my way in. He's reduced it by 3mm so it should fit pretty snugly now. What are you doing?

E: I can't get it off.

H: No! No! You're gonna be really pleased with it. Don't mess about, Eve.

E: No really. It's stuck!

H: Yeah, they've done a superb job.
Well, get it off!

E: I'm trying!

H: I know, I know. I can't wait to show it to your grandmother tonight.

Eve! I'm getting married in five days' time. When the vicar asks me to put the ring on my fiancée's finger it would be very nice if my secretary was not attached!

E: Oh!

H: No, nothing's wrong. Um, look I've gotta dash so I'll see you later.

E: Oh-oh …

H: Come on! Get pulling!

E: I'll er … get a plumber.

speakout memorable moments

5A Teach/Elicit *lighthouse* and *prawns*. Read the questions with the class and check Ss understand the situations. Ss listen and say which of the statements is not true. In feedback, elicit Ss' answers.

> **Answers:** 4 is not true. (They went to a blues concert.)

B Ss listen again and tick the phrases the speaker uses, then check their answers in pairs. In feedback, elicit Ss' answers and drill the phrases.

> **Answers:** ✓ One of the most memorable moments/ events in my life was … ; It all started one day when … ; I had absolutely no idea; Next thing … ; Next morning … ; That weekend is one of my happiest memories.

C Give Ss 5 mins to read the questions and choose which one they want to answer, then plan their answer alone. Remind them to use key phrases from Ex 5B. Monitor and help with vocabulary, writing any new words/phrases on the board.

D Ss tell their stories in small groups. Monitor and note down any common errors. In feedback, nominate Ss from each group to share one of their group's stories with the class and correct any common errors.

Unit 6 Recording 8

S=Stig Vatal

S: One of the most, er, memorable moments, or not moments rather events, in my life … er … was a couple of years ago. Erm … It all started one day when I was at work and my brother phoned me out of the blue and said, um, 'What are you doing the weekend of Sept 23rd?' or whatever it was. And I said, 'I don't know.' He said, 'Well, book a flight to Norway.' My brother lives in Norway and I live in England so I said, 'Why?', he said, 'Oh I'll let you know when you get there – it's a surprise.' So weeks went on and I tried to work out what this could be, but I had absolutely no idea. So the weekend in question came about … went to the airport, got on my flight and ah I was met there by somebody I'd never met before. He just came up and said, 'Are you Stig?'. I said, 'Yes.' And he said, 'OK. Come with me.' So I went with him to the car. We drove for a little while and I tried to kind of get it out of him where we were going, but he wouldn't tell me anything. He pulled up outside a hotel and there was my brother and my half brother and my two half sisters there waiting for me. I was thinking 'What on earth is going on?' And my brother just said, 'I realise we don't spend enough time together, so I've gathered you all here and I've planned a weekend for you.' We're like 'Oh, cool! So, what are we doing?' 'I'm not telling you.' 'OK fine.' Next thing we got on a boat and, er, he took us out to a lighthouse. And the first night we spent, er, eating Norwegian prawns drinking beer and we slept in a lighthouse. Next morning we got up, drove off in his car, we said, 'Where are we going?' He said, 'I'm not telling you.' He took us to a local shopping centre and said, er, 'I realise I've done OK in life. I've done better than you guys. Here have a load of money. I want you all to go shopping and buy stuff that you wouldn't normally buy with this money.' He said, 'The one condition is you're not allowed to buy a gift for me or my family.' So off we went in different directions, spent all his money and, er, bought some very nice things, met back again. In the evening, he took us out to a blues concert, then he took us for a five-course meal. And, er, we stayed that night in a very nice hotel. The next morning we had breakfast, I got back on a plane and went back to England. Yeah, that weekend is one of my happiest memories.

writeback a website entry

6A Ss read the website entry alone, then answer the questions in pairs. In feedback, elicit Ss' answers.

> **Answers:** People from around the world share their personal experiences and stories. Ross's car journey was special because it was a clear night with a full moon and he talked with his friends. The roads were empty and there was a feeling of adventure. The air was warm and he remembers the music they listened to.

B Make sure Ss choose a different question from Ex 5C than the one they spoke about in Ex 5D. Ss write their stories alone. Monitor and help with vocabulary where needed. When they have finished, Ss show their website entries to their partner.

> **Teaching tip**
>
> *Weaker Ss* may need more assistance with planning their website entries. Before they start writing, write the following on the board *When did this happen? Where were you? Which other people were involved? What happened? How did you feel? Why was it memorable? Has it happened again in your life? What was the best thing about the moment?* Give Ss 5 mins to take notes and plan their answers to the questions. Monitor and help with ideas where necessary. When they are ready, Ss can write their website entry as in Ex 6B.

Homework ideas
• **Ex 6B:** write a final draft of your website entry.

LOOKBACK

Introduction

Ss revise and practise the language of Unit 6. The notes below provide ideas for exploiting the exercises and activities but your approach will depend on your aim, e.g. whether you use the activities as a diagnostic or progress test or as revision/fluency practice. If done as a test then it would not be appropriate to monitor or help Ss.

-ING/-ED ADJECTIVES

1A In pairs, Ss use adjectives to describe how they feel in the given situations. With *weaker classes*, elicit the first one as an example. In feedback, elicit the adjectives and drill them.

> **Possible answers:** 1 annoyed 2 frightened 3 bored
> 4 embarrassed

B Read the examples with the class. Ss choose five of the adjectives and write a situation for each. Monitor and help with vocabulary and write any new words/phrases on the board.

C Ss read the situations out to their partner for them to guess the adjective. Make sure they don't say their adjective when reading out the situation. In feedback, nominate some Ss to read out their situations for the class to guess the adjective.

ZERO AND FIRST CONDITIONALS

2A Elicit the first answer as an example. Ss match the sentence halves alone, then check their answers in pairs. In feedback, elicit Ss' answers.

> **Answers:** 1 b) 2 f) 3 d) 4 c) 5 a) 6 g) 7 e)

B Ss complete the sentences alone, using their own ideas, then compare their endings in pairs. In feedback, nominate Ss to share their endings with the class.

> **Alternative approach**
> Once they have written alternative endings, Ss read out only the endings to their partner in random order. Their partner guesses which sentence they are finishing.

3 Demonstrate by writing on the board three things you want to achieve this year. Give Ss 2–3 mins to write three things they would like to achieve. Monitor and help with vocabulary where needed. Refer Ss back to your list on the board and elicit possible advice. Ss read out their goals and give advice in pairs. In feedback, ask Ss what advice they received.

VERB–NOUN COLLOCATIONS

4 Read the example with the class. Ss rearrange the letters alone, then check their answers in pairs. In feedback, elicit Ss' answers.

> **Answers:** 1 get seats 2 hold a sale 3 raise money
> 4 watch a programme 5 do experiments 6 cuts hair

> **Optional extra activity**
> In pairs, Ss discuss which of the sentences are true for them.

SECOND CONDITIONAL

5 Focus Ss attention on the A and B prompt boxes and read the example with the class. Ss use the prompts in the boxes to form second conditional sentences in pairs. In feedback, go through each of the phrases in the box, nominating a different pair each time to share their sentences with the class.

> **Answers:** If I was rich, I'd give money to charity. If there was no war, the world would be more peaceful. If there were more hours in the day, people would work more. If I had more energy, I'd dance all night. If nobody smoked, people would be healthier. If I gave up coffee, I'd sleep better. If I could paint well, I'd do a portrait of you.

GIVING NEWS

6A Read the example with the class and check Ss understand they may have to change the punctuation. Ss add the missing words alone, then check their answers in pairs. In feedback, elicit Ss' answers.

> **Answers:** 1 A: Bad news, *I'm* afraid. B: What's the matter? A: The computers aren't working. B: Not again! *That's* annoying. 2 A: You'll never *guess* what. B: What? A: I got the job B: Congratulations! That's *great/fantastic* news.
> 3 A: I've got some good news *for* you. B: What is it? A: I've been promoted. B: Well *done*. That's great news.
> 4 A: I'm *sorry* to have to tell you, but I'm leaving the company. B: What? Why? A: The company has got problems, so they're reducing the number of managers. B: I'm sorry to *hear* that. 5 A: You *know* that exam I did last week? B: Yes? A: Well, I passed. B: Congratulations! I'm so *pleased* for you.

B Ss practise the conversations in pairs. Monitor and check Ss are using natural intonation. In feedback, nominate Ss to perform one or two of the conversations for the class.

> **Optional extra activity**
> As an extension, give Ss 3 mins to work alone and think of any news they can give about things that have just happened or are going to happen in their lives, using the ideas in Lesson 6.3 Ex 1A to help. When they are ready, Ss mingle and share their own news. Monitor and encourage other Ss to ask follow-up questions and use the language for responding to news. In feedback, elicit ideas from one or two Ss.

> **Homework ideas**
> • Workbook Review and check 3, p42–44
> • Workbook Test 3, p45

OVERVIEW

BBC VIDEO PODCAST
What has been your greatest achievement?

This video podcast extends discussion of the unit topic to achievements. Ss can view people talking about their greatest achievements and how they did them. Use this video podcast at the start or end of Unit 7.

THE SECRET OF SUCCESS

Introduction

Ss learn and practise the present perfect simple and continuous in the context of success. They also learn verb phrases with prepositions.

SUPPLEMENTARY MATERIALS

Resource bank p156 and p157

Warm up

Write on the board *What's the best way to be successful at learning English?* Ss discuss the question in pairs, then join other pairs and share their ideas. Elicit Ss' ideas in feedback and see if everyone agrees.

SPEAKING

1A Ss read the quotes and discuss the questions in pairs. In feedback, check Ss understand the quotes and elicit which ones they agree/disagree with.

B Give Ss 2 mins to think of and write the names of three successful people. They could be famous people or people they know. If Ss are stuck for ideas, they can choose people from the photos at the foot of p80–81. They then write answers to the three questions.

VOCABULARY success

2A Read the example with the class. Ss complete the sentences alone, then check their answers in pairs. In feedback, elicit Ss' answers and drill the phrases.

Answers: 1 work hard 2 have a natural talent
3 believe in yourself 4 have the opportunity 5 practise
6 be a high achiever 7 focus on 8 get better at

Teaching tip

When Ss learn new words, it's a good idea for them to also learn which prepositions, verb patterns, etc. come after them. If they record new words as whole phrases, it makes them easier to retrieve correctly and it's more likely that Ss will learn and use them.

B Ss match the definitions to six of the phrases in Ex 2A. Make sure they understand that two of the phrases don't have definitions. In feedback, elicit Ss' answers and give further explanations/examples if necessary.

Answers: 1 believe in yourself 2 focus on 3 get better at
4 practise 5 have the opportunity (to do something)
6 be a high achiever

C First, give an example about yourself using one of the phrases. Ss choose two of the phrases and write a true sentence for each, then compare their sentences in pairs. In feedback, nominate Ss to share their partner's sentences with the class.

➡ **VOCABULARYBANK** p154 Success

1A Read the two examples, then Ss match the rest of the definitions to the expressions in pairs. In feedback, elicit Ss' answers.

B Focus attention on the pictures and elicit what Ss can see. Ss work alone to complete the captions, then check their answers in pairs.

Stronger classes can do the exercise at home.

Answers: 1A 1 b) 2 a) 3 c) 4 d) 5 f) 6 e) 7 g) 8 h) 9 j) 10 i) 1B 1 came 2 runner up 3 medal 4 prize 5 got 6 nominated 7 awarded 8 shortlist 9 award 10 winning

LISTENING

3A Focus attention on the title and elicit what Ss think the programme is about. Ss read and check their predictions, then discuss what they think the secret of success is. In feedback, elicit Ss' ideas.

B Ss listen to the recording, then check their predictions in pairs. In feedback, elicit the answer.

Answer: They all practised at least 10,000 hours.

C Ss complete the summary from memory. They then listen again and check. In feedback, elicit Ss' answers.

Answers: 1 common 2 practised 3 successful 4 skill 5 10,000 6 successful

4A Give Ss 3–4 mins to read the sentences and decide if they are true or false.

B Ss listen again and check their answers to Ex 4A in pairs. In feedback, elicit Ss' answers.

Answers: 1 T 2 F 3 T 4 T 5 F 6 F

Unit 7 Recording I

P=Presenter I=Ian

P: Hello and welcome back to the *Focus* podcast. I'm Jenny Osmond, the editor of Focus, the monthly science and technology magazine from the BBC.
He's the hugely influential author of *Blink* and the *Tipping Point*. His work is quoted by academics, presidents and your mates down the pub. And now Malcolm Gladwell has turned that deft mind of his to a new subject: the science of success. In his new book, *The Outliers*, Gladwell argues that if we want to be successful, we should think less about what successful people are like and more about where they have come from and the opportunities they have had along the way. Now, Ian's read the book and he joins me. Now … his new book is looking at success …

I: Yes and what he says is, erm, that if we think about somebody like Bill Gates, hugely successful person and we want to learn from, from his achievements, then what do we look at? We look at what that man is like, you know, what drives him, what does he do on a day-to-day basis, how can we be more like him? Erm … But what Gladwell argues in the new book is, is that we should pay less attention to that side of stuff and look at where Bill Gates came from. So, how did he get to where he got to, the opportunities he had along the way. Erm … And what he says is that Bill Gates has one thing in common with another group of very successful people, The Beatles.

P: So, what's that?

I: Well, they both practised what they do and they practised a lot.

P: Right, so how much is a lot?

I: A lot is 10,000 hours. That's like the magic number if you're going to become world-class at anything in the world, you need to put 10,000 hours' practice in.

P: Oh, OK.

I: So, The Beatles, they, they were doing gigs, you know, like all-night gigs in Hamburg, in these little clubs and just the number of hours that they put in on the stage, erm, allowed them to master their craft. And the same with Bill Gates. He, er, as he was growing up, got into computer programming and through a very fortunate series of events, he was able to programme and programme and programme, erm and again …

P: Because he had access to computers at a time when these things were developing.

I: Absolutely! … Exactly! The timing is so, so important. He happened to go to a university, erm, where he had access to er, a computer programming unit. I mean, this was back in the 60s and 70s when computers were the size of rooms and stuff. Erm and so what Gladwell does throughout the book is pick up on these little things that we really need to go back and look at again if we are to really understand why successful people are as successful as they are.

P: I think the 10,000 hours magic number is really interesting because, as you know, I used to play tennis professionally and I hit a load of tennis balls when I was younger. And I'm sure, I must have done 10,000 hours' worth, you know, I must have done four hours a day and stuff. And I remember speaking to Martina Hingis' mum about why she thought her kid was so good and such a prodigy and she basically said, 'My daughter has been hitting tennis balls since the age of three and she has hit X number of tennis balls for X number of hours and it's, you know, I'm sure she's … So once you're over that magic number of 10,000 … yeah

I: The same goes for people like Beethoven, erm … It's incredible how …

P: But at the end of the day you have to have talent.

I: You've got to have raw talent, you've got to have belief in what you can do and you have to have the will to put those hours in … but you also need the opportunity.

SPEAKING

5 Give Ss 2 mins to read the questions and think about their answers. Ss discuss the questions in small groups. Monitor and note down any common errors for later correction. In feedback, nominate Ss from each group to share their group's ideas with the class.

GRAMMAR present perfect simple versus continuous

6A First, do sentence a) as an example. Ss underline and circle the examples in the rest of the sentences alone, then check their answers in pairs. In feedback, elicit Ss' answers.

Answers:
a) Martina 's been playing tennis since she was three years old. b) She 's been going to ballet lessons since she was a child. c) I've known Max for years. d) How long have you been studying French? e) He's always enjoyed playing sport.

B Ss read the rules alone. Check Ss understand the rules, then elicit an example from Ex 6A that goes with rule 1. Make sure Ss understand that all the rules have more than one example. Ss match the examples alone, then check their answers in pairs. In feedback, elicit Ss' answers and give further examples if necessary. If Ss are still uncertain, ask them to read the rules in the **Language bank** on p140.

Answers: 1 sentences a), b) and d) 2 sentences c) and e) 3 sentences a), b), c) and d)

Teaching tip

The present perfect simple and continuous are difficult for Ss, both in terms of form and meaning. Ss need lots of exposure and practice before they will fully understand these tenses. The important thing is to keep practising them. Explain this to Ss and don't get frustrated if they are still making mistakes with these tenses long after you've taught them.

⮕ LANGUAGEBANK 7.1 p140–141

Stronger classes could read the notes and do the exercises at home. Otherwise, check the notes with Ss, especially the use of state verbs and the difference between *for* and *since*. In both exercises, elicit the first answer as an example. Ss can refer back to the notes to help. In feedback, elicit Ss' answers.

Answers: 1 1 've been sitting 2 've been studying 3 've been waiting 4 've (always) hated 5 's been doing 6 haven't been listening 7 's been teaching 8 have (you) been living 9 haven't been watching, 've been reading 10 haven't known
2 1 seen 2 known 3 met 4 've been playing 5 has been travelling 6 enjoyed 7 've been waiting 8 have been studying

PRACTICE

7A Elicit the first answer as an example. Ss complete the rest of the sentences alone, then check their answers in pairs. Monitor and check Ss are forming the tenses correctly. Don't elicit any answers at this stage.

Answers: 1 've been writing 2 've been playing 3 've (always) loved 4 hasn't been studying 5 have (you) known 6 've been learning 7 've had 8 heard

B Ss listen to the sentences and check their answers to Ex 7A. Play the recording again for Ss to decide if *have* is strong or weak. In feedback, elicit the answer. With *weaker classes*, before they listen to decide if *have* is strong or weak, write on the board *They've been playing football.* and *Have you seen my keys?* In another space on the board write /həv/ and /ev/. Read the sentences out naturally and ask Ss to match the phonemic transcriptions to the sentences.

Answer: *have* is weak except for *I haven't written a best seller yet* in sentence 1

8A Elicit the first question orally as an example. Ss write the questions alone, then check them in pairs. In feedback, elicit the correct questions and drill them, focusing attention on the weak form of *have*.

Answers: 1 How long have you known your best friend?
2 How long have you done/been doing your hobby for?
3 How long have you been studying English? 4 How long have you lived/been living where you live now? 5 How have you spent/been spending your days off recently?

B Read the example with the class and point out that we use the past simple to talk about further details. Ss ask and answer the questions in pairs. Monitor and note down any common errors with the present perfect. In feedback, nominate Ss to share their partner's answers with the class and correct any common errors.

VOCABULARY *PLUS* verb phrases

9A Introduce the topic by writing on the board *I like listening music.* Ask *What's wrong with this sentence?* (The preposition 'to' is missing.) Explain that we often use prepositions with verbs and which preposition we use depends on the verb. Ss choose the correct prepositions alone, then check their answers in pairs. In feedback, elicit Ss' answers.

Answers: 1 with 2 to 3 at 4 in 5 about 6 on 7 for

B Ss add the verbs from Ex 9A to the correct groups, then check their answers in pairs. In feedback, elicit Ss' answers.

Answers: 1 have (a lot) in common 2 think 3 have access 4 has a talent 5 pick up 6 be (good/world class) 7 put

speakout TIP

Read the tip with the class and highlight the importance of recording verbs with their prepositions. This will make it easier for Ss to recall and use the verbs correctly at a later stage. Ss work in pairs and add verbs to each group in Ex 9B. In feedback, elicit Ss' answers.

C Read the examples with the class, then give Ss 5 mins to write their three questions. Early finishers can write an extra question. Monitor and check Ss are forming the questions correctly and help with vocabulary where necessary.

D Ss ask and answer their questions in pairs. In feedback, nominate Ss to share their partner's answers with the class.

⮕ VOCABULARYBANK p154 Verb phrases

1A Elicit the first answer as an example. Ss work alone to complete the sentences, then check their answers in pairs. In feedback, elicit Ss' answers.

B In pairs, Ss match the definitions to the verb phrases in Ex 1A.

Stronger classes can do the exercise at home.

Answers: 1A 1 with 2 about 3 to 4 for 5 on 6 in
B a) write about b) care for c) stick to d) take part in e) work for f) lead to, result in g) work on h) part with i) go on j) cope with k) protest about

Homework ideas

- Ex 5: write about your answers to the questions.
- Language bank 7.1 Ex 1–2, p141
- Vocabulary bank p154
- Workbook Ex 1–7, p46–47

THE MEMORY MEN

Introduction

Ss learn and practise language to describe present and past ability in the context of people with extraordinary memory. They also practise writing a summary.

SUPPLEMENTARY MATERIALS

Resource bank p155 and p158

Warm up

Write on the board *the name of your first pet, what you were doing last Sunday at 4p.m., the name of the last person you spoke to before class, a joke* and *what we learnt last lesson*. In pairs, Ss discuss which of the things they can remember. In feedback, elicit some of the information.

SPEAKING

1 Tell Ss one thing you are good at and one thing you aren't very good at and encourage Ss to ask you questions about them. Read the examples with the class. Ss ask and answer their questions in pairs. In feedback, nominate Ss to share their partner's information with the class.

VOCABULARY   ability

2A Ss discuss the meanings in pairs. If possible, give out dictionaries for Ss to check their ideas. In feedback, elicit Ss' answers.

Answers: 1 with special skills or knowledge of a subject 2 having a natural ability to do something 3 the state of being able to do something 4 good at doing something that you have learned and practised 5 a natural ability or skill, especially in learning 6 have a natural ability to do something well 7 and 8 very bad at doing something

B Read the questions with the class and check they understand them. Ss answer the questions in pairs, then listen to the recording to check. In feedback, elicit Ss' answers.

Answers: 1 <u>ex</u>pert <u>gif</u>ted <u>a</u>bility <u>skil</u>ful <u>ap</u>titude <u>tal</u>ented <u>hope</u>less <u>use</u>less 2 expert gifted skilful hopeless useless The stress is normally on the first syllable.

C Play the recording again, but pause after each sentence for Ss to repeat. Listen and help with their pronunciation.

3A First give Ss some examples from your own life to demonstrate. Ss work alone and write down the names. Don't elicit any answers yet.

B Ss explain their answers in small groups. Encourage other Ss to ask follow-up questions. In feedback, nominate Ss from each group to share their group's answers with the class.

READING

4A Tell Ss to cover the text and look at the photo, then discuss the question in pairs. In feedback, elicit Ss' ideas.

B Put Ss into A/B pairs. Student As read the text on p83 and Student Bs read the text on p161 to see if any of their ideas are mentioned. Tell Ss not to worry about new vocabulary at this stage as they'll read the text again in Ex 4C. Set a strict time limit of 3 mins. In feedback, elicit Ss' answers.

C Ss read their texts again, working alone to answer the questions. Monitor and help with any vocabulary, but encourage them to try and work out meanings themselves.

Answers: 1 Stephen couldn't make friends. In fact, he talked to nobody, showed no interest in school subjects and wasn't able to sit still. Daniel couldn't make friends. Aged eight, he was able to calculate 82 × 82 × 82 × 82 in his head, but he couldn't tie his own shoe laces, or ride a bicycle. 2 Stephen is a brilliant artist. His eye for detail is perfect. He can see a building just once and remember everything about it. Daniel has an incredible ability with numbers. 3 Stephen appeared on a TV programme drawing a complicated building. Daniel appeared on a TV programme and recited 22,514 numbers from pi perfectly. 4 Stephen has been to London (England), Rome (Italy), Hong Kong and Tokyo (Japan). He drew pictures of the cities from a helicopter. Daniel went to Iceland and learned Icelandic in a week. 5 Stephen has published four books of his drawings. Daniel published a book, *Born on a Blue Day*. 6 Stephen works in his own art gallery in London. Daniel runs a language teaching business on the internet.

D Ss tell their partner about their text, using the answers to the questions in Ex 4C. Encourage Ss to ask further questions.

Teaching tip

The activity in Ex 4C and Ex 4D is called 'jigsaw reading'. It provides real communication and closely mimics real-life language use by integrating reading and speaking skills. Make sure Ss don't look at the texts when summarising for their partner, as this forces them to relay the information in their own words. Of course, if they get stuck, they can look back quickly.

GRAMMAR   present and past ability

5 Read the example with the class. Ss answer the questions alone, then check their answers in pairs. In feedback, elicit Ss' answers and give further explanations if necessary.

Answers: 1 present ability 2 past ability 3 past ability (negative) 4 present ability 5 past ability 6 past ability (negative) 7 present ability 8 past ability 9 past ability (negative)

⟩⟩⟩ **LANGUAGEBANK** 7.2 p140–141

Check the charts and the notes with Ss', especially the fact that we use *be able to* to talk about one particular situation.

1 Teach/Elicit *crawl*. Ss work alone to find the mistakes, then check their answers in pairs. Elicit Ss' answers.

2 Elicit the first sentence as an example. Ss work alone to write the sentences, then check their answers in pairs. In feedback, elicit Ss' answers and drill the sentences.

Answers: 1 Johnny isn't able *to* make full sentences but he *can* to *say* several words. He *is* able to understand …; he managed *to* crawl …; he sometimes manages to *draw* simple pictures. 2 1 She can ride 2 I can't play 3 weren't able to 4 Did you manage 5 Are you able 6 manage to sleep 7 Could you run 8 haven't managed to

PRACTICE

6 Ss complete the text alone, then check their answers in pairs. In feedback, elicit Ss' answers and ask them to explain why they are correct.

Answers: 1 managed 2 able 3 couldn't 4 can't 5 isn't 6 can 7 to 8 could

SPEAKING

7A Focus attention on the pictures and check that Ss understand the actions. Ss read the instructions and tick the activities alone, then check their answers in pairs.

B Ss share their experiences in small groups, using the questions to help. Encourage other Ss to ask follow-up questions.

WRITING a summary

8A Give Ss 2–3 mins to read the summary alone, then answer the questions in pairs. In feedback, elicit Ss' answers.

Answers: 1 yes 2 shorter 3 he/she uses his/her own words

B Read the example with the class to show how the details have been summarised. In pairs Ss find the details/missing information in the text. In feedback, elicit Ss' answers.

Answers: 2 p161 lines 8–14; 3 p161 lines 11–12 p83 lines 11–14; 4 p83 line 10 p161 last line; 5 p83 lines 2–5 p161 lines 4–17

LEARN TO make notes for a summary

Teaching tip
Note-taking is a useful skill, particularly if Ss want to study in English. Stress the importance of this skill before you begin.

9A Check Ss understand exactly what they are looking for. Ss find the examples alone, then check their answers in pairs. In feedback, elicit Ss' answers.

Answers: 1 info 2 a) & b) → 3 2 (to)
4 THE MEMORY MEN 5 The artist, The mathematician 6 things he sees, numbers

B Ss discuss the suggestions and change the bad ideas in pairs. In feedback, elicit Ss' answers.

Answers: Good ideas: 1, 2, 4, 5, 6, 8 Bad ideas: 3 (try to write down the key words), 7 (do use your own words)

10A Give Ss 1 min to read the words in the box and check they understand them. Ss listen and tick the things the people talk about, then check their answers in pairs. In feedback, elicit Ss' answers.

Answers: names, faces, dates, words, birthdays, directions to places, films, jokes, information about products

B Ss read the notes about Peggy and, in pairs, discuss what they can remember about John and Tim. Ss listen again and take notes. Play the recording again if necessary.

Answers: JOHN: Job: Actor Memory: needs 2 remember lines (words) & 'blocking' (where 2 stand or move), bad at birthdays & dates
TIM: Job: History student Memory: needs 2 remember dates & names, bad at jokes & films

C Ss compare their notes in pairs and use the words in the box to help them remember other details. In feedback, nominate Ss to share what they can remember with the class.

Unit 7 Recording 4

T=Tim J=John P=Peggy

T: So what about your memory, Peggy? How good is it?
P: It's OK, which is lucky 'cos I need to remember lots of things.
J: Like what?
P: Well, I'm a sales rep for a publishing company so I'm usually out visiting schools, trying to sell books.
J: So you need to remember … what exactly?
P: Oh, lots of things. The worst thing when I started was just trying to remember how to get to these schools in my car. I used to get lost all the time. I'm not very good at directions. Then once you're there you have to remember the names and faces of the people you're talking to. I once spent a whole hour calling this woman Sally when her name was Samantha.
T: And she didn't tell you?
P: For some reason she didn't tell me. And then there's all the product information.
J: Product information? What, the books?
P: Yes. We sell about five hundred different books and I have to know the difference between all of them. I mean, it gets easier, thank goodness, but I still make mistakes occasionally. What about you, John? You're an actor, right?
J: Yeah. The main thing I have to remember is my lines. Fortunately, I've got a good memory for words and I don't find it that hard to memorise them. So, I mean, yeah. The other thing you have to remember when you're in the theatre is the blocking.
T: What's that?
J: Blocking? It's where you stand or move to, y'know? Like, when you say your words you might have to walk quickly across the stage. Or move in front of someone. It's all planned and er, you have to remember it.
T: Oh, I see.
J: But it's funny: for, for other things I have a terrible memory. I'm totally useless. I always forget birthdays and dates. I'm always late for things. It's just … yeah … luckily, I'm OK with my lines.
P: What about you, Tim?
T: I'm probably the same as all other students. At least all other history students. I have to memorise dates and also names. But it's not that difficult because you read about them so much you can't really forget them. But for other things I have a really bad memory. I can never remember jokes or films. Sometimes I'm watching a film and after an hour I realise I've seen it already. I'm completely hopeless like that.
J: Oh, me too …

11A Ss discuss the questions in pairs. Make sure Ss take notes about their partner, as they'll write a summary later. Monitor and encourage them to ask follow-up questions to find out as much information as possible.

B Give Ss 10 mins to write their summaries. Tell Ss not to include the name of their partner. Monitor and help with vocabulary, writing any new words/phrases on the board. When they have finished, Ss swap summaries with their partner, who reads and checks they are correct. Then collect all the summaries and redistribute them to different Ss. Ss read them and guess who each summary is describing. In feedback, ask Ss if they found out anything interesting or surprising about a classmate.

Homework ideas
• Ex 7B: write about your abilities.
• Language bank 7.2 Ex 1–2, p141
• Workbook Ex 1–6, p48–49

ARE YOU QUALIFIED?

Introduction

Ss learn and practise how to clarify opinions and refer to what they said earlier in the context of qualifications.

SUPPLEMENTARY MATERIALS

Resource bank p159

Warm up

Explain the following dilemma: *You are the manager of a small company and are interviewing someone for a job as a researcher. All the other researchers in your company have a degree. The person you are interviewing has said on their CV that they have a degree, but you know this person from your school (they don't recognise you) and you know they left school at 16 with no qualifications. However, by the answers they gave to your questions, you also think that this person is able to do the job. What would you do?* In pairs, Ss discuss the options and what they would do. In feedback, elicit Ss' ideas.

VOCABULARY qualifications

1A Read the example with the class. Ss discuss the question and write a list of jobs in pairs. Monitor and help with vocabulary where needed. In feedback, elicit Ss' ideas and write the jobs on the board.

B Ss read the text, then answer the question in pairs. In feedback, elicit the answer.

Answers: Steve Eichel applied for and got, a number of diplomas and a degree in hypnotherapy for his cat because he was worried about the number of therapists with false diplomas and degrees and he wanted to see how easy it was to get these.

2A Focus attention on the words in bold. Ss discuss the meanings in pairs. Make sure they don't answer the questions yet. In feedback, elicit Ss' answers and ask *Which words can you see in the photos?*

Answers: 1 qualifications: if you have a qualification, you have passed an exam or course to show you have a particular level or skill in a subject 2 certificate: an official document that shows something is true or correct, e.g. a document showing the exams you have passed 3 driving licence: an official card that says you are legally allowed to drive a car; licence: an official document that gives you permission to do or own something 4 online course: a series of lessons done using computers 5 distance learning: a method of study that involves working at home and sending your work to your teacher; face-to-face learning: studying with another person, i.e. talking to them in the same room 6 do an apprenticeship: work for an employer for a fixed amount of time in order to learn a skill 7 degree: a qualification you get when you finish a course at university 8 MA: a university degree that you can study for after your first degree; PhD: the highest university degree Getting a degree, distance learning and face-to-face learning are shown in the pictures.

B Ss discuss the questions in groups. In feedback, nominate Ss to share their answers with the class.

Culture notes

In England and Wales, people usually take a General Certificate of Secondary Education (GSCE) in around 10 subjects at 16. If they want to go to university, then they study 3–4 A levels from 16–18, either at school or at college. People usually start university at 18 and most undergraduate degrees last 3–4 years. This leads to either a Bachelor of Arts (BA) or a Bachelor of Science (BSc) degree. After that, they can study for postgraduate degrees, such as an MA, MSc, MBA and/or PhD.

FUNCTION clarifying opinions

3A Ss discuss the question in pairs. In feedback, elicit Ss' ideas and have a brief discussion.

B Read the possible answers with the class. Ss listen and answer the question, then check it in pairs. Tell Ss not to worry if they don't understand everything at this stage as they'll listen again in Ex 3C. In feedback, elicit the answer.

Answers: b intelligent people

C Ss answer the questions in pairs, then listen again and check. In feedback, elicit Ss' answers.

Answers: 1 Because he can sell things in about fifteen languages; he guesses where you're from by looking at you; and he learned the languages by talking to tourists. 2 One friend built his own house. Another takes parts of old cars and makes new cars from them. 3 They show that you are motivated and committed enough to complete a course. 4 These give you an amazing education too.

Unit 7 Recording 5

M=Man W=Woman

M: It's interesting: one of the most intelligent people I know is a ten-year-old boy from Egypt. He doesn't go to school and he works on a street in Cairo, in one of the touristy areas. And he sells things like small statues of the pyramids, things like that, to tourists. Now, the reason I say he's intelligent is that he can sell you something in about fifteen languages. I once spent an afternoon watching him and it was incredible. Most of the time he uses English, but he guesses where you're from by looking at you and then he starts speaking. He can speak just a little bit of French, Spanish, Japanese, Italian, German, etcetera. It's amazing. He knows just enough in all these languages to say hello and sell you something.

W: How did he learn the languages?

M: I asked him that and he said he learned them by talking to tourists.

W: That is quite amazing.

M: So anyway, that's my example. Like I said, he doesn't go to school but, for me, he's super-intelligent. What about you?

W: I can think of loads of people who don't have any qualifications but are able to do really difficult things. I've got a friend, for example, who built his own house. He just taught himself how to do it, bought a piece of land, bought the materials and the equipment and just did it. No qualifications, no certificates, no university degree. In my view, that's a real practical kind of intelligence.

M: I couldn't do that.

W: Let me give you another example. I've got another friend who takes parts of old cars and makes new cars from them. He does it at the weekend as a way to relax. And the new car actually works!

M: I couldn't do that either.

W: I wouldn't know where to start. And this is someone who left school at fifteen to do an apprenticeship. But, you know, having said that, I do think qualifications are useful in some ways. I mean, for one thing, they show that you are able to complete a course, that you're motivated and committed enough.

M: Yeah, I think that's true.

W: But I must say real life experience, travelling, going out and meeting people, talking … I think these give you an amazing education, too.

M: Exactly. That's what I was saying. Just like the boy from Egypt.

4A Ss complete the phrases alone, then check in pairs. In feedback, elicit Ss' answers.

Answers: 1 reason 2 my 3 give 4 one

B Ss listen to the phrases, paying attention to which word is stressed, then check their answers in pairs. With *weaker classes*, you may also need to say the phrases yourself, exaggerating the stressed word. In feedback, elicit Ss' answers.

Answers: The second word is stressed.

Unit 7 Recording 6

1 In my view
2 I do think
3 I must say
4 For one thing

C Play the recording, pausing after each sentence for Ss to repeat. Make sure they are stressing the correct words.

Unit 7 Recording 7

1 In my view, that's a real practical kind of intelligence.
2 I do think qualifications are useful in some ways.
3 But I must say real life experience, travelling and meeting people give you an amazing education too.
4 For one thing, they show you are able to complete a course.

LANGUAGEBANK 7.3 p140–141

Stronger classes could read the notes and do the exercise at home. Otherwise, drill the sentences in the charts. Elicit the first answer in Ex 1 as an example. Ss work alone to choose the correct alternatives, then check their answers in pairs. In feedback, elicit Ss' answers.

Answers: 1 For example, 2 in my view 3 I must say 4 Let me give you an example: 5 I do think 6 for me, 7 The reason I say this is because 8 For another,

5 Read the example with the class. Ss complete the sentences alone, then check their answers in pairs and discuss if they agree with the sentences. In feedback, elicit Ss' answers and opinions and have a brief discussion.

Answers: 1 must, For example, 2 For, For one 3 In my, The reason I 4 I do, Let me give you

LEARN TO refer to what you said earlier

6 Read the questions with the class and check they understand them. Ss read the phrases and answer the questions in pairs. In feedback, elicit Ss' answers and drill the phrases.

Answers: 1 c) 2 a) 3 b)

7 Ss complete the conversation alone, then check it in pairs. In feedback, elicit Ss' answers and ask *Do you agree with the opinions?*

Answers: Having said that, Like I said, That's what I was saying.

SPEAKING

8A Give Ss 2 mins to read the advertisement and answer the question. In feedback, elicit Ss' answers.

Answers: tour guide licence, university degree, basic qualifications in biology/land management

B Put Ss into groups of three. If your class doesn't divide by three, have one or two pairs, who only read Candidate A and Candidate B's information. Ss read the profiles and answer the questions alone. Monitor and help with vocabulary where needed.

C Ss present their candidate's information to their group, then decide together who should get the job and why. In feedback, nominate Ss from each group to share their ideas with the whole class.

Homework ideas
• Language bank 7.3 Ex 1, p141
• Workbook Ex 1–2, p50

WATER SKI CHALLENGE

Introduction

Ss watch an extract from a BBC magazine show in which one of the presenters water skis across the English Channel for charity.

SUPPLEMENTARY MATERIALS

Ex 6B: if you have access to the internet in class, load up www.bbc.co.uk/my-story (correct at the time of going to press).

Warm up: write the words below on the board.

Warm up

Write on the board *bungee jumping, mountain climbing, snowboarding, white-water rafting, hanggliding* and *doing a parachute jump*. Ask *What do we call these types of sport?* (extreme sports). Ss discuss in pairs if they or anyone they know has done them and what it was like.

▶ DVD PREVIEW

1 Ss discuss the questions in small groups. Monitor and help with vocabulary and write any new words/phrases on the board. In feedback, nominate Ss from each group to share their ideas with the class.

2A Ss read the text and answer the questions alone, then check their answers in pairs. In feedback, elicit Ss' answers.

Answers: To water ski across the English Channel to France. She's doing it to raise money for Sport Relief. She had never water skied before, she does the crossing in the middle of winter and she's only had a few months of training.

Culture notes

Sport Relief is a biennial event which runs over one long weekend and is co-produced by BBC Sport. Celebrities take on sporting challenges in order to raise money for charity. It began in 2002 and was a joint venture between BBC Sport and Comic Relief. At the heart of the event is the Sport Relief Mile, where everyone around the country, regardless of age or physical ability, is invited to walk, run, wheel, bounce or crawl a mile to raise money for charity. If Ss are interested, they can find out more and get involved at www.sportrelief.com.

B Ss match the words/phrases in bold in the text with the definitions. In feedback, elicit Ss' answers and drill the words/phrases.

Answers: 1 tough 2 attempted 3 give up 4 a challenge 5 outstanding 6 determination

▶ DVD VIEW

3 Give Ss 1 min to read the summaries. Play the DVD. Ss watch and choose the correct summary, then check their answer in pairs. In feedback, elicit the correct summary.

Answer: summary 3

4A Give Ss a few minutes to read the statements. Play the DVD again. Ss watch and put the statements in the order they hear them. They then check their answers in pairs. In feedback, elicit Ss' answers.

Answers: a) 5 b) 4 c) 3 d) 6 e) 7 f) 1 g) 2

B From memory Ss try to decide who says which statements. Play the DVD again. Ss watch and check their answers, then check them in pairs. In feedback, elicit Ss' answers.

Answers: a) C b) T c) C d) C e) T f) T g) C

C Ss discuss the questions in small groups. In feedback, nominate Ss from each group to share their opinions with the class.

DVD 7 The One Show

CB=Christine Bleakley S=Supervisor AC=Adrian Chiles

CB: Ohhh. I'm doing it for real today.
S: This challenge is incredibly tough. She is gonna be operating in sub-zero temperatures for over 90 minutes. If she falls in the water too often … the challenge is over. If she makes this, it will be a true achievement and a true landmark for Sport Relief.
S: How are you feeling?
CB: I feel like I am in some sort of a … odd dream. I really do.
AC: All those nerves, all that adrenalin, it's all gonna come flowing out as soon as we get on the water.
S: Yeah, yeah. So … remove the fear and just keep focused on what you've gotta do and that is, land on that beach in Calais.
CB: Now it's just me against the Channel.
S: Go!
CB: I'm determined not to fall in but I soon realise determination might not be enough.
After several falls into the freezing water I already feel like I can't take much more.
S: We're just about a quarter of the way in and she's already fallen five times – now that … that is gonna take its toll without any shadow of a doubt in the later stages.
Every time she goes in I get a bit more worried. The weather's not looking good. There's white tops on the waves.
CB: But despite my best efforts, the wind and waves mean I can't stop myself falling.
S: She's fallen in ten times in just ten miles. That simply isn't good enough for this challenge. She has got to dig in now and start to focus.
CB: This could be an impossible challenge.
S: She is focused. She is in the zone. She's starting to fly now. Now we start to believe that she could truly make this challenge.
CB: My arms and body hurt so much but I just don't want to give up.
S: The hands have gone, the back's going, the legs are tired, but we've still got seven miles to go.
AC: She's turned it round here. The first half didn't go well. She's pulled it out of the bag.
CB: I can see France. And nothing is going to stop me.
AC: Five more minutes and you're there. Just enjoy this. Keep smiling. Come on! We're there!
CB: I did it! I did it! I could see this from out there. I thought wow! That looks fabulous.
S: Everybody around was worried whether she could make this or not. It is an incredibly tough challenge.
CB: Oh, that is a very welcome sight.
S: And the first woman to water-ski across the Channel in the winter, having only got on water-skis four months ago.
She is remarkable. It's a truly outstanding achievement.

speakout an achievement

5A Ss listen and answer the questions, then check their answers in pairs. In feedback, elicit Ss' answers.

> **Answers:** 1 To learn how to scuba dive. 2 It was a really good experience. 3 The classroom/theoretical training. 4 The practical stuff: she was very nervous, the water was freezing, she had trouble going under the water and her ears got blocked up. 5 Yes, she managed to do it eventually.

B Give Ss 2–3 mins to read the phrases. Ss listen again and tick the phrases they hear. In feedback, elicit Ss' answers and drill the phrases.

> **Teaching tip**
> Before Ss listen for phrases, ask them to read the phrases first, saying them in their head. This will give Ss an idea of what the phrases sound like, making it easier to recognise them in the recording.

> **Answers:** ✓ I found it really easy/quite difficult.
> It was the … I had trouble with.
> I was/We were very nervous.
> I tried to/experimented with … but it didn't work/I couldn't …
> I got very frustrated/annoyed/tired.
> I'm (so) glad/Eventually I managed it.
> It was a (really) difficult challenge/good experience …
> For me, it was quite an achievement.

Unit 7 Recording 8

T=Tracy Hackerman

T: A couple of years ago, er, I learned how to scuba dive which was, um, really exciting, really good experience and when you're learning half of the, the training is in the classroom and half is er, a practical in a swimming pool. So the classroom stuff was fine erm, I found it really quite easy. I was learning with my mum and she was really worried about doing the kind of more academic stuff and passing the exam but I found that part OK. It was the practical stuff that I had trouble with and she was really lucky, she was erm, really good. But you go and you learn all the technical stuff, you know how to go under the water, how to clear your mask if you get water in it, that kind of thing. And then you have to do two dives outside in a, in a kind of reservoir or a quarry or, you know, something like that. But obviously because I'm in the UK it was really, really cold and we woke up on the morning of our dive and there was ice on the water so when we got there we were very nervous and didn't want to get into the water. But once I was in it was so freezing that I tried to go under the water but the more I tried the harder it got and then I got very frustrated and started to cry and then all my ears got blocked up and I couldn't get under. But eventually I managed it and erm, went down, passed my test, did all of the skills that you need to do. Despite the fact that I was so terrible at it I managed to pass and now, erm, now I'm passed I can go anywhere I want so I'll make sure it will be somewhere very hot. So, erm, to sum up, although it was a really difficult, really difficult challenge, I'm so glad I managed it. Erm … For me, it was quite an achievement and and I'm proud of myself for having done it.

C Give Ss 5 mins to read the questions and make notes in preparation for their talk. Monitor and help with vocabulary and write any new words/phrases on the board.

D Ss share their experiences in groups. Encourage Ss to ask follow-up questions. When they have all finished, Ss discuss the question in their group. In feedback, nominate Ss from each group to share their experiences with the class.

> **Alternative approach**
> To encourage Ss to use the key phrases, nominate one student in each group to act as 'monitor'. As they listen to Ss describe their experiences, they tick which of the key phrases they hear used. In feedback, ask the monitors to tell the class who used the most key phrases in their group.

writeback an internet post

6A Elicit/Teach *enrol* and *to treasure sth*. Ss read the internet post and answer the questions alone, then check their answers in pairs. In feedback, elicit Ss' answers.

> **Answers:** He decided to learn Welsh because he was living in Wales and his wife spoke Welsh. He enrolled for a course at the university and practises in the local shop, where other people help him.

B Give Ss 10 mins to plan their ideas and write their posts. Monitor and help with vocabulary and write any new words/phrases on the board. When they have finished, Ss work in groups and show their posts to other Ss. In feedback, elicit Ss' favourite stories.

> **Optional extra activity**
> Ask the Ss to visit www.bbc.co.uk/my-story. When they have finished writing their stories, they could submit them to the website.

> **Teaching tip**
> There are various options for publishing Ss' written work, e.g. *a class web page, blogs, wikis, a social networking site, a class newspaper*, etc. It can be motivating for Ss to see their writing published.

> **Homework ideas**
> • Ex 6B: write a final draft of your internet post and submit it at www.bbc.co.uk/my-story (correct at the time of going to press).

LOOKBACK

Introduction

Ss revise and practise the language of Unit 7. The notes below provide ideas for exploiting the exercises and activities but your approach will depend on your aim, e.g. whether you use the activities as a diagnostic or progress test or as revision/fluency practice. If done as a test then it would not be appropriate to monitor or help Ss.

SUCCESS

1A Ss underline the alternatives alone, then check their answers in pairs. In feedback, elicit Ss' answers. In pairs, Ss discuss which quotes are important for them and why. In feedback, nominate Ss to share their partner's ideas with the class.

> **Answers:** 1 practising, practising 2 an opportunity 3 on 4 at

B Ss discuss the questions in pairs. In feedback, elicit Ss' ideas.

PRESENT PERFECT CONTINUOUS

2A Ss complete the sentences alone, then check their answers in pairs. With *weaker classes*, review how to form the present perfect continuous and elicit the first answer as an example. In feedback, elicit Ss' answers.

> **Answers:** 1 've been practising 2 've been visiting 3 've been marking 4 've been trying 5 've been researching

B Read the example with the class. Ss write their sentences alone. Monitor and check Ss are forming the present perfect continuous correctly. Don't elicit any answers yet.

> **Possible answers:** 1 an actor 2 a doctor/nurse 3 a teacher 4 a chef/housewife 5 a journalist

C In pairs, Ss read out their sentences in random order and their partner guesses the job. In feedback, nominate Ss to read out their sentences for the class to guess.

> **Optional extra activity**
> Ss write four sentences about what they have been doing in their own job or studies recently, two true and two false. When they are ready, they read out their sentences to the group, who ask follow-up questions, then guess which sentences are true and which are false. In feedback, nominate Ss from each group to read out their sentences for the class to guess.

ABILITY

3 Ss complete the text alone, then check their answers in pairs. In feedback, elicit Ss' answers.

> **Answers:** 1 hopeless 2 useless 3 have 4 expert 5 gifted 6 skilful 7 ability

> **Optional extra activity**
> In small groups, Ss discuss an inspirational teacher they had. Write on the board *Have you ever had a teacher who helped you develop an ability, or changed your life? What did they do?* Ss discuss the questions in small groups. In feedback, nominate Ss from each group to share their experiences with the class.

PRESENT AND PAST ABILITY

4A Ss underline the correct alternatives alone, then check their answers in pairs. In feedback, elicit Ss' answers.

> **Answers:** 1 can 2 couldn't 3 able to 4 was able to 5 'm not able 6 managed to

B Read the example with the class. Ss tick the sentences that are true for them, then compare/discuss their answers in small groups. In feedback, nominate Ss from each group to share their experiences with the class.

CLARIFYING OPINIONS

5A Ss complete the conversations alone. Tell Ss there are no correct answers and they should write their own opinions. Monitor and help with ideas if necessary.

B Ss share their opinions in small groups. Monitor and encourage Ss to ask follow-up questions. In feedback, nominate Ss from each group to share their opinions with the whole class.

OVERVIEW

8.1 NEIGHBOURS

GRAMMAR | articles and quantifiers

VOCABULARY | getting on

HOW TO | talk about where you live

COMMON EUROPEAN FRAMEWORK

Ss can scan longer texts in order to locate desired information and gather information from different parts of a text; can make his/her opinions and reactions understood, giving brief reasons and explanations.

8.2 MY PLACE IN CYBERSPACE

GRAMMAR | relative clauses

VOCABULARY | the internet

HOW TO | make recommendations

COMMON EUROPEAN FRAMEWORK

Ss can understand the information content of the majority of recorded or broadcast audio material on topics of personal interest; can write clear, detailed texts on a variety of subjects related to his/her field of interest.

8.3 MAKE YOURSELF AT HOME

FUNCTION | being a good guest

VOCABULARY | welcoming

LEARN TO | accept apologies

COMMON EUROPEAN FRAMEWORK

Ss can exchange, check and confirm accumulated factual information on familiar routine and non-routine matters within his/her field.

8.4 TRIBE ⊙ BBC DVD

speakout | design a community

writeback | a web advert

COMMON EUROPEAN FRAMEWORK

Ss can follow TV broadcast material delivered in standard dialect and can identify the speaker's mood, tone, etc.; can make his/her opinions and reactions understood, giving brief reasons and explanations; can write straightforward, detailed descriptions on familiar subjects within his/her field of interest.

8.5 LOOKBACK

Communicative revision activities

BBC VIDEO PODCAST

What makes a good neighbour?

This video podcast extends discussion of the unit topic to relationships. Ss can view people talking about their neighbourhood relationships. Use this video podcast at the start or end of Unit 8 .

NEIGHBOURS

Introduction

Ss learn and practise articles and quantifiers in the context of neighbours. They also learn and practise compound nouns.

SUPPLEMENTARY MATERIALS

Resource bank p160, p161 and p162

Ex 9C, speakout TIP: bring dictionaries for Ss to use.

Warm up

Explain the following dilemma: *You live in a block of flats and the people who live below you are always playing very loud music late at night, which stops you sleeping. In fact, you haven't slept properly for weeks. You have asked them many times not to play music after 10p.m. and they agree politely, but continue. What would you do?* Ss discuss the dilemma in pairs. In feedback, elicit Ss' answers.

VOCABULARY getting on

1 Ss discuss the questions in pairs. In feedback, nominate Ss to share their partner's answers with the class.

2A Read the example with the class. In feedback, elicit Ss' answers and check they understand the phrases in bold, giving further examples from your own experience.

Answers: 1 b) 2 e) 3 f) 4 d) 5 a) 6 c)

B In pairs, Ss discuss which sentences are true for them. Encourage Ss to ask follow-up questions. In feedback, nominate Ss to share their partner's answers with the class.

Teaching tip

Personalising new vocabulary by using the language to talk or write about themselves (as in Ex 2B) helps Ss internalise the phrases and gives them real meaning.

⟹ **VOCABULARYBANK** p155 Getting on

Elicit the first sentence with the class as an example, then Ss complete the definitions in pairs. *Stronger classes* can do the exercise at home.

Answers: 1A 1 b) 2 a) 3 d) 4 f) 5 c) 6 e)
B a) pops over b) unfriendly c) borrows d) lends me
e) helpful f) gossiping

READING

3A Ss circle the correct options alone, then compare their answers in pairs. In feedback, elicit Ss' predictions, but don't give any answers yet.

B Give Ss a strict time limit of 3 mins to scan the text for the answers. Tell them not to worry about new vocabulary at this stage as they'll read the text again in Ex 4. In feedback, elicit Ss' answers.

Answers: 1 c) 2 b) 3 c) 4 a)

4 Ss read the text more carefully and answer the questions, then check their answers in pairs. Monitor and help with vocabulary where necessary. In feedback, elicit Ss' answers and write any new words/phrases on the board.

> **Answers:** 1 How well do people know their neighbours neighbours ? 2 ICM is a research group. It asked people how well they know their neighbours. 3 RxKaren, Jilcove, Todd 4 Loobygraham

GRAMMAR articles

5 Focus attention on the underlined words. Ask Ss to read the rules, then match the words in the sentences to the rules. They then check their answers in pairs. In feedback, elicit Ss' answers and give further examples if necessary.

> **Answers:** 1 b) f) 2 a) d) 3 c) e)

Watch out!

With articles, exceptions to the rules can cause problems for Ss. Rules may be a throwback to former times, e.g. *I'm going to the bank* dates from the time when there was only one bank in each town. The best approach is to focus on the rules as 'rules of thumb'.

PRACTICE

6 Ss complete the comments alone, then check their answers in pairs. In feedback, elicit the answers and ask Ss to say why they are correct, referring to the rules in Ex 5.

> **Answers:** 1 a 2 a 3 a 4 the 5 the 6 a 7 – 8 – 9 an 10 The 11 the 12 the

> ⇒ **LANGUAGEBANK** 8.1 p142–143 Ex 1
>
> *Stronger classes* could read the notes about articles and do Ex 1 at home. Otherwise, check the notes about articles with Ss, especially the 'extra' rules not covered in Ex 5 on p92. Give further examples if necessary. Elicit the first answer as an example. Ss work alone to complete the exercise, then check their answers in pairs. In feedback, elicit Ss' answers.
>
> > **Answers:** 1 1 Why don't you come and join us? There are plenty *of* seats. 2 Bobby's girlfriend is *an* engineer. 3 Thousands of people were at the game, so there was *a* lot of noise. 4 Yesterday we saw a doctor about my illness. Fortunately, *the* doctor said it was nothing serious. 5 Laila was hungry so she ate a bit *of* bread. 6 *Women* live longer than men. 7 We went to the party but there weren't *many* people there. 8 We looked up and saw an aeroplane in *the* sky. 9 I can't buy it because I only have a *little* money left. 10 My wife and I have lived in *the* United States for several years.

GRAMMAR quantifiers

7A Read the example with the class. Ss underline the quantity words, then check their answers in pairs. In feedback, elicit Ss' answers.

> **Answers:** 1 lots of 2 plenty of 3 a few 4 no 5 all 6 Many

B Ss answer the questions in pairs. In feedback, elicit Ss' answers and give further examples if necessary.

> **Answers:** 1 lots of, plenty of, all, many 2 a few 3 no 4 a few, many

> ⇒ **LANGUAGEBANK** 8.1 p142–143 Ex 2
>
> *Stronger classes* could read the notes and do the exercise at home. Otherwise, check the notes about quantifiers, especially the meanings of *some* (to refer to a limited amount) and *any* (to refer to an unlimited amount). Also, check Ss' understand that *too* means 'more than necessary' and is not the same as *a lot*.
>
> > **Answers:** 2 1 An 2 A 3 the 4 many 5 much 6 lot 7 little 8 the 9 few 10 the

PRACTICE

8A Teach/Elicit *get on my nerves* and *a nuisance*. Ss underline the correct alternatives, then check their answers in pairs. In feedback, elicit Ss' answers.

> **Answers:** 1 many, None 2 plenty, some 3 much, a lot of 4 all of, a few 5 Several, a bit of

B Ss discuss the questions in small groups and say if they have had any similar experiences. In feedback, nominate Ss from each group to share their opinions with the class.

VOCABULARY PLUS compound nouns

9A Ss read the sentences and mark whether they are positive, negative or both. They then check their answers in pairs. In feedback, elicit Ss' answers.

> **Answers:** 1 – 2 + 3 + 4 +/–

B Focus attention on the example. Ss underline the compound nouns, then check their answers in pairs. In feedback, elicit Ss' answers.

> **Answers:** 1 main road 2 bookshop 3 swimming pool 4 window shopping

C Read the patterns with the class and check Ss' understand them. If you've brought dictionaries, give them out for Ss to use. Ss match the nouns to the patterns, then check their answers in pairs. In feedback, elicit Ss' answers.

> **Answers:** a) bookshop b) main road c) swimming pool d) window shopping

speakout TIP

Read the tip with the class. Write *shop*, *teacher* and *bag* on the board in three separate sections. Divide the class into three groups (one for each word). Ss brainstorm compound nouns containing the word, then check the spelling in a dictionary. In feedback, elicit Ss' answers, write them on the board and drill the compounds. Explain that it is difficult to know when compounds are written together, separately or with a hyphen (even for native speakers) and they should check the spelling in a dictionary.

10A Ss find one word which forms a compound with both of the words in each pair. Elicit the first answer as an example. Ss complete the compound nouns alone, then check them in pairs. In feedback, elicit Ss' answers but don't confirm them as they will listen to check in Ex 10B.

Answers: 1 traffic 2 car 3 shopping 4 market 5 school 6 centre 7 street 8 house 9 estate 10 shop

B Ss listen and check their answers to Ex 10A. Then, in pairs, ask Ss to work out which word in compound nouns is usually stressed. Play the recording again for Ss to check. Elicit the answer.

Answers: The first word is usually stressed.

C In pairs, Ss discuss which of the compound nouns are near their place of study. If your room has large windows, ask Ss to look out of them and say which they can see. In feedback, nominate Ss to share their ideas with the class.

Watch out!

If one of the components of a compound noun refers to its location, we usually stress the second word, e.g. *city centre, kitchen sink, back garden.*

Unit 8 Recording 1

1 traffic jam, traffic lights
2 car park, car rental
3 shopping centre, shopping mall
4 supermarket, outdoor market
5 primary school, language school
6 sports centre, city centre
7 high street, one-way street
8 semi-detached house, terraced house
9 housing estate, industrial estate
10 duty-free shop, gift shop

▶ VOCABULARY BANK p155 Compound nouns

1A Read the example and elicit where to put *office*. Ss work alone to put the words next to the correct key words to make compound nouns, then check their answers in pairs. If you've brought dictionaries, give them out for Ss to check the spelling of the compound nouns. In feedback, elicit Ss' answers and write them on the board.

B Ss put the key words in the correct places and use dictionaries to check the spelling. In feedback, elicit Ss' answers and write them on the board.

Stronger classes can do the exercise at home.

Answers: 1A 1 tennis racket, tennis player, tennis court 2 coffee shop, coffee machine, coffee cup 3 post office, postcode, postcard 4 language barrier, language lab, language learner 5 sun cream, suntan, sunglasses
B 1 running shoes, sports shoes, high-heeled shoes 2 chequebook, picture book, textbook 3 bedroom, dining room, changing room 4 sewing machine, washing machine, drinks machine 5 mobile phone, pay phone, cellphone

SPEAKING

11A Focus attention on the photos and elicit what each one shows. Give Ss 4–5 mins to think about where they live and make notes under the headings. Monitor and help with vocabulary and write any new words/phrases on the board.

B Read the examples with the class. Ss think about the questions and make notes alone.

C Ss compare their ideas from Ex 11A and Ex 11B in small groups and choose the best ideas. Monitor and note down any common errors. In feedback, nominate Ss from each group to share their group's best ideas with the class. Correct any common errors.

Homework ideas
• Ex 11C: write about the area you live in.
• Language bank 8.1 Ex 1–2, p143
• Vocabulary bank p155
• Workbook Ex 1–7, p51–52

MY PLACE IN CYBERSPACE

Introduction

Ss learn and practise relative clauses in the context of the internet. They also learn and practise using complex sentences when writing a website review.

SUPPLEMENTARY MATERIALS

Resource bank p163

Warm up

Explain the following situation: *Your government is offering a prize of 1,000 euros (or your country's currency) for the best idea for an internet company. If you win, you will be able to use the money to start up the company.* Ss work in pairs to come up with an idea for an internet company. When they are ready, Ss present their ideas to the class and Ss vote for the best one.

VOCABULARY the internet

1A Focus attention on the picture and elicit examples of each type of website. Ss match the questions to the websites alone, then check their answers in pairs. In feedback, elicit Ss' answers.

Answers: 1 news site 2 travel site 3 social networking site 4 photo sharing site 5 dating site 6 photo (video) sharing site 7 ratings site 8 corporate website 9 personal homepage 10 blog 11 wiki 12 search engine

B Ss discuss the questions in pairs and find out if they have any answers in common. In feedback, nominate Ss to share their answers with the class.

LISTENING

2A Check Ss understand *online community* and elicit some examples. Give Ss 1 min to read the questions and check they understand what information they need to listen for. Ss listen to the recording and answer the questions, then check their answers in pairs. In feedback, elicit Ss' answers.

Answers: 1 She started an artists' colony on the internet. 2 It's a very creative kind of community and she loves it. 3 Because it's a community of bloggers and no one knows one another personally. 4 They have 'a following', who are loyal readers. 5 A very small town. 6 It's cheap to shop online for things that they can't get locally and it saves them an hour's drive in the car. 7 She puts up pictures of her and her family and she writes messages. 8 At least once every day.

B Check Ss understand the words in the box. Play the recording again and pause after each speaker. Ss take it in turns to explain what the speaker said in pairs, using the words in the box as prompts. Monitor and check that Ss are explaining what the speakers said in their own words. In feedback, nominate Ss to summarise what the speakers said.

Unit 8 Recording 2

L=Lynn

L: In real life my husband and I are both artists, visual artists. We paint landscapes and portraits. Well, we've been using the website for about two years now. And about a year ago we started an artists' colony on the internet and it's been great. There are people like us, who work in the arts, but also other people. And we show our paintings and it's brought some business for us. It's a very creative kind of community and we love it. We really do.

R=Rick

R: There is definitely a community of bloggers. It's a very twenty-first century community, which means no one knows one another personally. Bloggers might tell you their thoughts but, er, you don't know them as people. The guy who wrote this, who says he's a fifty-year-old American university professor, might be a sixteen-year-old girl from Bombay – we just don't know. But the best blogs have a following, who are very loyal readers. These are people who log on every day. And they get really engaged in the content. Well, that, to me, is a community.

N=Nathan

N: The place where we live is very small. There's only one shop, which sells all sorts of things like food, newspapers and everything really. There's a small school, a pub and then not much else. Actually, our social life is based on the pub, where we have our town meetings. Anyway, when we need to buy other things we shop online. It's cheap and it saves us an hour's drive in the car. And yeah, I've bought all sorts of things there: furniture, clothes … stuff you just can't get where we live.

A=Abbie

A: The website which I use the most is a social networking site. It's like Facebook or MySpace. I put up pictures of me and my family and I write messages – but to be honest, I use it mostly to keep in touch with friends. And the thing that I like is you go onto your friend's homepage to see what they've been doing … and er, you, you can see pictures of all their friends. And then you see pictures of your friend's friends and it grows and grows so you meet new people. Erm, I think it's great. I check it at least once every day.

3 Ss discuss the questions in pairs. In feedback, nominate Ss to share their opinions with the class.

Optional extra activity

This would be a good point to set up a class group/page on one of the many social networking sites on the internet. They're free and easy to set up and join. You can ask Ss to post questions or homework there and set web tasks for them to do outside class. This will help Ss use English outside the classroom.

GRAMMAR relative clauses

4 Teach/Elicit *entrepreneurs*. Ss read the text, then answer the question in pairs. In feedback, elicit the answer.

Answers: The website became successful because of a number of features: links to the videos, which made them easy to email; tell-a-friend functions; a feature that allowed YouTube videos to be played on other social networking sites; and another feature that let users comment on the videos.

5A Ss read the sentences and identify the clauses, then check their answers in pairs. In feedback, elicit Ss' answers. With *weaker classes*, follow the procedure in the box below first.

Optional extra activity

Write on the board 1 *That's the website which I visit every day.* and 2 *YouTube, which is very popular, allows you to post your own videos.* Ask *Which sentence defines something?* and *Which gives us extra information?* (1 defines and 2 gives extra information). Explain that 1 has a defining relative clause and 2 has a non-defining clause. Ss then identify the relative clauses in Ex 5A.

Answers: a) non-defining relative clause b) defining relative clause

B Ss read the rules. They complete rule 3 alone, then check it in pairs. In feedback, elicit Ss' answers and give more examples if needed.

> **Answers:** *where, who, which, that*

C Ss find eight more relative clauses in the text and categorise them alone. They then check their answers in pairs. In feedback, elicit Ss' answers.

> **Answers:** who were also colleagues (ND), which would solve the problem (D), who follows the development of the internet (D), where dreams become reality (ND), which made them easy to email (ND), that allowed YouTube videos to be played on other social networking sites (D), that let users comment on the videos (D), where you posted videos (D)

> ➡️ **LANGUAGEBANK** 8.2 p142–143
>
> Check the notes with Ss, especially the rules concerning when we can omit the relative pronoun in *defining relative clauses* and when we can use *that*. In each exercise, elicit the first answer as an example. Ss work alone to complete the exercises, then check their answers in pairs. In feedback, elicit Ss' answers.
>
> > **Answers:** 1 1 whose 2 when 3 which 4 where 5 who 6 which 7 who 8 whose
> > 2 1 Is this the programme that you wanted to watch?
> > 2 Last year I met a translator who spoke six languages.
> > 3 It was 6 o'clock on the fifth of August when the world changed forever. 4 They gave Jodie an apple, which she ate quickly. 5 That's the apartment where Felipe lived.
> > 6 She spent a month in Manchester, which she loved.
> > 7 The boss, whose office is next to mine, is always shouting. 8 My boyfriend, who lives in Barcelona, is coming to visit me.

PRACTICE

6A Teach/Elicit *subscribers* and *go on and on about nothing*. Ss circle the correct alternatives, then check their answers in pairs. With **weaker classes**, elicit the first answer as an example. In feedback, elicit Ss' answers.

> **Answers:** 1 which was 2 which must be 3 which is called 4 that use 5 who works for 6 when online 7 where people go 8 who all use

B Ss discuss the questions in pairs. In feedback, nominate Ss to share their partner's answers with the class.

7A Explain that the commas in non-defining relative clauses signify where we pause when saying them. Ss listen and tick the sentences they hear, then check their answers in pairs. *Weaker classes* may need to listen twice. In feedback, elicit Ss' answers.

> **Answers:** 1 b) 2 a) 3 a) 4 b) 5 a)

B Demonstrate by reading out sentence 1b) and eliciting the answer. In pairs, Ss read out sentences for their partner to guess. In feedback, nominate one or two Ss to read out sentences for the class to guess.

SPEAKING

8A Read the example with the class. Give Ss 5 mins to write their ideas. Monitor and help with vocabulary and write any new words on the board. Don't elicit any answers yet.

B Ss share their ideas in small groups. Monitor and note down any common errors for later correction. In feedback, nominate Ss from each group to share their ideas with the class and correct any common errors.

WRITING a website review

9A Ss read the review, then answer the questions in pairs. In feedback, elicit Ss' answers.

> **Answers:** 1 a wiki 2 It has a range of subjects and a simple design which makes it easy to use. 3 Journalists (but there's something there for everyone)

B Ss refer to the review in Ex 9A and number the features alone, then check their answers in pairs. In feedback, elicit Ss' answers.

> **Answers:** a) 2 b) 4 c) 1 d) 3

C Ss underline the phrases alone, then check their answers in pairs. In feedback, elicit Ss' answers.

> **Answers:** One reason I'd recommend it is; The best thing about magportal.com is; Another excellent feature is

LEARN TO use complex sentences

10A Ss read the sentences alone, then discuss which sounds more fluent in pairs. In feedback, elicit the answer.

> **Answers:** The b) sentences sound more fluent.

speakout TIP

Read the tip with the class and elicit Ss' ideas about how the sentences have been made more complex (by using relative clauses and conjunctions). Explain that using more complex sentences can have a good effect on their speaking and writing.

B Ss rewrite the sentences alone. Monitor and help where necessary.

C Give Ss time to compare their sentences in pairs. In feedback, elicit their ideas.

> **Possible answers:** 1 The website is well-designed *and the* good design makes it user-friendly. 2 The site has too much animation, *which* makes it very slow *because* it takes a long time to upload. 3 The website's content comes from its users, *who* send in their photos. 4 The site feels friendly *because* it has user profile areas *where* users can say who they are.

11A Give Ss 5 mins to think about their answers and make notes. Monitor and help with vocabulary and write any new words on the board.

B Ss write their reviews alone. Monitor and correct errors. When they have finished, Ss show their reviews to other Ss. In feedback, nominate Ss to tell the class which websites they think sound interesting.

> **Optional extra activity**
> If you have access to computers with the internet, Ss can use them to present the features of their chosen website when showing their reviews.

> **Homework ideas**
> • Ex 11B: write a final draft of your review.
> • Language bank 8.2 Ex 1–2, p143
> • Workbook Ex 1–6, p53–54

MAKE YOURSELF AT HOME

Introduction

Ss learn and practise asking for advice and apologising in the context of being a guest in someone's home.

SUPPLEMENTARY MATERIALS

Resource bank p164

Warm up: write the questions below on the board.

Warm up

Write on the board *Do you ever have guests come to stay in your home? Who are they? Have you ever had any 'problem' guests? What did they do?* Ss discuss the questions in small groups. In feedback, nominate Ss from each group to share their experiences with the class.

VOCABULARY welcoming

1A Ss match the phrases to the situations alone, then check their answers in pairs. In feedback, elicit Ss' answers.

Answers: 1 d) 2 a) 3 e) 4 f) 5 c) 6 b)

B Focus attention on the example and play the first phrase in the recording. Play the rest of the recording, pausing after each phrase and eliciting how some of the words link together.

Teaching tip

Studying linking is useful because it can help Ss to distinguish between words when listening and to sound more fluent when speaking. Explain this to your Ss.

C Play the recording, pausing after each conversation for Ss to repeat the final line. Listen carefully to how Ss link the words and, if necessary, say the phrases again for Ss to repeat after you and then drill them.

Unit 8 Recording 5

Conversation 1

A: I'm really hungry. Can I have some of this?
B: Help yourself.

Conversation 2

A: Come on in.
B: Thanks.
C: Have a seat.

Conversation 3

A: Hi.
B: What a day! I'm so tired!
A: I'll make you some coffee. Put your feet up.

Conversation 4

A: Can I just quickly use your phone?
B: Be my guest.

Conversation 5

A: Welcome!
B: Thank you. What a nice room.
A: Make yourself at home.

FUNCTION being a good guest

2A Ss discuss the questions in pairs. In feedback, nominate Ss to share their partner's answers with the class.

B Teach/Elicit *empty-handed, shake hands* and *host*. Read the text and see if any of their ideas were mentioned. In feedback, elicit Ss' answers.

---

3 Ss discuss the questions in pairs. In feedback, elicit Ss' opinions and additional advice and ask them to give reasons if there is any advice they disagree with.

4 Ss listen and answer the questions, then check their answers in pairs. Tell Ss not to worry about vocabulary at this stage, as they'll listen again in Ex 5. In feedback, elicit Ss' answers.

Answers: Speakers in conversations 1, 3, 4 and 5 did something wrong. Speakers 2 and 6 are asking for advice.

5 Ss discuss the endings in pairs, then listen again and complete the sentences. In feedback, elicit Ss' answers.

Answers: 1 smoke in the house. 2 a dish. 3 ten minutes. 4 her shoes off. 5 wear a jacket. 6 meat.

Unit 8 Recording 6

Conversation 1

W=Woman M=Man

W: Hi Dave. Sorry. Do you mind?
M: Sorry?
W: We don't smoke in the house.
M: Oh, sorry about that. I didn't know.
W: That's all right. It's no problem.

Conversation 2

M1=1st man M2=2nd man

M1: So they've invited me to dinner at their home.
M2: Wonderful. And they're also from Morocco?
M1: The same as you. From Morocco.
M2: That'll be great.
M1: So, do I need to bring a dish? Like, bring some food?
M2: No, it's not necessary. You can bring a small gift if you want but you don't need to bring food.

Conversation 3

M=Man W=Woman

M: Hello?
W: Hello?
M: Hi, I'm Richard Davies. From Exeter? I'm here to visit your offices.
W: Ah hello.
M: I'm a bit early. Is this a bad time?
W: Umm.
M: I can come back later.
W: I wasn't expecting you so early. Can you come back in ten minutes? I just need to finish some work here, then I'll be able to show you around.
M: Of course. Sorry about that.
W: Not at all. It's fine.

Conversation 4

W1=1st woman W2=2nd woman

W1: So, I walked into your parents' house but I forgot to take my shoes off. Did I do something wrong?
W2: Oh, I see.
W1: My shoes weren't dirty or anything but I still felt really bad.
W2: It's OK – I'll tell my parents you forgot. Don't worry about it.
W1: I don't know. Should I call them up to apologise?
W2: No, it's nothing. You really don't have to apologise.

Conversation 5

W=Waiter C=Customer

W: Excuse me sir, would you mind putting this on?
C: What?
W: Put on your jacket. In this restaurant you have to wear a jacket.
C: My apologies. I didn't realise.

Conversation 6

W=Woman M=Man

W: So this American family are going to stay with us for Thanksgiving.

M: For what?

W: For Thanksgiving. You know, people from the United States celebrate it.

M: So what's the problem?

W: Americans always eat turkey on Thanksgiving, don't they? But we're vegetarians – we never eat meat. So, well, what should we do?

M: Um … if I were you, I'd tell them the problem and maybe they can cook a turkey while you and your family just eat something else.

6 Ss read the phrases and tick the ones they remember hearing, then check with the audio script on p173. In feedback, elicit Ss' answers and drill the phrases.

> **Answers:** ✓ What should we do? If I were you, I'd …
> Do I need to bring a dish? No, it's not necessary.
> Did I do something wrong? It's OK. Don't worry about it.
> Is this a bad time? I can come back later. Can you come back in ten minutes? Not at all. It's fine.
> Sorry about that. I didn't know.
> My apologies, I didn't realise.

> ➡ **LANGUAGEBANK** 8.3 p142–143
>
> *Stronger classes* could read the notes and do the exercises at home. *Weaker classes* can do the exercises in class.
>
> > **Answers:** 1 A: Do I need to shake everyone's hand? B: No, it's not necessary. 2 A: Is it OK if I take coffee into the meeting? B: Yes, of course. 3 A: I didn't realise I had to send the information by email. B: It's OK. We can sort it out. 4 A: Did I do something wrong? B: Don't worry about it. 5 A: What should I do if I am late? B: If I were you, I'd catch an earlier train. 6 A: Sorry about that. I didn't know you were here. B: No problem. 7 A: Is this a bad time? B: No, it's fine.

7A Elicit the missing words for the first conversation as an example. Ss add the rest of the missing words alone, then check their answers in pairs. In feedback, elicit Ss' answers.

> **Answers:** 1 A: Is *it* OK if I take a call during a meeting? B: Not really. It's considered a bit *rude*. 2 A: I just called the boss by his first name, John. Did I do something *wrong*? B: Not *at* all. That's normal here. 3 A: Sorry about *that*. I didn't know you were waiting. B: Don't worry *about* it. 4 A: My apologies. I didn't *realise* this was your seat. B: No, it's *OK*. You can sit there. 5 A: You know I can't eat butter or cheese, right? What *should* I do if they offer me these? B: If I *were* you, before your visit I'd tell them you don't eat dairy products.

B Ss practise the conversations with a partner. If there's time, Ss swap roles and practise the conversations again. In feedback, nominate one or two pairs to perform the conversation for the class.

LEARN TO accept apologies

8A Read the phrases with the class. Ss listen and put the phrases in order. In feedback, elicit Ss' answers and drill the phrases if necessary.

> **Answers:** a) 2 b) 3 c) 1 d) 6 e) 4 f) 5

B Give Ss 2 mins to read the situations and think about what to say. Ss practise apologising in pairs. Monitor and check Ss are using the phrases correctly. In feedback, nominate a different pair to perform each conversation for the class.

Unit 8 Recording 7

Extract 1

W=Woman M=Man

W: We don't smoke in the house.

M: Oh, sorry about that. I didn't know.

W: That's all right. It's no problem.

Extract 2

W=Woman M=Man

W: I wasn't expecting you so early. Can you come back in ten minutes? I just need to finish some work here, then I'll be able to show you around.

M: Of course. Sorry about that.

W: Not at all. It's fine.

Extract 3

W1=1st woman W2=2nd woman

W2: It's OK – I'll tell my parents you forgot. Don't worry about it.

W1: I don't know. Should I call them up to apologise?

W2: No, it's nothing. You really don't have to apologise.

SPEAKING

9A Ss read the situations, then discuss the questions in pairs. In feedback, elicit Ss' experiences and ideas.

B Put Ss into A/B pairs and give them 2–3 mins to complete the flow chart and think about what they're going to say. *Weaker classes* may need to write out the conversation before they practise. Ss practise the role-play in pairs. If there's time, Ss swap roles and practise the role-play again. In feedback, Ss perform their role-plays for the class.

> **Homework ideas**
> - Language bank 8.3 Ex 1, p143
> - Workbook Ex 1–3, p55

8.4 TRIBE

Introduction

Ss watch an extract from a BBC programme in which the presenter goes to live with a remote tribe on the Pacific island of Anuta. Ss learn and practise how to plan an ideal community and write a web advert.

SUPPLEMENTARY MATERIALS

Warm up: write the questions below on the board.

Warm up

Write on the board *What's the remotest place you've ever been to? Why did you go there? How did you travel there? Did you have any problems?* Ss discuss the questions in small groups. In feedback, nominate Ss from each group to share their answers with the class.

▶ DVD PREVIEW

1A Ss cover the text and look at the photos. Ask *Where do you think this is?* Ss discuss the questions in pairs. In feedback, nominate Ss to share their ideas.

B Give Ss 2 mins to read the programme information and answer the questions in pairs. In feedback, elicit Ss' answers.

Answers: He hopes to learn about the tribe's traditions and how they survive.

Culture notes

Anuta is a small volcanic island in the south-eastern part of the Solomon Islands' province of Temotu, the smallest permanently inhabited Polynesian island, with a diameter of only 750 metres. It has a population of around 300, divided between two villages, the *Mua* and *Muri*. An important concept in their society is *Aropa*, which roughly translates as 'compassion' and all the island's resources from fishing and agriculture are divided equally among its members.

Culture notes

The BBC programme *Tribe* was first aired in 2005 and is presented by Bruce Parry, a former British Royal Marine. Over three series, he has visited remote places and tribes all over the world, including Africa, Asia, South America and the Pacific Islands.

2 Ss match the words and definitions alone, then check their answers in pairs. In feedback, elicit Ss' answers and drill the words.

Answers: 1 bind (people together) 2 survive 3 customs 4 tribe 5 isolated 6 remote

Optional extra activity

If you think Ss need extra practice with the vocabulary, write the following questions on the board *Are there any tribes living in your country? Where do they live? Are there any remote areas in your country? Why are they remote? What customs would visitors to your country find difficult to adapt to? In what ways can customs bind people together? Can you think of any examples?* Ss discuss the questions in small groups. In feedback, nominate Ss from each group to share their ideas with the class.

▶ DVD VIEW

3 Read the sentences with the class and check they understand them. Play the DVD. Ss watch and number the scenes in the correct order, then check their answers in pairs. In feedback, elicit Ss' answers.

Answers: a) 2 b) 4 c) 6 d) 5 e) 1 f) 3

4A Ss discuss the correct answers in pairs. Don't elicit any answers yet.

B Play the DVD again for Ss to check their answers to Ex 4A. In feedback, elicit Ss' answers.

Answers: 1 a) 2 b) 3 b) 4 a)

5 Ss discuss the questions in pairs. In feedback, elicit their opinions and have a brief discussion.

DVD 8 Tribe

BP=Bruce Parry A=Anutan

BP: My name's Bruce Parry. I've been travelling to some of the world's most remote places to see how people there live and how they're adjusting to a rapidly changing world.

I believe there's only one way to really understand another culture and that's to experience it first hand, to become for a short while, one of the tribe.

After four days at sea, we sight a speck of land on the horizon. Half a mile wide, 75 miles from its nearest neighbour. This finally is my first sighting of the Island of Anuta.

How do people survive in such an isolated place? And could this really be paradise on earth?

The Island of Anuta is surrounded by a shallow reef. So our yacht anchors off-shore and I'm paddled towards the beach.

Anuta's one of the Solomon Islands, which used to be under British rule, but even so, I didn't expect this many people to speak English.

The entire community is here to greet me and I'm told that I must shake hands with each and every one of them.

This really is phenomenal. What a reception. Everyone is out, all smiling and … just a really warm feeling. And let's face it, look around, what an amazing place. I'm in paradise.

A couple of hundred handshakes later and I'm taken to meet the community leaders.

So tell me, what is the protocol? I must go in on my … very low, on my … on my knees?

I've heard it's customary to greet the chief in the Polynesian way, with a nose kiss.

OK. But I don't kiss him with my lip, or just my nose.

A: Yes, your nose.

BP: OK.

The chief tells me I can stay on Anuta.

Well, this is gonna be an amazing day, it's something I'm really looking forward to. It's a community fish drive. And what's happening is, every single member of the island is gonna gather together and we're gonna go out and force the fish into this area here where we dive and spear the lot of them. What could be more fun? Everyone's gonna be out there.

It's a pretty obvious system but it's deadly and productive at the same time. Essentially, this wall that we've all been rebuilding is here to stop the fish getting away so that when the wall of people beat towards us, the fish can't escape here and they go into the killing area. And that's where we spear them.

speakout design a community

6A Give Ss 2 mins to read the text, then discuss the questions in pairs. In feedback, elicit Ss' answers.

Answers: In the future, the Maldives will be under water because of global warming. No one will be able to live there and nothing will remain.

B Ss read the questions and note down their answers alone, adding any additional information they want to. Monitor and help with vocabulary and write any new words/phrases on the board.

7A Ss listen and note down the speakers' answers to the first three questions, then check their answers in pairs. In feedback, elicit Ss' answers.

Answers: 1 somewhere in France 2 a mix of people, fairly small 3 not to physically hurt someone else

B Read the phrases with the class. Ss listen again and tick the phrases they hear. In feedback, elicit Ss' answers and drill the phrases.

Answers: I'd probably choose …, They'd need to be able to …, Ideally, there would be …

Unit 8 Recording 8

B=Ben Jacques S=Sharon Hills

B: So Sharon, erm, imagine you had to start a brand new community. Er …

S: Yes?

B: I know it's a difficult question, but ideally where would it be?

S: Erm, I'd probably choose somewhere quite warm, so yeah, so you didn't have any issues of flooding, or you know, too much snow to deal with something like that. And then I'd choose another place most people would probably choose, not an island … erm ….

B: Where … where exactly?

S: But, I think, hmmmm …. somewhere in France, I don't know why.

B: Oh somewhere in France? OK and and who would be there: the French only or a mixture of people?

S: No, I … well, it would need to be a mix of people and they'd need to be able to help one another.

B: In what way?

S: Well, erm … I'd like to take one person who's an expert in one field, another person who's an expert in another field, so you have – you know – arty people, erm, manually skilled people, erm … good orators, good writers.

B: Ah, so a whole range of skills …

S: Exactly!

B: … all going into the melting pot.

S: Yes, but, I wouldn't have too many people to start with, although if it's too small a group then I suppose you risk, erm, falling out. But I think if you keep that group fairly small to begin with then you can draw up your own special laws, you know, to govern yourselves.

B: Would it need laws do you think … this, this utopian society?

S: Mmmm … well, ideally there'd be no laws but because people are human I think you would probably have to come up with some ground rules yes.

B: What would be the most important one?

S: Oh! Erm, I think, erm … not to physically hurt somebody else I suppose.

B: Right, so pretty much like we have at the minute …

S: Yes, I suppose …

8 Ss share their answers from Ex 6B in pairs, then plan their community together. When they have finished, Ss join another pair and present their community.

writeback a web advert

9A Ss read the text and answer the question in pairs. In feedback, elicit Ss' answers.

Answers: It's a village community that combines Fijian traditions with international ideas for environmentally-friendly living. Everyone helps maintain the island.

B Ss use the prompts to write the advert in pairs. Monitor and help with vocabulary, writing any new words/phrases on the board. When they have finished, Ss show their adverts to another pair and compare their adverts.

Homework ideas
• **Ex 8:** write a description of your community.
• **Ex 9B:** write a final draft of your web advert.

LOOKBACK

Introduction
Ss revise and practise the language of Unit 8. The notes below provide ideas for exploiting the exercises and activities but your approach will depend on your aim, e.g. whether you use the activities as a diagnostic or progress test or as revision/ fluency practice. If done as a test then it would not be appropriate to monitor or help Ss.

GETTING ON

1A Read the example with the class and explain that Ss can use the words as many times as they want. Give Ss 5 mins to make as many phrases as they can. In feedback, elicit Ss' answers and write the phrases on the board.

Answers: get on well with, get to know, get on your nerves, ask a favour, do a favour, disturb (people), make friends with (people), mind your own business, invite people over, keep yourself to yourself, be a nuisance, be nosy

Alternative approach
Do this as a brainstorming game. Divide the class into groups of three and give them 2 mins to make as many phrases as they can. In feedback, ask a representative from each group to write their phrases on the board and award a point for each correct phrase. The group with the most phrases wins.

B Read the example with the class. Ss write four questions alone, then stand up and ask other Ss the questions in a mingling activity. Monitor and encourage them to ask follow-up questions. In feedback, nominate Ss to share some of the answers they heard with the class.

ARTICLES AND QUANTIFIERS

2A Ss complete the text alone, then check their answers in pairs. In feedback, elicit Ss' answers.

Answers: 1 b) 2 b) 3 a) 4 b) 5 c) 6 c) 7 b) 8 a) 9 a) 10 c)

B In small groups, Ss discuss possible endings for the story in Ex 2A, then write down their sentences. In feedback, nominate Ss from each group to read out their endings and ask Ss to vote for their favourite endings.

Optional extra activity
When Ss have written their endings, they cross out all of the articles and quantifiers they've used. When they read out their endings, other Ss in the class guess the missing articles and quantifiers.

THE INTERNET

3A Ss complete the questions alone, then check their answers in pairs. In feedback, elicit Ss' answers.

Answers: 1 travel 2 video 3 search 4 networking 5 blog 6 sites

B Ss discuss the questions in pairs. Monitor and encourage them to ask follow-up questions. In feedback, nominate Ss to share their partner's answers with the class.

RELATIVE CLAUSES

4A Ss underline the correct alternatives alone, then check their answers in pairs. Tell them not to worry about the gaps yet. In feedback, elicit Ss' answers.

Answers: 1 when 2 where 3 that 4 when 5 who 6 whose

B Ss complete the sentences alone using the words in the box, then check their answers in pairs. In feedback, elicit Ss' answers.

Answers: 1 democracy 2 a zoo 3 friendship 4 rush hour 5 an expert 6 a banker

5 Do an example with the class first to demonstrate. In pairs, Ss give definitions for their partner to guess. Monitor and help with vocabulary where needed. In feedback, nominate Ss to share their definitions for the class to guess.

BEING A GOOD GUEST

6A Ss match the comments to the responses alone, then check their answers in pairs. In feedback, elicit Ss' answers.

Answers: 1 e) 2 b) 3 c) 4 d) 5 a)

B Ss cover the responses and read out the comments for their partner to respond. When they have finished, Ss swap roles and repeat the exercise. In feedback, elicit possible alternative responses.

Optional extra activity
When Ss have practised the responses in Ex 6B, elicit situations where Ss might hear each of the expressions and write them on the board. In pairs, Ss discuss if they have been in any of the situations themselves and what happened. In feedback, nominate Ss from each pair to share their experiences with the class.

Homework ideas
• Workbook Review and check 4, p56–58
• Workbook Test 4, p59

OVERVIEW

9.1 GIANT LEAPS

GRAMMAR | third conditional

VOCABULARY | history

HOW TO | talk about imaginary past situations

COMMON EUROPEAN FRAMEWORK

Ss can understand the description of events, feelings and wishes; can write short, simple essays on topics of interest.

9.2 IN OUR TIME

GRAMMAR | active vs passive

VOCABULARY | periods of time

HOW TO | talk about your personal history

COMMON EUROPEAN FRAMEWORK

Ss can understand the information content of the majority of recorded or broadcast audio material on topics of personal interest; can give clear, detailed descriptions on subjects related to his/her field of interest.

9.3 I HAVE NO IDEA!

FUNCTION | expressing uncertainty

VOCABULARY | describing people

LEARN TO | react to information

COMMON EUROPEAN FRAMEWORK

Ss can enter unprepared into conversations on familiar topics; can give feedback on and follow up statements and inferences in a discussion; can initiate, maintain and end discourse appropriately with effective turn taking.

9.4 MICHELANGELO ● BBC DVD

speakout | influential work

writeback | a wiki entry

COMMON EUROPEAN FRAMEWORK

Ss can understand most of a documentary in standard dialect; can present clear, detailed descriptions on subjects related to his/her field of interest.

9.5 LOOKBACK

Communicative revision activities

BBC VIDEO PODCAST

Do you think life is better now than in the past?

This video podcast extends discussion of the unit topic to historical events. Ss can view people describing what have been the most important historical events in their lifetime. Use this video podcast at the start or end of Unit 9 .

GIANT LEAPS

Introduction

Ss learn and practise the third conditional in the context of important historic moments. They also learn and practise vocabulary related to history and how to write a short essay.

SUPPLEMENTARY MATERIALS

Resource bank p167

Ex 10B: bring coloured pens/pencils for Ss to use.

Warm up

Ss discuss the most important events in their countries' histories. With monolingual classes, ask them to try and agree on the single most important event in their country's history. In feedback, elicit Ss' ideas.

VOCABULARY history

1A Focus attention on the photos at the top of the page and elicit what Ss can see in them. Ss discuss the questions in pairs. In feedback, elicit Ss' answers and write them on the board.

> **Answers:** Left to right: a civil rights march in the US in the sixties, the invention of the aeroplane, the industrial revolution, the discovery of DNA/genetics, the invention of the wheel

B Ss read the comments and see if any of their ideas are mentioned. In feedback, compare the ideas in the comments with the Ss' ideas on the board. Ask *Which ones do you agree with?* and have a brief discussion.

C Read the examples with the class and check Ss understand the definitions. Ss match the words and definitions alone, then check their answers in pairs. In feedback, elicit Ss' answers and drill the words.

> **Answers:** 1 revolution, turning point 2 development, invention, discovery 3 advance, progress 4 movement 5 foundation 6 spread

D Ss complete the sentences alone. Monitor and help with any new vocabulary. When they have finished, Ss compare answers in small groups and see if they have any answers in common. In feedback, nominate Ss from each group to share any common answers with the class.

⟹ **VOCABULARYBANK** p156 History

Elicit the first word with the class as an example, then Ss complete the definitions in pairs. *Stronger classes* can do the exercise at home.

> **Answers:** 1 invasion 2 historian 3 colony
> 4 democratic 5 liberate 6 discovery 7 leader 8 politics
> 9 developing 10 invention 11 founder 12 independence

READING

2A Give Ss 1 min to read the introduction. In pairs, Ss predict some 'alternative moments' that the historians might choose. In feedback, elicit Ss' ideas and write them on the board.

B Teach/Elicit *tails*, *hunting*, *verse*, *be found guilty* and *steam*. Refer Ss back to Ex 11 on p34 about making notes. Put Ss into A/B pairs. Student As read the texts on p105 and Student Bs read the texts on p159 and make notes using the question prompts. Monitor and make sure Ss only write notes and don't copy large chunks of text.

Answers: Learning to eat meat What? Learning to eat meat Where? Africa When? 2.5 million years ago Why was it important? It led to hunting, which led to us being imaginative and intelligent.
Teaching people to read What? Teaching people to read Where? France When? 1199 Why was it important? Reading became the foundation of modern education.
Exploring the sky What? Exploring the sky Where? Italy When? 1630 Why was it important? It changed our view of the universe.
Invention of the steam engine What? Invention of the steam engine Where? Britain When? 18th century Why was it important? It changed many things, e.g. transport, manufacturing and communication.

3A Ss cover their texts and share information with their partner from Ex 2B. Monitor and make sure they only use their notes and don't read out from their texts. In feedback, nominate Ss to summarise their partner's texts with the class.

B Ss answer the questions in pairs. If they get stuck, they can refer back to the texts they read. In feedback, elicit Ss' answers.

Answers: 1 *Doctrinale* and *Two World Systems* 2 De Villedieu's methods of teaching and Gallileo's discoveries about the universe. 3 The developments in teaching methods and in our understanding of the universe were because of one person. The development in humans learning to eat meat and the invention of the steam engine were because of many people.

C Rearrange Ss into small groups. Ss discuss the questions in their groups. In feedback, elicit Ss' answers and have a brief discussion.

GRAMMAR third conditional

4A Ss read the sentences, then answer the questions in pairs. In feedback, elicit Ss' answers.

Answers: The sentences describe an imaginary situation in the past.

B Read the chart with the class. Explain that this is the third conditional. Ss find another example in the texts in Ex 2B. In feedback, elicit the answer.

Answers: If he hadn't written *Doctrinale*, education would probably have remained the same for hundreds of years. If Galileo hadn't defended his theories, he would have been a free man, but we wouldn't have understood the science of our universe.

C Read the sentences with the class and elicit the answer.

Answers: The *if* clause and the *would* clause have changed places. The sentences begin with the *would* clause.

Alternative approach

To encourage a more student-centred approach to language clarification, Ss do Ex 4 (A, B and C) in pairs. In feedback, elicit Ss' answers and deal with any queries, providing further explanations and/or examples where necessary.

Teaching tip

It can be useful to think of past tenses as 'distant' and present tenses as 'near'. In this way, there are three things that affect our choice of tense: **time**, **register** and **reality**.

time: we use past tenses to describe past actions because they are distant in time (*I crashed the car yesterday.*)

register: we communicate with people we see as distant by using past tenses to sound more formal (*I was wondering if you could tell me how to get there?*)

reality: we speak hypothetically by using past tenses to indicate distance in reality (*If I had arrived earlier, I would have seen her.*)

The third conditional is made up of two pasts – one to express **non-reality** and one to express past **time**. Explaining this to your Ss with examples may give them a better understanding of hypothetical language.

LANGUAGEBANK 9.1 p144–145

Stronger classes could read the notes and do the exercises at home. Otherwise, check the notes with Ss, especially the use of the comma, depending on the order of the clauses. Drill the examples in the notes and make sure Ss are using the contractions. In each exercise, elicit the first answer as an example. Ss work alone to complete the exercises, then check their answers in pairs. In feedback, elicit Ss' answers and drill the sentences. Ss can refer to the notes when doing the exercises.

Answers: 1 1 d) 2 f) 3 c) 4 h) 5 g) 6 b) 7 a) 8 e)
2 1 If Maya's car hadn't broken down, she wouldn't have been late for the meeting. 2 She would have come to the concert if she hadn't felt ill. 3 If I had been qualified, I would have got the job. 4 They would have bought the house if they'd had enough money. 5 If our best player hadn't been injured, we wouldn't have lost the game.
6 I would have cooked a meal if you'd told me you were coming.

PRACTICE

5A Ss complete the sentences alone, then check their answers in pairs. With *weaker classes*, elicit the first sentence with the class as an example and write the forms on the board. Monitor and check Ss are forming the third conditional correctly. Don't elicit any answers yet.

Answers: 1 would have remained, hadn't explored 2 had been found, wouldn't have crashed 3 would have been, hadn't discovered 4 hadn't met, wouldn't have formed 5 wouldn't have been, hadn't invented 6 hadn't opened, would have remained

B Ss listen and check their answers. Pause after each sentence for Ss to make any changes if necessary. In feedback, elicit Ss' answers.

C Play the recording again and pause after each sentence for Ss to repeat. In feedback, elicit Ss' answers to the question and drill again if necessary.

Answer: *had not* and *would not* are contracted.

Watch out!

When it's used as an auxiliary, *have* is shortened to /əv/. (This is why native speakers often make the mistake of using *of,* instead.) Focus on this when drilling.

Unit 9 Recording 1

1 Machu Picchu would've remained unknown if Hiram Bingham hadn't explored the Andes in Peru.
2 If the 'I love you' virus had been found earlier, forty-five million computers wouldn't have crashed.
3 The first experiments in cloning would've been impossible if Gregor Mendel hadn't discovered genes.
4 If John Lennon hadn't met Paul McCartney, they wouldn't have formed The Beatles.
5 The invention of the mobile phone wouldn't have been possible if Alexander Graham Bell hadn't invented the telephone.
6 If the Nestor Film Company hadn't opened a film studio there in 1911, Hollywood would've remained a quiet community.

6 Demonstrate by writing on the board three things that have happened to you and eliciting third conditional sentences from the class. Ss then write their sentences for Ex 6 alone. Monitor and help with vocabulary and check Ss are forming the third conditional correctly. When they have finished, Ss compare their sentences in pairs and see if they have any answers in common. In feedback, nominate Ss to share their partner's ideas with the class.

SPEAKING

7A Elicit some ideas for big moments in history and write them on the board. Give Ss 5 mins to prepare notes on their chosen event. If they need help, put Ss into A/B pairs. Student A reads the notes on p163 and Student B reads the notes on p160. Monitor and help with vocabulary, writing any new words/phrases on the board.

Alternative approach

If you have a *multilingual class* with different nationalities in it, ask Ss to prepare information about a big moment in their country's history and share it in Ex 7B with Ss from other countries.

B Ss describe their big moments in pairs. Encourage Ss to ask follow-up questions. In feedback, nominate Ss to share their partner's information with the class.

WRITING a short essay

8 Introduce the topic by asking *What do you know about essays? Do/did you have to write them in your studies? What kind of topics do they describe? Have you ever written them in English?* In pairs, Ss put the stages in order. In feedback, elicit Ss' answers.

Answers: a) 5 b) 6 c) 1 d) 4 e) 2 f) 3

9 Teach/Elicit *gunpowder* and *compass.* Ss read the essay, then answer the question in pairs. In feedback, elicit Ss' answers and have a brief discussion based on their reactions to the ideas.

Answers: The writer thinks the Chinese would have seen the incredible size of the land and the riches in the ground, returned with more men, created new communities, brought their technology and farmed the land and got rich. The new Chinese colony would have grown and grown and perhaps they would have later spread to other lands.

LEARN TO structure paragraphs

10A Focus attention on the labelled paragraph and key. Ss complete the statements alone, then check their answers in pairs. In feedback, elicit Ss' answers, giving further explanations if necessary.

Answers: 1 topic sentence 2 supporting sentences 3 linking words

B Ss label the first paragraph of the essay in Ex 9 alone, then check their answers in pairs. If you have brought coloured pens/pencils, distribute them for Ss to use. In feedback, elicit Ss' answers.

Answers: Topic sentence: Once, China led the world in technology. Supporting sentence 1: Centuries before Europe, they had printing and gunpowder. Supporting sentence 2: They also had the compass, which meant they could navigate without relying on the position of the moon. Supporting sentence 3: Furthermore, they were brilliant ship builders. Linking words: also, furthermore

11A Give Ss 1 min to read the instructions and check they understand them. Ss work alone and follow the instructions to plan their essay. Monitor and help with vocabulary, writing any new words/phrases on the board.

Teaching tip

Allowing Ss to choose their own topic (as in Ex 11A) increases motivation, as Ss will be more interested in what they're writing about.

speakout TIP

Read the tip with the class and emphasise the importance of checking their writing. Give Ss 5 mins to follow the instructions and check their work. Monitor and help where necessary.

B Ss swap essays with a partner and check each other's work, following the instructions in the speakout tip. In feedback, nominate Ss to summarise their partner's text for the class.

Homework ideas
• Ex 11A: write a final draft of your essay.
• Language bank 9.1 Ex 1–2, p145
• Vocabulary bank p156 History
• Workbook Ex 1–6, p60–61

IN OUR TIME

Introduction

Ss learn and practise active versus passive forms in the context of personal histories. They also learn and practise vocabulary related to periods of time and common collocations.

SUPPLEMENTARY MATERIALS

Resource bank p165, p166 and p168

Ex 4A: bring dictionaries for Ss to use.

Warm up

Write on the board *toys*, *games*, *TV shows*, *films*, *music* and *places*. In pairs, Ss discuss what they can remember in each category from when they were very young. In feedback, nominate Ss to share their partner's answers with the class.

GRAMMAR active versus passive

1 Draw a word web on the board with teenagers in the middle. Elicit one or two ideas and write them on the board. Ss write three words alone, then compare their ideas in pairs. In feedback, elicit Ss' answers and write them on the board.

2A Give Ss a strict time limit of 2 mins to read the paragraph and choose the best title, then check their answer in pairs. Elicit the best title in feedback.

Answer: 2 How the young found their voice

B Ss read the sentences and answer the questions alone, then check their answers in pairs. Monitor and help Ss where necessary. In feedback, elicit Ss' answers.

Answers: 1 a) was invented b) had c) was rejected d) saw e) have been created 2 a) and e) 3 active verbs: b) and d); passive verbs: a), c) and e)

C Ss complete the rule alone, then check their answer in pairs. In feedback, elicit Ss' answers.

Answer: be

D Ss find and underline three more examples of the passive in the text, then check in pairs. In feedback, elicit Ss' answers.

Answers: James Dean, who <u>was killed</u> in a car crash … Magazines, cosmetics and cars <u>were designed</u> to appeal to teenagers, who <u>could usually be found</u> in coffee bars

> ⟱ **LANGUAGEBANK** 9.2 p144–145
>
> Check the notes with Ss, especially the different uses of the passive, giving further examples if necessary. In each exercise, elicit the first answer as an example. Ss work alone to complete the exercises, then check their answers in pairs. In feedback, elicit Ss' answers.
>
> **Answers:** 1 1 has been stolen 2 sent 3 are being built 4 hasn't been played 5 be removed 6 made 7 weren't employed 8 being repaired
> 2 1 is read, 's/is published 2 aren't filmed, works 3 was written, described 4 made, was bought 5 have been cleaned, have been painted 6 've/have been given, haven't moved 7 isn't being cooked, 're/are using 8 won't be spoken, won't speak

PRACTICE

3A Read the example with the class. Ss rewrite the sentences alone, then check their answers in pairs.

Answers: 1 Jeans are worn by people all over the world. 2 Mobile phones are being designed especially for teenagers. 3 Teenagers have always been influenced by the media. 4 A great film about a teenage vampire was made in Sweden. 5 In the past, children were seen as mini-adults. 6 In the future, people will be prevented from smoking until they are twenty-one. 7 In Mexico, a party called *quinceañera* is held when a girl reaches the age of fifteen. 8 Many of the computer games of the future will be designed by teenagers.

B Ss listen and check their answers. Pause the recording after each sentence for Ss to make any necessary changes. In feedback, elicit Ss' answers.

C Write *are*, *has been*, *was* and *were* on the board. Play the recording again and ask Ss to focus on these words when they listen. Elicit how the weak forms are pronounced. Play the recording again, pausing after each sentence for Ss to repeat.

Answers: The verb forms *are*, *has been*, *was* and *were* are pronounced as weak forms, with the schwa.

VOCABULARY periods of time

4A Ss put the words and phrases in the box in order, then check their answers in pairs. If you've brought dictionaries, give them out for Ss to use. With *weaker classes*, go through the words/phrases in the box first and elicit what period each one refers to. Ss then put them in order. In feedback, elicit Ss' answers and write them on the board in order.

Answers: a fortnight, a decade = the nineteen-seventies/eighties (1970s, 1980s) = the seventies/eighties, a generation = a quarter-century, an era = an age, a century, a millennium

B First, give Ss one or two examples with your own opinions. Ss complete the sentences alone. Monitor and help with vocabulary, writing any new words/phrases on the board.

C Ss compare their answers in pairs and find any common answers. In feedback, nominate Ss from each pair to share their opinions with the class and have a brief discussion.

LISTENING

5A Focus attention on the photos and elicit what Ss can see. Write any new words/phrases on the board. Elicit which decade each photo shows.

Answers: A 70s B 80s C 90s

B Write on the board *Decade? Positive or negative?* Ss listen and answer the questions for each speaker. Tell them not to worry if they don't understand all the vocabulary at this stage as they'll listen again in Ex 5C.

Answers: 1 90s, positive 2 70s, positive 3 80s, not very positive at the time, but positive now

speakout TIP

Read the tip with the class and explain that it's easier to understand something when we have a clear purpose for listening. Read the questions in Ex 5C with the class and elicit information to listen for e.g. Q3 – a country or city.

C Ss listen again and answer the questions, then check their answers in pairs. If necessary, play the recording again. In feedback, elicit Ss' answers.

> **Answers:** 1 film and music 2 Suggested answers: fireworks, parties 3 London, England 4 John Lennon 5 fashion and music 6 girls cutting their hair short

Unit 9 Recording 3

1   Yeah, <u>I grew up in the 90s. Erm, for me film and music are two important ah important aspects of my life and it was a fantastic decade for both of those.</u> In terms of films, there were some ah excellent ones that came out, erm, my favourites being *Forrest Gump*, *Pulp Fiction* and *The Shawshank Redemption*. In terms of the music … probably the most famous bands of the time was Oasis and Blur. Ah, <u>one of the most memorable moments of the 90s was Euro 96 … obviously the football tournament.</u> I was lucky enough to go to the opening ceremony myself. Obviously, as we was entering the end of the millennium the celebrations towards the end of the nineties were huge as were the actual celebrations on the night. Tony Blair was elected, erm, so he was the first sort of Labour government for, for a long time. Um and also Mother Teresa died, sort of Mother Teresa was, erm, the famous charitable missionary.

2   Ah, the 70s, well they were wonderful I think if, if I'm asked were they was it a good decade or a bad decade, personally I have to think it was a good decade to grow up in. I think it's very lucky I think of it as a very lucky experience when generally the world that I lived in, which was London and England, which was the post-war period and therefore an era of a certain amount of erm, restriction was all ending and things were freeing up and that happened just at the time that I was leaving home and finding my own independence. It all seemed as though it happened at the same time. <u>Erm, technology was er, changing and improving, um, everything seemed to be developing and getting better in many ways.</u> The fashion was getting rid of short hair and regimented kind of looks, erm, individuality was very much the order of the day. Great people were emerging in the arts. John Lennon, for example, was an icon for me I think as a creative artist with a message as well in his work. Great artists in film, Scorsese, *Taxi Driver*, Spielberg, *Duel* these were emerging artists of tremendous skill and artistry but they were just starting out then when I was.

3   I was a teenager in the 80s and I remember thinking that um <u>I didn't like a lot of the fashion and the music from back then but now it's obvious in retrospect that I did quite like it. I love looking back on like a nostalgia trip at the way we used to dress and how much hair gel I used and how much hair spray the girls used</u> and er, now in the 2000s there's sort of a trip back into that time you know, girls are wearing big earrings again and geometric patterns of their clothes. Erm, the music in the 80s became quite computerised sounding, quite electronic and er, disco faded away, although we did still have soul although people like Luther Vandross and Billy Ocean, erm, making soul music. Er, New Romantic was another style that came out in the early 80s where the men started wearing lots of make-up and had big shoulders and small waists and erm, there was Madonna was a big trendsetter for girls and er, at one point she cut her hair really short in the mid 80s and almost like a boy's and then all the girls started cutting their hair short, too. Erm, I wasn't very fashionable myself, I used to spend most of my money on records not clothes. Erm, there were some good films around in the 80s too things like *Back to the Future* with Michael J Fox, *Desperately Seeking Susan* with Madonna, *ET*, *Police Academy* … Um, I'm gonna be forty this year and I reckon my birthday party is going to be a big nostalgia trip back to the 80s.

6A Ss turn to audio script 9.3 on p173–174 and answer the questions using the underlined sentences to help them.

B Ss discuss their answers in pairs. In feedback, nominate one or two Ss to share their partner's answers with the class.

SPEAKING

7A Read the questions with the class and check Ss know what they have to do. Give them 5 mins to think about the topics and note down their ideas. Monitor and help with vocabulary, writing any new words/phrases on the board.

B Ss tell each other their personal histories in small groups. Encourage Ss to ask follow-up questions. In feedback, nominate Ss from each group to share ideas with the class.

VOCABULARY *PLUS* collocations

8A Teach/Elicit *theoretical physicist*, *drag* and *cave*. Read the questions with the class and elicit their predictions. Ss read the text and answer the questions alone, then check their answers in pairs. In feedback, elicit Ss' answers.

> **Answers:** 1 Because it is 'outside our imagination'. 2 Because humanity makes progress slowly and 'Stone Age man didn't have TV for entertainment.' 3 The people of the future might not know the answers to our problems.

B Highlight the example with the class. Ss read the text again and find two phrases for each verb. Elicit Ss' answers.

> **Answers:** have the same dream, have trouble, come naturally, makes progress, come back, make a mess, give us directions, give instructions

C Ss add the underlined phrases to the word webs. In feedback, elicit Ss' answers.

> **Answers:** see below

D Read the words in the box with the class and check Ss understand them. Ss complete the word webs alone, then check their answers in pairs. In feedback, elicit Ss' answers.

> **Answers:** <u>give</u>: instructions, a talk, me a call, directions; <u>have</u>: a good time, the same dream, trouble, a break; <u>make</u>: a decision, a mess, progress, a profit

> ▶ **VOCABULARYBANK** p156 Collocations
> Elicit the first answer as an example. Ss work alone to complete the word webs, then check their answers in pairs. In feedback, elicit Ss' answers.
>
> > **Answers:** 1 nearer, across the mountain, with instructions, to dinner 2 orders, a prize, permission, me a headache 3 100 calories, ideas, a cold, a chance 4 a film, an effort, an agreement, a living

9A Ss complete the headings alone, then check their answers in pairs. In feedback, elicit Ss' answers.

> **Answers:** 1 time 2 instructions 3 trouble 4 progress 5 directions 6 break 7 talk 8 profit 9 first 10 mess

B Ss choose one of the topics and prepare to give a talk on it. *Stronger Ss* can choose two. Monitor and help with vocabulary, writing any new words/phrases on the board.

C Ss give their talks in small groups. Encourage other Ss to ask follow-up questions. In feedback, nominate Ss from each group to share with the class anything they have learned.

> **Homework ideas**
> • Ex 7A/B: write about your childhood.
> • Language bank 9.2 Ex 1–2, p145
> • Workbook Ex 1–5, p62–63

I HAVE NO IDEA!

Introduction

Ss learn and practise how to express uncertainty and react to information in the context of describing historical figures.

SUPPLEMENTARY MATERIALS

Resource bank p169

Ex 3A: bring dictionaries for Ss to use.

Ex 7A: research some geography and history trivia on the internet to help Ss if they get stuck.

Warm up: prepare some questions similar to those on the website below, or load the website up ready to play the game with the class.

Warm up

If you have access to the internet in class, load up www. playtheshow.com/weakestlink (correct at time of going to press) and play it with the class. If not, before class, prepare some questions similar to those on the website and play the game with Ss answering the questions in teams.

SPEAKING

1 First, tell Ss about some famous game shows in your country as an example. Ss discuss the questions in pairs. In feedback, nominate one or two Ss to share their ideas with the class and have a brief discussion.

VOCABULARY describing people

2 Ask *Do you like history? How much do you know about the history of your country?* Ss do the quiz in pairs. Tell them not to worry if they don't know the answers and that they should guess. Monitor carefully and notice what language they are using when they don't know the answers. This will give you an idea of how well Ss can already express uncertainty at this stage. Tell Ss not to worry about the answers to the quiz at this stage, as they'll hear them in Ex 4A.

Alternative approach

Do the quiz as a class game show. Ss work in teams to answer the questions. In feedback, award points for correct answers. The team with the most correct answers wins.

Answers: 1 a) 2 a) 3 b) 4 b) 5 a) 6 c)

3A Ss look back at the quiz in Ex 2 and discuss the meaning of the words in bold. If you've brought dictionaries, give them out for Ss to use. In feedback, elicit the meanings and give further examples to clarify the meanings if necessary.

Answers: 1 original: able to produce things that are completely new and different 2 influential: able to influence what happens or what people think 3 innovative: good at introducing new ideas or methods; inspirational: good or successful so that people admire you and want to achieve something themselves 4 charismatic: able to attract and influence other people 5 brave: behaving with courage in a frightening situation; exemplary: good so that it can be used as an example for others to copy 6 creative: good at thinking of new ideas

B Read the example with the class. Ss think of one person for each adjective, then compare their ideas in pairs. In feedback, nominate Ss to share their ideas with the class and ask if other Ss agree.

FUNCTION expressing uncertainty

4A Ss listen to the conversation and tick the answers from the quiz in Ex 2 that the man knows, then check in pairs. In feedback, elicit Ss' answers and ask how many correct answers they got in the quiz.

Answers: 3 (Chaplin) and 6 (da Vinci)

B Ss cover the exercise. Ask *Can you remember any of the phrases the man used when he didn't know the answers?* and elicit their ideas. Ss complete the groups of phrases alone, then check their answers in pairs. In feedback, elicit Ss' answers and drill the phrases.

Answers: 1 I don't know 2 I'm not sure but I think 3 I know it isn't 4 I used to know

C Ss listen and tick the phrases they hear, then check their answers in pairs. In feedback, elicit Ss' answers.

Answers: 1 I have no idea, I haven't a clue 2 I'm not a hundred percent certain but it might be … I'm fairly sure it's … 3 It's definitely not 4 I can't remember, I'm sure it isn't

Unit 9 Recording 4

W=Woman M=Man

W: What about this first one? Who was once kidnapped in France?

M: I have no idea. Maybe Isabelle Allende?

W: It was Chaucer. I think he worked for the British government.

M: Did he? I didn't know that.

W: OK, what about the next one? Who was messy?

M: Umm … probably Machiavelli.

W: It was Karl Marx.

M: Oh really?

W: And the third one: who was stopped by the US government from entering the States?

M: I'm not a hundred percent certain but it might be Chaplin. I read somewhere that he had some political views that they didn't like in the States. I'm fairly sure it's Chaplin. Is that right?

W: You're right. It was Chaplin.

M: Yeah, I read something about that.

W: OK, number four. Who played the violin?

M: I haven't a clue. I'll guess it was Galileo.

W: It was Einstein. He was a very good violinist, apparently.

M: Was he? That's interesting.

W: Number five.

M: It's definitely not Mandela. Ermm … Joan of Arc?

W: Didn't you see that film about Che Guevara and his friend travelling across South America on their motorbikes?

M: I don't think I did, actually.

W: Yeah, Guevara was a medical student …

M: Oh yes, I knew that. I just couldn't remember.

W: Who went on a road trip with his friend?

M: Ah, that's right.

W: And the last one?

M: Umm, well I'm sure it isn't Picasso. Oh, it's da Vinci. He invented lots of stuff but never actually produced any of it, like … um … oh I can't remember, but I know he was an inventor as well as an artist.

W: Correct. It was da Vinci. He invented the parachute.

M: Oh yeah, I was just about to say that!

▦➡ **LANGUAGE**BANK 9.3 p144–145

Stronger classes could read the notes and do the exercise at home. Otherwise, drill the phrases in the notes with the Ss and elicit possible continuations for the sentences. Teach/ Elicit *PIN number*. Elicit the first answer as an example. Ss work alone to underline the correct alternatives, then check their answers in pairs. In feedback, elicit Ss' answers.

Answers: 1 I've forgotten 2 I'm sure it isn't
3 definitely not 4 fairly sure 5 haven't a clue 6 have no idea 7 can't remember 8 a hundred percent certain

5A Read the example with the class. Ss add the missing pairs of words alone, then check their answers in pairs. In feedback, elicit Ss' answers.

Answers: 1 A: Which sculptor is famous for the statue of David? Was it Leonardo da Vinci or Michelangelo? B: I *have no* idea. I don't know anything about art. 2 A: What's the name of that American politician who made a film about the environment? B: Oh, um, I *can't* remember. Was it Rumsfeld? No, um, Bush? 3 A: Who was the white South African leader who freed Mandela? B: I'm *fairly sure* it was Botha, wasn't it? 4 A: Who's that Mexican actor who was in *Amores Perros*? B: Oh, *I've forgotten* his name but I know who you mean. He's quite small and good-looking. 5 A: Which company invented the CD Rom? B: I'm not a hundred *percent certain* but it might be Sony. 6 A: Do you know who wrote *The Lord of the Rings*? Wasn't it William Golding? B: I don't know, but *it's definitely* not Golding. 7 A: Who won the last football World Cup? B: I'm *sure it* wasn't England. 8 A: What was the name of that Steven Spielberg film about dinosaurs? B: I *haven't a* clue. I don't watch Hollywood movies.

B Ss try to answer the questions in pairs. When they have finished, they can turn to p160 to find the answers. In feedback, ask *Which answers did you know? Did you find any answers surprising?*

Answers: 1 Michelangelo 2 Al Gore 3 F W de Klerk 4 Gael Garcia Bernal 5 Sony and Philips in a joint project 6 J R Tolkien 7 Spain (in 2010) 8 *Jurassic Park*

C Ss practise the conversations in pairs. Monitor and check their pronunciation of the phrases, noting any common problems for later drilling. If there's time, Ss swap roles and repeat the conversation. In feedback, correct any common pronunciation problems by drilling the phrases with the class.

LEARN TO react to information

6A Ss read the extracts, focusing on B's responses. Play the recording for Ss to listen to B's intonation.

Watch out!

Echo questions *Did he?* (in extract 1) and *Was he?* (in extract 3) echo the original statement and are similar in meaning to *Really?* when reacting to information you don't know. Write the following sentences on the board (or read them out) and ask Ss to provide the echo question:

– Margaret Thatcher was the first British female prime minister. (*Was she?*)

– Michelangelo was also a poet. (*Was he?*)

– Che Guevara went to medical school. (*Did he?*)

– My mother is an astronaut. (*Is she?*)

– Yoko Ono lived in the United States as a child. (*Did she?*)

B Ss answer the questions in pairs. In feedback, elicit the answers, then play the recording again, pausing after B's responses for Ss to repeat.

Answers: 1 B knew the answers to questions 4, 5 and 6. 2 The information in questions 1, 2 and 3 was new.

SPEAKING

7A Put Ss into A/B pairs. The As read the information on p111 and the Bs read the information on p162. Ss write two more questions of their own. Monitor and help with ideas. If Ss are stuck for ideas, give them the trivia you researched before class to help them write questions. Ss ask their questions in pairs. In feedback, find out who answered the most correct questions and nominate Ss to share any information they learned with the class.

Homework ideas
• Ex 1: write a description of a quiz show in your country.
• Language bank 9.3 Ex 1, p145
• Workbook Ex 1–3, p64

MICHELANGELO

Introduction

Ss watch an extract from a BBC documentary about the life and works of Michelangelo.

SUPPLEMENTARY MATERIALS

Warm up: write the questions below on the board.

Warm up

Write on the board *Who are the most famous artists/designers from your country? Do you like their work?* Ss discuss the questions in small groups. If you have access to the internet in class, Ss download some of the artists' work and show it to other Ss. In feedback, elicit Ss' ideas.

▶ DVD PREVIEW

1 Focus attention on the painting and elicit Ss' ideas, feeding in information from the **Culture notes**.

> **Answers:** The picture at the bottom of p113 shows part of *The Creation of Adam*, which is part of the ceiling of the Sistine Chapel. The Sistine Chapel ceiling was painted by Michelangelo between 1508 and 1512.

2 Ss read the sentences alone, then discuss the meanings of the words in pairs. In feedback, elicit Ss' answers.

> **Answers:** unique: nothing else like it; divine: inspired by god; eternal: lasts forever; extraordinary: amazing, much better than one would normally expect; mortal: will die one day; awe-inspiring: makes you stop and take notice, impressive; feat: an amazing achievement; ordinary: usual; aspirations: dreams, ambitions; quest: mission
> Opposites: ordinary/unique, mortal/eternal

3 Teach/Elicit *tempestuous*. Ss read the text, then discuss the question in pairs. In feedback, elicit Ss' answers.

> **Answers:** Michelangelo had a difficult, imperfect life, yet was able to produce perfect works of art, of stunning beauty.

Culture notes

Michelangelo di Lodovico Buonarroti Simoni was born on 6th March 1475, in Caprese, near Arezzo, Tuscany and is commonly referred to as Michelangelo. He was an Italian Renaissance painter, sculptor, architect, poet and engineer. He produced hundreds of perfectly-made works, many of which he created before he turned thirty. During his lifetime, he was often called *Il Divino*, 'the divine one' and many believed his work was an expression of god. He died on 18th February 1564, aged 88. Three of his most famous works are the David, the Sistine Chapel ceiling and the Basilica of Saint Peter.

▶ DVD VIEW

4A Ss read the sentences and make predictions in pairs. In feedback, elicit Ss' predictions, but don't give any answers yet.

B Play the DVD for Ss to check their answers alone and then in pairs. In feedback, elicit Ss' answers.

> **Answers:** 1 T 2 T 3 F (five hundred) 4 T 5 F (money was always tight) 6 F (he was appalled by his son's love of the arts)

5A Ss read the notes and work alone to complete with the missing words, then check their answers in pairs.

B Play the DVD again for Ss to check their answers. In feedback, elicit Ss' answers.

> **Answers:** 1 riches 2 beautiful 3 simple 4 unhappy 5 talent 6 earth

C Ss discuss the questions in small groups. In feedback, nominate Ss from each group to share their answers.

DVD 9 The Divine Michelangelo

V=Voice-over A=Actor

V: This is the story of a superstar, a sculptor, a painter an architect who strides the history of art like a Colossus. He was a tempestuous genius who would let nothing stand in the way of his quest for eternal fame and riches untold.

A: He doesn't know perfection when he sees it.

V: He was an outsider who created works so big and so beautiful that nobody believed they were produced by a mere mortal.

A: I've just created a giant.

V: He claimed he was divinely inspired ...

A: Heaven's own art.

V: ... yet stole from Popes, fought his rivals and struggled with his own demons.

His name was Michelangelo.

500 years ago, Michelangelo created three of the wonders of the world: the David, the most famous sculpture in history; the ceiling of the Sistine Chapel, the most awe-inspiring painting; and the dome of St Peters, the jewel in the crown on the Roman skyline. But what sort of man was capable of these incredible feats?

A: What do you think I am? An ordinary labourer? You think I'm the honest, simple stone-cutter who makes a living with his hands? Well look at that. What simple artisan could create something like that? Her face will live forever, not just from this century to the next, but on and on and on and on and on. Heaven's own art. Not mortal, but divine.

V: Within a month of Michelangelo's birth, his family moved to Florence. He had an unhappy childhood. His mother died when he was six, leaving his father Ludovico with five sons to bring up. Money was always tight.

Ludovico was a lowly paid local official with aspirations of grandeur. He was appalled by the young Michelangelo's love of the arts.

A: Moreover, he thought I would bring disgrace on the family. Of course this distressed me. But I would not turn back.

V: But for all his father's opposition, Michelangelo persevered and produced works which showed an extraordinary talent.

From the dome to the David, from the Pietà to the Sistine Chapel, Michelangelo had created a unique vision of heaven on earth.

speakout influential work

6A Teach/Elicit *novel*, *ghost*, *black humour* and *satire*. Ss listen and answer the questions, then check their answers in pairs. In feedback, elicit Ss' answers.

> **Answers:** She talks about Gabriel Garcia Marquez. Finding his work as a teenager made her become a 'reader'.

B Ss listen again and tick the phrases they hear. In feedback, elicit Ss' answers and drill the phrases.

> **Answers:** ✓ I fell in love with his novels. That book really made its mark on me. He's one of the best-known writers. I'm a big fan of that type of writing. The style is brilliant.

Unit 9 Recording 6

L=Lili Lowe

L: OK, well, someone whose work really influenced me is Gabriel Garcia Marquez. I like his short stories, but I fell in love with his novels, particularly *One Hundred Years of Solitude*. That book really made its mark on me. Anyway, erm, well, Marquez is a Colombian writer. I think he was born in 1928. He's a Nobel Prize winner – he won the Nobel Prize in Literature – and his books have been translated into dozens of languages. Erm … He's one of the best-known writers in the style of what's called magic realism. This means he writes kind of realistically but there's magic, I mean magical things happen in his books, like ghosts appear and kind of crazy things happen. I'm a big fan of that type of writing. Anyway, his novels are kind of funny but it's black humour or satire. He invents all these amazing, unforgettable characters, like um, corrupt officials and devoted lovers, vicious policemen and stupid revolutionaries and through it all you're laughing at the characters but you also see their world is falling apart. I haven't read his work in Spanish, only English, erm, but the style is brilliant. His dialogue is fast and funny and he writes amazing descriptions of places and people. And, um, well, it was finding Marquez's work as a teenager that really made me become a reader.

C Give Ss 5 mins to think of a person and prepare their ideas. Monitor and help with vocabulary, writing new words/phrases on the board.

D Ss share their descriptions in small groups. Monitor and note down any common errors for later correction. In feedback, nominate Ss from each group to share their descriptions with the class and correct any common errors.

> **Alternative approach**
> Ss describe the person who has influenced them, as in Ex 6D, but don't say who it is. Other Ss in the group try to guess who the person is. In feedback, nominate Ss from each group to describe their people for the class to guess.

writeback a wiki entry

7A Give Ss 2–3 mins to read the proposal. In feedback, ask *Who is the wiki entry about?* (world-famous, influential people in the arts and sciences); *How long should it be?* (no more than 200 words); *What information should it include?* (where they live(d), when they worked, their place in history, why they are/were influential and who they have influenced); and *Who can't you write about?* (political leaders, sports stars or businesspeople).

B Ss read the example and decide if it fits the requirements. In feedback, elicit Ss' answers.

> **Answers:** All the requirements are met in the example.

C Give Ss 10–15 mins to write their wiki entries. Monitor and help with vocabulary and check Ss are producing the language accurately. When they have finished, Ss show their writing to other Ss. In feedback, elicit Ss' favourite entries.

> **Alternative approach**
> If you have internet access, write the following prompts on the board: *name, when they live(d), where there were/are from, what they did, how they influenced you*. Ss research the person on the internet and make notes under the headings. They then use the notes to write their wiki entries.

> **Homework ideas**
> • **Ex 7C:** write a final draft of your wiki entry.

LOOKBACK

Introduction

Ss revise and practise the language of Unit 9. The notes below provide ideas for exploiting the exercises and activities but your approach will depend on your aim, e.g. whether you use the activities as a diagnostic or progress test or as revision/ fluency practice. If done as a test then it would not be appropriate to monitor or help Ss.

HISTORY

1A Organise Ss into small groups/teams. In each team, Ss appoint a secretary to write their sentences. With *weaker classes*, give/elicit an example first. Make sure Ss understand it is a race and the team to finish first wins. Monitor and check Ss are forming their sentences correctly.

B In each team, Ss appoint a spokesperson (a different person from the secretary in Ex 1A) to read out their sentences to the class. Encourage peer correction. When they have finished, ask Ss to vote for the best sentences.

> **Teaching tip**
> Peer correction is a good way to make correction more student-centred and build the group dynamic. When you hear an error, ask *Is there another way we can say that?* Elicit the correction and write it on the board.

THIRD CONDITIONAL

2A Ss complete the sentences alone. Make sure Ss write their sentences on a separate piece of paper (or in their notebooks), as they will give them to someone else in Ex 2B. Monitor and help with vocabulary, writing any new words/ phrases on the board.

B Read the example with the class. Ss exchange sentences with a partner for them to write third conditional sentences. With *weaker classes*, review the form of the third conditional first on the board. Monitor and check Ss are forming the sentences correctly. In feedback, nominate Ss to read out their sentences to the class.

> **Optional extra activity**
> Write the following sentence halves at the top of blank pieces of paper, one sentence half for each piece of paper:
>
> 1 If I hadn't been born in my country, …
>
> 2 If I hadn't got out of bed this morning, …
>
> 3 If I hadn't decided to study English at this school, …
>
> 4 I wouldn't have met my teacher if …
>
> 5 I would have become an astronaut if …
>
> Stick the pieces of paper on the walls around the class and ask Ss to walk round and complete each sentence however they wish. Monitor but don't correct any answers yet. When they have finished, collect the pieces of paper and put Ss in two large groups. Give each group a board pen. Look through Ss' answers and, each round, call out an incorrect sentence. One person from each group comes to the board to write the correction and the rest of their group can call out and help. The first team to correct the error gets a point and the group with the most points at the end wins.

PERIODS OF TIME

3A Ss complete the sentence alone and check their answers in pairs. In feedback, elicit Ss' answers and drill the words if necessary.

> **Answers:** 1 decade 2 nineteen-nineties 3 millennium 4 era 5 fortnight, century 6 generation

B Ss discuss the questions in pairs. In feedback, nominate Ss to share their partner's answers with the class.

THE PASSIVE

4A Read the example with the class. Ss complete the sentences alone, then check their answers in pairs. In feedback, elicit Ss' answers.

> **Answers:** 1 was discovered 2 identified 3 was built 4 climbed 5 was destroyed 6 was released 7 was assassinated 8 was elected 9 declared 10 became

B In pairs, Ss match the dates to the events. If they don't know, they should guess. Don't elicit any answers yet.

C Ss compare their answers in small groups. In feedback, elicit Ss' answers.

> **Answers:** 2 1984: US and French scientists identified the AIDS virus. 3 1961: A wall between East and West Germany was built. 4 1953: Edmund Hillary and Tenzing Norgay climbed Mount Everest. 5 1912: The Titanic was destroyed after hitting an iceberg in the North Atlantic. 6 1990: Nelson Mandela was released from prison. 7 1948: Mahatma Gandhi was assassinated by a terrorist. 8 1979: Margaret Thatcher, the UK's first female prime minister, was elected. 9 1939: The UK and France decleared war on Germany. 10 1908: Two-year-old Pu Yi became Emperor of China.

> **Optional extra activity**
> If you have internet access, Ss can research and write more historical events and their dates using the passive, making some dates true and some false, e.g. *The Berlin Wall was destroyed in 1986*. When they are ready, they read out their sentences for other Ss to guess if they are true or false. In feedback, nominate Ss to read out their facts for the class to guess.

EXPRESSING UNCERTAINTY

5A Ss put the words in order alone, then check their answers in pairs. With *weaker classes*, elicit the first answer as an example first. In feedback, elicit Ss' answers and drill the phrases.

> **Answers:** 1 Sorry, I have no idea 2 No, it's definitely not allowed here. 3 I'm fairly sure it opens at 7.00a.m. 4 I can't remember. 5 Sorry, I haven't a clue. 6 I'm not a hundred percent certain, but it might be Timothy. 7 I'm sure it isn't far. 8 Sorry, I've forgotten.

B Ss discuss the questions in pairs. In feedback, elicit how many questions they can answer and give the answers that they don't know.

OVERVIEW

🎧 BBC VIDEO PODCAST
What are the biggest problems facing the world today?

This video podcast extends discussion of the unit topic to global problems. Ss can view people talking about what they think are the biggest problems facing the world at the moment. Use this video podcast at the start or end of Unit 10.

ETHICAL MAN

Introduction
Ss learn and practise reported speech in the context of environmental issues. They also learn and practise word-building using prefixes.

SUPPLEMENTARY MATERIALS
Resource bank p170, p171 and/or p172
Ex 1B: bring dictionaries for Ss to use.
Warm up: write the questions below on the board.

Warm up
Write on the board *What are the biggest environmental problems facing your country at the moment? How serious are they? What is being done to improve things? What else could be done?* Ss discuss the questions in pairs. In feedback, elicit Ss' answers and have a brief class discussion.

VOCABULARY the environment

1A Check Ss understand 'green living' by eliciting examples and writing them on the board, e.g. *recycling, saving energy*, etc. Ss discuss the question in pairs. In feedback, nominate Ss to share their ideas with the class.

B In pairs, Ss discuss the meanings of the words in bold. If you've brought dictionaries, give them out for Ss to use. In feedback, elicit the definitions and provide further examples if necessary.

Answers: 1 pre-prepared – prepared and packaged by someone else; processed – has had some factory treatment; organic – produced without the use of chemicals
3 energy-saving light bulbs – light bulbs which use less energy than traditional light bulbs 4 insulated – protected from the heat/cold with a layer of material; double-glazed – with two layers of glass 5 on standby – it can still be switched on using a remote control 6 packaging – the wrapping around the product 7 secondhand items – things which are not new, but have been used by someone else
8 recycled – not thrown away as rubbish, but used again

C Ss read the questions in Ex 1B and note down their answers. Monitor and provide support as necessary.

D Ss compare their answers in pairs. In feedback, nominate Ss to tell the class how 'green' their partner is.

➡ VOCABULARYBANK p157 The Environment

1A Teach/Elicit *carbon dioxide*. Read the example and elicit the second answer. Ss work alone to complete the text, then check their answers in pairs. In feedback, elicit Ss' answers.

B Ss work alone to complete the table, then check their answers in pairs. In feedback, elicit Ss' answers.

Stronger classes can do the exercises at home.

Answers: 1A 1 global warming 2 natural resources
3 harmful 4 pollution 5 destroys the environment
6 industrial waste 7 factory smoke 8 car exhaust fumes
9 aerosol cans 10 destruction of the rainforest
11 protect 12 environmentally-friendly
B 1 destruction 2 protect 3 pollution 4 damage
5 waste

READING

2A Read the question with the class and give Ss 3–4 mins to discuss the possible changes in pairs. In feedback, elicit Ss' ideas and write them on the board.

B Ss read the text, then check their ideas from Ex 2A in pairs. In feedback, elicit Ss' answers and tick any ideas on the board that were mentioned.

Answers: He changed the light bulbs in his house to energy-saving light bulbs; changed the way he heats and powers his home; stopped flying and got rid of the car; walked; used bicycles; took public transport; did his supermarket shopping online; ate organic vegetables; stopped eating meat (for a month). His wife walked two miles to the hospital in the middle of the night to have her baby. They went on a twelve-hour train journey instead of taking a two-hour flight.

C Ss discuss the questions in pairs, then read the text again to check their answers. In feedback, elicit Ss' answers.

Answers: 1 His boss asked him to. 2 No (He says, 'I put my family through hell.') 3 They changed the light bulbs and how they heat and power their home. They also changed how they travelled and shopped and ate. 4 Other journalists do things like report from war zones, analyse complex economic data, or work with criminals. 5 Yes, by 37 percent. 6 Yes, many of the changes will remain.

D In pairs, Ss discuss reasons why the experiment was/wasn't a good idea. In feedback, elicit Ss' ideas and have a brief class discussion.

3 Ss find the words in the text alone, then check their answers in pairs. Draw attention to the paragraph numbers next to the definitions to help them. In feedback, elicit Ss' answers and give further examples/explanations if necessary.

Answers: 1 our impact on the environment 2 got rid of 3 nightmarish 4 heatwave 5 put my family through hell 6 being compelled

GRAMMAR reported speech

4A Ss complete the chart alone, then check in pairs. Don't elicit their answers yet.

Teaching tip

With *weaker classes*, do an example first to demonstrate how to report speech. Ask a student: *(Maria), Did you recycle anything last week?* (Yes). Elicit how to report this and write on the board *(Maria) said she had recycled something last week*. Draw attention to the change in tense. Ss complete the chart in Ex 4A.

B Ss check their answers to Ex 4A in the text in Ex 2. In feedback, elicit Ss' answers.

Answers: 1 aren't 2 will 3 walked 4 thought 5 's (has) 6 have 7 liked

C Ss study the table and complete the rules alone, then check in pairs. In feedback, elicit Ss' answers and give further examples if necessary.

Answers: 1 back (backshift) 2 keep the tenses the same 3 pronouns and time references 4 the same as

➡ **LANGUAGEBANK** 10.1 p146–147

Stronger classes could read the notes and do the exercises at home. Otherwise, check the notes with Ss, especially when not to change the tense and the word order in questions. In each exercise, elicit the first answer as an example. Ss work alone to complete the exercises, then check their answers in pairs. In feedback, elicit Ss' answers. Ss can refer to the notes to help.

Answers: 1 1 they were 2 said, there 3 had, their 4 had, next 5 she, her 6 told, was 7 they had 8 couldn't, had
2 1 She said that she thought La Tasca's was her favourite restaurant. 2 He told me he was going to meet Mr Susuki that afternoon. 3 He said that Maja had called him the day before. 4 They told us that they'd meet us there the next day. 5 We told her that we hadn't received her application. 6 She told Matt that she might see him at the party. 7 He said that he'd already sent me an email explaining the situation. 8 She told her boss that she couldn't type very fast.

PRACTICE

5A Read the example with the class. Ss complete the sentences alone, then check their answers in pairs. Don't elicit the answers yet.

B Ss listen to the recording and check their answers. Check Ss' understand the sentences and deal with any questions. Play the recording again and pause after each sentence for Ss to shadow the answers.

Answers: 1 his 2 had 3 they 4 was 5 they 6 had 7 hadn't 8 had

SPEAKING

6A Organise Ss into two groups, Group A and Group B. If you have a *large class*, further divide each group into smaller groups of three or four. Ss read the fact file for their group and discuss the questions in their groups. Monitor and help with any new vocabulary and write it on the board. Monitor each group and check their answers before moving on to Ex 6B.

B Pair Ss from different groups. Ss summarise their discussions for their partner and ask if they agree. In feedback, nominate Ss to share their opinions with the class and have a brief discussion.

VOCABULARY PLUS word-building (prefixes)

7A Write *national* on the board and ask *Does this refer to one country or more than one?* (one). Ask *How can we change it so that it refers to more than one country?* (international). *What have we added here?* (a prefix). Ss underline the prefixes in the sentences, then check their answers in pairs. In feedback, elicit Ss' answers.

Answers: 1 <u>un</u>usual 2 <u>un</u>real 3 <u>re</u>cycled 4 <u>re</u>usable 5 <u>dis</u>agrees 6 <u>dis</u>obey 7 <u>mis</u>understand 8 <u>mis</u>pronounce 9 <u>under</u>weight 10 <u>over</u>cooked

B Ss match the prefixes with the meanings. Encourage them to use the context of the sentences to find the answers. In feedback, elicit Ss' answers.

Answers: 1 un- and dis- 2 re- 3 over- 4 under- 5 mis-

Watch out!

Suffixes never change the meaning of a word, but they can change the stress (*photograph*, *photographic*). Prefixes never change the stress of a word, but they do change the meaning (*national*, *international*). Learning the meaning of common prefixes can greatly widen Ss' vocabulary.

8 Ss complete the sentences alone, then check their answers in pairs. In feedback, elicit Ss' answers.

Answers: 1 unbelievable 2 misjudge 3 disappeared 4 overcook 5 unethical 6 misunderstood 7 untidy 8 disability

speakout TIP

Read the tip with the class. Ss discuss the meanings of the words in bold in Ex 9 in pairs. In feedback, elicit Ss' answers.

9 Ss discuss the questions in pairs. In feedback, nominate Ss to share their opinions with the class and have a brief discussion.

Answers: 1 not trust, or trust very little 2 not known 3 make new again, validate 4 estimate too much, estimate too little 5 not approve

VOCABULARYBANK p157 Word-building

1 Elicit the first answer as an example. Ss work alone to complete the sentences, then check their answers in pairs. In feedback, elicit Ss' answers.

Stronger classes can do the exercise at home.

Answers: 1 inaccurate 2 ex-wife 3 impossible 4 irregular 5 impolite 6 immature 7 inappropriate 8 irresponsible 9 ex-boss 10 irrational 11 inadequate 12 immobile

Homework ideas
- Ex 6A/B: research and write about another environmental problem.
- Language bank 10.1 Ex 1–2, p147
- Vocabulary bank p157
- Workbook Ex 1–6, p65–66

10.2 WORLD FOOD

Introduction

Ss learn and practise verb patterns with reporting verbs in the context of food around the world. They also practise writing a restaurant review.

SUPPLEMENTARY MATERIALS

Resource bank p173

Warm up

In small groups, Ss describe their favourite dish and how to make it. In *multilingual classes*, Ss could discuss famous, or their favourite, dishes from their countries. In feedback, nominate Ss from each group to share their answers with the class.

READING

1 Ss cover the text, focus on the pictures and discuss the questions in pairs. In feedback, elicit Ss' answers and nominate Ss to share their partner's opinions with the class.

Answer: A Italy, the UK or France B China or South-East Asia C India or Thailand

2A Teach/Elicit *bursting*, *instant noodles* and *bankrupt*. Ss read the text then answer the question in pairs. In feedback, elicit the answer.

Answer: Because it has so many amazing places to eat, many selling dishes which were invented in the city, like sushi and instant noodles.

B Ss read the text again, then check their answers in pairs. In feedback, elicit Ss' answers.

Answers: 1 sushi and instant noodles 2 All around the city (including food halls and restaurants) 3 'kuidaore' (eat until you are bankrupt)

LISTENING

3A Ss read the sentences and predict whether the sentences refer to Hiroshima or Madrid. Elicit Ss' predictions but don't give any answers yet. Ss listen and check their predictions. In feedback, elicit Ss' answers.

Answers: 1 M 2 H 3 H 4 M 5 H

B Ss complete the sentences from memory, then listen again and check. After listening, Ss turn to p174–175 and check their answers in the audio script. In feedback, elicit Ss' answers and ask *Have you ever visited any of these cities? If not, would you like to? Do you agree with the speakers?*

Answers: 1 offer 2 famous 3 vegetables 4 ten 5 wonderful/sensational 6 dessert 7 worst

C Ss read the phrases in the box. Check they understand the phrases. Give Ss 5 mins to plan their ideas and make notes. Monitor and help with vocabulary and write any new words/phrases on the board.

D Ss share their experiences in small groups. Monitor and note down any common errors for later correction. In feedback, nominate Ss from each group to share their experiences with the class and correct any common errors.

Unit 10 Recording 2

1   My favourite food city is ah Hiroshima, in Japan … Umhmm … Ah they've got all sorts of food. They've of course got the really famous sushi that everyone thinks about when they think of Japanese food, but they've got so much else to offer. Ah, Hiroshima's really famous for its *okonomiyaki* which is like a cross between a pancake and a pizza … and it's kind of egg and like a flour mixture with cabbage and noodles and meat and sometimes cheese. It's really good. One of my favourite restaurants is a place called, ah, Daikichi, which specialises in grilled chicken you can get grilled chicken with cheese, grilled chicken with plum sauce, ah and a really good soup with rice and ginger in it. I'd love to take you to Daikichi, you'd love it. They do good beer, too. Erm, but also you can get *tempura* in Hiroshima, which is like prawns and vegetables deep fried in a really light, fluffy batter … it's really good. And then, ah, you have also the informal restaurants that are called Izakaya where you go with a group of friends and you order lots of dishes and everyone shares and eats from the middle of the table so it's a great way to try lots of different kinds of food. Actually I know a really good Izakaya that I should take you to.

2   Well, my favourite food city would be Madrid. I lived in Madrid, in Spain for around ten years on and off and the quality of the food is, is wonderful – it's sensational. Spanish people always say that, ah, Spanish food is the best in the world and I always argued while I lived there, that, er, I felt there was a lot more variety of food in the UK, but when I moved back to the UK I really started to miss the richness, the quality of food in Spain. I think my favourite restaurant in Spain was a tiny little, um, Galician which is a part in the north west of Spain, seafood restaurant in a small little bar, it was a very, it wasn't posh or expensive, it was cheap and basic but just served the most wonderful seafood followed by lots of white wine and er, a great *Tarta de Santiago*, a great pastry dessert, afterwards. Another great thing, obviously about Spanish food which you'll've heard of is 'tapas' where everyone gets together on a Sunday lunchtime before lunch to have a few bites to eat and and a few beers together and it's a lovely social atmosphere and it's nice to go out and try a variety of different food. I tried once, ah, pig's ear, which I have to say was possibly the worst thing I've ever tasted, but generally the quality was sensational.

VOCABULARY reporting verbs

4A Read the example with the class. Ss match the verbs and statements alone, then check their answers in pairs. In feedback, elicit Ss' answers.

Answers: 1 b) 2 c) 3 a)

B Refer Ss back to the rules for reported speech in Ex 4A on p117 and explain that when we report speech, we often use reporting verbs instead of *say* to make it sound more natural. Ss complete the sentences with the verbs in the box alone, then check their answers in pairs. With *weaker classes*, check Ss' understand the verbs in the box before they complete the sentences. In feedback, elicit Ss' answers.

Answers: 1 warned 2 invited, offered 3 promised 4 suggested 5 explained 6 refused

GRAMMAR verb patterns

5A Focus attention on the sentences and explain that the reporting verb you use affects the pattern of the words that follow. Read the examples with the class. Ask Ss to complete the chart alone, then check their answers in pairs. In feedback, elicit Ss' answers and give further examples if necessary.

Answers: 1 b) 2 d) 3 c) 4 e) 5 a)

B Ss listen and underline the stressed words. In feedback, elicit Ss' answers.

> **Answers:** She <u>offered</u> to <u>show</u> us <u>around</u>. He <u>agreed</u> to <u>show</u> us <u>around</u> <u>Palermo</u>. They <u>promised</u> to <u>cook</u> for us. They <u>recommended</u> <u>taking</u> the <u>bus</u>. She <u>suggested</u> <u>trying</u> some of the <u>local</u> <u>dishes</u>. They <u>invited</u> us to <u>stay</u>. He <u>warned</u> us <u>not</u> to <u>eat</u> the <u>chillies</u>. She <u>decided</u> that <u>she</u> would <u>stay</u>. We <u>explained</u> that it was our <u>first</u> <u>trip</u> to the <u>area</u>.

C Ss listen again and pay attention to the weak forms. Pause the recording after each sentence for Ss to repeat. If necessary, isolate the weak forms for Ss to practise.

D Read the example with the class. Ss identify the verbs alone, then check their answers in pairs. In feedback, elicit Ss' answers.

> **Answers:** promise (*to* or *that*), suggest (*that* or *-ing*)

▶ **LANGUAGEBANK** 10.2 p146–147

Stronger classes could read the notes and do the exercises at home. Otherwise, check the notes with Ss. In each exercise, elicit the first answer as an example. Ss work alone to complete the exercises, then check their answers in pairs. In feedback, elicit Ss' answers. Ss can refer to the notes to help them.

> **Answers:** 1 1 He refused to pay for the meal.
> 2 She explained that he needed to show his passport to immigration. 3 She suggested booking/that we book our tickets in advance. 4 He offered to pick me up on the way to the station. 5 She invited us all to come for lunch on Sunday. 6 He promised to cook something for dinner. 7 She warned us to hold on to our bags at the station. 8 He agreed to have the meeting on Tuesday.
> 2 1 The company has agreed ~~that~~ *to* pay for the trip.
> 2 correct 3 I suggested ~~to~~ *that she look/looking* for another job. 4 She suggested ~~to call~~ *calling* an ambulance. 5 We offered ~~helping~~ *to help*, but there was nothing we could do. 6 The manager refused *to* let us leave the hotel before we met his wife. 7 We promised to ~~sending~~ *send* her a postcard. 8 correct

---

PRACTICE

6 Ss complete the sentences alone, then check their answers in pairs. Monitor and make sure Ss are using the correct forms. With *weaker classes*, elicit the first sentence as an example. In feedback, elicit Ss' answers.

> **Answers:** 1 explained (to us) that 2 suggested visiting/ suggested that we visit 3 warned, to eat 4 promised to take 5 offered to show

---

SPEAKING

7A Ss read the comments alone and answer the question. In feedback, elicit their ideas and have a brief discussion.

B Ss discuss their opinions in pairs. Monitor and help with vocabulary and write any new words/phrases on the board.

C Ss work with a different partner and tell them about their previous partner. In feedback, nominate Ss to share their opinions with the class and say who has the most similar opinions to them.

WRITING a restaurant review

8A Tell Ss to close their books. Draw a word web on the board and write *a restaurant review* in the middle. Elicit Ss' ideas about what to include in a review and write them on the board. Ss open their books and compare their ideas with the headings in Ex 8A. Ss match the headings to the questions alone, then check their answers in pairs. Monitor and help with vocabulary in if necessary.

> **Answers:** 1 c) 2 e) 3 b) 4 d) 5 a)

B Teach/Elicit *stylish*, *reasonably priced*, *vegan*, *cosy* and *cater for*. Ss read the reviews then discuss the questions in pairs. In feedback, elicit Ss' ideas and preferences.

LEARN TO link ideas

9A Explain that it's important to link our ideas well when writing and there are a number of linking words we can use to do this effectively. Ss read the examples and answer the questions alone, then check their answers in pairs. In feedback, elicit Ss' answers.

> **Answers:** 1 although, while 2 so … that, such … that 3 unless

B Ss read the reviews and underline the linking words. In feedback, elicit Ss' answers.

> **Answers:** Review 1: such … that (line 3), Whilst (line 5)
> Review 2: Although (line 2), so … that (lines 4–5)
> Review 3: such … that (lines 7–9)

C Elicit the first sentence orally as an example. Ss connect the sentences with the linking words alone, then check their answers in pairs. In feedback, nominate one student per sentence to come to the board and write their answer.

> **Answers:** 1 Starbucks has been so successful that now they want to open new stores in China. 2 The restaurant has had such bad reviews that nobody wants to go there. 3 I won't go back there again unless they get a new chef. 4 Although the food was delicious, the service was poor. 5 While the restaurant had a good atmosphere, the food was disappointing.

10 Ss plan and write their reviews. Monitor and help with vocabulary and write any new words/phrases on the board. When they have finished, Ss show their reviews to other Ss and choose which one they would like to visit.

> ### Homework ideas
> - Ex 10: write a final draft of your restaurant review.
> - Language bank 10.2 Ex 1–2, p147
> - Workbook Ex 1–8, p67–68

WHEN YOU TRAVEL, ...

Introduction

Ss learn and practise giving advice and warnings and making generalisations in the context of airports.

SUPPLEMENTARY MATERIALS

Resource bank p174

Warm up: prepare a story about when you had a problem while travelling (or use the one provided below).

Warm up

Tell Ss about a time when you had a problem while travelling. If you can't think of one, tell them the following story (and pretend it's true for you): *Last year, I was coming back from holiday, when the air-traffic controllers decided to go on strike. All flights were cancelled and I had to be back home in two days' time to start a new job. In the end, we had to pay a driver 500 euros to drive us over 1,000 miles back home. When we got home, we found out on the internet that the strike had been called off and the airport reopened just one hour after we'd left! I was furious!* Ask comprehension questions to check Ss understand the story, then Ss discuss their own problem travel experiences in small groups. In feedback, nominate Ss from each group to share their experiences with the class.

VOCABULARY airports

1A Ss discuss the questions in pairs. In feedback, elicit Ss' answers and have a brief class discussion.

B Before doing the exercise, ask *What different things do you have to do at an airport before getting on a plane?* and write Ss' ideas on the board. Ss look at the box and see if any of their ideas are mentioned. Ss complete the sentences alone, then check their answers in pairs. In feedback, elicit Ss' answers and drill the words, especially *aisle*.

Answers: 1 passport 2 gate 3 priority 4 aisle 5 boards
6 card 7 check 8 hand 9 proceed 10 X-ray

C In pairs, Ss put the phrases in the order they would usually hear them. In feedback, elicit Ss' answers but allow for some variation, as the order might vary in different airports around the world.

Suggested answer: 1, 7, 8, 4, 2, 5, 10, 9, 3, 6

FUNCTION giving advice/warnings

2A Tell Ss to close their books. Divide the board into two sections. At the top of section 1, write *Things you must do in an airport*; at the top of section 2, write *Things you mustn't do in an airport*. Divide the class in half. One group creates a list for section 1 and the other group creates a list for section 2. Monitor and help with vocabulary as needed. In feedback, elicit the groups' ideas and write them on the board.

B Ss read the text and compare it with the ideas on the board. In feedback, elicit which of their ideas were mentioned and any other ideas they read about.

C Ss discuss the questions in pairs. In feedback, nominate Ss to share their opinions/experiences with the class. If Ss have experienced any of these problems, encourage them to elaborate and tell their stories.

3A Read the situations with the class and check Ss understand them. Ss listen and match the conversations to the situations, then check their answers in pairs. In feedback, elicit Ss' answers.

Answers: 1 d) 2 b) 3 c) 4 a)

B Ss listen again and identify the problems, then check their answers in pairs. In feedback, elicit Ss' answers.

Answers: 1 unlicensed taxi drivers 2 tube delays
3 mosquitoes and malaria, drinking unpurified water
4 street crime

Unit 10 Recording 4

Conversation 1

W=Woman M=Man

W: Is there anything I should know for when I arrive at the airport?

M: Yes, watch out for the taxi drivers who tend to hang around outside the airport. Most of them aren't licensed, so you shouldn't really use them.

W: OK.

M: If you do use one, make sure you find out how much the journey is supposed to cost. Don't get in until you've agreed the price with the driver, or else you could find that you have to pay three or four times the amount you should pay for the journey.

W: Oh right. That's good to know.

Conversation 2

M=Man W=Woman

M: Hi – I'm going to Heathrow tomorrow and my plane leaves at 3p.m. Latest check in time is 1.40. What time do you think I should leave central London?

W: For Heathrow? Well, you'd better leave plenty of time, because often there are delays on the tube. Are you going on the tube or the train?

M: The tube, I think.

W: The tube? If I were you, I'd allow about an hour and a half. So, if you want to be at the airport at 1.30, then you'd better leave at about twelve o'clock.

M: OK. That's great. Thanks.

Conversation 3

M1=1st man M2=2nd man

M1: Be careful when you take trips into the jungle in the north. Generally, there are a lot of mosquitoes there, so remember to take mosquito nets and insect cream. It's a good idea to wear long trousers and shirts with sleeves in the evening. And don't forget to take your malaria tablets.

M2: Oh yes, I must remember those.

M1: And whatever you do, don't drink the water, or you'll get a bad stomach.

M2: Oh, I didn't know that.

M1: Yes, always be sure to boil the water first, or drink bottled water. You have to be careful when you eat raw food, too, like fruit, if it's been washed in water.

M2: OK.

Conversation 4

W1=1st woman W2=2nd woman

W1: We're going there on holiday and I've heard that there's a lot of street crime. Is that true?

W2: Not really no. I mean, it's like any big city. You need to watch out for groups of young children on the streets. They try to distract you and then sometimes take your bag.

W1: Oh. Right.

W2: It's not very common, but don't walk around the city obviously carrying money in a big money belt or anything.

W1: Of course.

W2: The most important thing is to remember to hold on to your handbag and things like that, but no, there isn't really much crime. On the whole, it's a pretty safe city.

W1: That's useful, thanks.

4A Ss match the sentence halves alone, then check their answers in pairs. Don't elicit the answers yet.

B Ss listen and check their answers. In feedback, elicit Ss' answers. Play the recording again and pause after each sentence for Ss to repeat, paying attention to the stressed words.

Answers: 1 d) 2 b) 3 h) 4 g) 5 e) 6 a) 7 j) 8 f) 9 c) 10 i)

Unit 10 Recording 5

1 Watch out for the taxi drivers who tend to hang around outside the airport.

2 Make sure you find out how much the journey is supposed to cost,

3 Don't get in until you've agreed the price with the driver, or else …

4 You'd better leave plenty of time.

5 If I were you, I'd allow about an hour and a half.

6 Be careful when you take trips into the jungle.

7 Don't forget to take your malaria tablets.

8 Whatever you do, don't drink the water.

9 You need to watch out for groups of young children on the streets.

10 The most important thing is to remember to hold on to your handbag.

⟱ **LANGUAGEBANK** 10.3 p146–147

Stronger classes could read the notes and do the exercise at home. Otherwise, drill the phrases in the notes and elicit possible continuations. Elicit the first answer in Ex 1 as an example. Ss work alone to make sentences, then check their answers in pairs. In feedback, elicit Ss' answers.

Answers: 1 Don't forget to set the alarm. 2 You need to buy a ticket before you get on the train. 3 If I were you, I'd call them before you leave. 4 Watch out for speed cameras. There are lots on the road. 5 Make sure you apply for a visa. 6 Whatever you do, don't leave valuable items in the room. 7 The most important thing is to check your flight times. 8 Don't forget to take your mobile phone.

---

5 Elicit the mistake in the first sentence as an example. Ss correct the mistakes alone, then check their answers in pairs. In feedback, elicit Ss' answers.

Answers: 1 The most important thing to remember is not going *to go* out alone. 2 If I were you I'll *I'd* bring waterproof clothes. 3 Make sure if you wear a helmet when you ride a motorbike. 4 Be carefully when you're on the main roads. They're very busy. 5 Don't forgetting to keep your luggage with you at all times. 6 Whatever you are do, don't buy food from the street sellers. It's terrible. 7 Watch out for people try *trying* to sell you fake watches. 8 You'll *You'd* better leave your valuables in the hotel.

LEARN TO make generalisations

6A Elicit the incorrect alternative in the first sentence as an example. Make sure Ss understand that two of the alternatives are correct. In feedback, elicit Ss' answers.

Answers: The following are not possible: 1 are tend to 2 never 3 Always 4 On the whole 5 For the whole

B Ss listen and underline the alternatives the speakers use. In feedback, elicit Ss' answers and drill the phrases.

Answers: 1 tend to 2 often 3 Generally 4 It's not very common 5 On the whole

speakout TIP

Read the tip with the class. Nominate Ss to make a generalisation about their country using a different phrase from Ex 6A each time.

7 Read the example with the class. Ss write the sentences alone, then compare their answers in pairs. In feedback, elicit Ss' answers.

Answers: 1 Men tend to use the internet more than women. 2 On the whole, I go to bed early in the winter. 3 The beaches are generally clean and safe./Generally, the beaches are clean and safe. 4 It's not common for the trains to the airport to be delayed. 5 Criminals have a tendency to target tourists. 6 English people often complain about the weather.

SPEAKING

8A Put Ss into A/B pairs and give them 3–4 mins to read the information and think about what to say. Monitor and help with vocabulary as necessary. When they are ready, Ss practise the role-plays in pairs. Monitor and note down any common errors for later correction.

B Ss swap roles and repeat the procedure in Ex 8A. Monitor and note down any common errors for later correction. In feedback, nominate one or two pairs to perform their role-plays for the class. Correct any common errors with the class.

Homework ideas
- Language bank 10.3 Ex 1, p147
- Workbook Ex 1–3, p69

THE GREAT MELT

Introduction

Ss watch an extract from a BBC nature documentary about the growing difficulties for polar bears when arctic ice melts.

SUPPLEMENTARY MATERIALS

Warm up: write the questions below on the board.

Warm up

Write on the board *What are the effects of climate change on the world? Has your country been affected as a direct result of climate change? What can we do to prevent it?* Ss discuss the questions in pairs. In feedback, elicit Ss' answers.

▶ DVD PREVIEW

1 Focus attention on the photos and ask *Where do you think this is?* (the Arctic) *Do you know who the man in the photo is?* (Sir David Attenborough) Ss read the text alone, then work in pairs to predict why life is difficult for the polar bears. In feedback, elicit Ss answers and ask *Do you know of any other animals which are endangered? What are the causes?*

Culture notes

The BBC nature documentary *Nature's Great Events* was first aired in 2009 and looks at how annual changes in the patterns of movement of the sun lead to some of the world's greatest natural events. This programme looks at the annual summer thaw in the Arctic oceans. In recent years, due to climate change, more and more ice has been melting each year. As polar bears travel out on the ice to hunt for seals, more and more of the ice breaks up. Polar bears then become trapped on ice floes, floating in the sea and have to swim greater distances between the ice and to safety, which is swiftly decreasing their numbers.

The programme is directed by Sir David Attenborough, who is widely recognised as the face of British nature documentaries, having presented them for over 50 years. He has won countless awards for his work. If Ss are interested, they can find out more at www.bbc.co.uk/naturesgreatevents/.

▶ DVD VIEW

2 Read the questions with the class and elicit their predictions. Play the DVD. Ss watch and check their predictions, then compare their answers in pairs. Check the answers.

Answers: 1 Because they can become trapped at sea, starve, or drown in the open sea. 2 Yes, it's worse.

3A Check Ss understand the words in the box, especially *flicker* and *drown*. Ss complete the sentences alone, then check their answers in pairs. Don't elicit any answers yet.

B Ss watch the DVD again and check their answers. In feedback, elicit Ss' answers.

Answers: 1 flicker 2 sea 3 rises 4 summer 5 islands 6 ice 7 drown

Optional extra activity

If you think Ss need more practice with the vocabulary, write on the board *Can you think of any other things which flicker? When does the sun rise in winter in your country? And in summer? are there any islands which are part of your country?* Ss discuss in small groups. In feedback, nominate Ss from each group to share their ideas with the class.

4 Ss discuss the questions in small groups. In feedback, nominate Ss from each group to share their opinions with the class and have a brief discussion.

DVD 10 Nature's Great Events: The Great Melt

DA=David Attenborough

DA: Winter in the Arctic. The northern lights flicker across the sky. It's a land of continuous night, where temperatures plummet to minus 40.

Polar bears are in their element, hunting for seals on the frozen sea.

But the long night is coming to an end. In February the sun rises for the first time in four months.

In the coming weeks the strength of the sun will power an enormous change, but for now its rays offer only a little warmth.

At the height of summer even the permanent ice-caps are touched by the power of the sun.

As July draws on, the great melt reaches its peak.

The greatest seasonal change on the planet has taken place.

The sea ice that once extended all the way to the horizon is now open ocean.

In just three months the sun has won its battle with the ice.

Over seven million square kilometres of ice has melted away, uncovering thousands of islands surrounded by open ocean. But in recent years the scale of this melt has been growing. And for one animal, this is a critical issue.

A mother bear and her adolescent cub rest on a fragment of sea ice. With the melt, they're forced to swim ever greater distances to hunt for seals.

Their Arctic home is increasingly vulnerable to a changing climate and this year there has been even less ice than normal.

If future melts are as extreme as this one, bears like these may starve or drown, lost at sea.

This is one of the last pieces of ice now adrift in the open ocean. The polar bear's icy world has melted away.

speakout an endangered place

5A Read the questions with the class and check Ss know what they are listening for. Ss listen and answer the questions, then check their answers in pairs. In feedback, elicit some of the Ss' answers.

Answers: 1 Venice 2 It is slowly sinking. 3 Because many people think it is one of the most romantic cities in the world – it has beautiful bridges and no cars. 4 answer not given 5 We can put pressure on the government to find a permanent solution.

B Give Ss 1 min to read the phrases. Ss listen again and tick the phrases they hear. In feedback, elicit Ss' answers and drill the phrases.

> **Answers:** ✓ The problem is that … We have an opportunity to … … before it's too late.

Unit 10 Recording 7

R=Rob Hustin

R: One place that I think everyone should have the chance to see is Venice. But the problem is that this beautiful and charming city is slowly sinking. Ever since the fourteenth century engineers have tried to work out a way to stop the floods in Venice, but so far nobody has managed. Sometimes there are as many as forty floods per year between March and September and Venice is actually sinking at a rate of two and a half inches every decade. It's very possible that your grandchildren and their grandchildren will never have the chance to see this fragile city. Everyone should have the chance to enjoy the city, to walk across its famous bridges, through its ancient squares. There are no cars in Venice and many people think it helps this to be one of the most romantic cities in the world. So, can it be saved?

Well, they are trying. Barriers are being put in to try and stop the water getting too high. This is viewed as a temporary measure, although they should last a hundred years, so the problem is finding a permanent solution. If you want my advice, go there while you still can and then together we can put pressure on the government to spend the money it needs to find a permanent way to keep this beautiful and historic city for future generations. We have an opportunity now to save this city and we must, before it's too late.

6A If you have access to the internet, give Ss 10 mins to research a place/animal first. If not and Ss need help, they can turn to p163 and choose one of the places there. Ss plan their talks, using the questions to help them and make notes. Monitor and help with vocabulary and write any new words/ phrases on the board.

B When giving a presentation, it's important to practise delivery as well as content. Ss have a chance to practise this here. Ss practise their presentations in pairs, with their partner making notes on how they can improve. When they have finished, they give each other feedback. Monitor and help, providing suggestions where possible.

C Ss give their presentations to the class. Make sure all Ss are paying attention and offer lots of praise and encouragement. In feedback, elicit which of the places Ss would like to visit.

> **Teaching tip**
>
> Giving a presentation can be nerve-racking. Encourage Ss to do their best and offer plenty of support. When each student has given their presentation, encourage the class to give a round of applause.

writeback email for action

7A Teach/Elicit *cobbled street* and *demolish*. Ss read the email and answer the questions. In feedback, elicit Ss' answers.

> **Answers:** Little Green Street is just outside the centre of London. A developer plans to build a car park nearby and the writer is worried that the heavy machinery and lorries will destroy the street and the house in it.

B Ss choose one of the places they talked about in Ex 6 (their own or someone else's) and write their emails. Monitor and help with vocabulary and write any new words/phrases on the board. When they have finished, Ss show their emails to other Ss and they choose the best one.

> **Optional extra activity**
>
> When Ss have finished their drafts, collect them in. Arrange Ss in small groups and explain the following *You are members of your government's environmental protection agency and have been given enough money to solve the problem in one of the emails for action.* Ss read the emails and then discuss which of the problems they will choose to spend money on and why. In feedback, nominate Ss from each group to share their decisions and reasons with the whole class.

> **Homework ideas**
> * Ex 6C: write about the place you gave a presentation on.
> * Ex 7B: write a final draft of your email for action.

LOOKBACK

Introduction

Ss revise and practise the language of Unit 10. The notes below provide ideas for exploiting the exercises and activities but your approach will depend on your aim, e.g. whether you use the activities as a diagnostic or progress test or as revision/fluency practice. If done as a test then it would not be appropriate to monitor or help Ss.

THE ENVIRONMENT

1A Ss complete the words/phrases alone, then check their answers in pairs. In feedback, elicit Ss' answers.

Answers: 1 organic 2 pre-prepared 3 energy-saving 4 insulated 5 recycle 6 on standby 7 secondhand 8 processed

B Give two examples about yourself to demonstrate. Ss write their sentences alone, then compare them in pairs and see if they have any answers in common. In feedback, nominate Ss to share their ideas with the class.

REPORTED SPEECH

2 Read the example with the class. Ss write the conversation in direct speech, then check it in pairs. Monitor and check Ss are using the correct tenses/verb forms. In feedback, nominate a pair to read the conversation out to the class.

Answers: Samantha: Franco, this is Tom. **Tom**: Pleased to meet you. **Franco**: It's a pleasure to meet you, too. I hope you're enjoying your stay in Milan. **Tom**: I think Milan is a beautiful city and I have very much enjoyed my stay here. I've met lots of wonderful people and eaten some delicious food. **Franco**: Have you had the chance to do any sightseeing? **Tom**: Unfortunately, I haven't had very much time at all, but I enjoyed seeing the cathedral. **Franco**: Do you plan to come and visit Italy again soon? **Tom**: I would love to, but Italy is a long way from Queensland. **Franco**: That's true. Would you like to come and have a coffee with us before you go to the airport? **Tom**: I'd love to. Thank you.

3A Ss ask and answer the questions in pairs. Monitor and make sure Ss note down their partner's answers.

B Rearrange Ss into new pairs. Ss report their previous partner's answers and see if they have any answers in common. Monitor and check Ss are reporting correctly. In feedback, nominate Ss to share their answers with the class.

REPORTING VERBS

4 Read the example with the class. Ss take it in turns to test each other in pairs. In feedback, nominate Ss to demonstrate their sentences for the class to guess the verbs.

Optional extra activity
Arrange Ss in pairs. Give them 5 mins to write a short dialogue using two of the actions represented by the verbs in Ex 4. Monitor and help with vocabulary, writing any new words/expressions on the board. When they are ready, Ss perform their dialogues for the class and other Ss decide which two action were included.

VERB PATTERNS

5A Ss circle the correct alternatives alone, then check their answers in pairs. In feedback, elicit Ss' answers.

Answers: 1 to give 2 to answer 3 to stay 4 to pay 5 that it was 6 that they wanted

B Ss discuss the questions in pairs. In feedback, nominate Ss to share their partner's answers with the class.

GIVING ADVICE/WARNINGS

6A Elicit the first answer as an example. Ss complete the advice/warnings alone, then check their answers in pairs. Monitor and check that Ss have formed the advice/warnings correctly. In feedback, elicit Ss' answers.

Answers: 1 Whatever you do 2 Don't forget to 3 Make sure 4 Don't … or else 5 I were you 6 Be careful 7 'd better 8 You need to

B Ss match the situations with the advice/warnings alone, then check their answers in pairs. In feedback, elicit some of the Ss' answers.

Answers: a) 1 b) 5 c) 7 d) 6 e) 8 f) 3 g) 2 h) 4

C Ss cover the phrases in Ex 6A and take it in turns to give each other advice using the situations in Ex 6B. Monitor and prompt Ss to use the phrases. In feedback, elicit what advice Ss gave for each situation.

Optional extra activity
In pairs, Ss look at the situations in Ex 6B and think about times when they have been in these, or similar situations. Ss discuss what they did and compare with the advice from Ex 6A. In feedback, nominate Ss to share their experiences with the class.

Homework ideas
• Workbook Review and check 5, p70–72
• Workbook Test 5, p73

PAGE	UNIT	PHOTOCOPIABLE	LANGUAGE POINT	TIME
125	1	Who you know	**Vocabulary: family and relationships** • review vocabulary of family and relationships • practise speaking skills by asking and answering questions	25–30
126	1	Collocation dominoes	**Vocabulary plus: collocations with *take, get, do, go*** • review collocations with *take, get, do* and *go*	25–30
127	1	Similarities	**Grammar: question forms** • practise forming questions • practise speaking skills by asking questions to find similarities	30–40
128	1	Queens and kings	**Grammar: review of verb tenses** • use the present simple, present continuous, past simple and past continuous • practise speaking skills by asking and answering questions	30–40
129	1	Jobs fair	**Functional language: talking about yourself** • practise functional language for talking about yourself in the context of jobs	30–40
130	2	You're the director	**Vocabulary: types of story and the news** • review vocabulary of types of story and the news • practise speaking skills by discussing and presenting ideas for a film	30–40
131	2	Shapes of you	**Vocabulary plus: prepositions** • review prepositions and expressions of time • practise speaking skills by guessing and explaining information	25–30
132	2	Celebrity facts	**Grammar: present perfect/past simple** • practise the present perfect and past simple in a true/false activity	30–40
133	2	In your dreams	**Grammar: narrative tenses** • use the past simple, past continuous and past perfect • practise speaking skills by describing and asking about a dream	30–40
134	2	What happened next?	**Functional language: telling a story** • practise functional language for telling a story and keeping a story going	30–40
135	3	What did you say?	**Vocabulary: communication** • review vocabulary of communication	20–30
136	3	Idiom wars	**Vocabulary plus: idioms** • review idioms in the context of a game	25–30
137	3	The contract of life	**Grammar: the future (plans)** • practise future forms for making plans	20–30
138	3	Inventions	**Grammar: the future (predictions)** • use future forms for making predictions • practise speaking skills by discussing and presenting an invention	30–40
139	3	Sorry, I didn't catch that	**Functional language: dealing with misunderstandings** • practise functional language for dealing with misunderstandings in role-play situations	30–40
140	4	Three jobs	**Vocabulary: personal qualities** • review vocabulary of personal qualities • practise speaking skills by finding out and giving information about jobs	30–40
141	4	Finding the right words	**Vocabulary plus: confusing words** • review vocabulary of confusing words in the context of a correction activity • practise speaking skills by discussing statements	25–35
142	4	Top tips	**Grammar: *must, have to, should*** • use modals of obligation *must, have to* and *should* to give advice	30–40
143	4	Those were the days	**Grammar: *used to, would*** • use *used to* and *would* in the context of talking about your childhood • practise speaking skills by asking about people's childhoods	30–40
144	4	Coalition government	**Functional language: reaching agreement** • practise functional language for reaching agreement in a role-play situation	30–40
145	5	Give us a clue	**Vocabulary: technology** • review vocabulary of technology • practise speaking skills by describing types of technology	25–35
146	5	Word-building race	**Vocabulary plus: word-building: adjectives** • review adjective suffixes in the context of a board game	30–40
147	5	Which phone?	**Grammar: comparatives/superlatives** • use comparatives and superlatives to compare phones • practise speaking skills by discussing and comparing information on phones	30–40
148	5	You're not French, are you?	**Grammar: question tags** • use question tags • practise rising and falling intonation in question tags to check information	25–30
149	5	What's the problem?	**Functional language: polite requests** • practise functional language for polite requests in role-play situations	30–40

RESOURCE BANK

Index of photocopiables

PAGE	UNIT	PHOTOCOPIABLE	LANGUAGE POINT	TIME
150	6	How emotional are you?	**Vocabulary: -ing/-ed adjectives** • review -ing/-ed adjectives in the context of a questionnaire	30–40
151	6	Guess the verb	**Vocabulary plus: multi-word verbs** • review multi-word verbs • practise speaking skills by describing the meaning of multi-word verbs	25–30
152	6	Conditionals race	**Grammar: zero and first conditionals** • practise zero and first conditionals in the context of a board game	30–40
153	6	Why would you do that?	**Grammar: second conditional** • use the second conditional in the context of a game	30–40
154	6	Mixed emotions	**Functional language: giving news** • practise functional language for giving news and responding to news	30–40
155	7	Gifted!	**Vocabulary: success and ability** • review vocabulary of success and ability • practise speaking skills by asking questions about success and ability	30–40
156	7	All about you	**Vocabulary plus: verb phrases with prepositions** • review verb phrases with prepositions • practise speaking skills by asking personal questions	30–40
157	7	Guess the film star	**Grammar: present perfect simple vs continuous** • practise present perfect simple vs continuous in the context of a guessing game	30–40
158	7	Mixed abilities	**Grammar: present and past ability** • practise *can, can't, could, couldn't, be able to* and *manage to* for present and past ability • practise speaking skills by asking about abilities	30–40
159	7	Sound investments	**Functional language: clarifying opinions** • practise functional language for clarifying opinions in a role-play situation	30–40
160	8	Do you get on?	**Vocabulary: getting on** • review vocabulary of getting on • practise speaking skills by asking and answering questions about getting on	30–40
161	8	Pelmanism	**Vocabulary plus: compound nouns** • review compound nouns in the context of a game	25–30
162	8	Where I live	**Grammar: articles and quantifiers** • practise articles and quantifiers • practise speaking skills by discussing statements about where you live	25–35
163	8	Internet relativity	**Grammar: relative clauses** • practise relative clauses by finishing sentences	25–35
164	8	Making yourself at home	**Functional language: being a good guest** • practise functional language for being a good guest in role-play situations	30–40
165	9	The history of my country	**Vocabulary: history and periods of time** • review vocabulary of history and periods of time • practise speaking skills by discussing and presenting the history of a country	30–40
166	9	Guess my collocation	**Vocabulary plus: collocations with *come, give, have, make*** • review collocations with *come, give, have* and *make* in a guessing game	25–35
167	9	Bad decisions	**Grammar: third conditional** • practise the third conditional in the context of reflecting on bad decisions made in history	30–40
168	9	Amazing facts	**Grammar: active vs passive** • practise forming active and passive sentences in a true/false activity	25–30
169	9	School quiz	**Functional language: expressing uncertainty** • practise functional language for expressing uncertainty	30–40
170	10	'Green test' your school	**Vocabulary: the environment** • review vocabulary of the environment in the context of a questionnaire • practise speaking skills by discussing recommendations	50–60
171	10	Do you agree?	**Vocabulary plus: word-building (prefixes)** • review word-building using prefixes • practise speaking skills by discussing whether you agree or disagree with statements	30–40
172	10	At the races	**Grammar: reported speech** • practise reported speech in the context of a game	30–40
173	10	Report that!	**Grammar: verb patterns** • use verb patterns in reported speech in the context of a game	30–40
174	10	When in Rome …	**Functional language: giving advice/warnings** • practise functional language for giving advice and warnings to visitors to a place you know well	30–40

Worksheet A

1 **Read out the sentences for your partner to correct the underlined words.**

1 When I was at junior school, I was a very good <u>employee</u>.

2 When I meet up with my <u>team-mates</u> after school, we speak English together to get more practice.

3 I'm a <u>partner</u> of several clubs in my home town.

4 <u>I'm related to</u> my mother – we look the same and have a similar personality.

5 I think a good <u>mentor</u> is always ready to listen to his or her employees.

6 No one has ever asked me to be the <u>great-grandmother</u> of their child.

7 I've never <u>inherited</u>. I'm still waiting for the right person to come along!

8 I don't live with my <u>family history</u>, but they all live quite near so I see them often.

9 I don't know much about my mother's <u>roots</u> of the family.

10 I don't get to see my <u>ancestors</u> very often. Most of them live in a different city.

2 **Are the sentences true or false for you? Discuss with your partner.**

Worksheet B

1 **Read out the sentences for your partner to correct the underlined words.**

1 I like team sports, but success often depends on your <u>classmates</u>.

2 If I owned a company and an <u>pupil</u> was always late, I would fire them.

3 My <u>relatives</u> came to my country in the 1800s.

4 I never knew my <u>godmother</u> – she died a long time before I was born.

5 I don't know much about my <u>extended family</u> – only back to the 1950s.

6 To be a good <u>boss</u>, I think you need to know how your pupils learn best.

7 In class, I like working with a <u>member</u> more than working on my own.

8 My family's <u>side</u> are in the town which I grew up in.

9 I <u>take after</u> someone famous – well, my brother was in the local newspaper once!

10 I've never <u>had a fiancé/fiancée</u> anything.

2 **Are the sentences true or false for you? Discuss with your partner.**

a course	get	a degree	take	after someone	go
for a drink	take	a taxi	go	for a walk	go
for a meal	do	exercise	go	off something	do
housework	get	here	do	research	take
responsibility for	get	married	get	on with someone	go
grey	do	some work	get	a job	do
someone a favour	go	home	take	part in something	do

1 Complete the information about yourself. Add three more facts.

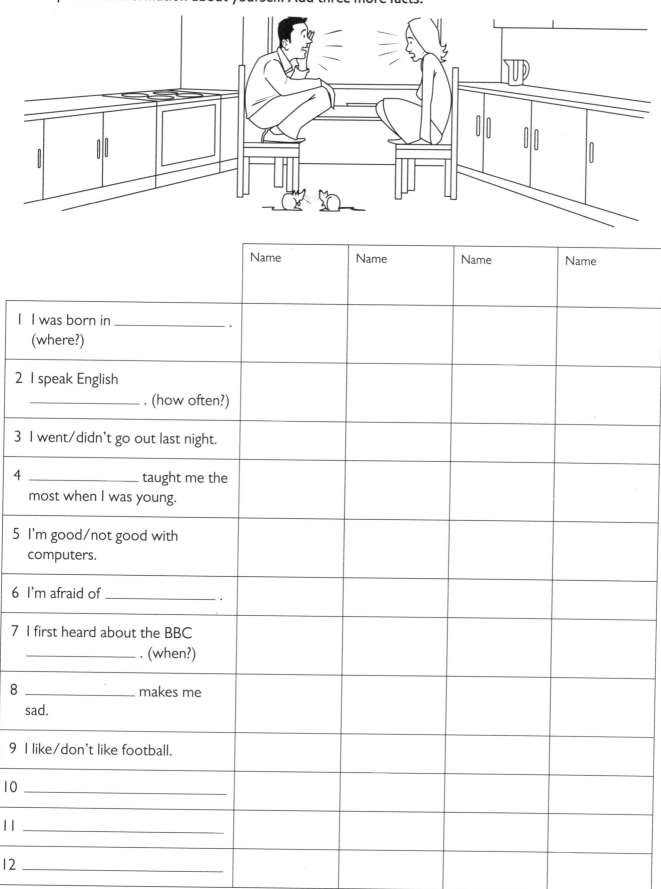

	Name	Name	Name	Name
1 I was born in _____ . (where?)				
2 I speak English _____ . (how often?)				
3 I went/didn't go out last night.				
4 _____ taught me the most when I was young.				
5 I'm good/not good with computers.				
6 I'm afraid of _____ .				
7 I first heard about the BBC _____ . (when?)				
8 _____ makes me sad.				
9 I like/don't like football.				
10 _____				
11 _____				
12 _____				

2 Ask some of your classmates the questions. Tick ✓ if they are the same or cross ✗ if they are different.

QUEENS AND KINGS

Grammar: review of verb tenses

Worksheet A

Ask your partner questions to complete the text about Queen Elizabeth II. Then answer your partner's questions about King Juan Carlos I.

Queen Elizabeth II of the United Kingdom

Queen Elizabeth II of the United Kingdom was born in London on the [1] _____ . She has one sister, Princess Margaret. She is married to [2] _____ . They got married on the 20th of November 1947, when they received [3] _____ from around the world. She later had her first child, Prince Charles, while they were [4] _____ in 1948.

While she was [5] _____ in 1952, her father died and she became queen.

In 1977 she celebrated her [6] _____ (twenty-five years), and in 2002 she celebrated her [7] _____ (fifty years). At the moment, she is hoping to become [8] _____ in British history. (This will actually happen on the 10th of September 2015.)

She lives at Buckingham Palace, but it is reported that she prefers [9] _____ .

Currently, she is working hard to [10] _____ .

King Juan Carlos I of Spain

King Juan Carlos I of Spain was born in Rome on the 5th of January 1938. He got married in 1962 to Sofía of Greece and Denmark, and they have three children and eight grandchildren.

In 1969, the dictator Francisco Franco named Juan Carlos as his successor. In 1974 and 1975, while the dictator was suffering from health problems, Juan Carlos was temporary head of state. On the 22nd of November 1975, two days after the death of Franco, Juan Carlos became king.

At the moment he is enjoying popular support from Spanish people, and in 2008 he was voted the most popular leader in all Ibero-American states. At present he is working hard to promote Ibero-American relations.

He speaks Spanish, English, French, Italian and Portuguese. He likes sport and while the Spanish football team were celebrating their 2010 World Cup victory, he told them 'You made our best dreams come true.'

Worksheet B

Ask your partner questions to complete the text about King Juan Carlos I. Then answer your partner's questions about Queen Elizabeth II.

King Juan Carlos I of Spain

King Juan Carlos I of Spain was born in [1] _____ on the 5th of January 1938. He got married in 1962 to [2] _____ , and they have three children and [3] _____ grandchildren.

In 1969, the dictator Francisco Franco named Juan Carlos as [4] _____ . In 1974 and 1975, while the dictator was [5] _____ , Juan Carlos was temporary head of state. On the 22nd of November 1975, two days after the death of Franco, Juan Carlos [6] _____ .

At the moment he is enjoying [7] _____ , and in 2008 he was voted the most popular leader in all Ibero-American states. At present he is [8] _____ Ibero-American relations.

He speaks [9] _____ . He likes sport and while the Spanish football team were celebrating [10] _____ , he told them 'You made our best dreams come true.'

Queen Elizabeth II of the United Kingdom

Queen Elizabeth II of the United Kingdom was born in London on the 21st of April 1926. She has one sister, Princess Margaret. She is married to Prince Philip, the Duke of Edinburgh. They got married on the 20th of November 1947, when they received 2,500 wedding gifts from around the world. She later had her first child, Prince Charles, while they were living near Windsor in 1948.

While she was visiting Kenya in 1952, her father died and she became queen.

In 1977 she celebrated her Silver Jubilee (twenty-five years), and in 2002 she celebrated her Golden Jubilee (fifty years). At the moment, she is hoping to become the longest-reigning queen in British history. (This will actually happen on the 10th of September 2015.)

She lives at Buckingham Palace, but it is reported that she prefers Windsor Castle.

Currently, she is working hard to promote her 600 charities and organisations.

Role card 1

You are an exhibitor at a jobs fair. You are looking to recruit suitable people to train and work for your company. Competition between companies at the jobs fair to recruit new people is high, so think about how you can persuade people to work for you.

First decide on the following information:

Position available: _____

Main duties/tasks of the position: _____

Qualifications needed: _____

Experience required: _____

Personal qualities you are looking for: _____

Typical hours: _____

Working environment: _____

Best things about the position: _____

When you are ready, take your place at the jobs fair and ask and answer questions about the position.

Role card 2

You are looking for a new job and have decided to go to a jobs fair, where different companies are looking to recruit people for positions in their companies. You want to find the best job possible.

First decide on the following information:

Type of job you are looking for: _____

Qualifications you have: _____

Experience you have: _____

Your top three personal qualities: _____

Which **three** of the following are important to you, and why?

working outside	working in an office	working with people	caring for people
using computers	physical work	challenging work	being creative selling things
managing people	training people	being competitive	other (say which)

_____

_____

When you are ready, visit the companies and ask questions about the positions available. Choose one you would like to apply for.

1   Choose a type of film and some events.

Types of film

> biopic   docudrama   disaster   romantic comedy   period drama   fantasy/science fiction
> mystery/crime   action/adventure   psychological thriller

Events

> a crash happens   someone attacks the hero   a lot of violence occurs   a fugitive is caught
> an earthquake hits the city   X and Y fall in love   the queen dies   X is destroyed
> workers go on strike   hostages are taken/released   X gets shot
> X causes an economic collapse   Lord X falls ill   X has an affair   other (say which)

2   Complete the storyboard then present your ideas to the class.

1	2	3
Background	Main characters	Problem

4	5	6
Solution	Further problem	Ending – happy or sad?

1 **Make notes on these topics randomly in the shapes.**

- something you usually do at the weekend

- a good programme on TV in your country at the moment

- the last time you were in a hurry – and why

- where you were on New Year's Day this year

- a place where you like going for a walk

- the name of a song by your favourite singer/band

- the last time you travelled by boat

- where you were in 2008

- something you like doing on your own

- a person you met by chance

- what you usually do in the evening

- the last time you went for a run

- something you did on purpose and regretted

- the last person you spoke to on the phone

- something you have made by hand

- if you are usually on time or late

Fold ─

2 **Look at your partner's notes and guess what they refer to.**

Worksheet A

Read out your celebrity facts, choosing the correct verb form. Then listen to your partner's facts and say if they are true or false.

1 At the age of ten, Justin Timberlake **has won/won** the 1991 pre-teen Mr America contest. (true)

2 Christina Aguilera **has recorded/recorded** an album in Spanish, but she doesn't speak the language. (true)

3 When he was a child, Jim Carrey **has worn/wore** tap shoes to bed, in case his parents needed cheering up in the middle of the night. (true)

4 Drew Barrymore **has never directed/never directed** a film. (false – she directed her first film *Whip It* in 2009)

5 Samuel L. Jackson **has first appeared/first appeared** in a film when he was two years old. (false – Samuel L. Jackson first appeared in the film *Together for Days* in 1972, when he was twenty-four)

6 Jack Black **has been/was** an actor since 1969. (false – he was born in 1969)

7 The film *Titanic* **has never been/was never** translated into any languages other than English. (false – it has been translated into many languages)

8 Janis Joplin, Jimi Hendrix, Jim Morrison and Kurt Cobain **have all died/all died** when they were twenty-seven. (true)

9 James Bond is a real agent in the British secret service. He **has worked/worked** there for over twenty years. (false – James Bond is a fictional character)

10 Tom Cruise **has studied/studied** to be a priest. (true)

Worksheet B

Listen to your partner's facts and say if they are true or false. Then read out your celebrity facts, choosing the correct verb form.

1 Quentin Tarantino **has directed/directed** but never acted in films. (false – he has appeared in many of his own films)

2 Jennifer Lopez **has started/started** singing and dancing lessons at the age of five. (true)

3 Cuba Gooding Jr's first job **was/has been** as a break-dancer for Lionel Richie at the 1984 Olympics. (true)

4 George Clooney **has had/had** a pet lion when he was a boy. (false – but he did have a pet pig!)

5 Brad Pitt **has never won/never won** an Oscar. (true – but he has been nominated for two)

6 Ex-President Ronald Reagan **has appeared/appeared** in over fifty films from the 1930s to the 1960s. (true)

7 John Wayne **has made/made** more than 200 films before he died in 1979. (true)

8 Steven Spielberg **has appeared/appeared** in the 1984 film *ET*. (false – he directed it)

9 Harrison Ford **has had/had** a species of spider named after him. (true)

10 Jennifer Aniston **has dated/dated** all of the male actors in *Friends* in real life. (false – but she has dated Brad Pitt, who once appeared in *Friends*)

Think of a dream you had recently and make notes in the word webs. Describe your dream to your group. Listen and ask questions to find out more about other students' dreams.

Things you did/ate the day before

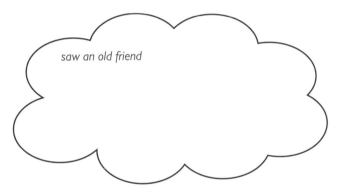

saw an old friend

Background of the dream

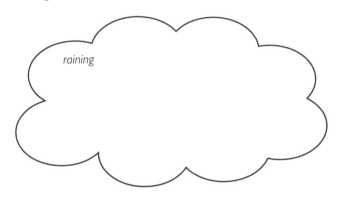

raining

Places in the dream

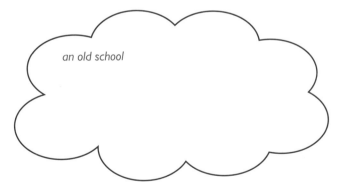

an old school

Clothes you were wearing

a beautiful dress

Main events of the dream

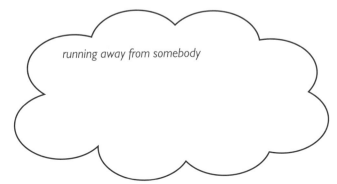

running away from somebody

The end/After the dream

woke up feeling scared

Worksheet A

Two ugly sisters lived in a flat in London.

Suzerella was a university student who worked part-time as a cleaner for the two ugly sisters. The two ugly sisters were very cruel and made her work very hard.

A new nightclub opened, and a very handsome celebrity was going to open it. The ugly sisters and Suzerella really wanted to go and meet him.

The ugly sisters bought their tickets, but wouldn't let Suzerella go. They made her stay at home and clean the floors.

On the opening night, Suzerella was at home, cleaning and feeling very sad. Suddenly, an angel appeared …

Worksheet B

Joe and his mother were very poor. They lived together in a very small house, and didn't have enough food to eat.

One day, they went to a market, so they could sell their TV to buy some food.

While they were there, Joe's mother went to see the other things for sale and asked Joe to stay and try and sell the TV.

A man came up and asked Joe to sell him the TV for some 'magic' beans. Joe thought this was an excellent idea, and sold it to him.

When Joe's mother returned, she was very angry, and couldn't believe Joe had done that. When they got home, she threw the beans into the garden.

The next morning, when Joe woke up, a huge, tree had grown in the garden. Joe decided to climb it …

Compliment everyone on their hair.	Moan about the weather.
Gossip about your teacher.	Boast about your English.
Try to argue with everyone, saying food from your country is better than anywhere else.	Warn everyone not to eat British food.
Chat with everyone about the weather.	Apologise to everyone for arriving late today.
Compliment everyone on their English.	Moan about your job/studies.
Gossip about another student in the class.	Boast about your job/studies.
Try to argue with everyone about the best way to study English.	Warn everyone not to go out at the weekend.
Chat with everyone about TV programmes.	Apologise to everyone for not hearing what they said.

Student A

Put these idioms somewhere in the grid, one word per square:

We're in hot water.   It's not my cup of tea.   We're working against the clock.
He's a bit of a dark horse.   Can you keep an eye on her?

Student B

Put these idioms somewhere in the grid, one word per square:

I really put my foot in it.   It's a piece of cake.   We're running out of time.
I've had enough of the rat race.   Could you give me a hand?

	1	2	3	4	5	6	7	8
A								
B								
C								
D								
E								
F								
G								
H								

Miss!

Hit '…'!

You've hit the idiom '…'!

	1	2	3	4	5	6	7	8
A								
B								
C								
D								
E								
F								
G								
H								

Miss!

Hit '…'!

You've hit the idiom '…'!

The Contract of Life

I, _____ , hereby promise that:

This weekend I'm ____-ing _____ .

Before the end of the month I'm going to _____ .

This year I'll definitely _____ .

Next week I might _____ .

In the next ten years I'm going to _____ .

This evening I might _____ .

Next year I'll definitely _____ .

Tomorrow I'm ____-ing _____ .

Before I'm sixty-five _____ .

(your own promise) _____ .

(your own promise) _____ .

Signed _____

Witness 1

Name _____   Signed _____

Witness 2

Name _____   Signed _____

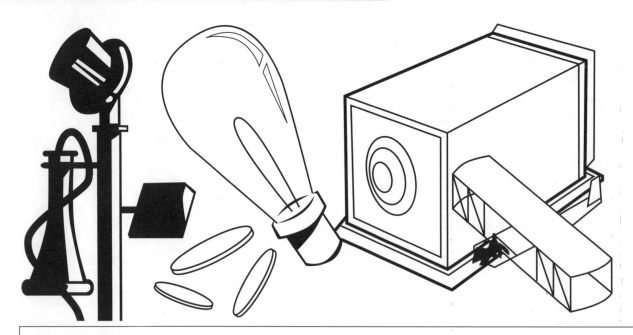

Name of invention _____

What your invention looks like:

What will your invention do? _____
_____

How is it going to transform the way we live? _____
_____

Is it likely to be popular for everybody, or will it be a luxury product? _____
_____

Which current inventions could it be more popular than? _____
_____

Other details _____
_____

Role card 1A

You are a market researcher. You need to ask people in the street answers to these questions. If they do the questionnaire, they can win a free mobile phone. Be polite!

Market research questionnaire

1 How old are you?
   - a) under 20
   - c) 36–49
   - b) 21–35
   - d) over 50

2 Which profession do you work in?
   - a) food and drink
   - c) manufacturing
   - b) education
   - d) administration

3 How many people do you live with?
   - a) alone
   - b) my immediate family
   - c) my extended family

4 What do you use the internet for?
   - a) email
   - c) social networking
   - b) news
   - d) shopping

5 How much do you earn?
   - a) under 20,000 a year
   - b) 20,000–35,000 a year
   - c) over 35,000 a year

Role card 2A

Your name is Jane/John. You called your friend Louisa/Louis earlier, but they weren't in, so you left a message with their flatmate. You were calling to see if your friend had the receipt for some pink shoes they bought you for your birthday. The shoes don't fit. You can go over to your friend's place to pick up the receipt later, if it's convenient. You finish work at 7p.m. and would like to go over then.

Additional information:

- It's really important that you get the receipt tonight. The only chance you have to take the shoes back is tomorrow morning before work.
- The shoes actually fit perfectly, but you just don't like them. Don't let your friend know this, though.

Role card 1B

You are in a hurry as you're late for work. A market researcher stops you and asks you to do a questionnaire. You don't really want to, but if you do, you might win a mobile phone, and your current one is very old. Answer the questions, but try to be as quick as possible.

This is your profile:

- You are twenty years old, but it's your birthday tomorrow.
- You are a business management consultant (you give advice to managers of small businesses).
- You live with your husband/wife, and their son from a previous marriage.
- You only ever use the internet for business research.
- Your salary varies. You get paid for each project you work on – about 10,000 per project. You do three to four projects a year.

Role card 2B

Your name is Louisa/Louis. You have just got home and found the following phone message, taken down by your flatmate. Call your friend Jane/John to check the details.

Your friend Joan?/Shaun? called to ask if you have the recipe for pigs' feet, which you made for their birthday. If you do, can you take it over to their place at 7a.m. before they go to work?

See you later.

Additional information:

- You're going out with friends in a few minutes, and won't be back until very late.
- You love giving your friends gifts, and if they don't like them, you get very upset. You are usually really good at buying presents, though.

Role card 1A

You are a Human Resources Manager for a company that produces new technology for the computer industry. Read about these three jobs that are available at your company, then answer your partner's questions.

Trainer

The successful candidate will be responsible for training new staff in company practices, giving workshops and writing a training program. He/She will be decisive, a good communicator and a good leader.

Inventor

We are looking for an inventor, who will work as part of a team to create new technology for the computer industry, and help develop existing technology. The ideal person must be able to think outside the box, highly motivated and hard-working.

Sales representative

We need someone to work in our sales team, finding new customers and selling new technology to our existing customers. He/She must be competitive, a real risk-taker and ambitious

Role card 2A

You are interested in working for six months on a cruise ship. You know that these three jobs are available, and you want to find out more information. Ask your partner – a recruitment agent at the cruise company – questions to get the missing information. Then decide which job you will apply for.

Entertainments manager

Main duties:

Personal qualities needed:

Deckhand/Caretaker

Main duties:

Personal qualities needed:

Travel agent

Main duties:

Personal qualities needed:

Role card 1B

You are interested in working for a company which produces new technology for the computer industry. You know that these three jobs are available, and you want to find out more information. Ask your partner – the Human Resources Manager – questions to get the missing information. Then decide which job you will apply for.

Trainer

Main duties:

Personal qualities needed:

Inventor

Main duties:

Personal qualities needed:

Sales representative

Main duties:

Personal qualities needed:

Role card 2B

You are a recruitment agent for a cruise company. Read about these three jobs that are available on a six-month cruise of the Pacific islands, then answer your partner's questions.

Entertainments manager

We are looking for an entertainments manager for our wonderful entertainment program. You will find new acts and plan interesting activities for the guests for the six-month cruise. You will be a good leader, a risk-taker and able to think outside the box.

Deckhand/Caretaker

The successful candidate will be responsible for the general maintenance of the ship, with duties to include cleaning and repairs. He/She will be hard-working and motivated.

Travel agent

This job will involve selling the cruise package before departure and finding new customers. After the cruise departs, this person will be available on board to help guests with their questions. He/She must be a good communicator, competitive and decisive.

Worksheet A

1 Read out your sentences.

1   I like being busy. When I have a lot of <u>job</u> to do, it stops me getting bored. ✗
    (work)

2   I'm quite forgetful. I always have to get other people to <u>remember</u> me to do things. ✗
    (remind)

3   I sometimes find it difficult to <u>listen</u> what people say to me in English. ✗
    (hear)

4   I never <u>forget</u> people's birthdays. ✓

5   For me it's more important to have an enjoyable job than to <u>win</u> a lot of money. ✗
    (earn)

6   We had a <u>fun</u> day out last Saturday – we went to a music festival. ✓

2 Listen to your partner's sentences and say if they are right or wrong.

3 Discuss which sentences are true for you.

Worksheet B

1 Listen to your partner's sentences and say if they are right or wrong.

2 Read out your sentences.

1   I've never <u>earnt</u> any money in the lottery. ✗
    (won)

2   I'd like to try lots of different <u>jobs</u> in my lifetime. ✓

3   I always <u>remember</u> to charge my mobile phone battery. ✓

4   I like <u>hearing</u> classical music. ✗
    (listening to)

5   I <u>forgot</u> my book at home today, by mistake. ✗
    (left)

6   My teacher is <u>fun</u> – he/she always tells good jokes. ✗
    (funny)

3 Discuss which sentences are true for you.

How to _____

1 You must _____
_____

2 You don't have to _____
_____

3 You shouldn't _____
_____

4 You mustn't _____
_____

5 You should _____
_____

6 You have to _____
_____

How to _____

1 You must _____
_____

2 You don't have to _____
_____

3 You shouldn't _____
_____

4 You mustn't _____
_____

5 You should _____
_____

6 You have to _____
_____

How to _____

1 You must _____
_____

2 You don't have to _____
_____

3 You shouldn't _____
_____

4 You mustn't _____
_____

5 You should _____
_____

6 You have to _____
_____

How to _____

1 You must _____
_____

2 You don't have to _____
_____

3 You shouldn't _____
_____

4 You mustn't _____
_____

5 You should _____
_____

6 You have to _____
_____

Grammar: *used to, would*

Write sentences about when you were a child, using *used to* or *would*.
Then ask questions to find people with the same information.

	Name
Pets	
1 _____ .	_____
Home	
2 _____ .	_____
3 _____ .	_____
Family	
4 _____ .	_____
5 _____ .	_____
What you were(n't) afraid of	
6 _____ .	_____
7 _____ .	_____
Sports and games	
8 _____ .	_____
9 _____ .	_____
Ambitions and dreams	
10 _____ .	_____
11 _____ .	_____
Food	
12 _____ .	_____

Worksheet A

The Education party

You are the leader of the Education party. You have just won equal votes in the recent general election in Politicaria, and must now form a coalition government with the Freedom party. You both need to agree on the country's new laws, but first, decide what your priorities are.

You want the following:

• More money spent on state education, and less on hospitals.
  Reasons:

• Higher taxes for the rich.
  Reasons:

• Strong law and order, with more money spent on the police.
  Reasons:

• Big investment in the environment and renewable energy.
  Reasons:

Worksheet B

The Freedom party

You are the leader of the Freedom party. You have just won equal votes in the recent general election in Politicaria, and must now form a coalition government with the Education party. You both need to agree on the country's new laws, but first, decide what your priorities are.

You want the following:

• More money spent on hospitals, and less on state education.
  Reasons:

• Lower taxes for everyone.
  Reasons:

• More freedom for people in general, restricting the powers of the police.
  Reasons:

• Big investment in nuclear power.
  Reasons:

Crossword A

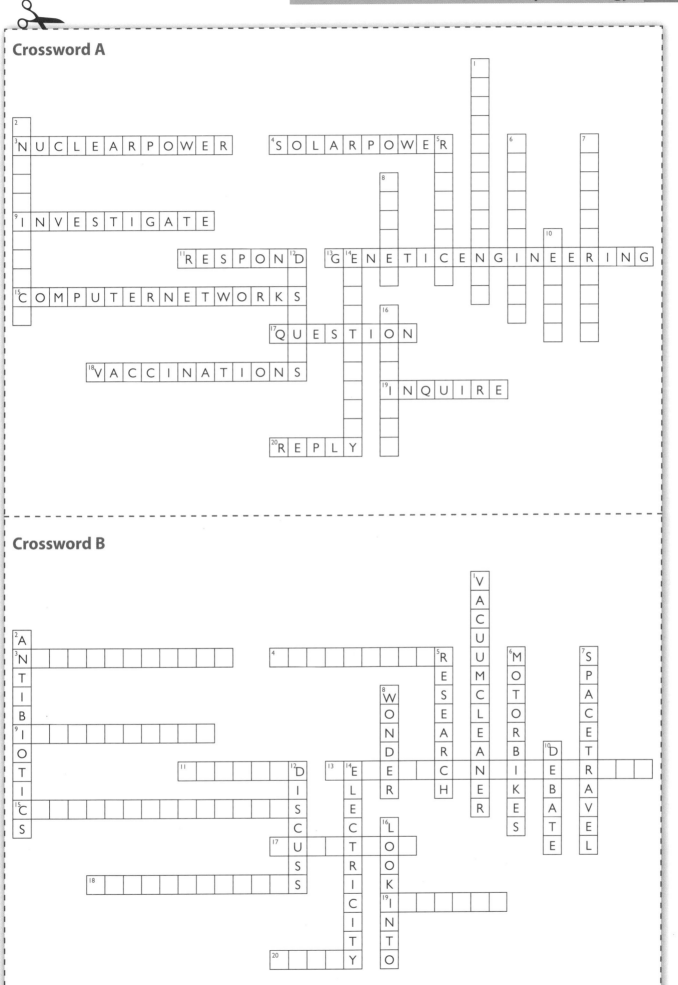

3. NUCLEARPOWER
4. SOLARPOWER
9. INVESTIGATE
11. RESPOND
13. GENETICENGINEERING
15. COMPUTERNETWORKS
17. QUESTION
18. VACCINATIONS
19. INQUIRE
20. REPLY

Crossword B

I love cats: they're so cute and (love).

-less

I like films which are (drama).

There aren't many (home) people in my country.

The most (effect) plans are often the simplest.

Free square!

I hate horror films. They're too (scare).

I'm a very (talk) person — I talk too much sometimes!

-ful

English grammar is always (logic).

-ic/-ical

I think I'm a (response) person.

Free square!

I can't cook. When I do, my food is never (eat)!

Going to the dentist can be (pain).

There are some very (poet) traditional stories from my country.

There have been a lot of (explode) scandals in my country recently.

I like work that is (create).

-able/-ible

I have a friend who is a (care) driver. He/she's always nearly having accidents.

I'm (hope) that my English will improve in the next year.

I'm quite a (mess) person!

Art classes at school were (use). I never learnt anything!

Happiness is more (value) than money.

FINISH

-y

Learning English is (ease).

I'm (hope) at music. I can't sing or play any instruments.

My favourite kind of holiday is one which is (peace) — I like to relax.

START

It doesn't matter what job you do, as long as you are (success).

-ive

I love (rain) days.

Free square!

I'd love to travel and do (biology) research — just like Darwin!

Role card 1

You are looking for a new mobile phone. You want a phone with a lot of different functions, but you also want one that's very small, and that you can carry around easily. You don't want to spend too much money, but you don't mind paying a bit more for extra functions.

Compare the information below with your partner's phones. Then choose which phone you are going to buy.

Role card 2

You are looking for a new mobile phone. You don't have much money, so you can't buy a very expensive phone. You travel a lot, so you want a phone that can connect to the internet almost anywhere. You also like playing games on your phone on long bus journeys.

Compare the information below with your partner's phones. Then choose which phone you are going to buy.

Econofon 3000

Price: *$10.00*

Size: *15cm x 7cm*

Easy/difficult to use: *very easy*

Functions: *calls and text messages only*

Battery life: *12 hours*

Internet speed: *no internet*

Gamesmart 999

Price: *$299.99*

Size: *12cm x 15cm*

Easy/difficult to use: *easy*

Functions: *calls, text messages, internet, lots of games*

Battery life: *5 hours*

Internet speed: *medium*

Supertech 7120i
Price: *$699.99*

Size: *10cm x 7cm*

Easy/difficult to use: *very difficult*

Functions: *calls, text messages, internet, email, camera, video camera, organizer, games and many more*

Battery life: *8 hours*

Internet speed: *fast*

Micro 272X
Price: *$350.00*

Size: *5cm x 3cm*

Easy/difficult to use: *medium*

Functions: *calls, text messages, camera, video*

Battery life: *9 hours*

Internet speed: *no internet*

Surfista XS
Price: *$150.00*

Size: *10cm x 6cm*

Easy/difficult to use: *quite difficult*

Functions: *calls, text messages, internet, email, camera, video*

Battery life: *10 hours*

Internet speed: *very fast*

Traveller 900

Price: *$99.99*

Size: *8cm x 6cm*

Easy/difficult to use: *easy*

Functions: *calls, text messages, camera, video, simple games; internet available on the 901 model, which costs 250.00*

Battery life: *24 hours*

Internet speed: *slow, where available*

Complete the sentences with the names of your classmates.
Use question tags to check the information.

	✓ or ✗?
1 _____ came to class by car today.	
2 _____ likes studying English.	
3 _____ doesn't like eating fish.	
4 _____ went out with friends last night.	
5 _____ has got a boy/girlfriend.	
6 _____ is a student.	
I'm fairly sure …	
7 _____ .	
8 _____ .	
9 _____ .	
I'm not sure …	
10 _____ .	
11 _____ .	
12 _____	

Worksheet A

Role card 1A

You have just bought a new computer, which was very expensive. When you got home, you set it up, following the instructions. You switched it on, but nothing happened. You have tried everything, and connected all the cables correctly, but nothing has worked. Call the support line and ask for help. You either want a new computer or a full refund.

Role card 2A

You work for a mobile phone company. A customer calls to complain that the payment for their bill has left their bank four days early. It is because of a problem with your computer system. However, don't tell them this, and tell them it's not your company's policy to give refunds. Suggest another solution.

Role card 3A

You recently bought a new MP3 player, and the shop assistant told you it would work with any computer. However, when you got home and tried to connect it, a message came up saying 'Player not compatible with this software'. Your computer uses Supersystem1 software. Take it back to the shop to complain, and ask for a refund.

Worksheet B

Role card 1B

You are a computer engineer and work for the support line of a computer company. You have nearly finished for the day, and are keen to get home quickly because it's your daughter's birthday today. A customer calls you to complain about a new computer that she can't get to work. Ask her questions to find out what's wrong and make sure she checks all the cables are connected. After trying everything, it still won't work. However, your company doesn't give refunds or replacement computers, so try to find another solution.

Role card 2B

You are having a bad day. First your alarm clock didn't go off this morning, and so you were late. Then you just missed the bus and had to walk two kilometres to work. You were late for work and your boss was angry. You have just checked your bank statement and noticed that the payment for your mobile phone bill has come out of your account four days early, leaving you with no money for the weekend until you get paid on Monday. Call the mobile phone company to complain, and ask them to refund you.

Role card 3B

You work in an electronics shop. A customer recently bought an MP3 player, which you know can be used with any computer. However, it is only compatible with Supersystem2 software. The customer comes to your shop to complain that it wouldn't work with their computer. Find out as much as you can and try to solve the problem. Your company doesn't give refunds, though.

Worksheet A

1 Underline the correct adjective, and write one more question.

1 It's Thursday. You have to finish a project by the end of the week. How do you feel?
   a) **Relaxed/Relaxing**. You'll get it done.
   b) A bit **stressing/stressed**, but you'll get it finished somehow.
   c) Very, very **worried/worrying**. You don't have enough time left.

2 You've just seen a new horror film at the cinema.
   a) It was **boring/bored**. Not scary at all.
   b) You feel **embarrassing/embarrassed**. You think your friends saw you were scared.
   c) It was so **frightening/frightened** that you won't be able to sleep tonight!

3 Someone jumps the queue in front of you at the supermarket.
   a) You're **surprised/surprising** that someone could do that, but it's OK.
   b) It's a bit **annoying/annoyed**, but you don't say anything.
   c) You're **disgusting/disgusted** at their behaviour, and tell them angrily to wait.

4 You find out that your English teacher is giving you a test this week. How do you feel?
   a) **Pleased/Pleasing**. It will be good to see your progress.
   b) A bit **confusing/confused**. You're not sure what to study.
   c) **Terrified/Terrifying**. You hate tests!

5 _____
_____
_____
_____

Student B's answer:
_____

2 Look at your partner's answers and read the analysis. Do you agree?

Mostly c) answers
You're a very passionate person, but need to learn to control your emotions. Slow down sometimes!

Mostly b) answers
You manage your emotions well, and you don't let them get out of control. Perhaps you should become a therapist!

Mostly a) answers
You're a very calm person who rarely gets excited. You're good in a crisis, but you should open up at times – don't let life get boring!

Worksheet B

1 Underline the correct adjective, and write one more question.

1 It's Friday afternoon. How do you feel?
   a) **Pleased/Pleasing**, because it's the end of the week.
   b) This time of the week is **excited/exciting**. Here comes the weekend!
   c) I feel absolutely **exhausting/exhausted**. It's been a very emotional week (again)!

2 Your friend calls you to tell you his/her pet has just died.
   a) You're **confusing/confused** about why he/she is so upset. It's only a pet.
   b) The situation is a little **worrying/worried**. You know your friend is going to be upset.
   c) You're **devastated/devastating**. Why did it have to die?

3 It's your birthday, but nobody remembered.
   a) It's fine. In fact, you're quite **pleased/pleasing** because you don't like lots of attention.
   b) It's not a problem; it's just a bit **annoyed/annoying** that nobody remembered.
   c) You are **disgusting/disgusted** with them. They call themselves 'friends'?

4 You arrive at a party and don't know anyone.
   a) You know it's going to be **bored/boring**. You have nobody to talk to, so you leave.
   b) You feel a little uncomfortable, but it's **interesting/interested** to meet new people.
   c) You feel really **embarrassed/embarrassing** about being alone and panic!

5 _____
_____
_____
_____

Student A's answer:
_____

2 Look at your partner's answers and read the analysis. Do you agree?

Mostly c) answers
You're a very passionate person, but need to learn to control your emotions. Slow down sometimes!

Mostly b) answers
You manage your emotions well, and you don't let them get out of control. Perhaps you should become a therapist!

Mostly a) answers
You're a very calm person who rarely gets excited. You're good in a crisis, but you should open up at times – don't let life get boring!

Worksheet A

Describe each multi-word verb to your partner but do <u>not</u> use the words in italics. Your partner will try and guess the verb.

chat somebody up *talk speak man woman like*	**scroll up** *website computer mouse move top*	**dress up** *clothes formal wear smart down*
get on *like friend relationship good well*	**click on** *mouse computer icon link move*	**try on** *clothes shop test fit size*

Worksheet B

Describe each multi-word verb to your partner but do <u>not</u> use the words in italics. Your partner will try and guess the verb.

settle down *old family calm home live*	**shut down** *computer finish off power close*	**take off** *clothes remove finish bed on*
go off somebody *stop like relationship finish friend*	**log off** *website computer close leave exit*	**dress down** *clothes informal up wear jeans*

6

If you practise English every day, …	I'll be embarrassed if …	**FREE SQUARE**	When it's really hot, …	If I get a (new) job next year, …	**FINISH**
If my favourite team wins a game …	I always … when I get home.	I'll go to bed early tonight if …	If you don't eat enough vegetables, …	**FREE SQUARE**	If someone says something bad about me, …
I could go abroad next year if …	If you do exercise every day, …	**FREE SQUARE**	When I next speak to my parents, …	When I next go on holiday, …	If you visit my country, …
When I see a sad story on the news, …	**FREE SQUARE**	When I next see my family, …	I'll be really happy if …	If there's nothing interesting on TV tonight, …	**FREE SQUARE**
I get annoyed when …	I might go out tonight if …	If my teacher gives me lots of homework today, …	If I study/work hard this year, …	I find it relaxing when …	I won't be happy if …
If I feel confused in class …	**FREE SQUARE**	When I go to bed tonight …	When I feel exhausted …	If I'm late for class, …	If I get home early tonight, …
START	I feel relaxed when …	If it rains this weekend, …	When I have lots of work to do …	I can save time in the mornings if …	**FREE SQUARE**

paint yourself blue	shout 'Hello!' in the middle of the street	cry in class	tell your teacher to be quiet
kiss a stranger	play with children's toys	shout at a police officer	stand on a bus when there are free seats
move to the arctic	fail a test on purpose	sing a song to the class	cycle 1,000km
climb a tall tree	steal a penguin from the zoo	dance in the street	start a fire in your house
sit on a dog	bark like a dog	run through the supermarket	eat a book
walk in the middle of the road	drink water from the sea	break a window in your house	sing during an exam

MIXED EMOTIONS

Functional language: giving news

You've just passed your driving test.	You've seen your friend's boy/girlfriend holding hands with someone else.	You have the opportunity to study abroad next year.	You've lost your friend's book which you borrowed.
You've been offered a great new job.	You've met a new boy/girlfriend.	Your favourite sports team has just won a game.	You've just got a pay rise in your job.
You're going on holiday next week.	You're getting married.	You've lost your dog.	The class party has been cancelled.
You've lost your job.	You've split up with your partner.	You've crashed your friend's car.	Your computer has 'died'.
You've failed an important exam.	You've had a big argument with your parents.	The concert you were going to has been cancelled.	Your wallet has been stolen.

Worksheet A

1 Ask your partner questions using the prompts below.

	Partner 1	Partner 2
1 / work / hard / school?		
2 How often / practise / _____ ?		
3 / know anyone / expert / _____ ?		
4 / aptitude / computers?		
5 / believe / ability / succeed?		
6 Who / most / talented musician / you know?		
7 / know anyone / ability / _____ ?		
8 / anything / you / hopeless / ?		

2 Now change partners and ask your questions again. Do they have anything in common?

Worksheet B

1 Ask your partner questions using the prompts below.

	Partner 1	Partner 2
1 What things / practise / regularly?		
2 / know anyone / natural talent / languages?		
3 For which jobs / need to be / skillful communicator?		
4 / know anyone / gifted / art?		
5 / find it easy / focus / problems?		
6 / you / high achiever / school?		
7 / ever have / opportunity / _____ ?		
8 / anything / you / useless / ?		

2 Now change partners and ask your questions again. Do they have anything in common?

	My answer	Name
1 Who do you most depend _____ in your life?		
2 How many hours a day do you put _____ to your work/studies?		
3 Who do you have a lot in common _____ ?		
4 Do you believe _____ ghosts?		
5 What do you have a talent _____ ?		
6 Who was the last person you argued _____ ?		
7 What was the last TV show you laughed _____ ?		
8 Who in your family do you usually agree _____ ?		
9 What sport is your country world-class _____ ?		
10 Do your parents have access _____ the internet at home?		
11 What kind of art/photography do you like looking _____ ?		
12 Does your work/Do your studies give you a lot to think _____ at the moment?		
13 On a date, do you think the man, woman, or both should pay _____ the meal?		
14 What organisations/clubs do you belong _____ ?		
15 Who did you rely _____ most when you were younger?		
16 What one thing in your life do you worry _____ most?		
17 Are you good at picking up _____ other people's problems?		
18 If you receive bad service in a shop/restaurant, do you usually complain _____ it?		

Worksheet A

Film star 1A

1 She was born on 30th August 1972 in San Diego, USA.

2 She / previously / work / model.

3 She / act / major roles / since / first appeared in *The Mask* in 1994.

4 She / win / many awards / but / never win / an Oscar.

5 She / previously / date / Justin Timberlake and Matt Dillon.

6 She / recently / appear / *There's Something About Mary, Charlie's Angels* and *Shrek* in comedy roles.

Answer:
Cameron Michelle Diaz

Student B's score: _____

Film star 2A

1 He was born on 19th March 1955 in Idar-Oberstein, Germany.

2 As well / acting, he / also work / nuclear power plant.

3 He / go bald / since / 1980s.

4 He / previously / be married / Demi Moore.

5 He / win / many awards / but / never win / an Oscar.

6 He / appear / many action films / *Armageddon* and *The Sixth Sense,* and sitcoms such as *Moonlighting* and *Friends*.

Answer:
Walter Bruce Willis

Student B's score: _____

Film star 3A

1 She was born on 5th October 1975 in Reading, England.

2 She / act / major roles / since / first appeared in *Sense and Sensibility* in 1995.

3 She married Sam Mendes / 2003 / but they / recently / split up.

4 She / recently / win / an Oscar / *The Reader*.

5 She / act / one of / best-selling films of all time / Leonardo DiCaprio.

6 She / appear / other films / *Iris, Enigma* and *Flushed Away*.

Answer:
Kate Elizabeth Winslet

Student B's score: _____

Worksheet B

Film star 1B

1 He was born on 17th August 1943 in New York, USA.

2 He / be / member of a real street gang.

3 He / be married / Grace Hightower / since 1997.

4 Since 1989 / he / invest / TriBeCa district of New York.

5 He / win / two Oscars / *The Godfather II* and *Raging Bull*.

6 He / mainly / act / serious roles / but recently / act / comedy roles / *Meet the Fockers* and *Stardust*.

Answer:
Robert De Niro, Jr.

Student A's score: _____

Film star 2B

1 She was born on 26th March 1985 in Teddington, England.

2 She / act / major roles / since / first appeared in *Bend it Like Beckham* in 2002.

3 She / always / want / act / since she was three.

4 She / recently / do / charity work / Amnesty International.

5 Although she / be nominated / she / never win / an Oscar.

6 She / act / major series of films about pirates with Johnny Depp and Orlando Bloom.

Answer:
Keira Christina Knightley

Student A's score: _____

Film star 3B

1 He was born on 23rd July 1989 in London, England.

2 He / act / 'with magic' / since 2001.

3 He / act / in films, on TV and at the theatre.

4 He / win / many awards / but / never win / an Oscar.

5 He / appear / Sunday Times Rich List as one of the richest young people in England.

6 He / recently / act / in the theatre.

Answer:
Daniel Jacob Radcliffe

Student A's score: _____

tell a joke in English	play a musical instrument	get to sleep quickly
get home early	remember people's birthdays	say 'hello' in five languages
speak a foreign language (not English) fluently	juggle	do difficult mathematics in your head
ride a bike	sail a boat	cook
drive a car	run fast	pass a difficult exam
do yoga	get to class on time	use the present perfect

Role card 1

You are one of the directors of *Y-Starz*, a clothing company aimed at the teenage market. Last year you made record profits, and now you have to decide how you are going to spend the money this year.

You believe the best option is to spend at least 75% of the money on paying rewards to shareholders, for the following reasons:

- You didn't pay them last year, and they are expecting to receive some money this year.
- The economy is going to get worse this year, and if you don't pay them, they might sell their shares.

- _____
- _____

Role card 2

You are one of the directors of *Y-Starz*, a clothing company aimed at the teenage market. Last year you made record profits, and now you have to decide how you are going to spend the money this year.

You believe the best option is to spend at least 75% of the money on improving the environmental aspects of the company, such as eco-friendly machinery, reducing pollution, etc. for the following reasons:

- Your competitors have recently invested a lot of money in this, and if you don't, you might get a bad reputation with your customers.
- The government has announced plans to give tax cuts to companies investing in the environment, and you would receive this money next year if you invest now.

- _____
- _____

Role card 3

You are one of the directors of *Y-Starz*, a clothing company aimed at the teenage market. Last year you made record profits, and now you have to decide how you are going to spend the money this year.

You believe the best option is to 'go global', by spending at least 75% of the money on setting up factories and shops in places such as China and Brazil, for the following reasons:

- These markets are growing, and it would mean growing the business over the next few years.
- The economy in the country where you are based is predicted to get worse this year.

- _____
- _____

Role card 4

You are one of the directors of *Y-Starz*, a clothing company aimed at the teenage market. Last year you made record profits, and now you have to decide how you are going to spend the money this year.

You believe the best option is to spend at least 75% of the money on new technology, for the following reasons:

- There have been a number of new innovations in machinery for producing clothes, which can cut costs.
- Your competitors are also doing this at the moment.

- _____
- _____

Worksheet A

1 **Read out the questions and replace the underlined phrase with the one your partner gives you.**

   1 Are you good friends with your neighbours, or do you prefer to <u>be alone</u>?

   2 Are you a <u>very curious</u> person?

   3 Do you find it easy to <u>start a good relationship with</u> new people you meet?

   4 Do you have any neighbours who <u>interrupt your privacy</u>?

   5 Have you <u>helped</u> anyone recently?

   6 What kind of behaviour <u>annoys you</u>?

2 **Now listen to your partner's questions and give them the correct phrase from the box.**

   | get on well with | mind their own business | a nuisance | invite your neighbours over |
   | ask a favour of | get to know | | |

3 **Discuss your answers to the questions.**

Worksheet B

1 **Listen to your partner's questions and give them the correct phrase from the box.**

   | keep yourself to yourself | disturb you | gets on your nerves | make friends with |
   | done favours for | nosy | | |

2 **Now read out the questions and replace the underlined phrase with the one your partner gives you.**

   1 Do you <u>have a good relationship with</u> everyone in your family?

   2 Do you ever <u>ask your neighbours if they want to come to your house</u> for a coffee?

   3 When you have a problem, do you like people to help or do you prefer them to <u>not get involved</u>?

   4 In your work/studies, is there anything which is <u>annoying</u>?

   5 How do you <u>find out about</u> people you've just met?

   6 Do you find it easy to <u>ask for help from</u> other people?

3 **Discuss your answers to the questions.**

traffic	traffic	jam	lights	car	car
park	rental	super	outdoor	market	market
primary	school	shopping	shopping	centre	mall
sports	city	centre	centre	high	one-way
street	street	semi-detached	terraced	house	house
housing	industrial	estate	estate	duty-free	gift
shop	shop	main	road	book	shop
swimming	pool	window	shopping	clothes	shop

Worksheet A

1 Read out the sentences. Your partner will try to correct them.

1 There aren't much primary schools in my area.
(~~much~~ – many)

2 I have a good local supermarket close to where I live. It's a best in the area.
(~~a~~ – the)

3 In my city there are lot of housing estates.
(~~lot of~~ – a lot of)

4 There are none swimming pools in my area.
(~~none~~ – no)

5 How many graffiti is there in your area? A little bit or a lot of?
(~~many~~ – much, ~~a lot of~~ – a lot)

6 High Street in my town gets very busy at the weekend. Plenty people come there to do their shopping.
(~~High Street~~ – The High Street, ~~Plenty~~ – plenty of)

7 Every the buildings in my city are modern.
(~~Every~~ – All)

8 There aren't much car parks in my area, and parking is a problem.
(~~much~~ – many)

2 Now listen to your partner's sentences and try to correct them.

3 Discuss which sentences are true for you.

Worksheet B

1 Listen to your partner's sentences and try to correct them.

2 Now read out the sentences. Your partner will try to correct them.

1 There is the big park in the centre of my city.
(~~the~~ – a)

2 My city gets plenty tourists in the summer, but in the winter there are no.
(~~plenty~~ – plenty of, ~~no~~ – none)

3 How much shopping centres are there in your area?
(~~much~~ – many)

4 There are lots of one-way streets in my area, and we get so many traffic during rush hour.
(~~many~~ – much)

5 I like buying food at an outdoor market. A one where I live is small, but there are several types of food available.
(~~A~~ – The)

6 I have a nicest neighbour in the world. She's an teacher!
(~~a~~ – the, ~~an~~ – a)

7 The New York is much more famous than my city.
(~~The New York~~ – New York)

8 There aren't much things for young people to do in my area in the evening.
(~~much~~ – many)

3 Discuss which sentences are true for you.

Worksheet A

1 Read out the sentence halves for your partner to complete.

1 YouTube <u>is a website where you can</u> …

2 <u>I visit my favourite website, which is</u> flash.com, …

3 <u>My mother, who is a</u> web designer, …

4 Findit.com <u>is the website which I always use for</u> …

5 <u>The internet company which I most respect is</u> …

6 <u>Today's children, who spend too long on the internet,</u> …

2 Now listen to your partner's sentence halves and complete them with your endings.

A … help you with technical problems related to your computer.

B … information about a particular company.

C … every day.

D … humour online.

E … has a lot of animation.

F … share opinions on your favourite websites.

3 Using the underlined phrases, make sentences that are true for you.

Worksheet B

1 Listen to your partner's sentence halves and complete them with your endings.

A … at least three times a day.

B … loves her job.

C … share videos.

D … searches.

E … will have problems with communication later in life.

F … savetheplanet.com.

2 Now read out the sentence halves for your partner to complete.

1 <u>My personal homepage, which I use for</u> homework projects, …

2 Cyberforum.com <u>is a new website where you can</u> …

3 <u>A</u> support technician <u>is a person who can</u> …

4 SN.com, <u>which is a social networking website, is the first website I visit</u> …

5 LOL, <u>which means</u> 'laughing out loud', <u>is the best way to express</u> …

6 <u>A</u> corporate <u>website is a place where you can go to find out</u> …

3 Using the underlined phrases, make sentences that are true for you.

Worksheet A

Situation 1A
You're having a party at your house. Student B starts smoking, and you'd like them to go outside.

Situation 2A
You are sitting on the train, reading the newspaper, when Student B enters.

Situation 3A
You invite Student B over to your house, and they arrive an hour late.

Situation 4A
You buy something in a shop and the shop assistant (Student B) gives you too much change.

Situation 5A
You call Student B for a chat, but they sound really busy.

Situation 6A
You are at Student B's house for a dinner party. They offer you a dish which has taken them ages to prepare, but you can't eat it as you don't like it.

Situation 7A
You are in class and Student B wants to open the window. You are cold and want to keep it closed.

Situation 8A
You arrive at a party at Student B's house and everyone is wearing smart clothes. You are wearing jeans and a T-shirt.

Situation 9A
You are sitting in your car, about to drive away from a car park, when Student B's car hits yours. There isn't much damage.

Situation 10A
You borrow a DVD from Student B, but accidentally break it.

Situation 11A
You are waiting to be served in a shop, when Student B goes in front of you.

Situation 12A
You are in a meeting with Student B and put your feet up on the desk.

Worksheet B

Situation 1B
You're at a party at Student A's house. You've just finished dinner, relax and smoke a cigarette.

Situation 2B
You get on the train and want to sit down, but Student A is taking up two seats.

Situation 3B
Student A invites you over to their house and you arrive an hour late.

Situation 4B
You are working in a shop and the customer (Student A) tells you you've given them too much change.

Situation 5B
Student A calls you for a chat, but you are very busy and can't talk right now.

Situation 6B
You are having a dinner party. You have prepared a dish which took you ages, but Student A doesn't want to eat it.

Situation 7B
You are in class and are really hot. You want to open the window.

Situation 8B
You are having a formal party at your house, and everyone is wearing smart clothes. Student A arrives, wearing jeans and a T-shirt.

Situation 9B
You accidentally hit Student A's car while trying to park. There isn't much damage.

Situation 10B
Student A borrows a DVD from you, but when they return it, it's broken.

Situation 11B
You are next in line in a shop and start talking to the shop assistant.

Situation 12B
You are in a meeting with Student A, when they put their feet up on the desk. You think this is very rude and don't want them to do it.

1 **Work in pairs. Invent the name of a country and think of the main events in its history. Use the ideas in the box to help you, and add your own ideas.**

progress in _____	the discovery of _____	the foundation of _____ , which caused _____
was invaded by _____	was colonised by _____	the invention of _____ , by _____
the _____ movement	advances in _____	the spread of _____ a period of development
a great turning point the _____ revolution	independence	under the leadership of _____
_____ , the founder of _____		

The history of _____ (name of country)

The 1700s: The age of _____

The 1800s: The _____ era

The early 1900s: A period of _____

The 1950s to the 1990s: The modern era

The new millennium: The _____

2 **Present your history to the class.**

GUESS MY COLLOCATION

Vocabulary plus: collocations with *come*, *give*, *have* and *make*

A

B

C

D
1

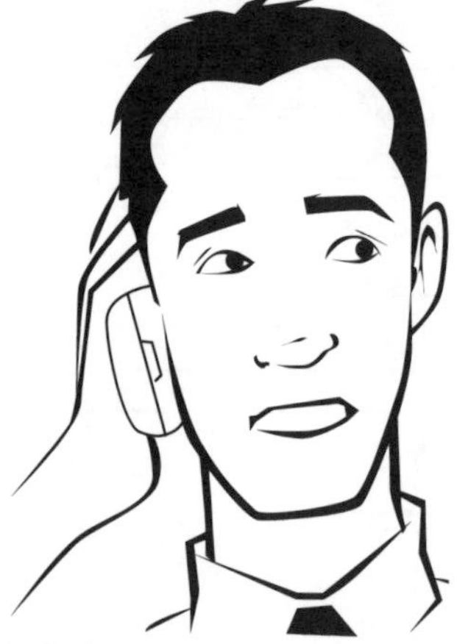

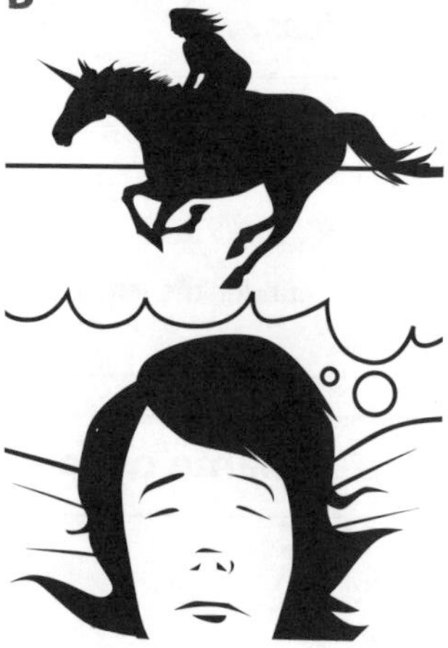

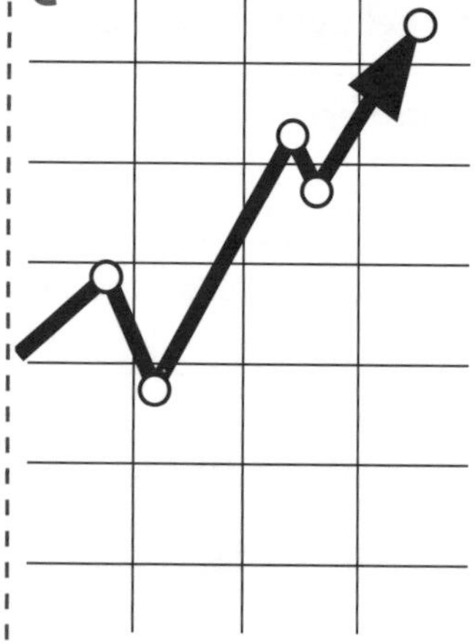

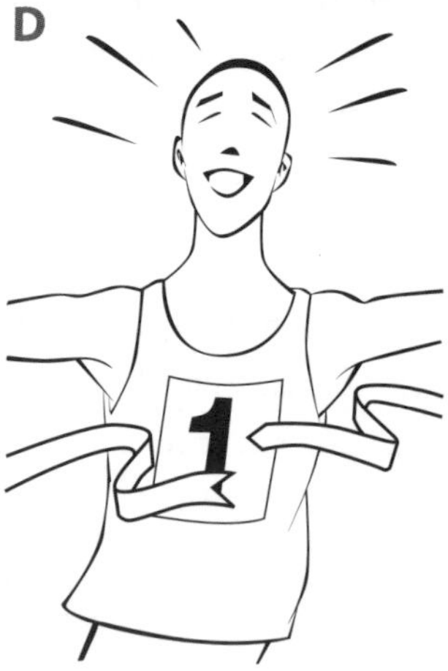

E
WELCOME HOME!

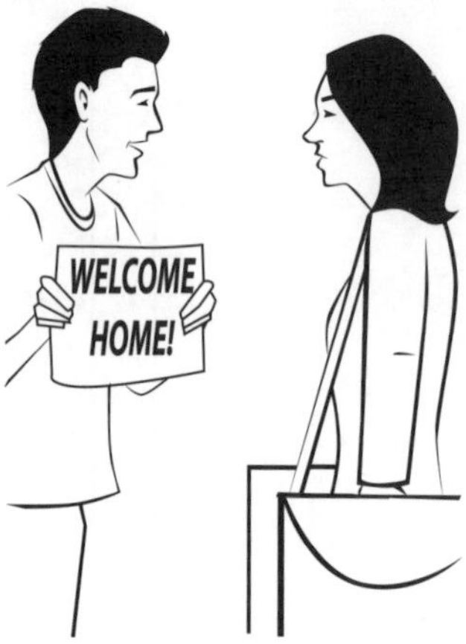

F

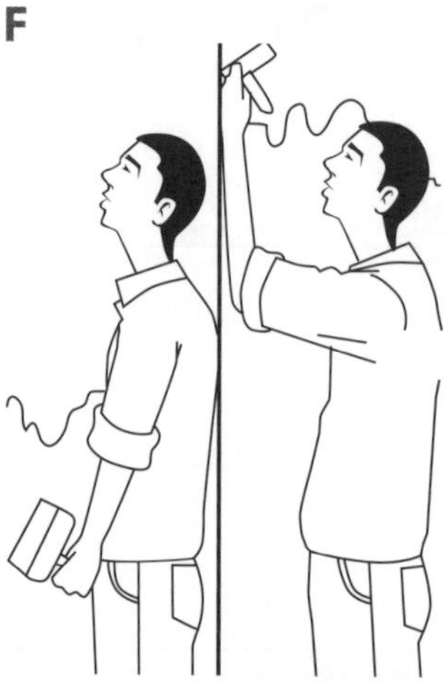

G

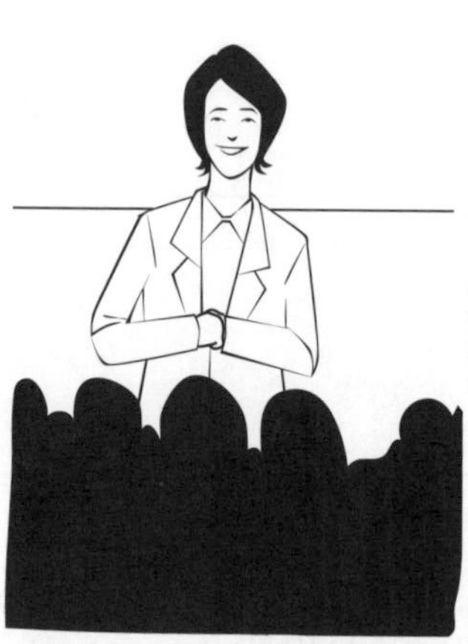

H

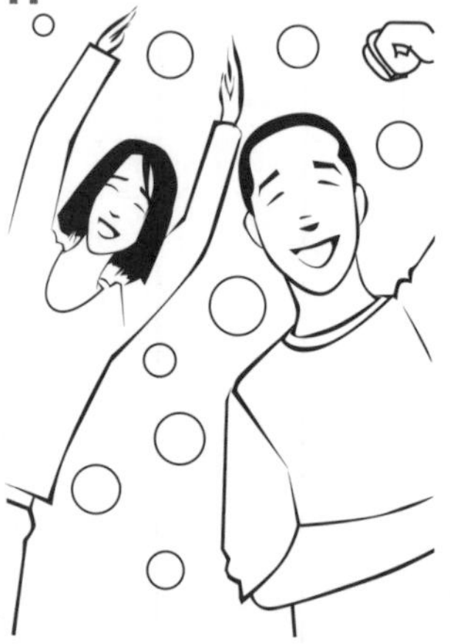

I

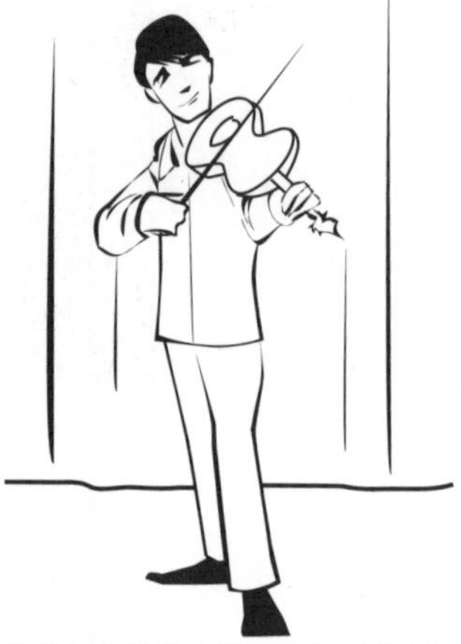

J
FIRST YOU ADD THE ONIONS...

K

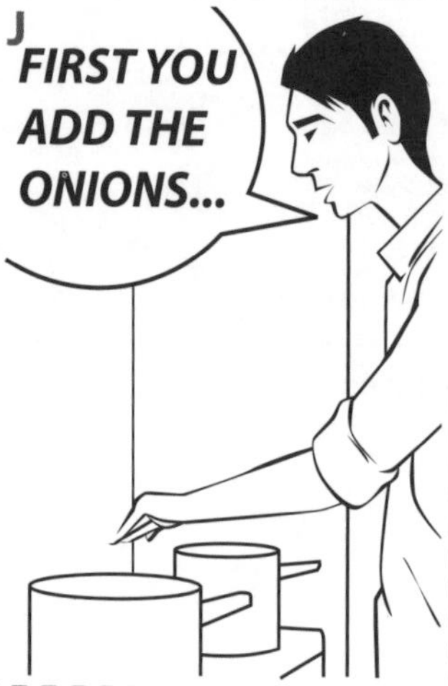

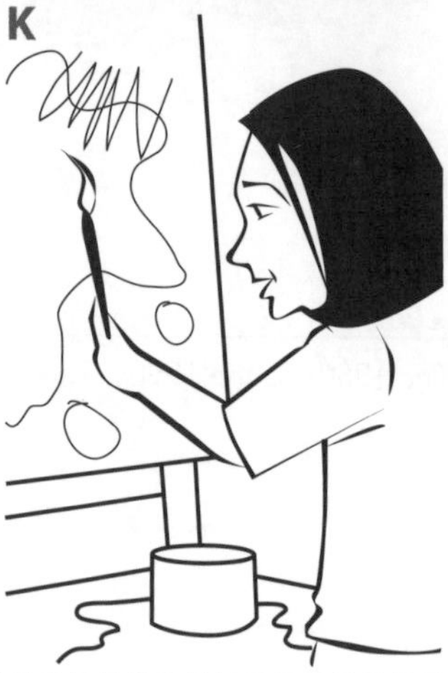

L
?

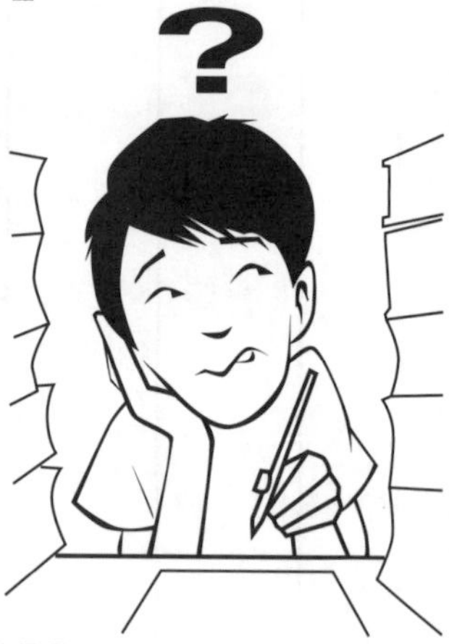

M

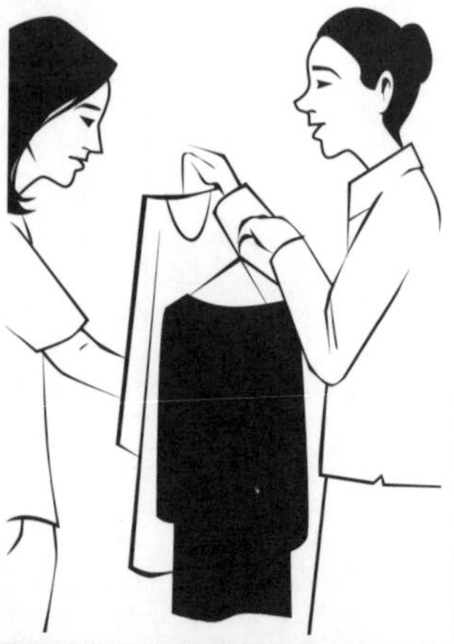

N

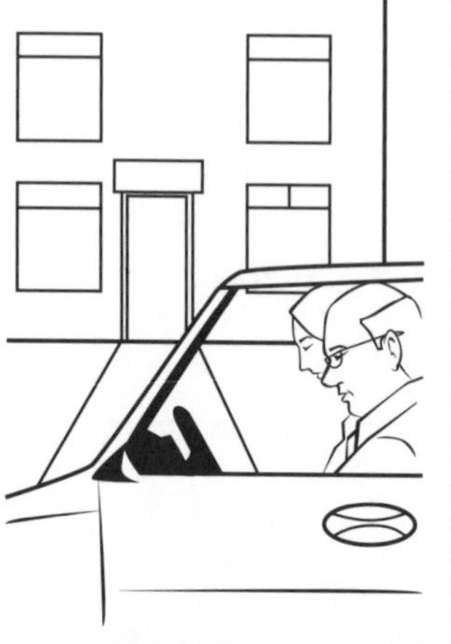

O

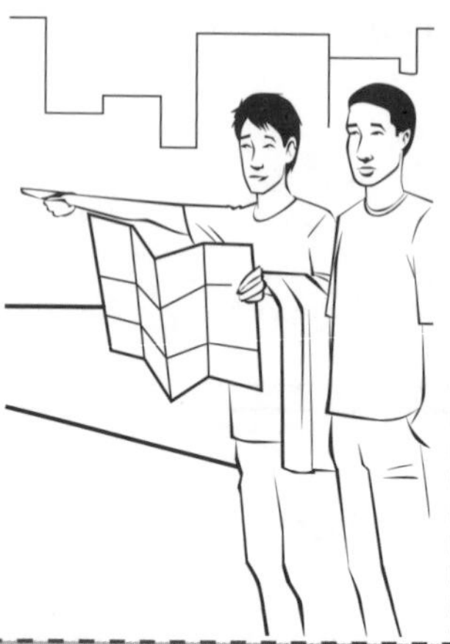

P

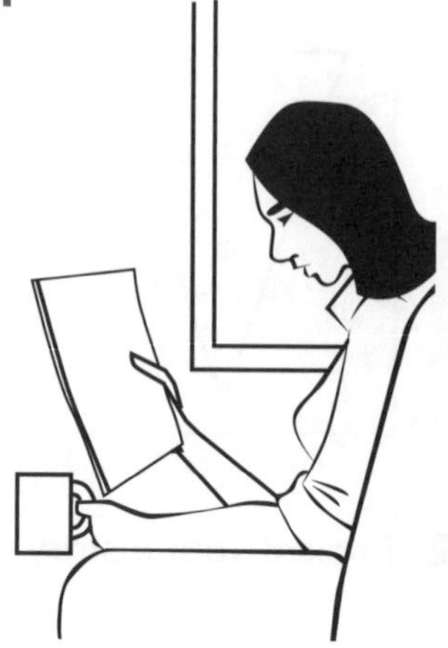

✂

1

When: 12th Century BC

Where: Troy (west coast of modern day Turkey)

Who: The Trojans

What: After ten unsuccessful years of war, the Greeks decided to build a huge wooden horse as a 'gift' to the Trojans to end the war. The Trojans accepted this 'gift' and allowed the horse to be pushed into the city, with thirty Greek soldiers inside.

If the Trojans had(n't)

_____ .

I would(n't) have

_____ .

2

When: 1173

Where: Pisa, Italy

Who: unknown

What: One of Italy's biggest tourist attractions was actually a huge mistake, after the decision was taken to build a fifty-metre-tall tower on soft soil.

If they had(n't)

_____ .

I would(n't) have

_____ .

3

When: 1876

Where: the USA

Who: William Orton, President of the Western Union Telegraph Company

What: When Alexander Graham Bell presented his idea for the telephone to Orton, he replied, 'while it is a very interesting novelty … it has no commercial possibilities' Bell patented his invention himself and founded his own company, AT&T. It went on to become the most valuable patent ever.

If William Orton had(n't)

_____ .

I would(n't) have

_____ .

4

When: 1920

Where: the USA

Who: United States government

What: After World War I, people were worried about social decline and a drop in moral standards in the USA. The government decided the problem was with alcohol and made it illegal. Alcohol consumption over the next ten years actually increased, along with organised crime, and they dropped the law in 1933.

If the government had(n't)

_____ .

I would(n't) have

_____ .

5

When: 1962

Where: London, England

Who: Dick Rowe, Decca Records

What: After listening to *The Beatles* Dick Rowe contacted *The Beatles*' manager, Brian Epstein, and told him he wasn't interested, and that guitar music was 'finished'. The Beatles then went on to become one of the most famous bands of all time.

If Dick Rowe had(n't)

_____ .

I would(n't) have

_____ .

6

When: 1979

Where: the USA

Who: Ross Perot

What: Perot saw Bill Gates' Microsoft company as having a good future, and offered to buy it for a figure between $6 million and $15 million. Bill Gates wanted $40–$60 million. Perot thought this was too much and walked away. Microsoft is now worth billions of dollars.

If Perot (or Gates) had(n't)

_____ .

I would(n't) have

_____ .

Worksheet A

Read out the sentences using the correct tense and form of the verb in brackets (active or passive). Your partner will guess if they are true or false.

1 Acuncture _____ (first use) in 2700 BC by Chinese Emperor Shen Nung. (true)

2 Christmas _____ (become) a national holiday in the USA in 1918. (false, all states recognised it as a holiday by 1890)

3 In the Middle Ages, it _____ (believe) the heart was the centre of intelligence. (true)

4 In 1892, Italy _____ (raise) the minimum age of marriage for girls to 16. (false, it was 12)

5 Roman coins _____ (discover) in the USA. (true)

6 One percent of the world's surface _____ (permanently cover) by ice. (false, it's ten percent)

7 More than half of the world's oxygen _____ (produce) by the Amazon rainforest. (false, it's twenty percent)

8 According to a US journal, by 2040 the Arctic Ocean _____ (have) no ice. (true)

Worksheet B

Read out the sentences using the correct tense and form of the verb in brackets (active or passive). Your partner will guess if they are true or false.

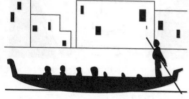

1 The first coins _____ (use) by the Romans. (false, it is thought the first coins were used by the Lydians, around 600 BC)

2 National beauty contests _____ (cancel) in Canada in 1992. (true)

3 John F Kennedy _____ (visit) China in 1972, the first US President to do so. (false, it was Richard Nixon)

4 The 'Black Death' _____ (reduce) the population of Europe by half from 1347 to 1351. (false, it was by one third)

5 The first modern Olympics _____ (hold) in Athens in 1896. (true)

6 All gondolas in Venice _____ (paint) red. (false, they are painted black)

7 Mount Everest _____ (grow) by five millimetres every year. (true)

8 According to National Geographic, in twenty years the Amazon rainforest _____ (reduce) by forty percent. (true)

The _____ **School Quiz**

Team name: _____

1 How many teachers are there in your school?	
2 How many students are there in your school?	
3 When did your school first open?	
4 When is your teacher's birthday?	
5 How many levels of general English does your school offer?	
6 Does your school offer any specialist English courses? If so, which ones?	
7 Does your school have any other branches? If so, where?	
8 Is your school open all year round?	
9 Has your teacher worked in any other countries? If so, which ones?	
10 How many classrooms does your school have?	
11 Does your school have computers for students to use? If so, how many?	
12 How many secretaries are there?	
13 Does your school have a course for complete beginners?	
14 Is there a minimum age to study at your school? If so, what is it?	
15 Is there a maximum age to study at your school? If so, what is it?	
16 What is the school director's name?	
17 Can you name five teachers who work at your school?	
18 What exams can you study for at your school?	
19 How many TVs are there in your school?	
20 What time does your school open in the morning?	

		Yes	No
1	Is there somewhere to recycle paper?		
2	Is there somewhere to recycle glass?		
3	Is there somewhere to recycle plastic?		
4	Is there somewhere to recycle aluminium cans?		
5	Is there somewhere to recycle food waste?		
6	Does the school sell secondhand books?		
7	Are there enough litter bins?		
8	Does your teacher switch off the lights when he/she leaves the classroom?		
9	Is the food in the canteen organic?		
10	Does your teacher avoid driving a car to school?		
11	Are the windows double-glazed? *Or*, If your school is in a hot climate, do the classrooms have fans (instead of air-conditioning)?		
12	Does the school do anything to promote environmental awareness?		
13	Do all the classrooms have energy-saving light bulbs?		
14	_____ ?		
15	_____ ?		

Recommendations

I'd make my school more eco-friendly by …

- _____
- _____
- _____
- _____
- _____

Worksheet A

1 Read out the sentences and replace the phrase in brackets with the word your partner gives you.

	Me ✓ or ✗	Partner ✓ or ✗
1 I always (process so that it can be used again) food packaging.		
2 I'm quite an (messy) person. I don't clean up as often as I should.		
3 If I had a (physical problem), I think I would cope with it.		
4 I'm terrible at cooking. I always (leave in the oven for too long) things.		
5 I find speaking English difficult as I often (say the sounds of words incorrectly) words.		
6 My hometown is (not familiar) to most of the world.		
7 I was quite a naughty child and would often (not follow the instructions) my parents.		
8 I should be more confident. Sometimes I (think they are less than they really are) my own abilities.		

2 Now listen to your partner's sentences and give them the correct word and prefix from the boxes.

re-	dis-	mis-	under-	over-	un-

weight	judge	understand	believable	estimate	agree	new	appear

3 Do you agree with the sentences? Does your partner agree? Mark the boxes with a ✓ or a ✗.

Worksheet B

1 Listen to your partner's sentences and give them the correct word and prefix from the boxes.

re-	dis-	mis-	under-	over-	un-

cook	cycle	estimate	tidy	obey	pronounce	ability	known

2 Now read out the sentences and replace the phrase in brackets with the word your partner gives you.

	Me ✓ or ✗	Partner ✓ or ✗
1 I think being (not heavy enough) is unattractive.		
2 Some of my government's policies at the moment are (impossible to take seriously).		
3 If I (don't understand properly) someone in English, I sometimes just pretend I've understood.		
4 If I (have a different opinion) with someone, I always tell them.		
5 I think experts (calculate as too high) the negative effects of eating fast food.		
6 Many types of animals will (not exist) in the future if we don't look after them.		
7 In my country you have to (make valid again) your passport every five years.		
8 I hate it when people (have the wrong idea about) me.		

3 Do you agree with the sentences? Does your partner agree? Mark the boxes with a ✓ or a ✗.

Grammar: reported speech

Horse: _____	**Total:** $1000

1 'I'm having lunch with my mum tomorrow.'
(two days later) She said she was having lunch with her mum tomorrow.
_____ $ _____

2 'We won't know the full effects for a long time.'
They said they wouldn't know the full effects for a long time.
_____ $ _____

3 'I've never been to Egypt.'
He said that he never goes to Egypt.
_____ $ _____

4 'I go running every day.'
She said she went running every day.
_____ $ _____

5 (Father to Son) 'I've told you twice already.'
(Son) Dad said he'd told you twice already.
_____ $ _____

6 'What do you want for your birthday?'
She asked me what did I want for my birthday.
_____ $ _____

7 'Have you ever seen anything so ridiculous?'
He asked me had I ever seen anything so ridiculous.
_____ $ _____

8 'Next year I'm going to study abroad.'
(the same year) She told us that she was going to study abroad next year.
_____ $ _____

9 'I sent it last week.'
(a week later) She said she had sent it last week.
_____ $ _____

10 'Will you marry me?'
She asked me if I will marry her.
_____ $ _____

11 'I haven't eaten broccoli for years.'
He said he didn't eat broccoli for years.
_____ $ _____

12 'How was your holiday?'
He asked me how my holiday had been.
_____ $ _____

✂

1 Would you like me to help you with your homework? *Hint:* offer	2 If I were you, I'd leave early. *Hint:* recommend	3 If you want, you can stay with me while you're in town. *Hint:* invite
4 Black shoes or blue shoes? I know, I'll wear the black ones. *Hint:* decide	5 You want a lift home? Of course it's no problem! *Hint:* agree	6 I'll definitely do my homework for tomorrow. *Hint:* promise
7 Why don't you hire a car? *Hint:* suggest	8 No! I won't eat my broccoli! *Hint:* refuse	9 If you stay in a hostel it will be cheaper. *Hint:* explain
10 If you're going out at night, you should be careful. *Hint:* warn	11 I'll help you with your bags, if you like. *Hint:* offer	12 What about going to the cinema tonight? *Hint:* suggest
13 I'll always love you. *Hint:* promise	14 Would you like to come with me? *Hint:* invite	15 I think I'll have fish for lunch. *Hint:* decide
16 I wouldn't take a taxi, if I were you. *Hint:* warn	17 It's my first visit here. *Hint:* explain	18 You should visit the fantastic local restaurants. *Hint:* recommend

1 Complete the sentences to make advice for visitors to a country, city or region you know well. Use the ideas in the box to help you.

crime	taxis	health	food and drink	public transport	time
climate	complaining	making jokes	shopping	going out alone	animals

If you visit _____ for the first time ...

1 Make sure you _____

2 You need to _____

3 Be careful _____

4 Don't _____

5 Watch out for _____

6 You'd better _____

7 Whatever you do, _____

   or else you could _____

8 The most important thing is to _____

9 If I were you, I'd _____

10 Don't forget to _____

11 _____

12 _____

2 Share your ideas with your group.

Unit 1

WHO YOU KNOW
Materials: One copy of worksheet A and worksheet B per pair of students

Arrange Ss into A and B pairs and distribute the worksheets. Explain that in each of their sentences the underlined word is wrong, and their partner has a sentence with the correct word in it. Ss take it in turns to read out a sentence. Their partner has to find the sentence that contains the correct word and read it back to them. Ss can then swap the underlined words to correct their sentences. Demonstrate the activity by reading out Student A's first sentence and asking one of the stronger Student Bs to find the sentence that contains the correct word. You may wish to write both sentences on the board to ensure that Ss understand the activity.

Monitor and help Ss with vocabulary if necessary. When Ss have finished, check the answers and encourage Ss to explain the differences in meaning between each pair.

Answers:

Worksheet A: 1 pupil   2 classmates   3 member
4 take after   5 boss   6 godmother   7 had a fiancé/fiancée
8 extended family   9 side   10 relatives

Worksheet B: 1 team-mates   2 employee   3 ancestors
4 great-grandmother   5 family history   6 mentor
7 partner   8 roots   9 'm related to   10 inherited

Then ask Ss to go through the sentences and discuss with their partner which are true and false for them. Tell Ss they can change the false ones, making them true for them. Encourage the Ss to ask follow-up questions to find out more information. Elicit any interesting information they found out for feedback.

COLLOCATION DOMINOES
Materials: One set of dominoes per group

Draw a simple sketch of a domino on the board and ask Ss if they know this game and what it's called in their language.

Arrange Ss into groups of three (or groups of four if you have a large class) and give each group a set of dominoes. Explain the game and demonstrate. One student deals the dominoes and each player places their dominoes face up in front of them. One student starts the game by putting down a domino in the middle. Ss take it in turns to add a domino to either side, forming correct collocations. If they place a domino to the left, it needs to be the correct verb. If they place a domino to the right, it needs to be the correct word(s) to complete the collocation. If they can't go, they miss a turn. The winner is the first player to put down all their dominoes.

While they are playing, go round and check that Ss are forming correct collocations, and answer any questions they have.

As a follow-up, Ss can discuss some of the collocations in their groups. Tell Ss they will have to think carefully about how to use the collocations in questions. Remind Ss of question forms they might need, e.g. *When did you last take a taxi? Have you got a degree? Do you take after anyone? Have you ever done any research? Are you going to do any housework this weekend?* etc. Elicit any interesting information they found out for feedback.

SIMILARITIES
Materials: One worksheet per student

Explain that Ss are going to ask questions to find out about each other. Distribute the worksheets. Check that Ss understand the sentences, and what kind of information they need to supply. Ask Ss to work alone and complete the sentences with true information about themselves. When they have finished, ask them to write three more interesting facts about themselves in the spaces provided. For late finishers, this could be reduced to one or two sentences. Go round and check their sentences before they start the activity.

Arrange Ss into pairs. Elicit what questions they need to ask in order to find out the same information about their partner (including *What's your name?* and *How do you spell that?* for the top of the column). Tell Ss they should put a tick in the box if their partner's answer is the same as their own, or put a cross in the box if it is different. While they are asking each other the questions, monitor carefully and note down any errors and examples of good language you hear for later feedback.

When they have finished one column, tell Ss to find another partner and repeat the process. When they have done this with four different partners (or three if you are short of time), ask Ss to add up the number of ticks they have for each partner to find out who they are most compatible with. Elicit a few answers. In feedback, go through any common errors with the class and draw Ss' attention to any examples of good language that you heard.

QUEENS AND KINGS
Materials: One copy of worksheet A and worksheet B per pair of students

Lead into the topic by asking Ss some questions related to queens and kings, e.g. *Does your country have a king or queen, or a president? What are the advantages of having a king or queen as the head of state? What are the disadvantages?*

Arrange Ss into A and B pairs and distribute the worksheets. Give Ss a few minutes to read their texts before they start the activity. Both Ss have the same texts but information is missing from one of them.

Tell Ss to ask their partner questions in order to complete the information in their text. With **weaker students**, give them time to write down the questions they need.

Possible questions:

Worksheet A: 1 When was she born?   2 Who is she married to?   3 What did they receive?   4 What were they doing in 1948?   5 What was she doing in 1952?   6 What did she celebrate in 1977?   7 What did she celebrate in 2002?   8 What is she hoping to become at the moment?   9 What does she prefer?   10 What is she currently working hard to do?

Worksheet B: 1 Where was he born?   2 Who did he get married to in 1962?   3 How many grandchildren do they have?   4 What did the dictator Francisco Franco name Juan Carlos as in 1969?   5 What was the dictator doing in 1974 and 1975?   6 What did Juan Carlos do on the 22nd of November 1975? / What did Juan Carlos do two days after the death of Franco?   7 What is he enjoying at the moment?   8 What is he doing at present?   9 What languages does he speak?   10 What were the Spanish football team celebrating?

Monitor to ensure that Ss are using verb tenses correctly. When they have finished, they can check their answers by comparing texts.

JOBS FAIR
Materials: One set of role cards per pair of students

Lead into the activity by asking if Ss have ever been to a jobs fair, and if this is a common way for companies to recruit new staff in their country.

Divide the class in half and distribute role card 1 to one half of the class and role card 2 to the other half. Go through the situation on the cards and give Ss time to prepare the information they need. Go round helping with language and ideas, and encourage Ss to be creative. The Ss with role card 2 (the job seekers) can either be honest or invent information about themselves.

When the Ss are ready, review the language for talking about yourself from unit 1.3. Then position the students with role card 1 (the exhibitors) around the class. Remind those Ss that they are the exhibitors at the jobs fair. The students with role card 2 (the job seekers) walk around asking questions about the jobs and answering questions about themselves. Monitor carefully, prompting Ss where necessary, and taking notes on their use of language for later feedback/correction. At the end of the activity, ask Ss which jobs were chosen.

Unit 2

YOU'RE THE DIRECTOR
Materials: One worksheet per group

Arrange Ss into groups of three and distribute one worksheet to each group. Explain that Ss are going to plan and present their ideas for their own film. Check that Ss understand the types of film and the events at the top of the worksheet. In their groups, Ss first choose the type of film they want to make, and choose as many events from the second box as they want. Before they complete their storyboards, ask Ss to brainstorm their ideas on the background, main characters, first problem, solution, further problem and the ending. They then complete the storyboard with simple sketches to illustrate what happens in the film. Instead of drawing pictures, Ss can simply write notes, but make sure they don't write full sentences.

When they are ready, ask the groups to present their ideas to the class. Ss can then vote for the best film idea.

SHAPES OF YOU
Materials: One worksheet per student

Distribute the worksheets and ask Ss to read the topics and write notes, randomly, in the shapes below. Tell Ss that they should write only one or two words for each topic. They should not look at each other's notes yet. Monitor and help Ss with any vocabulary they need.

When they are ready, ask the Ss to fold their worksheet in half. Arrange Ss into pairs. Tell Ss to show each other their notes. Their partner tries to guess what topics the information refers to. If they get stuck and need help, they can have another look at the topics at the top of the worksheet. Early finishers can discuss the topics they didn't write notes on. When they have finished, elicit any interesting information from the pairs.

CELEBRITY FACTS
Materials: One copy of worksheet A and worksheet B per pair of students; pictures of the celebrities, if you do the warmer

Optional warmer: bring to the class pictures of the celebrities in the sentences, and pin them up on the walls. Ask Ss to walk round and guess the names of the celebrities.

Preteach *tap shoes, cheering up* and *break-dancer*. Divide the class in half and give worksheet A to one half of the class and worksheet B to the other half. Give the Ss a few minutes to read their sentences and choose the correct verb forms. Go round and check their answers.

> **Answers:**
>
> Worksheet A: 1 won   2 has recorded   3 wore   4 has never directed   5 first appeared   6 has been   7 has never been   8 all died   9 has worked   10 has studied
>
> Worksheet B: 1 has directed   2 started   3 was   4 had   5 has never won   6 appeared   7 made   8 appeared   9 has had   10 has dated

Arrange Ss into pairs. Ask them to read out the film star facts for their partner to guess if they are true or false. Each false answer has an explanation so that Ss know why those facts are false. Tell Ss to keep a note of how many correct guesses their partner makes. When they have finished, find out how much the Ss knew.

As a follow-up, you could ask Ss to find out about other celebrities and write similar true/false sentences for others to guess, making sure they use the past simple and present perfect correctly.

IN YOUR DREAMS
Materials: One worksheet per student

Start by writing the following questions on the board:

How often do you remember your dreams?

What kinds of things can affect our dreams?

Do you believe that our dreams can tell us about our personality?

Do you believe dreams can predict the future?

Arrange Ss into pairs to discuss the questions, but ask them not to discuss any of their actual dreams yet. When they have finished, invite Ss to share some of their answers.

Distribute the worksheets and ask Ss to think of a dream they can remember. If they can't remember any of their dreams, they can invent one. Give Ss enough time to make notes in the word webs with the details of their dream. Tell Ss they don't have to use the examples given: these are just to help Ss think of ideas. Go round and help where necessary.

When they have finished, arrange Ss into groups of three. Ss describe their dreams to the other group members, who listen and ask follow-up questions. When they have all finished, they can work together to try and interpret what they think their dreams mean/meant. Monitor and check their use of narrative tenses. For feedback, elicit any interesting dreams.

WHAT HAPPENED NEXT?
Materials: One copy of worksheet A and worksheet B per pair of students

Lead into the topic by eliciting some examples of common fairy tales and find out which are the same in the Ss' countries. Divide the class in half and give worksheet A to one half of the class and worksheet B to the other half. Explain to Ss that they have the basic facts of the beginning of a story, and they are going to continue it and finish it. Give Ss enough time to think about how they will tell the story and how they will finish it, and go round giving help where necessary.

When they are ready, arrange Ss into pairs. Review the language for telling a story and keeping a story going from unit 2.3. Ss tell each other their stories, and their partner listens and responds, using the language you've reviewed. When they have finished, invite some Ss to tell you how they ended their stories and ask Ss which they found the most interesting.

Unit 3

WHAT DID YOU SAY?
Materials: One card per student

Distribute one card to each student, and tell Ss not to show their card to anyone else. If you have more than sixteen Ss, you will need to double up some of the cards. Explain the activity. Ss read their card and think about what they are going to say. Give Ss enough time to prepare and go round and help if necessary. When they are ready, Ss walk around and do what's on their card. Tell Ss they have to speak to everyone in the class, and ask them to try and remember what other students say to them (without writing anything down). Monitor and note down any common errors for later correction.

When they have finished, arrange Ss into groups of three and give them five minutes to write down as many of the things other students said as they can remember. Elicit each group's answers and award a point for each correctly remembered sentence. The group with the most points wins.

IDIOM WARS
Materials: One set of instructions (Student A or B) and two grids per student

Arrange Ss into A and B pairs and distribute the A and B instructions and grids. Explain and demonstrate the rules of the game, using a grid on the board, similar to the one on the worksheets. Students secretly write the sentences from the box in one of their grids (the other grid will be used to record the words they find in their partner's grid). Each sentence contains an idiom. The sentences can be written horizontally, vertically or diagonally (but not backwards). Contractions (e.g. *It's*) count as one word.

When they are ready, tell Ss that they have to find their partner's idioms. To do this, Ss take turns calling out grid references to each other, e.g. Student A starts and calls out G3. If there is nothing written in that square on Student B's grid, they say *Miss!* and Student A should record the miss as an X in their blank grid. If there is a word in Student B's grid, they say *Hit!* as well as the word that is in the square. Student A records the word in their grid. Then it is Student B's turn to call out a grid reference. This continues until one student has found all five idioms.

Once Ss start 'hitting' words, the process becomes much easier and a student can guess the whole idiom from the words if they think they know it. If they are correct, the other student replies *Yes, you've hit the idiom '…'*.

When they have finished, check that Ss understand the meaning of the idioms by giving a definition and asking Ss to supply the correct idiom.

THE CONTRACT OF LIFE
Materials: One worksheet per student

Introduce the topic of New Year's resolutions, and tell Ss some of yours. Ask Ss to tell the class some of their resolutions, and if they kept them. Explain that Ss are going to make some plans for themselves, and then sign a contract to make sure they stick to their plans. Distribute the worksheets and give Ss enough time to complete the sentences with real plans for themselves. Go round and help as necessary.

When Ss have finished, ask them to sign their contract and show it to two other Ss, who sign as witnesses. Encourage the witnesses to ask follow-up questions on the reasons for their plans.

At the end of the activity, invite Ss to share some of their plans.

INVENTIONS
Materials: One worksheet per pair of students

Write the following inventions on the board: *the internet, washing machines, microwave ovens, cloning, nanotechnology* and hold a brief discussion on how each one has changed our lives. Ask Ss what inventions they would like to see in the future.

Arrange Ss into pairs and distribute a worksheet to each pair. Explain that they now have the chance to invent something for the future, which they will then present to the class. Give Ss enough time to discuss a name for their invention, produce a simple sketch (they could omit this if they don't want to draw), make notes to answer the questions and add any other details.

Monitor and help with ideas where necessary. Encourage Ss to be creative, but if they are having difficulty you could suggest some ideas (e.g. *fingerprint credit cards, exercise pills, virtual reality films,* etc).

When they are ready, ask each pair to present their invention to the class. The other Ss then vote for their favourite invention.

SORRY, I DIDN'T CATCH THAT
Materials: One set of role cards per pair of students

Arrange Ss into A and B pairs and distribute the A and B role cards. Tell Ss not to look at each other's role cards. Give Ss a few minutes to read through the information on role cards 1A and 1B, check what they need to do and think about the functional language they need. Remind Ss of the language for dealing with misunderstandings from unit 3.3, putting it on the board for Ss to refer to during the activity, if necessary.

When they are ready, ask Ss to role-play the situation. Monitor and help where necessary.

When they have finished, ask Ss to do the same for role cards 2A and 2B. At the end of the activity, invite some Ss to tell the class how they resolved the situations.

Unit 4

THREE JOBS
Materials: One set of role cards per pair of students

Lead into the topic by finding out how many Ss in the class have jobs, what they are and what qualities they need. Tell Ss that they are now going to do two role-plays that involve finding out or giving information about jobs.

TEACHER'S NOTES

Arrange Ss into A and B pairs and distribute the A and B role cards. Tell Ss not to look at each other's role cards. Give Ss a few minutes to read through the information on role cards 1A and 1B. Explain that Student A has to answer Student B's questions and provide information, and Student B has to ask for the information that is missing from his/her role card and then complete the role card. When they are ready, ask Ss to role-play the situation. Monitor and help where necessary.

When they have finished, ask Ss to swap roles and do the same for role cards 2A and 2B. At the end of the activity, ask Ss to choose which job they would like to apply for, and why.

As a follow-up you could review the strong adjectives vocabulary from unit 4.1, and ask Ss, in pairs, to use different adjectives to describe the jobs. Elicit their ideas for feedback.

Answers:

Role card 1B: Trainer: Main duties: training new staff, giving workshops, writing a training program

Personal qualities: decisive, a good communicator, a good leader

Inventor: Main duties: creating new technology, developing existing technology

Personal qualities: able to think outside the box, highly motivated, hard-working

Sales representative: Main duties: finding new customers, selling new technology to existing customers

Personal qualities: competitive, a risk-taker, ambitious

Role card 2A: Entertainments manager: Main duties: finding new acts, planning the entertainments program

Personal qualities: a good leader, a risk-taker, able to think outside the box

Deckhand/Caretaker: Main duties: general maintenance, cleaning, repairs

Personal qualities: hard-working, motivated

Travel agent: Main duties: selling the cruise package, finding new customers, helping guests with their questions during the cruise

Personal qualities: a good communicator, competitive, decisive

FINDING THE RIGHT WORDS

Materials: One copy of worksheet A and worksheet B per pair of students

Write the following incorrect sentence on the board and ask Ss to correct it:

I never remind to phone my mother on her birthday.

Tell Ss that they are going to try to identify whether their partner's sentences are correct or incorrect. Arrange Ss into pairs, and distribute the worksheets. Tell Ss not to look at each other's worksheets.

Student A reads out his/her sentences to Student B, who decides if they are correct or incorrect. If a sentence is incorrect, Student B should try to correct it. Student A keeps a note of how many times Student B is successful. Then Ss swap roles.

Remind Ss to read slowly and clearly to each other and that they should correct confusing words and not grammar. Monitor and help where necessary. In feedback, elicit some answers and ask Ss to explain why the incorrect sentences are wrong.

Then ask Ss to discuss which sentences are true for them, and explain their answers to their partner. At the end of the activity, invite Ss to share some of their answers.

TOP TIPS
Materials: One worksheet per group

Write the following on the board:

How to _____

You shouldn't be afraid of making mistakes.

You must learn new vocabulary.

You don't have to live in London.

You mustn't give up too easily.

Elicit the missing words from the title (*How to learn English*). Arrange Ss into groups of three (or groups of four if you have a large class), distribute one worksheet to each group, and ask each group to appoint a 'secretary', who will write down the group's answers. Explain that you are going to read out a situation (*How to …*), and each team must race to write good advice for that situation, completing the sentences in the box. Tell Ss that you will read out four situations so they will have a total of four races.

Choose from the following situations: *How to drive safely, How to become a millionaire, How to succeed at a job interview, How to be a good teacher, How to do well in exams, How to keep healthy*. Alternatively, you could use other situations that you are confident your class will be able to think of advice for.

The first group to complete their sentences wins the race. Ask the winning group to read out their advice and check that they formed correct sentences containing good advice.

When all four races have finished, the groups can join to form larger groups and compare what advice they wrote. Elicit any interesting answers for feedback.

THOSE WERE THE DAYS
Materials: One worksheet per student

Set the scene by telling Ss a few facts about you when you were a child, using *used to* and *would*. Distribute the worksheets and ask Ss to think back to their childhood, and write twelve true sentences using *used to* and *would* under the categories provided. Encourage them to write both positive and negative sentences. Go round and check their language, helping where necessary.

When they are ready, tell Ss to mingle with the objective of finding people with the same answers. To do this, Ss will have to ask other students questions based on their own sentences. When they find someone with the same answer, they write their name in the column on the right.

Monitor and check that Ss are forming the questions correctly, and encourage them to ask follow-up questions. When they have finished, arrange Ss into pairs to compare their sentences. Elicit any interesting answers from the class for feedback.

COALITION GOVERNMENT
Materials: One copy of worksheet A and worksheet B per pair of students

Introduce the topic by asking Ss about the political system in their country, e.g. *Is it a parliamentary or presidential system? What type of voting system do you have at elections? Do you have one clear party in government, or is it usually a coalition?*

Divide the class in half and give worksheet A to one half of the class and worksheet B to the other half. Give Ss five minutes to read the information and check they understand the activity and the vocabulary. Tell Ss in each half of the class to work together to plan two or three reasons for each priority. Explain that each student should write their own notes as they will work with a student from the other group later.

Arrange Ss into A and B pairs and tell them not to look at each other's worksheet. Review the functional language for reaching agreement from unit 4.3. Ss discuss the points and try to reach agreement on each issue. Monitor and help where necessary. At the end of the activity, find out if and how they managed to agree.

Unit 5

GIVE US A CLUE

Materials: One copy of crossword A and crossword B per pair of students

Arrange Ss into pairs and distribute the worksheets. Sit Ss face-to-face and tell them not to show their worksheets to each other. Tell Ss that they each have half of the answers to a crossword and they are going to work together to complete the crossword. Ss take it in turns to describe a word to their partner. They should also give the number in the grid, e.g. *3 across, 8 down*. If the other student guesses the word correctly, they can write it in the correct place in the crossword. If the student does not know the answer, he/she can try another one.

With **weaker classes**, before you arrange Ss into pairs, give them some time to prepare clues for their words.

When they have finished, tell Ss to look at each other's worksheets to check their answers are correct.

WORD-BUILDING RACE

Materials: One copy of the board and a dice or coin per group and one counter per student

Arrange Ss into groups of three and give each group a board (A3 size if possible), a dice or coin and a counter for each student. If Ss use a coin, explain *heads* and *tails* and that if the coin falls heads-up they move their counter forward two squares, and if it falls tails-up they move one.

Tell Ss to put their counters on the START square and to take it in turns to move around the board. If Ss land on a square with a sentence, they must say the sentence using the correctly formed adjective from the word in brackets. Point out that the suffixes they need to form the adjectives are on the board in the jigsaw squares. If Ss land on a square with a suffix, they must say five adjectives containing that suffix. If they are unsuccessful, they move back to the square they came from. If Ss land on a free square, they don't do anything. The winner is the first player to reach the FINISH square.

While Ss are playing the game, go round and help where necessary.

Answers:

From START to FINISH: easy useless painful logical talkative lovely/lovable dramatic homeless effective scary edible creative messy peaceful biological rainy successful hopeless valuable careless poetic responsible explosive hopeful

Suffix squares (example answers): *-able/-ible*: responsible lovable profitable (in)edible valuable *-less*: homeless useless careless hopeless restless *-ful*: painful peaceful thankful hopeful careful *-y*: messy hairy quickly easy flashy *-ive*: effective explosive creative effective cooperative *-ic/-ical*: poetic biological dramatic historical scientific

WHICH PHONE?

Materials: One set of role cards per pair of students

Lead into the topic by asking Ss what things they look for when buying a new mobile phone. You could write the categories from the role cards on the board to help **weaker classes** (*price, size, easy/difficult to use, functions, battery life, internet speed*). Tell Ss they are now going to do a role-play that involves describing and comparing different mobile phones.

Arrange Ss into pairs and distribute the worksheets. Give them time to read their roles and the information about the phones they have. Check that Ss know how to express sizes in speech, e.g. *seventeen by five centimetres*.

When they are ready, Ss describe the phones they have and compare them with the phones their partner has. After they have made comparisons, Ss choose which phone they want to buy, based on the role they are playing. Encourage them to give reasons for their choices, using comparatives and superlatives. At the end of the activity, invite Ss to share their choices.

Ss can then compare their own mobile phones in small groups, using the categories on the worksheet.

YOU'RE NOT FRENCH, ARE YOU?

Materials: One worksheet per student

Write two sentences on the board about two students in the class, one that contains a fact you are sure of and one that contains a fact you are not sure of, e.g. *Alessandra is a doctor; Julio doesn't like cheese*. Elicit the correct question tags for each sentence and model the correct intonation for checking the information, e.g.

Alessandra, you're a doctor, aren't you? Use falling intonation because you are sure of the answer.

Julio, you don't like cheese, do you? Use rising intonation because you are not sure of the answer.

Distribute the worksheets and ask Ss to complete the first six sentences with names of their classmates. Tell Ss not to look at each other's sentences. Ss then write six more sentences about their classmates, three that they're sure of, and three that they're not sure of. Monitor and help where necessary.

When Ss have finished, ask them to go and find their classmates and check the information using question tags.

Answers:

1 (*Name*), you came to class by car today, didn't you?
2 (*Name*), you like studying English, don't you?   3 (*Name*), you don't like eating fish, do you?   4 (*Name*), you went out with friends last night, didn't you?   5 (*Name*), you've got a boy/girlfriend, haven't you? / (*Name*), you have a boy/girlfriend, don't you?   6 (*Name*), you're a student, aren't you?

Monitor Ss' pronunciation of the question tags carefully and note any errors for later feedback. When they've finished, ask Ss how many they guessed correctly, and go through any common errors with the class.

WHAT'S THE PROBLEM?
Materials: One copy of worksheet A and worksheet B per pair of students

Arrange Ss into pairs, and give one set of role cards to each pair. Tell Ss not to look at each other's role cards. Review the language for polite requests and responses from unit 5.3. Focus Ss' attention on the first two situations (ignore the third for now), and give them enough time to prepare what they are going to say.

In pairs, Ss role-play the situations. Monitor and help where necessary. When they have finished, ask Ss what solutions they came up with.

Repeat the process for situation 3, but allow Ss to choose which role they want, and swap role cards if necessary.

Unit 6

HOW EMOTIONAL ARE YOU?
Materials: One copy of worksheet A and worksheet B per pair of students

Divide the class in half and give worksheet A to one half of the class and worksheet B to the other half. Explain that Ss are going to do a questionnaire to find out how emotional they are. First, ask Ss to read through the questions and answers, and choose the correct adjective in italics in each answer. Go round and check the answers. Ask Ss to write one more question of their own that could test how emotional a person is.

Answers:

Worksheet A: 1 a) Relaxed   b) stressed   c) worried
2 a) boring   b) embarrassed   c) frightening   3 a) surprised
b) annoying   c) disgusted   4 a) Pleased   b) confused
c) Terrified

Worksheet B: 1 a) Pleased   b) exciting   c) exhausted
2 a) confused   b) worrying   c) devastated   3 a) pleased
b) annoying   c) disgusted   4 a) boring   b) interesting
c) embarrassed

When they ready, arrange Ss into A and B pairs. Ss ask each other their questions and note their partner's answers. For question 5, they write their partner's answer in the space provided. When they have finished, ask Ss to note if their partner gave mostly a), b) or c) answers and to decide which category they fall into. Ss can also use the answer to question 5 to decide on the category. Ss then read the analysis and decide if they agree or not. Elicit some answers for feedback.

GUESS THE VERB
Materials: One copy of worksheet A and worksheet B per pair of students

Arrange Ss into pairs and distribute the worksheets. Tell Ss not to look at each other's worksheet. Explain the activity. Ss take it in turns to describe the multi-word verbs in bold to their partner, but they can't use any of the words in italics in their descriptions. The other student tries to guess the multi-word verb. Demonstrate the activity with a stronger student. While they are working, go round and help where necessary. For feedback, elicit some descriptions.

CONDITIONALS RACE
Materials: One copy of the board and a dice or coin per group and one counter per student

Arrange Ss into groups of three (or groups of four if you have a large class) and give each group a board (A3 size if possible), a dice or coin and a counter for each student. If Ss use a coin, they move one space for heads and two spaces for tails.

Tell Ss to put their counters on the START square and to take it in turns to move around the board.

If Ss land on a square with a sentence, they must finish the sentence correctly with true information about themselves. If Ss don't finish the sentence correctly, they move back to the square they came from. If Ss land on a free square, they don't do anything. The winner is the first player to reach the FINISH square.

While Ss are playing the game, go round and help, correcting/adjudicating where necessary.

WHY WOULD YOU DO THAT?
Materials: One set of cards per group

Write on the board: *make a noise like a cat,* and ask Ss to give you possible reasons why they would or wouldn't do this, e.g. *If I had a cat, and I wanted to get its attention, I would make a noise like a cat.* Arrange Ss into groups of three (or groups of four if you have a large class), and give each group a set of cards, placed face down in the middle. Ss take it in turns to take a card and read it out to the rest of the group. The other Ss try to give a good reason why they would or wouldn't do this. The first student to give a correctly formed reason wins the card. Go round and help with vocabulary and adjudicate where necessary.

For feedback, nominate a student from each group to give the most interesting answers to the class, forming full second conditional sentences.

MIXED EMOTIONS
Materials: Four copies of the worksheet, cut into cards

To prepare for the activity, make enough copies of the worksheet to provide three or four cards per student. Cut up the cards, then shuffle them all together. Distribute three or four cards to each student. Tell Ss not to look at each other's cards.

Review the language for giving good and bad news and responding to it from unit 6.3. Give Ss a few minutes to think about how they will tell people their good and bad news, then ask them to walk around and share their news with other Ss. Encourage Ss to respond using the expressions in unit 6.3 and ask follow-up questions. When they have finished, elicit some of the news they came up with.

As an extension, Ss could discuss which of the situations have really happened to them, and what happened.

Unit 7

GIFTED!

Materials: One copy of worksheet A and worksheet B per pair of students

Lead into the topic by writing the following on the board: *To be successful you need to …* and elicit ideas from the class. Arrange Ss into pairs and distribute the worksheets. Ss take it in turns to ask each other questions using the prompts, and write their partner's answers in the *Partner 1* column. With **weaker classes**, ask Ss to write out the questions first, and go round checking that they are forming the questions correctly. Monitor carefully and help where necessary.

When Ss have finished, ask them to find a new partner and ask their questions again, writing the answers in the *Partner 2* column. When they have finished, elicit any common answers for feedback.

ALL ABOUT YOU

Materials: One worksheet per student

Distribute the worksheets and ask Ss to read the questions and add the missing prepositions. If they get stuck, they can look back at unit 7.1 for help. When they have finished, check the answers.

Answers:
1 on   2 in   3 with   4 in   5 for   6 with   7 at   8 with   9 at   10 to   11 at   12 about   13 for   14 to   15 on   16 about   17 on   18 about

Ask Ss to write their own answers to the questions in the *My answer* column. When they have finished, Ss mingle and ask questions to find other people with the same answers. They write the name of the person with the matching answer next to the relevant question, in the *Name* column. Monitor carefully and encourage Ss to ask follow-up questions. Elicit any interesting answers for feedback.

GUESS THE FILM STAR

Materials: One copy of worksheet A and worksheet B per pair of students

Arrange Ss into pairs and explain the rules. Student A reads out the first fact about his/her first film star, using the prompts and the present perfect simple or continuous. If both tenses are possible, Ss should use the continuous. Student B then tries to guess who the film star is. (With **weaker classes**, ask Ss to write out the questions first, and go round checking that they are forming the tenses correctly.) If Student B can't guess, Student A reads out the next fact, and so on until he/she has read out all six facts. Ss score points for guessing the film star as follows:

After one clue 10 points; after two clues 8 points; after three clues 6 points; after four clues 5 points; after five clues 3 points; after six clues 1 point.

Ss take it in turns reading out facts and guessing until both Ss have done this with their three film stars. Give Ss enough time to complete the activity, then ask them how many points they scored.

Answers:

Film star 1A: 2 She has previously worked as a model. 3 She has been acting in major roles since she first appeared in *The Mask* in 1994.   4 She has won many awards, but has never won an Oscar.   5 She has previously dated Justin Timberlake and Matt Dillon.   6 She has recently appeared in *There's Something About Mary*, *Charlie's Angels* and *Shrek* in comedy roles.

Film star 2A: 2 As well as acting, he has also worked at a nuclear power plant.   3 He has been going bald since the 1980s.   4 He has previously been married to Demi Moore. 5 He has won many awards, but has never won an Oscar. 6 He has appeared in many action films, such as *Armageddon* and *The Sixth Sense*, and sitcoms such as *Moonlighting* and *Friends*.

Film star 3A: 2 She has been acting in major roles since she first appeared in *Sense and Sensibility* in 1995.   3 She married Sam Mendes in 2003, but they have recently split up.   4 She has recently won an Oscar for *The Reader*. 5 She has acted in one of the best-selling films of all time, with Leonardo DiCaprio.   6 She has appeared in other films such as *Iris*, *Enigma* and *Flushed Away*.

Film star 1B: 2 He has been a member of a real street gang. 3 He has been married to Grace Hightower since 1997. 4 Since 1989, he has been investing in the TriBeCa district of New York.   5 He has won two Oscars for his roles in *The Godfather II* and *Raging Bull*.   6 He has mainly acted in serious roles, but recently he has been acting in comedy roles in films such as *Meet the Fockers* and *Stardust*.

Film star 2B: 2 She has been acting in major roles since she first appeared in *Bend it Like Beckham* in 2002.   3 She has always wanted to act, since she was three.   4 She has recently been doing charity work for Amnesty International. 5 Although she has been nominated, she has never won an Oscar.   6 She has acted in a major series of films about pirates with Johnny Depp and Orlando Bloom.

Film star 3B: 2 He has been acting 'with magic' since 2001. 3 He has acted in films, on TV and at the theatre.   4 He has won many awards, but has never won an Oscar.   5 He has appeared in the Sunday Times Rich List as one of the richest young people in England.   6 He has recently been acting in the theatre.

MIXED ABILITIES

Materials: One set of cards per group

Start by reviewing the language of past and present abilities from unit 7.2 and write some examples on the board for Ss to refer to during the activity. Arrange Ss into groups of four and give each group a set of cards, positioned face down, in the middle.

Demonstrate the activity. Ss take it in turns to take a card and decide if they are going to ask about the present or past. They then ask the other Ss about their abilities, using the prompt on the card. The other Ss in the group can either lie or tell the truth. The student who asked the question must then ask follow-up questions to work out if the other Ss are lying or telling the truth. Monitor and help out where necessary. Elicit any interesting information for feedback.

SOUND INVESTMENTS
Materials: One set of role cards per group

Lead into the activity by eliciting things a company may need to invest in. Review the language for clarifying opinions from unit 7.3 and write some examples on the board for Ss to refer to during the activity. Arrange Ss into groups of four (or if you don't have the right number of Ss, have some groups of three and omit role card 4). Give out a role card to each member of the group, and give Ss time to read their role and think of two more reasons for their choice. Go round and help with vocabulary and ideas.

When they are ready, Ss carry out the role-play, giving their reasons and trying to reach a decision on how the money can be spent. They could choose to invest it all in one or two of the options, but they must spend at least 75% of the money on one of the options. Monitor and check Ss are using the language correctly. Elicit their decisions for feedback.

Unit 8

DO YOU GET ON?
Materials: One copy of worksheet A and worksheet B per pair of students

Arrange Ss into A and B pairs and distribute the worksheets. Tell Ss not to look at each other's worksheets. Explain that in each of their questions, the underlined phrase must be replaced by a phrase that their partner gives them. Student A reads out their question, and Student B responds by choosing the correct replacement phrase from their box and saying it to Student A, who writes it down. Ss don't give any answers to the questions yet. When they have finished, they change roles and complete Student B's questions. Check the answers with the class.

Answers:

Worksheet A: 1 keep yourself to yourself 2 nosy 3 make friends with 4 disturb you 5 done favours for 6 gets on your nerves

Worksheet B: 1 get on well with 2 invite your neighbours over 3 mind their own business 4 a nuisance 5 get to know 6 ask a favour of

Then ask Ss, in their pairs, to discuss their answers to the questions. Go round and help where necessary. Elicit some interesting answers for feedback.

PELMANISM
Materials: One set of cards per group

Prepare for the activity by cutting up one set of cards for each group of three Ss (or one set for each group of four Ss if you have a large class). Arrange Ss into groups of three or four, and give one set of cards to each group. Ask the Ss to spread out the cards, face down, on a flat surface in the centre of the group. Ss take it in turns to turn over two cards at a time. If they turn over a pair of words that form a compound noun (e.g. *sports centre*), they can keep the cards. If they don't, they must turn the cards back over, making sure they put them back in the same place. Ss keep going until no more pairs can be found. While Ss are doing the activity, go round and help where necessary. The student with the most pairs at the end wins.

WHERE I LIVE
Materials: One copy of worksheet A and worksheet B per pair of students

Arrange Ss into pairs and distribute the worksheets. Tell Ss not to look at each other's worksheets. Explain to the Ss that they are going to identify and correct the error in each sentence that their partner reads out.

Student A reads out their sentences to Student B, who must listen and correct the mistake(s) with articles and/or quantifiers. When they have finished, Student B does the same with his/her sentences. Go round and help where necessary.

When they have finished, ask Ss to discuss in pairs which sentences are true for them. Elicit any interesting answers for feedback.

INTERNET RELATIVITY
Materials: One copy of worksheet A and worksheet B per pair of students

Arrange Ss into A and B pairs and distribute the worksheets. Tell Ss not to look at each other's worksheets. Explain the activity. Student A reads out a sentence half to Student B, who must listen and choose the correct ending from the list on his/her worksheet. Student A continues until he/she has read out all the sentence halves. When they have finished, they repeat the process with Student B's sentence halves. When they have finished, check the answers with the class.

Answers:

Worksheet A: 1 C 2 A 3 B 4 D 5 F 6 E
Worksheet B: 1 E 2 F 3 A 4 C 5 D 6 B

Then ask Ss, in their pairs, to make sentences that are true for them, using the underlined phrases and finishing them with their own ideas. Elicit any interesting answers for feedback.

MAKING YOURSELF AT HOME
Materials: One copy of worksheet A and worksheet B per pair of students

Review the language from unit 8.3 for being a good guest and write some examples on the board for Ss to refer to during the activity. Arrange Ss into A and B pairs and distribute the worksheets. Explain that Ss are going to do some role-plays involving situations relating to being a good guest. Give Ss time to read their situations, and go round helping with any vocabulary where necessary.

When they are ready, Ss work through the situations, taking it in turns to apologise/use questions. Monitor and check they are using the expressions correctly. Ask some pairs to act out some of the situations for feedback.

Unit 9

THE HISTORY OF MY COUNTRY
Materials: One copy of worksheet per pair of students

Review the vocabulary in unit 9.1, asking Ss if any of these things have happened in the history of their country/ies. Explain that they are now going to invent the history of a fictional country and give a short presentation on it. Arrange Ss into pairs and distribute one worksheet to each pair. Ss first think of a name for their country, then use the words in the box and their own ideas to invent its history. Tell Ss that they don't have to use all of the ideas in the box, and they don't have to complete all of the sections, as long as they include events from a range of time periods. Encourage them to make the history as interesting as possible and go round and help where necessary.

When Ss are ready, ask each pair to present their history to the class. The other Ss listen and choose the most interesting one.

GUESS MY COLLOCATION
Materials: One set of cards per group

Arrange Ss into groups of three (or groups of four if you have a large class) and give each group a set of cards, positioned face down in the middle. Explain that each card has a picture on it that describes a collocation with *come, give, have* or *make* from unit 9.2. Write the collocations from the answer key on the board in random order for students to refer to. Ss take it in turns to pick up a card and match the picture on it with the correct collocation. Anyone in the group can try to guess the collocation. Whoever guesses correctly first keeps the card. Go round and help where necessary, supplying Ss with the collocation if they get stuck. At the end of the activity, the student with the most cards in each group is the winner.

Answers:

A give someone a call B have a dream C make a profit
D come first E come back F make progress
G give a talk H have a good time I come naturally
J give instructions K make a mess L have trouble (with something) M make a decision N come by car O give directions P have a break

When Ss have finished, go through the answers with the class, then ask Ss to discuss the last time they did some of the things in the pictures. Elicit any interesting answers for feedback.

BAD DECISIONS
Materials: Two sets of cards

Prepare for the activity by making two copies of the worksheet (A3 size if possible) and cutting them up into cards. Stick the cards up on the walls around the classroom. (If you can't stick them on the walls, arrange them on desks or chairs around the classroom.) Arrange Ss into pairs and explain that they are going to read about some bad decisions in history and say what they would have done. Ss walk around the class in pairs, reading the situations and coming up with two third conditional sentences for each, using the prompts at the bottom of each card. With **weaker students**, you could ask them to write down their sentences for you to check. Go round and help with vocabulary where necessary.

For feedback, elicit the Ss' sentences. As an extension, you could ask Ss if they can tell you any other bad decisions made in history (or recently) and make third conditional sentences about those decisions.

AMAZING FACTS
Materials: One copy of worksheet A and worksheet B per pair of students

Arrange Ss into A and B pairs and distribute the worksheets. Explain the activity. Student A reads the sentences out to his/her partner, filling the gap with the correct active or passive

form of the verb in brackets in the correct tense. Student B has to guess if the sentence is true or false. Student A notes down all of Student B's correct guesses. Ss then follow the same procedure for Student B's sentences. With **weaker classes**, you could give Ss a few minutes to write out the sentences first, and check their answers before they start the activity. Monitor and correct any incorrect use of tense or form and any irregular past participle errors. When they have finished, Ss add up their partner's score. The student with the most correct guesses wins. At the end of the activity, ask Ss to tell the class which facts they found surprising.

Answers:

Worksheet A: 1 was first used 2 became 3 was believed 4 raised 5 have been discovered 6 is permanently covered 7 is produced 8 will have

Worksheet B: 1 were used 2 were cancelled 3 visited 4 reduced 5 were held 6 are painted 7 grows 8 will be reduced

SCHOOL QUIZ
Materials: One copy of the worksheet per group and one copy of the worksheet with the answers, for the teacher

To prepare for the class, you will need to find out the answers to the questions on the worksheet in advance.

Arrange Ss into groups of three (or groups of four if you have a large class) and distribute one copy of the worksheet to each group. Ask the Ss to complete the title of the quiz with your school's name and to think of a name for their team. Write the team names in a list on the board. Review the functional language for expressing uncertainty from unit 9.3. Give Ss enough time to work together to answer the questions, using the functional language in their discussions. Tell Ss not to look at the other groups' answers.

When they have finished, go through each question and elicit an answer from each group. Award a point for each correct answer and write the scores up on the board. If none of the answers are correct, award a point to the group that is the closest. Add the points up to find the winning team.

Unit 10

'GREEN TEST' YOUR SCHOOL
Materials: One copy of worksheet per student

Explain to Ss that they are going to carry out a 'green test' of their school (or the building your class is in). Distribute one worksheet per student and ask them to read the questions, then think of two more questions they can ask and write them in the spaces provided.

When they are ready, Ss go round the school and find out the answers to the questions on their worksheet. Encourage them to ask people they come across. When they have finished, Ss come back to the classroom and share the answers with the class. Ask them how well they think the school did in the test.

Then arrange Ss into pairs. Ask them to write some recommendations to make their school more eco-friendly in the space provided on the worksheet. Elicit their answers for feedback.

TEACHER'S NOTES

DO YOU AGREE?
Materials: One copy of worksheet A and worksheet B per pair of students

Arrange Ss into A and B pairs and distribute the worksheets. Tell Ss not to look at each other's worksheets. Explain that in each of their sentences, the phrase in brackets must be replaced by a word with a prefix that their partner gives them. Student A reads out their sentence, and Student B responds by choosing the correct word and prefix from their boxes and saying it to Student A. Tell Ss that they can use the prefixes more than once, but they can use the words in the right-hand box once only. Ss don't give any answers to the questions yet. When they have finished, they change roles and complete Student B's sentences. Check the answers with the class.

Answers:

Worksheet A: 1 recycle   2 untidy   3 disability
4 overcook   5 mispronounce   6 unknown   7 disobey
8 underestimate

Worksheet B: 1 underweight   2 unbelievable
3 misunderstand   4 disagree   5 overestimate   6 disappear
7 renew   8 misjudge

After checking the answers, Ss put a tick or a cross in the column headed 'Me' to indicate whether they agree or disagree with each statement. Rearrange the Ss so they are working with a different partner. Ask them to discuss whether they agree or disagree with each statement, and mark the column headed 'Partner' with a tick or a cross. Go round and help where necessary. Elicit some interesting answers for feedback.

AT THE RACES
Materials: One copy of the worksheet per group

Arrange Ss into groups of three (or groups of four if you have a large class) and ask each group to appoint a 'secretary', who will be responsible for writing their sentences. Explain that there are going to be twelve 'horse races'. In each one, the group has to bet on what they think is the correct sentence of reported speech.

Distribute the worksheets and explain that each item of direct speech is followed by a sentence in which the speech is reported: some of the speech is reported correctly, and some sentences have mistakes. Give Ss enough time to look through the sentences and decide which ones are correct. They should write *correct* on the worksheet, or mark the corrections to make the sentence correct. They then have to decide how much money to bet on each answer, and should write this on the sheet. They have $1000 to bet in total, and can bet up to half of it on any one horse. They do not have to bet on every sentence.

Go through the sentences as a class, and write the correct sentences on the board. Ss double their money if they have identified a correct sentence or made any necessary corrections to the sentence. If their sentence is not correct they lose the money. Once all the sentences have been corrected, teams calculate their winnings by first doubling, then adding together all the bets they have won, and adding on any money they didn't bet.

Answers:
1 the next day/the following day   2 correct   3 has/had never been   4 correct   5 told me   6 what I wanted   7 if I'd ever seen   8 correct   9 the week before/the previous week   10 I would/I'd   11 he hadn't eaten   12 correct

REPORT THAT!
Materials: One set of cards per group

Arrange Ss into groups of three (or groups of four if you have a large class) and give each group one set of cards, positioned face down in the middle. Don't worry if the cards are not in order. Review the grammar from unit 10.2, then explain the activity. Each turn, a student takes a card and reads out the sentence at the top. The other Ss in the group try to report the sentence using a reporting verb in the correct form, and changing any other parts of the sentence (e.g. pronouns, time references) to report it correctly. If Ss get stuck, the student who picked up the card reads out the reporting verb as a hint. The first student in the group to say the sentence correctly keeps the card. The student with the most cards at the end wins. Go round while Ss are doing the activity and prompt/adjudicate where necessary.

At the end of the activity, elicit the answers from the class. Note that the suggested answers below are provided only as a guideline, as several alternatives may be possible in each case.

Suggested answers:
1 He/She offered to help me/us with my/our homework. 2 He/She recommended leaving early.   3 He/She invited me/us to stay with him/her while I was/we were in town. 4 He/She decided to wear the black shoes/ones.   5 He/She agreed to give me/us a lift home.   6 He/She promised to do his/her homework for tomorrow.   7 He/She suggested hiring a car.   8 He/She refused to eat his/her broccoli.   9 He/She explained that it would be cheaper to stay in a hostel.   10 He/She warned us to be careful if we were/are going out at night.   11 He/She offered to help me/us with my/our bags.   12 He/She suggested going to the cinema tonight/that night.   13 He/She promised he'd/she'd always love us/me.   14 He/She invited me/us to go with him/her.   15 He/She decided to have fish for lunch. 16 He/She warned me/us not to take a taxi.   17 He/She explained that it was his/her first visit here/there.   18 He/She recommended visiting the fantastic local restaurants.

WHEN IN ROME ...
Materials: One copy of the worksheet per student

Introduce the topic by preparing some pieces of advice for visitors to your country. Share the advice with the class and ask if any of it surprises the Ss. Distribute one worksheet to each student and ask them to think of a country, city or region they know well (preferably not their own, but don't insist on this if Ss don't know other places well enough), and write the name at the top of the worksheet. Ss then write ten pieces of advice for visitors to that country, city or region. Ss can use the topics in the box for ideas. Go round and help where necessary.

When they have finished, arrange Ss into groups of three (or groups of four if you have a large class) to share their ideas. The other Ss listen and guess which country, city or region they are describing. Elicit any interesting ideas for feedback.

184

Tests index

LISTENING

1 ▶ **44 Listen and circle the correct answer: a), b) or c).**

1 Jo thinks she could be ____ Native American.
   a) 5%   b) 15%   c) 50% ⟵(circled)

2 The woman felt the bed moving so she got up and ____.
   a) got under the table   b) went outside   c) got dressed

3 The girl's going to save ____ to go to the Moon.
   a) $1m   b) for a long time   c) for 25 years

4 Jack ____ Nick's idea for a new business.
   a) likes   b) agrees with   c) doesn't agree with

5 The shop doesn't have a ____.
   a) price list   b) computer   c) dishwasher

6 The woman says she couldn't live without a ____.
   a) fridge   b) cooker   c) tin opener

[| 10]

PRONUNCIATION

2 ▶ **45 Listen and cross out the word with a different vowel sound in bold.**

1 family   ~~drama~~   married   ambitious
2 inquiry   risk   science   fiction
3 romantic   forgot   comedy   job
4 genetic   remember   engineering   period
5 hear   earn   leader   freeze
6 fun   discussion   furious   wonderful

[| 5]

VOCABULARY AND GRAMMAR

3 Match the compound nouns.

1 great-   _d_   a) power
2 romantic   ____   b) taker
3 washing   ____   c) family
4 risk   ____   d) ~~grandparents~~
5 psychological   ____   e) networks
6 solar   ____   f) comedy
7 genetic   ____   g) drama
8 extended   ____   h) fiction
9 period   ____   i) machine
10 computer   ____   k) thriller
11 science   ____   l) engineering

[| 5]

4 Underline the correct preposition.

1 I'm meeting them _at_ / in lunchtime.
2 He complimented her _on_ / of her new hairstyle.
3 I dialled the wrong number for / by mistake.
4 We can't possibly predict what changes will take place in / on ten years' time.
5 You haven't said a word for an hour. What's at / on your mind?
6 He couldn't stop for a chat because he was from / in a hurry.
7 I warned him about / from the traffic jams.
8 She had to apologise on / for forgetting the time of the meeting.
9 He couldn't finish the exam because he ran up / out of time.
10 I think the situation will get slightly worse of / in the short term.
11 She forgot to switch up / off the lights when she left the house.

[| 5]

5 Complete the sentences. Use the correct form of the word in capitals.

1 He's been ___unemployed___ for six months. He can't find a job. EMPLOY
2 They're trying to find a _____ solution to the conflict. PEACE
3 I can't use my mobile. The battery needs _____. CHARGE
4 They had to close the business because it had become _____. PROFIT
5 There are fewer _____ people sleeping on the streets now there are more shelters for them. HOME
6 Commuting to work in big cities is more _____ than it used to be. EXHAUST

[| 5]

6 Correct <u>two</u> mistakes in each sentence.

1 My students don't hear me and that's why they do mistakes.

   My students don't **listen to** *me and that's why they* **make** *mistakes.*

2 My ancestors are coming for lunch today. My uncle says very funny stories.

   _____.

3 He got fired from his boss so he's looking for a new work.

   _____.

4 I said him I'd be late because I forgot my purse at home.

   _____.

5 You didn't remember me about Alan's birthday and now I'm in boiling water!

   _____.

6 She made medical research after university, but she didn't win much money.

   _____.

   `5`

7 Write questions for the answers in *italics*.

1 He was *talking on his mobile* when I saw him.
   What <u>was he doing when you saw him</u> _____?

2 I used to play *tennis and hockey* before I broke my leg.
   Which _____?

3 They were looking for *you* just now.
   Who _____?

4 *The Arsenal football team* is likely to win the championship.
   Which _____?

5 He realised *later* that he'd given her the wrong address.
   When _____?

6 *Maria* sent me a beautiful card for my birthday.
   Who _____?

   `5`

8 Complete the second sentence so that it means the same as the first. Use the word in brackets.

1 You can't smoke in the office. (must)
   You <u>mustn't smoke in the office</u> _____.

2 His flat's not as messy as it used to be. (less)
   His flat _____.

3 The plane will probably be late. (likely)
   The plane _____.

4 This one's a bit more expensive. (slightly)
   This one _____.

5 I told him not to forget to buy the bread. (remind)
   I _____.

6 We used to have a family lunch every Sunday. (would)
   We _____.

   `5`

9 Circle the correct answer: a), b), c) or d).

1 You _____ eat so much junk food.
   a) might   (b) shouldn't) c) must   d) have to

2 We _____ to stay with friends when we get to Sydney.
   a) will   b) would   c) likely   d) 're going

3 I've never been to China, but I _____ to Japan last year.
   a) went   b) 've been   c) used to go   d) gone

4 He _____ her name now.
   a) isn't remembering   b) don't remember
   c) doesn't remember   d) remember

5 When she got to the airport, she realised she _____ her passport at home.
   a) left   b) forgot
   c) 'd forgotten   d) 'd left

6 We met them _____ we were living in Tanzania.
   a) during   b) until   c) while
   d) as soon as

7 My ancestors _____ from Ireland.
   a) came   b) comes
   c) lived   d) are coming

8 Have you seen his latest play _____?
   a) just   b) yet   c) ever   d) last night

9 When we were children, we _____ in the garden all day.
   a) 'd played   b) 'd play
   c) were playing   d) 've played

10 You _____ to go now. You can go later.
   a) don't have b) must   c) mustn't   d) ought

11 The house was _____ more beautiful than he remembered.
   a) very   b) little bit   c) far   d) not as

   `5`

10 Complete the article with <u>one</u> word in each gap.

New words from old

The English [1] *language* is constantly growing in response to changes in the world around us, and new [2]_____ are added every day. The word 'framily' for example, first came into use in 2006 and is made [3]_____ two words: 'family' and 'friends'. It refers to close friends who [4]_____ become like a family, providing company and support to each other.

The concept has probably developed as a result [5]_____ changes in our society, where people don't live as near to [6]_____ families as they [7]_____ to. The word 'framily' has been used in the USA [8]_____ quite a while, especially by younger people living [9]_____ cities, as reflected in popular TV shows like *Friends*. If you like being with both 'framily' and family, you might want [10]_____ try 'togethering', which means to go on holiday with both your extended [11]_____ and friends!

   `5`

READING

11 Match gaps 1–6 in the text with sentences a)–f) opposite.

LIVING TOMORROW

If you want to find out what houses might look like in the future, you should visit the *Living Tomorrow* exhibition. It's a permanent exhibition near Brussels in Belgium, where you can see for yourself how tomorrow's technologies will integrate into our daily lives.

¹ _c_. Everything works via remote control, from warming up food, to authorising access to the supermarket delivery man. The living room has touch screens which control the light, music and windows. You might want to read, relax or just chat to friends there. ² ___. You'll find out why when you go upstairs.

The kitchen can be whatever you want it to be. Appliances like the oven, fridge and dishwasher slide in or out of view as needed. They even change colour automatically when you adjust the lighting. ³ ___. The only thing that doesn't move here is the flat screen on the wall. Among other things, you can use this screen to do your shopping easily and safely online.

Upstairs is the 'home theatre', with specialised acoustics and large screens. The latest 3D technology makes watching TV a whole new experience! ⁴ ___.

The bathroom, which has water-free toilets and voice-controlled taps, is also equipped with an 'intelligent mirror'. This acts as both a mirror and an electrically controlled screen. ⁵ ___. The mirror will even check your blood pressure and temperature, and remind you to take your medicine if necessary!

Finally, there's the 'home office'. ⁶ ___. This means that the office will become much more central to our lives. In fact, in 'the house of the future', it will hardly be necessary to leave home at all!

a) You can watch the news on it, check the weather forecast or listen to music while you clean your teeth.

b) Next to this, in the 'sleeping space', you can try out a bed that adapts to your size and shape.

c) ~~The 'House of the Future' consists of a living room, bathroom, kitchen, home theatre, sleeping space and office.~~

d) Thanks to tomorrow's interactive multimedia technology, more and more people will be working from home.

e) The oven and microwave are designed to recognise different kinds of food and decide automatically how to cook them.

f) However, you won't see a TV there.

	10

12 Read the text in Exercise 11 again and circle the correct answer: a), b) or c).

1 The Living Tomorrow exhibition ___ .
   a) shows what daily life will be like in the future
   b) is only going to be on for a short time
   c) shows you what houses will be like in the future

2 In the 'House of the Future', you ___ .
   a) won't have to switch the lights on
   b) can watch TV in the living room
   c) will have to open the door when your shopping is delivered

3 In the kitchen, ___ .
   a) the fridge and dishwasher are white
   b) you can move the domestic appliances around
   c) the oven decides what food you'll eat

4 There's a 'home theatre' upstairs ___ .
   a) where you can watch 3D TV
   b) which has an 'intelligent mirror'
   c) where you can sleep

5 In the bathroom, ___ .
   a) the taps turn on automatically
   b) music starts playing when you clean your teeth
   c) you can check what the weather is like outside

6 In the future, ___ .
   a) people won't be able to go outside very much
   b) the 'home office' will be more essential than it is now
   c) people won't need to work

	5

SPEAKING

13 Cross out the response that is not possible.

I So should I dress smartly for the interview?
~~a) I see.~~   b) Of course.   c) That's right.

2 Anyway, in the end, we had to sleep in the airport!
a) I don't believe it.   b) You must be joking.
c) What did you do?

3 A: I'm sorry, sir, but we have no more rooms available.
B: ___ you didn't get my booking?
a) Do you mean to say   b) Didn't you say
c) So you're saying

4 Would you mind calling a taxi for me?
a) Sure.   b) Yes, please.   c) Of course not.

5 ___ the name of our new product.
a) Let's sum up   b) Let's focus on
c) I think we need to come back to

6 Do you know if the train's on time?
a) I'm not sure.   b) Yes, I can.   c) I think so.

[5]

14 Match gaps 1–11 in the conversation with a)–k) below.

A: First of ¹ _a_ , we need to decide when to have the conference.

B: I think June's the best time – before the summer holidays start.

A: Yes, ² ___ a good point. May's too early.

B: Exactly. But ³ ___ me, the most important thing is *where* to have it. The way I see it, we should book somewhere as soon as possible.

A: Yes, I ⁴ ___. We'll need a hotel with conference facilities for fifty people.

B: How ⁵ ___ I call James? He works at the Plaza. He'll be able to advise us.

A: OK, go ahead. That's OK ⁶ ___ me.

B: So moving ⁷ ___ the next point. Who are we going to invite as speakers?

A: You've ⁸ ___ now. I thought *we* were going to do all the presentations?

B: Did ⁹ ___ that? Well, I think we need someone who specialises in marketing.

A: I'm ¹⁰ ___ I agree, actually. I have plenty of marketing experience.

B: OK. Why don't ¹¹ ___ back to that later? Let's recap: what have we decided so far?

a) ~~all~~
b) I say
c) about if
d) that's
e) lost me
f) not sure
g) for
h) we come
i) on to
j) by
k) agree

[10]

WRITING

15 Underline the correct alternative.

I In *general / the whole*, the good points outweigh the bad points.

2 I like eating pre-prepared food. *However / Although*, it isn't very healthy.

3 He never gets up *while / until* his alarm clock goes off.

4 *As soon as / By the time* I got home, it had stopped raining.

5 We talked on the phone *for / during* hours last night.

6 *Although / As well as that* he knows he should find a better job, he isn't ambitious enough.

[5]

16 Write an essay about the advantages and disadvantages of mobile phones. Use the prompts below to help you. Write 120–150 words.

It's easy to see the advantages of mobile phones in our everyday lives. ___

___

One of the main advantages ___

___

The problem is that, on the other hand, ___

___

In my opinion, ___

___

[10]

Total: [100]

LISTENING

1 ▶ 44 **Listen and circle the correct answer a), b) or c).**

1 Jo thinks she could be ____ Native American.
   a) 5%   b) 15%   (c) 50%)

2 The floor stopped moving after the woman ____.
   a) got dressed   b) went outside   c) got under the table

3 The girl's going to save ____ to go to the Moon.
   a) $1m   b) for 50 years   c) for a long time

4 Jack thinks Nick's idea for a new business is ____.
   a) great   b) original   c) mad

5 The shop doesn't have a ____.
   a) computer   b) price list   c) dishwasher

6 The woman thinks the most important invention for the kitchen is a ____.
   a) tin opener   b) cooker   c) fridge

[10]

PRONUNCIATION

2 ▶ 45 **Listen and cross out the word with a different vowel sound in bold.**

1 family ~~drama~~ married ambitious
2 inquiry risk science fiction
3 romantic forgot comedy job
4 genetic remember engineering period
5 hear earn leader freeze
6 fun discussion furious wonderful

[5]

VOCABULARY AND GRAMMAR

3 **Match the compound nouns.**

1 great-   ____   a) power
2 risk   ____   b) ~~grandparents~~
3 computer   ____   c) thriller
4 science   ____   d) engineering
5 psychological ____   e) networks
6 extended   ____   f) fiction
7 period   ____   g) cleaner
8 romantic   ____   h) taker
9 vacuum   ____   i) family
10 nuclear   ____   j) comedy
11 genetic   ____   k) drama

[5]

4 **Underline the correct preposition.**

1 I'm meeting them <u>at</u> / in lunchtime.
2 She's always gossiping about / from other people.
3 He apologised on / for forgetting to call me.
4 I couldn't finish the test because I ran out of / of the time.
5 The situation will improve at / in the long term.
6 Don't forget to switch on / up the computer before you start.
7 He complimented the students on / of their excellent exam results.
8 Some authors write their novels in / by hand.
9 You can't predict what changes will take place a long time of / from now.
10 She's hardly opened her mouth tonight. What's at / on her mind?
11 He couldn't stay because he was from / in a hurry to get to work.

[5]

5 **Complete the sentences. Use the correct form of the word in capitals.**

1 He's been ___unemployed___ for 6 months. He can't find a job. EMPLOY

2 Fewer _____ people are living on the streets because there are special places for them to sleep. HOME

3 Commuting to work every day is making me feel completely _____. EXHAUST

4 I hope they find a _____ solution to the conflict. PEACE

5 My mobile's not working. It must need _____. CHARGE

6 This new detergent is much more _____ than the old one. EFFECT

[5]

6 Correct two mistakes in each sentence.

1 My students don't hear me and that's why they do mistakes.

My students don't **listen to** me and that's why they
**make** mistakes.

2 You forgot to remember me about mum's birthday, so I'm on hot water now!

_____.

3 She made her best with the project, but it looked a bit short when she printed it on.

_____.

4 I don't like many of my ancestors much, but my Uncle Tom is great funny to be with.

_____.

5 He used to win a good salary, but then he lost his work. Now he's unemployed.

_____.

6 I said her I'd be late because I had to make some shopping.

_____.

[5]

7 Write questions for the answers in *italics*.

1 He was *talking on his mobile* when I saw him.
What _was he doing when you saw him_ ?

2 She realised *later* that she'd given him the wrong phone number.
When _____ ?

3 *David* sent me these beautiful flowers.
Who _____ ?

4 He used to play *rugby and tennis* before he had the accident.
Which _____ ?

5 I was looking for *my friends*.
Who _____ ?

6 *The Barcelona football team* is likely to win the championship.
Which _____ ?

[5]

8 Complete the second sentence so that it means the same as the first. Use the word in brackets.

1 You can't smoke in the office. (must)
You _mustn't smoke in the office_ .

2 I told him to remember to buy cheese. (remind)
I _____ .

3 We used to meet for lunch every Sunday. (would)
We _____ .

4 His room's not as messy as mine. (less)
His room _____ .

5 They'll probably be late again. (likely)
They _____ .

6 The red ones are a bit cheaper. (slightly)
The red ones _____ .

[5]

9 Circle the correct answer: a), b), c) or d).

1 Have you seen his latest play ____?
a) just   b) yet   c) ever   d) last night

2 My parents ____ from Ireland.
a) lived   b) are coming   c) come   d) comes

3 When we were children, we ____ outside all the time.
a) 'd play   b) 'd played
c) were playing   d) 've played

4 You ____ eat so much junk food.
a) might   b) shouldn't   c) must   d) have to

5 The house was ____ smaller than he remembered.
a) very   b) little bit   c) far   d) not as

6 We ____ to stay in a hotel when we get to Toronto.
a) will   b) would   c) likely   d) 're going

7 I've never been to India, but I ____ to China last year.
a) went   b) 've been
c) used to go   d) gone

8 They ____ her address any more.
a) aren't remembering   b) don't remember
c) doesn't remember   d) remember

9 You ____ to go now. You can go later.
a) don't have   b) must   c) mustn't   d) ought

10 When he got to the airport, he realised he ____ his plane ticket.
a) left   b) forgot
c) 'd forgotten   d) 'd left

11 He met them ____ he was living in Warsaw.
a) during   b) until
c) while   d) as soon as

[5]

10 Complete the article with one word in each gap.

New words from old

The English [1] _language_ is constantly growing in response to changes in the world around us, and [2] _____ words are created every day. The word 'framily', for example, first came into use in 2006 and is made from [3] _____ words: 'family' and 'friends'. It refers to close friends [4] _____ have become like a family, providing company and support. The concept has probably developed [5] _____ a result of changes in our society, where people [6] _____ live as near to their families as they used [7] _____. The word framily has been used in the USA for quite a while, especially by younger [8] _____ living in cities; this is reflected [9] _____ popular TV shows like *Friends*. If you like being with both 'framily' and family, you might want to try 'togethering', which [10] _____ to go on holiday with both your extended family and [11] _____!

[5]

READING

11 Match gaps 1–6 in the text with sentences a)–f) opposite.

LIVING TOMORROW

If you want to find out what houses might look like in the future, you should visit the *Living Tomorrow* exhibition. It's a permanent exhibition near Brussels in Belgium, where you can see for yourself how tomorrow's technologies will integrate with our daily lives.

¹ _b_ . Everything works via remote control, from warming up food, to authorising access to the supermarket delivery man. The living room has touch screens which control the light, music and windows. You might want to read, relax or just chat to friends there. However, you won't see a TV. ² ___.

The kitchen can be whatever you want it to be. Appliances like the oven, fridge and dishwasher slide in or out of view as needed. ³ ___. The oven and microwave are designed to recognise different kinds of food and decide automatically how to cook them. The only thing that doesn't move here is the flat screen on the wall – which, among other things, allows you to do your shopping easily and safely online.

Upstairs is the 'home theatre', with specialised acoustics and large screens. ⁴ ___. Next to this, in the 'sleeping space', you can try out a bed that adapts to your size and shape.

The bathroom, which has water-free toilets and voice-controlled taps, is also equipped with an 'intelligent mirror'. ⁵ ___. You can watch the news on it, check the weather forecast or listen to music while you clean your teeth. The mirror will even check your blood pressure and temperature, and remind you to take your medicine if necessary!

Finally, there's the 'home office'. Thanks to tomorrow's interactive multimedia technology, more and more people will be working from home. ⁶ ___. In fact, in 'the house of the future', it will hardly be necessary to leave home at all!

a) This means that the office will become much more central to our lives.

b) ~~The 'House of the Future' consists of a living room, bathroom, kitchen, home theatre, sleeping space and office.~~

c) This acts as both a mirror and an electrically controlled screen.

d) The latest 3D technology makes 'watching TV' a whole new experience.

e) You'll find out why when you go upstairs.

f) They even change colour automatically when you adjust the lighting.

	10

12 Read the text in Exercise 11 again and circle the correct answer: a), b) or c).

1 The Living Tomorrow exhibition ____.
  - (a) shows what houses will be like in the future)
  - b) shows what daily life will be like in the future
  - c) is only showing for a short time

2 In the 'House of the Future', you ____.
  - a) will have your shopping delivered automatically
  - b) won't have to know how to cook much
  - c) can watch TV in the living room

3 In the kitchen, ____.
  - a) you can move the domestic appliances around
  - b) the oven decides what food you'll eat
  - c) the fridge and dishwasher are white

4 There's a 'home theatre' upstairs ____.
  - a) which has an 'intelligent mirror'
  - b) where you can sleep
  - c) where you can watch films

5 In the bathroom, ____.
  - a) music starts playing when you clean your teeth
  - b) you can check if it's raining outside
  - c) the taps turn on automatically

6 In the future, ____.
  - a) the 'home office' will be more essential than it is now
  - b) people won't have to work
  - c) people won't be able to go outside very much

	5

SPEAKING

13 Delete the response that is **not** possible.

1 So should I dress smartly for the interview?

~~a) I see.~~ b) Of course. c) That's right.

2 ____ the name of our new company.

a) Let's focus on b) I think we need to come back to
c) Let's sum up

3 Do you know if the train's left yet?

a) Yes, I can. b) I think so. c) I'm not sure.

4 Anyway, in the end, we had to sleep on the floor!

a) You must be joking. b) What did you do?
c) I don't believe it.

5 A: Sorry, sir, but we have no tables available.

B: ____ you didn't get my booking?

a) Didn't you say b) So you're saying
c) Do you mean to say

6 Would you mind calling him for me?

a) Of course not. b) Yes, please. c) Sure.

| | 5 |

14 Match gaps 1–11 in the conversation with a)–k)
below.

A: First of ¹_a_, we need to decide when to have the
conference.

B: I think June's the best time – before the summer holidays
start.

A: Yes, that's a good ²____. May's too early.

B: ³____. But for me, the most important thing is *where* to
have it. The ⁴____ see it, we should book somewhere at
once.

A: Yes, ⁵____. We'll need a hotel with conference facilities for
fifty people.

B: How about if I call James? He works at the Plaza. He'll be
able to advise us.

A: OK, go ⁶____. That's OK by me.

B: So ⁷____ to the next point. Who are we going to invite as
speakers?

A: You've lost me now. I thought *we* were going to do all the
presentations?

B: ⁸____ say that? Well, I think we need someone who
specialises in marketing.

A: I'm not ⁹____ agree, actually. I have plenty of marketing
experience.

B: OK. Why ¹⁰____ come back to that later? ¹¹____ recap:
what have we decided so far?

a) ~~all~~	g) way I
b) ahead	h) point
c) Exactly	i) Did I
d) I agree	j) sure I
e) Let's	k) moving on
f) don't we	

| | 10 |

WRITING

15 Underline the correct alternative.

1 In *general* / *the whole*, the good points outweigh the bad
points.

2 We talked on the phone *for* / *during* hours last night.

3 *Although* / *As well as that* he isn't ambitious, he knows he
should find a better job.

4 I like eating organic food. *However* / *Although*, it's much
more expensive.

5 They never listen to music *while* / *during* they're studying.

6 *As soon as* / *By the time* he got home, it was nearly
midnight.

| | 5 |

16 Write an essay about the advantages and
disadvantages of mobile phones. Use the prompts below
to help you. Write 120–150 words.

It's easy to see the advantages of mobile phones in our
everyday lives. _____
_____
_____
_____
_____
_____

One of the main advantages _____
_____
_____
_____
_____
_____

The problem is that, on the other hand, _____
_____
_____
_____
_____
_____

In my opinion, _____
_____
_____
_____
_____
_____

| | 10 |

| **Total:** | 100 |

LISTENING

1 ▶ 38 Listen to a teacher talking about a school trip and complete the notes.

> **Visit to the Science Museum**
>
> Date: ¹ _27th May_
> Coach leaves at: ² ____ a.m.
> Museum opens: ³ ____ a.m. to 6p.m.
> 1st guided tour at: ⁴ _____
> Name of exhibition: Antenna
> ⁵ _____ break at: 11a.m.
> Number of themed galleries: 20
> Recommended: ⁶ _____ the Modern World
> and The Secret Life of the ⁷_____
> Lunch: in picnic area at ⁸_____ p.m.
> IMAX film at: 1.15p.m.
> Name of film: ⁹_____ Station
> 2nd guided tour at: 2.45p.m.
> Name of exhibition: Fast ¹⁰_____
> Free time: ¹¹____ to 5.30p.m.
> Home by: 8.00p.m.

[ ] 5

2 Listen again. Are the sentences true (T) or false (F)?

1 The teacher advises his students to be in the car park by 7.30a.m. _F_
2 They've all been to the museum before. ____
3 The Wellcome Wing had been closed until last week. ____
4 The teacher recommends two exhibitions about gadgets in the home. ____
5 They'll watch a film about what it's like to live and work in space. ____
6 The afternoon guided tour is about the development of Formula One cars. ____

[ ] 5

PRONUNCIATION

3 ▶ 39 Listen and write the number of words in each sentence. Contracted forms count as one word.

1 _7_   4 ____
2 ____   5 ____
3 ____   6 ____

[ ] 5

VOCABULARY AND GRAMMAR

4 Match 1–6 with a)–f).

1 organic _d_   a) learning
2 traffic ____   b) out
3 search ____   c) taker
4 print ____   d) ~~food~~
5 high ____   e) pass
6 period ____   f) engine
7 distance ____   g) lights
8 risk ____   h) on
9 driving ____   i) achiever
10 try ____   k) drama
11 boarding ____ l) licence

[ ] 5

5 Complete the sentences with the prepositions in the box. Use some words more than once.

> with   at   in   to   on   by   down   up

1 I haven't made friends __with__ many people at work.
2 We try to save energy by not leaving electrical appliances _____ standby.
3 The letter didn't arrive because it was delivered to the wrong house _____ mistake.
4 Do you believe _____ magic?
5 You'll get better _____ playing the piano if you practise every day.
6 Unfortunately, speaking a foreign language doesn't come naturally _____ me.
7 If you got up earlier, you might arrive _____ time.
8 You shouldn't forget to shut _____ your computer at night.
9 Did you know that Ben's split up _____ Jo?
10 When I get home from work, I like to relax and put my feet _____.
11 He succeeded _____ passing the exam after a lot of hard work.

[ ] 5

6 Complete the sentences. Use the correct form of the word in capitals.

1 She's been __unemployed__ for six months. She can't find a job. EMPLOY
2 The job market for university graduates is much more _____ these days. COMPETE
3 My son wants to specialise in _____ engineering. GENE
4 I heard a _____ talk about the meaning of dreams. FASCINATE
5 They were sent home from school for _____ the teacher. OBEY
6 I didn't get an interview because I didn't have the right _____. QUALIFY

[ ] 5

7 Correct **one** mistake in each question.

1 What for did you do that?
   What did you do that for?

2 Who did gave you those lovely flowers?
   _____

3 If you saw him, what would you said?
   _____

4 Where were made these shoes?
   _____

5 Who's the man that he stole your bag?
   _____

6 Have you speak to her last night?
   _____

       | 5 |

8 Circle the correct answer: a), b), c) or d).

1 We don't ____ eat out on Tuesdays.
   a) easily   b) early   c) usually   d) never

2 I couldn't leave at six because I ____ finished the report.
   a) had   b) hadn't
   c) wasn't   d) wouldn't

3 We talked for hours about ____ we used to live.
   a) where   b) which   c) that   d) which

4 She ____ to get promoted before me.
   a) should   b) might not
   c) won't   d) isn't likely

5 Your order ____ sent by first class post and will arrive tomorrow.
   a) is being   b) has being   c) will   d) is

6 He asked me what time ____ arrive.
   a) we'll   b) we'd   c) would we d) we have

7 If I'd seen you, I ____ hello.
   a) 'd say   b) 'll say
   c) would've said   d) had said

8 We ____ them since we were children.
   a) know   b) knew
   c) 've been knowing d) 've known

9 While we ____ to check in, they announced that our plane was delayed.
   a) waited   b) are waiting
   c) were waiting d) had waited

10 He's been working there since ____.
   a) five months b) March
   c) two years   d) a long time.

11 ____ we arrived, the concert had started.
   a) While   b) Until
   c) As soon as d) By the time

       | 10 |

9 Complete the second sentence so that it means the same as the first.

1 We last saw each other six months ago.
   We _haven't seen each other_ for six months.

2 There aren't many nice places to eat here.
   There are only _____.

3 If sales don't improve, I'll lose my job.
   Unless _____.

4 They're building a new factory near the river.
   A new factory _____.

5 He told them they shouldn't smoke so much.
   He warned_____.

6 I wasn't able to get in touch with her.
   I didn't _____.

       | 5 |

10 Complete the text about popular words with **one** word in each gap.

Do you tweet on Twitter?

It [1] _will_ probably come as no surprise that not only was Twitter the fastest growing website [2] _____ 2009, but 'twitter' was also the most widely used word in the media. 'Obama' was in [3] _____ place and 'H1N1', the name of the swine flu virus that spread all over [4] _____ world, was in third. More surprisingly, the success of Stephanie Meyer's _Twilight_ series of [5] _____ and films pushed the word 'vampire' into fifth place.

The popularity of the [6] _____ 'twitter' summed up the rise of social networking on the internet. It was also a 'fun' word, [7] _____ led to the creation of a whole new set of vocabulary. For example, 'tweet', 'tweetaholic' and even 'tweet up', which means to arrange to [8] _____ up with your friends.

If further proof of social networking as [9] _____ huge cultural force was needed, the New Oxford American Dictionary chose 'unfriend' as its 2009 Word of the [10] _____. To 'unfriend' means to remove someone as a friend on a social networking [11] _____ like Facebook. Have you unfriended anyone recently?

       | 5 |

READING

11 Match gaps 1–6 in the text with sentences a)–g) opposite. There is <u>one</u> extra sentence you do not need.

Teenage boy climbs Everest

In May 2010, American teenager Jordan Romero made history by becoming the youngest person to climb the highest peak in the world, Mount Everest (8,848m). ¹ _e_ . The first thing he did when he reached the summit was to make a phone call, saying, 'Mom, I'm calling you from the top of the world!'

Jordan made the climb with his father Paul, his stepmother Karen Lundgren and three Sherpa guides, all experienced mountaineers. However, despite Jordan's age, he was by no means an inexperienced climber. In fact, this was his sixth major achievement in his dream to climb the Seven Summits, the highest peaks on all seven continents.

² ____ . Between 2007 and 2009, he climbed five others in North and South America, Australia and Europe. Having climbed the Asian one, this left only the Vinson Massif (4,892m) in Antarctica to achieve his dream of being the youngest person to climb all seven.

³ ____ . There was a painting on a corridor wall in his California school which showed the highest point on every continent, and it fascinated him. He did some research and then one day he said to his father, 'Dad, I want to climb the Seven Summits.' His father immediately started training him and the following year they climbed Kilimanjaro.

Despite Jordan's achievements, the Everest climb also attracted criticism from people who said he was too young to take such risks. It is true that climbing at such high altitudes can be dangerous. ⁴ ____ Furthermore, a previous record holder for the youngest person to climb Mount Everest, 16-year-old Temba Tsheri from Nepal, lost five fingers from frostbite during his climb due to the extreme cold.

But Jordan's father rejected the criticisms, saying, 'We were so prepared, everything went absolutely perfectly. ⁵ ____ '. He said they'd spent several weeks getting used to the high altitude. He thought Jordan had trained hard and had been ready for the challenge.

Jordan himself said, 'I'm the one who started this project. ⁶ ____ . I know it's a big goal and luckily for me, my family is supporting me every step of the way. In fact my family is my team.'

He hopes his adventure will inspire young people around the world to set themselves challenges – to get fit and aim high.

a) The cold and the lack of oxygen has killed many climbers in the past.
b) It's my dream we are following.
c) Their knowledge and experience of the mountain will help keep us all safe.
d) He conquered the first one, Mount Kilimanjaro (5,895m), in Africa when he was ten.
e) ~~Jordan was 13 years old.~~
f) Age has nothing to do with anything.
g) Jordan says he was first inspired to climb at the age of nine.

```
                    10
```

12 Read the text again and choose the correct answer: a), b) or c).

1 When Jordan got to the top of Everest, he called his ____ .
 a) father
 b) friends
 c) mother ⟵(circled)
2 He'd already climbed ____ of the highest mountains in the world.
 a) five
 b) six
 c) seven
3 Jordan climbed Kilimanjaro when he was ____ .
 a) seven
 b) nine
 c) ten
4 Some people thought Jordan shouldn't climb Everest because ____ .
 a) he would get frostbite
 b) the mountain was too high
 c) he wasn't old enough
5 Before the climb, ____ .
 a) Jordan trained very hard
 b) he spent several months on Everest
 c) his father was very worried
6 Jordan would like ____ .
 a) everybody to climb mountains
 b) to inspire other teenagers
 c) to find more challenges

```
                    5
```

SPEAKING

13 Cross out the option or response that is not possible.

1 So should I dress smartly tonight?

~~a) I see.~~   b) Of course.   c) That's right.

2 I'm afraid the party's been cancelled.

a) Really?   b) Well done.   c) That's a shame.

3 A: Do you recommend taking a sweater?

B: Yes, ____ quite cold in the evenings.

a) it's generally   b) on the whole, it's
c) it tends to

4 A: That was a fantastic meal, wasn't it?

B: Yes, but I ____ the food was overpriced.

a) for one thing   b) do think   c) must say

5 Did you know that if you listen to Bach, it helps you to learn better?

a) Oh, really?   b) I have no idea.
c) Does it? That's interesting.

6 What should we get Harry and Sara for their wedding anniversary?

a) Don't forget to buy them a plant.
b) I don't know.
c) If I were you, I'd just send them a card.

☐ 5

14 Match gaps 1–11 in the conversation with a)–k) below.

A: ¹Have _a_ my car keys, Anna?

B: I'm ²____ sure I left them on the table.

A: No, I've looked there. Did you put them in your handbag?

B: Maybe. I ³____. Where *is* my handbag anyway?

A: I haven't got ⁴____. You know, I think we should buy a red carpet!

B: ⁵____? Why red?

A: I read an article about it. Apparently red helps you remember details better.

B: You've ⁶____.

A: Well, ⁷____ thing, we're getting very forgetful these days.

B: Yes, but ⁸____ I see it, that's because we spend too much time using computers.

A: Exactly! I think I'll try using a red screen on mine.

B: OK, but whatever ⁹____, don't buy a red carpet!

A: Don't worry. Hey, you'll ¹⁰____ what!

B: You found the keys?

A: Yes, in my pocket …

B: ¹¹____ joking!

a) ~~you seen~~   g) Really
b) the way   h) a clue
c) you do   i) lost me
d) fairly   j) can't remember
e) never guess   k) for one
f) You're

☐ 10

WRITING

15 Underline the correct alternatives.

The best meal of my life!

What's the ¹*more / most* delicious food you've ever eaten? Mine was chicken soup. ²*In general / In all likelihood* it wasn't just the soup itself, but where and ³*what / when* it was eaten. It happened when I was working in Morocco ⁴*while / during* Ramadan, when Muslims don't eat ⁵*or / but* drink anything from sunrise to sunset, and never complain.

⁶*Although / However* I'm not a Muslim, I admired the willpower of my friends so much ⁷*than / that* one day I decided to share the experience with them. It was one of the most memorable days of my life, full of unexpected feelings and emotions.

⁸*Finally / By the time* the sun was setting, I'd joined the crowds of people in the square, ⁹*which / where* the cafés had prepared bowls of steaming chicken soup ¹⁰*as well as / also* deliciously sweet desserts. Everyone had a bowl of soup in front of them and held their spoons ready to eat. ¹¹*After that / As soon as* the sun went down, we lifted our spoons. Food had never tasted so good.

☐ 5

16 Choose one of the topics below and write an essay / a story on a separate piece of paper. Use the paragraph notes to help you. Write 130–150 words.

Topic A

If you could choose to be a famous person from history, who would you choose?

Para 1: say who the person is and what they are famous for

Para 2: give two or three reasons why you would like to be them

Para 3: say what things you would do differently from them, and why

Topic B

Write a story beginning with these words:

It was the most important day of my life.

Para 1: say why the day was important

Para 2: describe what happened on this day

Para 3: say what the conclusion was – positive or negative

☐ 10

| Total: | 100 |

LISTENING

1 ▶ 38 Listen to a teacher talking about a school trip and complete the notes.

Visit to the Science Museum

Date: ¹ _27th May_

Coach leaves at: ² ____ a.m.

Museum opens: 10a.m. to ³ ____ p.m.

1st guided tour at: ⁴ _____

Name of exhibition: Antenna

Coffee break at: ⁵ _____ a.m.

Number of themed galleries: ⁶ _____

Recommended: Making the ⁷ _____ World and The Secret Life of the Home

Lunch: in ⁸ _____ area at 12.30p.m.

IMAX film at: 1.15p.m.

Name of film: Space ⁹ _____

2nd guided tour at: 2.45p.m.

Name of exhibition: ¹⁰ _____ Forward

Free time: 3.45 to ¹¹ _____ p.m.

Home by: 8.00p.m.

`5`

2 Listen again. Are the sentences true (T) or false (F)?

1 The teacher advised his students to be in the car park by 7.30a.m.   _F_

2 The Wellcome Wing has exhibitions about modern art and science.   ____

3 The teacher recommended two permanent exhibitions about contemporary science.   ____

4 The students will watch a film about daily life on the International Space Station.   ____

5 *Fast Forward* is an exhibition about how Formula One technology is being adapted for use in daily life.   ____

6 The visit will end with a guided tour of some interesting new galleries.   ____

`5`

PRONUNCIATION

3 ▶ 39 Listen and write the number of words in each sentence. Contracted forms count as one word.

1 _7_   4 ____

2 ____   5 ____

3 ____   6 ____

`5`

VOCABULARY AND GRAMMAR

4 Match 1–6 with a)–f).

1 organic   _d_   a) money
2 natural   ____   b) off
3 hand   ____   c) course
4 dating   ____   d) ~~food~~
5 genetic   ____   e) research
6 romantic   ____   f) luggage
7 log   ____   g) talent
8 raise   ____   h) estate
9 online   ____   i) site
10 council   ____   k) comedy
11 do   ____   l) engineering

`5`

5 Complete the sentences with the prepositions in the box. Use some words more than once.

with	in	to	on	down	up	for	at

1 I haven't made friends ____with____ many people at work.

2 Please come in and make yourself _____ home.

3 Ben's always had an aptitude _____ cooking.

4 I don't think it'll work. She has so little in common _____ him.

5 Since they got back from Singapore, they haven't been able to settle _____ again.

6 His teacher thinks Tim's not paying enough attention _____ his homework.

7 If they'd left earlier, they would've been able to check _____ for their flight on time.

8 I was embarrassed because I was wearing my jeans, but everybody else had dressed _____ for the party.

9 I wouldn't rely _____ him if I were you.

10 I know you didn't do it _____ purpose.

11 Unfortunately, dancing doesn't come naturally _____ him.

`5`

6 Complete the sentences. Use the correct form of the word in capitals.

1 She's been ____unemployed____ for six months. She can't find a job. EMPLOY

2 They _____ the teacher so they had to do extra homework. OBEY

3 The problem is that she's too good. She's _____ for the job. QUALIFY

4 I think he's got a very _____ job in the government. INFLUENCE

5 Please accept my apologies. I _____ what you said. UNDERSTAND

6 If you'd arrived on time, he wouldn't have been so _____. ANNOY

`5`

7 Correct <u>one</u> mistake in each question.

I What for did you do that?

   What did you do that for?

2 Who's the woman that she was so rude to you?

   _____

3 Have you see them last weekend?

   _____

4 Who did sent you that lovely card?

   _____

5 If he'd spoke to you, what would you have done?

   _____

6 How is made this table?

   _____

   [ ] **5**

8 Circle the correct answer: a), b), c) or d).

I We don't ____ eat out on Tuesdays.

   a) easily   b) early   (c) usually)   d) never

2 She ____ them since she was at primary school.

   a) knows   b) knew
   c) 's been knowing d) 's known

3 While they ____ at the gate, they found out the flight would be five hours late.

   a) waited   b) are waiting
   c) were waiting d) had waited

4 I've been working here for ____.

   a) five months   b) March
   c) two years ago d) last year

5 ____ we arrived, the concert started.

   a) While   b) Until
   c) As soon as d) By the time

6 He couldn't leave work early because he ____ asked his boss.

   a) had   b) hadn't
   c) wasn't   d) wouldn't

7 We talked for hours about ____ we used to play together in a band.

   a) when   b) which   c) that   d) which

8 I ____ to get promoted before him.

   a) should   b) might not
   c) won't   d) 'm not likely

9 Your order ____ sent by first class post and will arrive tomorrow.

   a) 's been   b) has being   c) will   d) is

10 She asked them what time ____ leave.

   a) they'll   b) they'd
   c) would they d) they have

11 If I'd met you, we ____ had lunch.

   a) would   b) won't have   c) could've   d) might

   [ ] **10**

9 Complete the second sentence so that it means the same as the first.

I We last saw each other six months ago.

   We *haven't seen each other* for six months.

2 They're delivering the furniture tomorrow.

   The furniture _____.

3 She told us it would be a good idea to take a taxi.

   She advised _____.

4 The quality isn't as good as it used to be.

   The quality is _____.

5 There wasn't much food left after the party.

   There was only _____.

6 If it doesn't stop raining, we won't be able to go for a walk.

   Unless _____.

   [ ] **5**

10 Complete the text with <u>one</u> word in each gap.

Do you tweet on Twitter?

It [1] *will* probably come as no surprise that not only was Twitter [2]_____ fastest growing website in 2009, but 'twitter' was also the [3]_____ widely used word in the media. 'Obama' was in second place and 'H1N1', the name of the swine flu virus that spread all over the world, was in [4]_____. More surprisingly, the success of Stephanie Meyer's *Twilight* series of books and [5]_____ pushed the word 'vampire' into fifth place.

The popularity of the word 'twitter' summed up the rise of [6]_____ networking on the internet. It was also a 'fun' word, which led to the creation of a whole new set of vocabulary. For example, 'tweet', 'tweetaholic' and even 'tweet up', [7]_____ means to arrange to meet [8]_____ with your friends.

If further proof of social networking as a huge cultural force was needed, [9]_____ New Oxford American Dictionary chose 'unfriend' as its 2009 Word of the Year. To 'unfriend' means to remove someone as a [10]_____ on a social networking site like Facebook. [11]_____ you unfriended anyone recently?

   [ ] **5**

READING

11 Match gaps 1–6 in the text with sentences a)–g) opposite. There is <u>one</u> extra sentence you do not need.

Teenage boy climbs Everest

In May 2010, American teenager Jordan Romero made history by becoming the youngest person to climb the highest peak in the world, Mount Everest (8,848m). ¹ _a_ . The first thing he did when he reached the summit was to make a phone call, saying, 'Mom, I'm calling you from the top of the world!'

Jordan made the climb with his father Paul, his stepmother Karen Lundgren and three Sherpa guides, all experienced mountaineers. However, despite Jordan's age, he was by no means an inexperienced climber. In fact, this was his sixth major achievement in his dream to climb the Seven Summits, the highest peaks on all seven continents.

² ___ . Between 2007 and 2009, he climbed five others in North and South America, Australia and Europe. Having climbed the Asian one, this left only the Vinson Massif (4,892m) in Antarctica to achieve his dream of being the youngest person to climb all seven.

³ ___ . There was a painting on a corridor wall in his California school which showed the highest point on every continent, and it fascinated him. He did some research and then one day, he said to his father, 'Dad, I want to climb the Seven Summits.' His father immediately started training him and the following year they climbed Kilimanjaro.

Despite Jordan's achievements, the Everest climb also attracted criticism from people who said he was too young to take such risks. It is true that climbing at such high altitudes can be dangerous. ⁴ ___ . Furthermore, a previous record holder for the youngest person to climb Mount Everest, 16 year old Temba Tsheri from Nepal, lost five fingers from frostbite during his climb due to the extreme cold.

But Jordan's father rejected the criticisms, saying, 'We were so prepared, everything went absolutely perfectly. ⁵ ___ .' He said they'd spent several weeks getting used to the high altitude. He thought Jordan had trained hard and had been ready for the challenge.

Jordan himself said, 'I'm the one who started this project. ⁶ ___ . I know it's a big goal and lucky for me, my family is supporting me every step of the way. In fact my family is my team.'

He hopes his adventure will inspire young people around the world to set themselves challenges – to get fit and aim high.

a) ~~Jordan was 13 years old.~~
b) Age has nothing to do with anything.
c) Jordan says he was first inspired to climb at the age of nine.
d) The cold and the lack of oxygen has killed many climbers in the past.
e) It's my dream we are following.
f) Their knowledge and experience of the mountain will help keep us all safe.
g) He conquered the first one, Mount Kilimanjaro (5,895m), in Africa when he was ten.

| | **10** |

12 Read the text again and choose the correct answer: a), b) or c).

1 When Jordan got to the top of Everest, he called his ___ .
   a) father
   b) friends
   c) mother

2 He hasn't climbed the highest mountain in ___ yet.
   a) Africa
   b) Asia
   c) Antarctica

3 Jordan first got interested in climbing when he was ___ .
   a) at school
   b) seven
   c) a teenager

4 The main criticism of Jordan's Everest climb was ___ .
   a) the cold
   b) his age
   c) the lack of oxygen

5 Before the climb, ___ .
   a) Jordan did a lot of training
   b) Jordan's father was very worried
   c) Jordan had frostbite

6 Jordan wanted to climb Everest because ___ .
   a) it was what he dreamt of
   b) his family wanted him to do it
   c) he wanted to encourage young people to keep fit.

| | **5** |

SPEAKING

13 Cross out the option or response that is **not** possible.

1 So should I dress smartly tonight?
   ~~a) I see.~~   b) Of course.
   c) That's right.

2 Did you know that if you miss breakfast, you can't concentrate so well?
   a) Oh, really?   b) I have no idea.
   c) Can't you?

3 What should I get them as a wedding present?
   a) Don't forget to send them a card.
   b) I don't know.
   c) If I were you, I'd give them some money.

4 I'm afraid our flight has been cancelled.
   a) You can't be serious. b) Well done.
   c) That's terrible!

5 A: Would you suggest taking a swimsuit?
   B: Yes, ____ quite hot in June.
   a) it's generally   b) on the whole, it's
   c) it tends to

6 A: That was a fantastic play, wasn't it?
   B: Yes, but I ____ the seats were overpriced.
   a) for one thing   b) do think   c) must say

   [ ] **5**

14 Match gaps 1–11 in the conversation with a)–k) below.

A: [1] Have _a_ my car keys, Anna?

B: I'm fairly [2]____ I left them on the table.

A: No, I've looked there. Did you put them in your handbag?

B: It's [3]____. I can't remember. Where *is* my handbag anyway?

A: I [4]____ a clue. You know, I think we should buy a red carpet!

B: Really? Why red?

A: I read an article about it. Apparently red helps you remember details better.

B: What exactly [5]____ mean?

A: Well, for one [6]____, we're getting very forgetful these days.

B: Yes, but the way I [7]____, that's because we spend too much time using computers.

A: [8]____! I think I'll try using a red screen on mine.

B: OK, but [9]____ you do, don't buy a red carpet!

A: OK, don't worry. Hey! [10]____ guess what!

B: You found the keys?

A: Yes, they were in my pocket …

B: You're [11]____!

a) ~~you seen~~   g) Exactly
b) whatever   h) joking
c) possible   i) haven't got
d) thing   j) do you
e) You'll never   k) see it
f) sure

   [ ] **10**

WRITING

15 Underline the correct alternatives.

The best meal of my life!

What's the [1]*more / most* delicious food you've ever eaten? Mine was chicken soup. [2]*In all probability / On the whole,* it wasn't just the soup itself, but where and when it was eaten. It happened [3]*during / while* I was working in Morocco during Ramadan, [4]*which / when* Muslims don't eat or drink anything from sunrise [5]*until / by* sunset, and never complain.

I'm not a Muslim, [6]*however / also* I admired the willpower of my friends [7]*so / such* a lot that one day I decided to share the experience with them. It was one of the most memorable days of my life, full of unexpected feelings [8]*or / and* emotions.

[9]*Finally / As* the sun was going down, I joined the crowds of people in the square, [10]*which / where* cafés had prepared bowls of steaming chicken soup and sticky, sweet desserts. Everyone had a bowl of soup and held their spoons, ready to eat. [11]*As soon as / As well as* the sun set, we lifted our spoons. Food had never tasted so good.

   [ ] **5**

16 Choose **one** of the topics below and write an essay / a story on a separate piece of paper. Use the paragraph notes to help you. Write 130–150 words.

Topic A

If you could choose to be a famous person from history, who would you choose?

Para 1: say who the person is and what they are famous for

Para 2: give two or three reasons why you would like to be them

Para 3: say what things you would do differently from them, and why

Topic B

Write a story beginning with these words:
It was the most important day of my life.

Para 1: say why the day was important

Para 2: describe what happened on this day

Para 3: say what the conclusion was – positive or negative

   [ ] **10**

   | **Total:** | **100** |

Mid-course Test A

LISTENING

1

Audioscript

1

A = Jo   B = Marta

A: Have you ever had your family tree done, Marta?

B: Yes, I have. And you, Jo?

A: Yes, I've just had it done. Fascinating! I discovered that one of my ancestors had been a minister for King Charles the second in the seventeenth century. Now I'm thinking of having a DNA test.

B: Whatever for?

A: Because it could be very exciting! I know my family originally came from France. But who knows, I might be 50% Native American, or 15% sub-Saharan African!

B: In my opinion, it doesn't really matter, does it? You know your family history and where your ancestors came from. The rest is a waste of money!

2

A: Did you see the news about the big earthquake?

B: Yes, isn't it awful?

A: It reminds me of when I was in Argentina – when they had that big earthquake in Chile.

B: Really? What happened?

A: Well, I was in a hotel in a small town just over the border from Chile. I woke up in the middle of the night because the bed was moving around.

B: I don't believe it! What did you do?

A: I didn't know *what* to do. They say you should get under a table or something, and not go outside – but I was so scared, I started putting on my clothes.

B: What happened next?

A: By the time I got dressed, the floor had stopped moving. Then I switched on the TV and saw there'd been a very big earthquake on the other side of the Andes mountains, in Chile.

B: How awful!

A: Yes, I've never been so scared in my life!

3

A: I'm definitely going to the Moon.

B: Sorry? Can you say that again?

A: I'm going to the Moon!

B: You've lost me. I don't get what you're saying.

A: It's simple! They're selling flights to the Moon now. I've always wanted to go there.

B: But they cost millions of dollars!

A: I know. But they'll get cheaper in twenty or thirty years' time. I'm going to save all my money and one day, I'll go there.

B: Do you mean to say that you're not going to spend any money for years and years, just to go to the Moon?

A: Yes. It's my dream. And I believe that dreams can come true….

B: Well, who knows, you might be right…

4

A = Nick   B = Jack

A: The way I see things, we should start our own business, Jack. It's the only way to escape the rat race.

B: That's a great idea, Nick. But what kind of business? We need an original idea – one nobody's thought of.

A: Well, I suggest we do something with computers. Everyone has one now, you know.

B: Right. Do you have anything in mind?

A: How about if we have an online translation service?

B: I'm not sure that's a very good idea, Nick.

A: Why not?

B: Because we don't speak any foreign languages.

A: I know that! But you can do anything these days with technology. We'll use online dictionaries!

B: Honestly, Nick, you must be mad! It'll never work.

5

A = Customer   B = Sales assistant

A: Excuse me.

B: Yes, madam? How can I help you?

A: Could you tell me which dishwasher is better? This smaller one, or that bigger one?

B: They're both very good, madam. But I think the smaller one is slightly more expensive.

A: Really? The smaller one should be cheaper, shouldn't it?

B: I'm not sure, madam. Would you mind waiting a minute while I go and check?

A: Of course not.

B: I'm sorry to keep you waiting, madam, but our computer's crashed.

A: Do you mean to say you don't have a price list?

B: I'm afraid not, madam. All the prices are on the computer. I'll have to wait until they sort it out. Could you come back in half an hour?

A: I'm afraid I can't. I'm having a big dinner party for 30 people tonight and I need a new dishwasher now!

6

A = Alex   B = Gary

A: Would you mind opening this tin of tuna for me, Gary?

B: Sure. Where's the tin opener?

A: In the drawer over there.

B: Are you sure it's in this drawer, Alex? I can't see it.

A: It should be there. I remember using it yesterday to open a tin of tomatoes.

B: Well, I can't find it.

A: Oh no, don't say I threw it away when I was clearing up. What are we going to do? We can't live without a tin opener. It's the most important invention for the kitchen in the last 100 years.

B: You must be joking. What about the cooker, the fridge and….

A: No, I'm perfectly serious. I love my cooker, and the fridge is a wonderful invention too, but have you ever tried to open a tin without a tin opener? It's absolutely impossible. I couldn't live without it.

2 c)   3 b)   4 c)   5 a)   6 c)

PRONUNCIATION

2

2 science   3 romantic   4 period   5 earn
6 furious

VOCABULARY AND GRAMMAR

3

2 f)   3 i)   4 b)   5 k)   6 a(7 l)   8 c)
9 g)   10 e)   11 h)

4

2 on   3 by   4 in   5 on   6 in   7 about
8 for   9 out   10 in   11 off

5

2 peaceful   3 (re)charging   4 unprofitable
5 homeless   6 exhausting

6

2 My **relatives** are coming for lunch today. My uncle **tells** very funny stories.

3 He got fired **by** his boss so he's looking for a new **job**.

4 I **told** him I'd be late because I **left** my purse at home.

5 You didn't **remind** me about Alan's birthday and now I'm in **hot** water!

6 She **did** medical research after university, but she didn't **earn** much money.

7

2 Which sports did you use to play before you broke your leg?

3 Who were they looking for just now?

4 Which football team is likely to win the championship?

5 When did he realise he'd given her the wrong address?

6 Who sent you a beautiful birthday card?

8

2 His flat's less messy than it used to be
3 The plane's likely to be late.
4 This one's slightly more expensive.
5 I reminded him to buy the bread.
6 We'd / We would have a family lunch every Sunday.

9

2 d) 3 a) 4 c) 5 d) 6 c) 7 a) 8 b)
9 b) 10 a) 11 c)

10

2 words 3 from 4 have 5 of 6 their
7 used 8 for 9 in 10 to 11 family

READING

11

2 f) 3 e) 4 b) 5 a) 6 d)

12

2 a) 3 b) 4 a) 5 c) 6 b)

SPEAKING

13

Delete: 2 c) 3 b) 4 b) 5 a) 6 b)

14

2 d) 3 g) 4 k) 5 c) 6 j) 7 i) 8 e)
9 b) 10 f) 11 h)

WRITING

15

2 However 3 until 4 By the time 5 for
6 Although

16

(sample answer: 150 words)

It's easy to see the advantages of mobile phones in our everyday lives. It's hard to imagine what life was like before we had them.

One of the main advantages is that you can get in touch with people at all times. This is particularly useful if you have children and you want to know where they are. Texting also makes it very easy to organise meetings with friends at the last minute.

The problem is that, on the other hand, mobiles can be very annoying. Although I couldn't live without mine, I find it quite irritating to be interrupted by calls when I'm out with friends. As well as that, I hate sitting next to people who have loud phone conversations on buses.

In my opinion, however, the advantages outweigh the disadvantages. I think the mobile phone is one of the most important inventions of the last 100 years.

Mid-course Test B

LISTENING

1

Audioscript
See test A.
2 a) 3 c) 4 c) 5 b) 6 a)

PRONUNCIATION

2

2 science 3 romantic 4 period 5 earn
6 furious

VOCABULARY AND GRAMMAR

3

2 h) 3 e) 4 f) 5 c) 6 i) 7 k) 8 j)
9 g) 10 a) 11 d)

4

2 about 3 for 4 of 5 in 6 on 7 on
8 by 9 from 10 on 11 in

5

2 homeless 3 exhausted 4 peaceful
5 (re)charging 6 effective

6

2 You forgot to **remind** me about mum's birthday, so I'm **in hot water** now!
3 She **did** her best with the project, but it looked a bit short when she printed it **out**.
4 I don't like many of my **relatives** much, but my Uncle Tom is great **fun** to be with.
5 He used to **earn** a good salary, but then he lost his **job**. Now he's unemployed.
6 I **told** her I'd be late because I had to **do** some shopping.

7

2 When did she realise that she'd given him the wrong phone number?
3 Who sent you those beautiful flowers?
4 Which sports did he use to play before he had the accident?
5 Who were you looking for?
6 Which football team is likely to win the championship?

8

2 I reminded him to buy cheese.
3 We'd / We would meet for lunch every Sunday.
4 His room's less messy than mine.
5 They're likely to be late again.
6 The red ones are slightly cheaper.

9

2 c) 3 a) 4 b) 5 c) 6 d) 7 a) 8 b)
9 a) 10 c) 11 c)

10

2 new 3 two 4 who 5 as 6 don't
7 to 8 people 9 in 10 means
11 friends

READING

11

2 e) 3 f) 4 d) 5 c) 6 a)

12

2 b) 3 a) 4 c) 5 b) 6 a)

SPEAKING

13

Delete: 2 c) 3 a) 4 b) 5 a) 6 b)

14

2 h) 3 c) 4 g) 5 d) 6 b) 7 k) 8 i)
9 j) 10 f) 11 e)

WRITING

15

2 for 3 Although 4 However 5 while
6 By the time

16

(sample answer: 150 words)

It's easy to see the advantages of mobile phones in our everyday lives. It's hard to imagine what life was like before we had them.

One of the main advantages is that you can get in touch with people at all times. This is particularly useful if you have children and you want to know where they are. Texting also makes it very easy to organise meetings with friends at the last minute.

The problem is that, on the other hand, mobiles can be very annoying. Although I couldn't live without mine, I find it quite irritating to be interrupted by calls when I'm out with friends. As well as that, I hate sitting next to people who have loud phone conversations on buses.

In my opinion, however, the advantages outweigh the disadvantages. I think the mobile phone is one of the most important inventions of the last 100 years.

End of Course Test A

LISTENING

1

Audioscript

T=Teacher

T: Good morning everybody. Before we start the class today, I need to give you some information about our field trip on the 27th of May – next Friday, in fact. As you know, we're spending the day at the amazing Science Museum in London. The coach will pick us up in the school car park. We'll leave at 8 o'clock so plan to be here at least 15 minutes before that – 7.45 at the latest. You'd better set your alarms for 6.30, OK?

Our visit's been confirmed by the museum and I've just received the itinerary and information about the activities they've organised for us. If you've visited the Science Museum before, you'll know that it's enormous and we can't possibly see everything in one day. You may want to take some notes now – though I'll also put the info on the class website later on. The museum opens from 10a.m. to 6p.m. If all goes well, we hope to arrive by 10.15 latest, when we'll have our first guided tour of the day – there are two, by the way. If you read the newspaper last Sunday, you'll have seen the article about the re-opening of the Wellcome Wing last week. It now has three state-of-the-art galleries which deal only with contemporary science. We're going to have a guided tour of one of them – an exhibition called *Antenna*, which is about how the latest scientific discoveries could change our lives. You'll also have the opportunity to give your opinions about the latest ideas. Remember, the museum has lots of hands-on multimedia stuff so you won't get bored – I'm sure you'll find it fascinating.

Then at 11 o'clock we'll have a coffee break and you'll be free to visit the permanent exhibitions until 12.30. There are twenty galleries with different themes so you'll only have time to see two or three properly. If I were you, I wouldn't miss the one called *Making the Modern World* – which is marvellous. It shows the development of the modern industrial world in a really entertaining and creative way. Also watch out for *The Secret Life of the Home*. It's great fun and you'll be amazed by all the gadgets people used to use in the house – and will use in the future!

Then it's lunchtime. We've ordered a picnic from the café, which we'll eat in the picnic area on the first floor. We'll all meet up there at 12.30 so don't be late – we have to go to the cinema at 1.15! Yes, but not an ordinary cinema – an IMAX 3D cinema! At quarter past one, we're booked to have a 3D experience called *Space Station*. You'll blast off into space with astronauts from the USA and Russia, and experience life on the International Space Station, 220 miles above Earth. How does that sound?

Great. OK, then we have our second guided tour at 2.45 – quarter to three – to see one of the special temporary exhibitions called *Fast Forward*. It's about twenty ways that Formula One technology is being used in our hospitals, homes and work places. For example, the materials and machines they've developed for the Formula One cars are now being used to make racing bikes, and sophisticated machines to monitor hospital patients. The tour should take about an hour – until 3.45. And I'm pleased to tell you that you'll then be free for the rest of the afternoon! You'll be able to go back to any galleries you're particularly interested in, or see something new. We'll leave the Museum at half past five so tell your parents you should be home by about 8p.m.

I think that's all for now. Oh, one last thing, check out the Science Museum website before we go. The more you read about it, the more interesting the visit will be.

2 8 3 10 4 10.15 5 coffee 6 Making
7 Home 8 12.30 9 Space 10 Forward
11 3.45

2
2 F 3 T 4 F 5 T 6 F

PRONUNCIATION
3
2 7 3 11 4 9 5 12 6 8

VOCABULARY AND GRAMMAR
4
2 g) 3 f) 4 b) 5 i) 6 k) 7 a) 8 c)
9 l) 10 h) 11 e)

5
2 on 3 by 4 in 5 at 6 to 7 on
8 down 9 with 10 up 11 in

6
2 competitive 3 genetic 4 fascinating
5 disobeying 6 qualifications

7
2 Who **gave** you those lovely flowers?
3 If you saw him, what would you **say**?
4 Where were **these shoes made**?
5 Who's the man **that stole** your bag?
6 **Did** you speak to her last night?

8
2 b) 3 a) 4 d) 5 a) 6 b) 7 c) 8 d) 9 c)
10 b) 11 d)

9
2 There are only a few nice places to eat here.
3 Unless sales improve, I'll lose my job.
4 A new factory is being built near the river.
5 He warned them not to smoke so much.
6 I didn't manage to get in touch with her.

10
2 in 3 second 4 the 5 books 6 word
7 which 8 meet 9 a 10 Year 11 site

READING
11
2 d) 3 g) 4 a) 5 f) 6 b)
(sentence c is not needed)

12
2 a) 3 c) 4 c) 5 a) 6 b)

SPEAKING
13
Delete: 2 b) 3 c) 4 a) 5 b) 6 a)

14
2 d) 3 j) 4 h) 5 g) 6 i) 7 k) 8 b)
9 c) 10 e) 11 f)

WRITING
15
2 In all likelihood 3 when 4 during 5 or
6 Although 7 that 8 By the time
9 where 10 as well as 11 As soon as

16
(sample answer: 145 words)
If I could, I'd choose to be King Henry VIII of England. He's most famous for having six wives, but that's not the reason I'd like to have been him. I admire him because he had a lot of courage and made a lot of changes in Great Britain.

I'd like to be like him because he was brave, innovative and charismatic. He was king at

a very dangerous time in British history and it was important for him to have sons to become king when he died. For this reason, he divorced his first wife and married five more times. However, he had many enemies who didn't agree with this.

It's easy to say I'd do things differently but I would try to trust people more than he did, and not execute them. His people suffered too much when he was king.

End of Course Test B
LISTENING
1
Audioscript
See test A.
2 8 3 6 4 10.15 5 11 6 20
7 Modern 8 picnic 9 Station 10 Fast
11 5.30

2
2 F 3 F 4 T 5 T 6 F

PRONUNCIATION
3
2 7 3 11 4 9 5 12 6 8

VOCABULARY AND GRAMMAR
4
2 g) 3 f) 4 i) 5 l) 6 k) 7 b) 8 a)
9 c) 10 h) 11 e)

5
2 at 3 for 4 with 5 down 6 to 7 in
8 up 9 on 10 on 11 to

6
2 disobeyed 3 overqualified 4 influential
5 misunderstood 6 annoyed

7
2 Who's the woman **that was** so rude to you?
3 **Did** you see them last weekend?
4 Who **sent** you that lovely card?
5 If he'd **spoken** to you, what would you have done?
6 How is **this table made**?

8
2 d) 3 c) 4 a) 5 c) 6 b) 7 a) 8 d)
9 a) 10 b) 11 c)

9
2 The furniture's being delivered tomorrow.
3 She advised us to take a taxi.
4 The quality is worse than it used to be.
5 There was only a little food left after the party.
6 Unless it stops raining, we won't be able to go for a walk.

10
2 the 3 most 4 third 5 films 6 social
7 which 8 up 9 the 10 friend
11 Have

READING

11

2 g) 3 c) 4 d) 5 b) 6 e)
(sentence f is not used)

12

2 c) 3 a) 4 b) 5 a) 6 a)

SPEAKING

13

Delete: 2 b) 3 a) 4 b) 5 c) 6 a)

14

2 f) 3 c) 4 i) 5 j) 6 d) 7 k) 8 g)
9 b) 10 e) 11 h)

WRITING

15

2 In all probability 3 while 4 when
5 until 6 however 7 such 8 and 9 As
10 where 11 As soon as

16

(sample answer: 145 words)

If I could, I'd choose to be King Henry VIII of England. He's most famous for having six wives, but that's not the reason I'd like to have been him. I admire him because he had the courage to challenge the Pope in Rome and change the religion of Great Britain.

I'd like to be like him because he was brave, innovative and charismatic. He was king at a very dangerous time in British history and it was important for him to have sons to become king when he died. For this reason, he divorced his first wife and married five more times. However, he had many enemies who didn't agree with this.

It's easy to say I'd do things differently but I would try to trust people more than he did, and not execute them. His people suffered too much when he was king.

Pearson Education Limited
Edinburgh Gate
Harlow
Essex CM20 2JE
England
and Associated Companies throughout the world.

www.pearsonelt.com

First published 2011

Fourth impression 2013

ISBN: 978-1-4082-1665-1

Set in Gill Sans Book 9.75/11.5

Printed in Malaysia (CTP-PJB)

Illustrated by Sean@kja-artist.com

Every effort has been made to trace the copyright holders and we apologise in advance for any unintentional omissions. We would be pleased to insert the appropriate acknowledgement in any subsequent edition of this publication.